Using and Administering Linux: Volume 3

Zero to SysAdmin: Network Services

David Both

Apress®

Using and Administering Linux: Volume 3

David Both
Raleigh, NC, USA

ISBN-13 (pbk): 978-1-4842-5484-4   ISBN-13 (electronic): 978-1-4842-5485-1
https://doi.org/10.1007/978-1-4842-5485-1

Managing Director, Apress LLC: Welmoed Spahr
Acquisitions Editor: Louise Corrigan
Development Editor: James Markham
Coordinating Editor: Nancy Chen

Cover designed by eStudioCalamar

Cover image designed by Freepik (www.freepik.com)

Distributed to the book trade worldwide by Springer Science+Business Media New York, 233 Spring Street, 6th Floor, New York, NY 10013. Phone 1-800-SPRINGER, fax (201) 348-4505, e-mail orders-ny@springer-sbm.com, or visit www.springeronline.com. Apress Media, LLC is a California LLC and the sole member (owner) is Springer Science + Business Media Finance Inc (SSBM Finance Inc). SSBM Finance Inc is a **Delaware** corporation.

For information on translations, please e-mail rights@apress.com, or visit http://www.apress.com/rights-permissions.

Apress titles may be purchased in bulk for academic, corporate, or promotional use. eBook versions and licenses are also available for most titles. For more information, reference our Print and eBook Bulk Sales web page at http://www.apress.com/bulk-sales.

Any source code or other supplementary material referenced by the author in this book is available to readers on GitHub via the book's product page, located at www.apress.com/9781484254844. For more detailed information, please visit http://www.apress.com/source-code.

Printed on acid-free paper

This book – this course – is dedicated to all Linux and open source course developers and trainers.

:(){ :|:& };:

Table of Contents

About the Author

David Both is an open source software and GNU/Linux advocate, trainer, writer, and speaker. He has been working with Linux and open source software for more than 20 years and has been working with computers for over 45 years. He is a strong proponent of and evangelist for the "Linux Philosophy for System Administrators." David has been in the IT industry for over 40 years.

Mr. Both worked for IBM for 21 years and, while working as a Course Development Representative in Boca Raton, FL, in 1981, wrote the training course for the first IBM PC. He has taught RHCE classes for Red Hat and has worked at MCI WorldCom, Cisco, and the State of North Carolina. In most of the places he has worked since leaving IBM in 1995, he has taught classes on Linux ranging from Lunch'n'Learns to full 5-day courses. Helping others learn about Linux and open source software is one of his great pleasures.

David prefers to purchase the components and build his own computers from scratch to ensure that each new computer meets his exacting specifications. Building his own computers also means not having to pay the Microsoft tax. His latest build is an ASUS TUF X299 motherboard and an Intel i9 CPU with 16 cores (32 CPUs) and 64GB of RAM in a Thermaltake Core X9 case.

He has written articles for magazines including *Linux Magazine*, *Linux Journal*, and *OS/2* back when there was such a thing. His article "Complete Kickstart," co-authored with a colleague at Cisco, was ranked 9th in the *Linux Magazine* Top Ten Best System Administration Articles list for 2008. He currently writes prolifically and is a volunteer community moderator for Opensource.com. He particularly enjoys learning new things while researching his articles.

David currently lives in Raleigh, NC, with his very supportive wife and a strange rescue dog that is mostly Jack Russell. David also likes reading, travel, the beach, old M*A*S*H reruns, and spending time with his two children, their spouses, and four grandchildren.

David can be reached at LinuxGeek46@both.org or on Twitter @LinuxGeek46.

About the Technical Reviewer

Klaatu Einzelganger is a UNIX geek, open source enthusiast, D&D nerd, and free-culture advocate. He has worked in the film and computing industry, often at the same time. He is one of the maintainers of the Slackware-based multimedia production project, `http://slackermedia.info`, and podcasts at gnuworldorder.info and hackerpublicradio.org.

Acknowledgments

Writing a book is not a solitary activity, and this massive three-volume Linux training course required a team effort so much more than most.

The most important person in this effort has been my awesome wife, Alice, who has been my head cheerleader and best friend throughout. I could not have done this without your support and love.

I am grateful for the support and guidance of Louise Corrigan, senior editor for open source at Apress, who believed in me and my vision for this book. This book would not have been possible without her.

To my coordinating editor, Nancy Chen, I owe many thanks for her hours of work, guidance, and being there to discuss many aspects of this book. As it grew and then continued to grow some more, our discussions were invaluable in helping to shape the final format of this work.

And to Jim Markham, my development editor, who quietly kept an eye and a guiding hand on the vast volume of material in these three volumes to ensure that the end result would meet the needs of you – my readers – and most importantly, you as the student.

Klaatu, my technical reviewer for this volume, has done a great job to ensure its technical accuracy. Due to the major changes made in some parts of the course as its final form materialized, he agreed to take on the task of technical reviewer for this volume late in the process. Nevertheless, he did an amazing job of keeping this highly technical volume on track.

Of course, any remaining errors and omissions are my responsibility alone.

Introduction

First, thank you for purchasing *Using and Administering Linux: Volume 3 – Zero to SysAdmin: Network Services.* The Linux training course upon which you have embarked is significantly different from other training that you could purchase to learn about Linux.

About this course

This Linux training course, *Using and Administering Linux – Zero to SysAdmin*, consists of three volumes. Each of these three volumes is closely connected and they build upon each other. For those new to Linux, it's best to start with Volume 1, where you'll be guided through the creation of a virtual laboratory – a virtual network and a virtual machine – that will be used and modified by many of the experiments in all three volumes. More experienced Linux users can begin with later volumes and download the script that will set up the VM for the start of Volumes 2 and 3. Instructions provided with the script will provide specifications for configuration of the virtual network and the virtual machine.

Refer to the following volume overviews to select the volume of this course most appropriate for your current skill level.

This Linux training course differs from others because it is a complete self-study course. Newcomers should start at the beginning of Volume 1 and read the text, perform all of the experiments, and complete all of the chapter exercises through to the end of Volume 3. If you do this, even if you are starting from zero knowledge about Linux, you can learn the tasks necessary to becoming a Linux system administrator, a SysAdmin.

Another difference this course has over others is that all of the experiments are performed on one or more virtual machines (VMs) in a virtual network. Using the free software VirtualBox, you will create this virtual environment on any reasonably sized host, whether Linux or Windows. In this virtual environment, you are free to experiment on your own, make mistakes that could damage the Linux installation of a hardware host, and still be able to recover completely by restoring the Linux VM host from any one of multiple snapshots. This flexibility to take risks and yet recover easily makes it possible to learn more than would otherwise be possible.

I have always found that I learn more from my mistakes than I ever have when things work as they are supposed to. For this reason, I suggest that rather than immediately reverting to an earlier snapshot when you run into trouble, you try to figure out how the problem was created and how best to recover from it. If, after a reasonable period of time, you have not resolved the problem, that would be the point at which reverting to a snapshot would make sense.

Inside, each chapter has specific learning objectives, interactive experiments, and review exercises that include both hands-on experiments and some review questions. I learned this format when I worked as a course developer for IBM from 1978 through 1981. It is a tried and true format that works well for self-study.

These course materials can also be used as reference materials. I have used my previous course materials for reference for many years and they have been very useful in that role. I have kept this as one of my goals in this set of materials.

Note   Not all of the review exercises in this course can be answered by simply reviewing the chapter content. For some questions, you will need to design your own experiment in order to find a solution. In many cases there will very probably be multiple solutions, and all that produce the correct results will be the "correct" ones.

Process

The process that goes with this format is just as important as the format of the course – really even more so. The first thing that a course developer must do is generate a list of requirements that define both the structure and the content of the course. Only then can the process of writing the course proceed. In fact, many times I find it helpful to write the review questions and exercises before I create the rest of the content. In many chapters of this course I have worked in this manner.

These volumes present a complete, end-to-end Linux training course for students like you who know before you start that you want to learn to be a Linux system administrator – a SysAdmin. This Linux course will allow you to learn Linux right from the beginning with the objective of becoming a SysAdmin.

Many Linux training courses begin with the assumption that the first course a student should take is one designed to start them as users. Those courses may discuss the role of root in system administration but ignore topics that are important to future SysAdmins. Other courses ignore system administration altogether. A typical second course will introduce the student to system administration, while a third may tackle advanced administration topics.

Frankly, this baby step approach did not work well for many of us who are now Linux SysAdmins. We became SysAdmins, in part at least, due to our intense desire – our deep need – to learn as much as possible as quickly as possible. It is also, I think in large part, due to our highly inquisitive natures. We learn a basic command and then start asking questions, experimenting with it to see what its limits are, what breaks it, and what using it can break. We explore the man(ual) pages and other documentation to learn the extreme usages to which it might be put. If things don't break by themselves, we break them intentionally to see how they work and to learn how to fix them. We relish our own failures because we learn more from fixing them than we do when things always work as they are supposed to.

In this course, we will dive deep into Linux system administration almost from the very beginning. You will learn many of the Linux tools required to use and administer Linux workstations and servers – usually multiple tools that can be applied to each of these tasks. This course contains many experiments to provide you with the kind of hands-on experiences that SysAdmins appreciate. All of these experiments guide you one step at a time into the elegant and beautiful depths of the Linux experience. You will learn that Linux is simple and that simplicity is what makes it both elegant and knowable.

Based on my own years working with Unix and Linux, the course materials contained in these three volumes are designed to introduce you to the practical, daily tasks you will perform as a Linux user and, at the same time, as a Linux system administrator – SysAdmin. But I do not know everything – that is just not possible – no SysAdmin does. Further, no two SysAdmins know exactly the same things because that, too, is impossible. We have each started with different knowledge and skills; we have different goals; and we have different experiences because the systems on which we work have failed in different ways, had different hardware, were embedded in different networks, had different distributions installed, and many other differences. We use different tools and approaches to problem-solving because the many different mentors and teachers we had used different sets of tools from each other; we use different Linux distributions; we think differently; and we know different things about the hardware on which Linux runs. Our past is much of what makes us what we are and what defines us as SysAdmins.

So I will show you things in this course – things that I think are important for you to know – things that, in my opinion, will provide you with the skills to use your own curiosity and creativity to find solutions that I would never think of to problems I have never encountered.

What this course is not

This course is not a certification study guide. It is not designed to help you pass a certification test of any type. This course is intended purely to help you become a good or perhaps even great SysAdmin, not to pass a test.

There are a few good certification tests. Red Hat and Cisco certifications are among the best because they are based on the test-taker's ability to perform specific tasks. I am not familiar with any of the other certification tests because I have not taken them. But the courses you can take and books you can purchase to help you pass those tests are designed to help you pass the tests and not to administer a Linux host or network. That does not make them bad – just different from this course.

Content overview

Because there are three volumes to this course, and because I reference other chapters, some of which may be in other volumes, we need a method for specifying in which volume the referenced material exists. If the material is in another volume, I will always specify the volume number, that is, "Chapter 2 in Volume 3" or "Volume 2, Chapter 5." If the material is in the same volume as the reference to it, I may simply specify the chapter number; however, I may also reference the current volume number for clarity.

This quick overview of the contents of each volume should serve as a quick orientation guide if you need to locate specific information. If you are trying to decide whether to purchase this book and its companion volumes, it will give you a good overview of the entire course.

Using and Administering Linux: Volume 1
Zero to SysAdmin: Getting Started

Volume 1 of this training course introduces operating systems in general and Linux in particular. It briefly explores *The Linux Philosophy for SysAdmins*[1] in preparation for the rest of the course.

Chapter 4 then guides you through the use of VirtualBox to create a virtual machine (VM) and a virtual network to use as a test laboratory for performing the many experiments that are used throughout the course. In Chapter 5, you will install the Xfce version of Fedora – a popular and powerful Linux distribution – on the VM. In Chapter 6, you will learn to use the Xfce desktop which will enable you to leverage your growing command line interface (CLI) expertise as you proceed through the course.

Chapters 7 and 8 will get you started using the Linux command line and introduce you to some of the basic Linux commands and their capabilities. In Chapter 9, you will learn about data streams and the Linux tools used to manipulate them. And in Chapter 10, you will learn a bit about several text editors which are indispensable to advanced Linux users and system administrators.

Chapters 11 through 13 start your work as a SysAdmin and take you through some specific tasks such as installing software updates and new software. Chapters 14 and 15 discuss more terminal emulators and some advanced shell skills. In Chapter 16, you will learn about the sequence of events that take place as the computer boots and Linux starts up. Chapter 17 shows you how to configure your shell to personalize it in ways that can seriously enhance your command line efficiency.

Finally, Chapters 18 and 19 dive into all things file and filesystems.

1. Introduction

2. Introduction to operating systems

3. The Linux Philosophy for SysAdmins

4. Preparation

5. Installing Linux

6. Using the Xfce desktop

7. The Linux command line

---

[1]Both, David, *The Linux Philosophy for SysAdmins*, Apress, 2018

8. Core utilities

9. Data streams

10. Text editors

11. Working as root

12. Installing updates and new software

13. Tools for problem-solving

14. Terminal emulator mania

15. Advanced shell topics

16. Linux boot and startup

17. Shell configuration

18. Files, directories, and links

19. Filesystems

Using and Administering Linux: Volume 2
Zero to SysAdmin: Advanced Topics

Volume 2 of *Using and Administering Linux* introduces you to some incredibly powerful and useful advanced topics that every SysAdmin must know.

In Chapters 1 and 2, you will experience an in-depth exploration of logical volume management – and what that even means – as well as the use of file managers to manipulate files and directories. Chapter 3 introduces the concept that, in Linux, everything is a file. You will also learn some fun and interesting uses of the fact that everything is a file.

In Chapter 4, you will learn to use several tools that enable the SysAdmin to manage and monitor running processes. Chapter 5 enables you to experience the power of the special filesystems, such as /proc, that enable us as SysAdmins to monitor and tune the kernel while it is running – without a reboot.

Chapter 6 will introduce you to regular expressions and the power that using them for pattern matching can bring to the command line, while Chapter 7 discusses managing printers and printing from the command line. In Chapter 8, you will use several tools to unlock the secrets of the hardware in which your Linux operating system is running.

Chapters 9 through 11 show you how to do some simple – and not so simple – command line programming and how to automate various administrative tasks.

You will begin to learn the details of networking in Chapter 12, and Chapters 13 through 15 show you how to manage the many services that are required in a Linux system. You will also explore the underlying software that manages the hardware and can detect when hardware devices such as USB thumb drives are installed and how the system reacts to that.

Chapter 16 shows you how to use the logs and journals to look for clues to problems and confirmation that things are working correctly.

Chapters 17 and 18 show you how to enhance the security of your Linux systems, including how to perform easy local and remote backups.

1. Logical volume management

2. File managers

3. Everything is a file

4. Managing processes

5. Special filesystems

6. Regular expressions

7. Printing

8. Hardware detection

9. Command line programming

10. Automation with BASH scripts

11. Time and Automation

12. Networking

13. systemd

14. dbus and udev

15. Using logs and journals

16. Managing users

17. Security

18. Backups

Using and Administering Linux: Volume 3
Zero to SysAdmin: Network Services

In Volume 3 of *Using and Administering Linux*, you will start by creating a new VM on the existing virtual network. This new VM will be used as a server for the rest of this course, and it will replace some of the functions performed by the virtual router that is part of our virtual network.

Chapter 2 begins this transformation from simple workstation to server by adding a new network interface card (NIC) to the VM so that it can act as a firewall and router, then changing its network configuration from DHCP to static. This includes configuring both NICs so that one is connected to the existing virtual router so as to allow connections to the outside world, and so that the other NIC connects to the new "inside" network that will contain the existing VM.

Chapters 3 and 4 guide you through setting up the necessary services, DHCP and DNS, that are required to support a managed, internal network, and Chapter 5 takes you through configuration of SSHD to provide secure remote access between Linux hosts. In Chapter 6, you will convert the new server into a router with a simple yet effective firewall.

You will learn to install and configure an enterprise class email server that can detect and block most spam and malware in Chapters 7 through 9. Chapter 10 takes you through setting up a web server, and in Chapter 11, you will set up WordPress, a flexible and powerful content management system.

In Chapter 12, you return to email by setting up a mailing list using Mailman. Then Chapter 13 guides you through sharing files to both Linux and Windows hosts. Sometimes accessing a desktop remotely is the only way to do some things, so in Chapter 14 you will do just that.

Chapter 15 shows you how to set up a time server on your network and how to determine its accuracy. Although we have incorporated security in all aspects of what has already been covered, Chapter 16 covers some additional security topics.

Chapter 17 discusses package management from the other direction by guiding you through the process of creating an RPM package for the distribution of your own scripts and configuration files.

Finally, Chapter 18 will get you started in the right direction because I know you are going to ask, "Where do I go from here?"

1. Server preparation

2. Server configuration

3. DHCP

4. Name services

5. Remote access with SSH

6. Routing and firewalls

7. Introducing email

8. Email clients

9. Combating spam

10. Apache web server

11. WordPress

12. Mailing lists

13. File sharing

14. Remote desktop access

15. Network time protocol

16. Security

17. Advanced package management

18. Where do I go from here?

Taking this course

Although designed primarily as a self-study guide, this course can be used effectively in a classroom environment. This course can also be used very effectively as a reference. Many of the original course materials I wrote for Linux training classes I used to teach as an independent trainer and consultant were valuable to me as references. The experiments became models for performing many tasks and later became the basis for automating many of those same tasks. I have used many of those original experiments in parts of this course, because they are still relevant and provide an excellent reference for many of the tasks I still need to do.

You will see as you proceed through the course that it uses many software programs considered to be older and perhaps obsolete like Sendmail, Procmail, BIND, the Apache web server, and much more. Despite their age, or perhaps because of it, the software I have chosen to run my own systems and servers and to use in this course has been well-proven and is all still in widespread use. I believe that the software we will use in these experiments has properties that make it especially valuable in learning the in-depth details of how Linux and those services work. Once you have learned those details, moving to any other software that performs the same tasks will be relatively easy. In any event, none of that "older" software is anywhere near as difficult or obscure as some people seem to think that it is.

Who should take this course

If you want to learn to be an advanced Linux user and SysAdmin, this course is for you. Most SysAdmins have an extremely high level of curiosity and a deep-seated need to learn Linux System Administration. We like to take things apart and put them back together again to learn how they work. We enjoy fixing things and are not hesitant about diving in to fix the computer problems that our friends and co-workers bring us.

We want to know what happens when some part of computer hardware fails so we might save defective components such as motherboards, RAM memory, and hard drives. This gives us defective components with which we can run tests. As I write this, I have a known defective hard drive inserted in a hard drive docking station connected to my primary workstation and have been using it to test failure scenarios that will appear later in this course.

Most importantly, we do all of this for fun and would continue to do so even if we had no compelling vocational reason for doing so. Our intense curiosity about computer hardware and Linux leads us to collect computers and software like others collect stamps or antiques. Computers are our avocation – our hobby. Some people like boats, sports, travel, coins, stamps, trains, or any of thousands of other things, and they pursue them relentlessly as a hobby. For us – the true SysAdmins – that is what our computers are. That does not mean we are not well-rounded and do not do other things. I like to travel, read, go to museums and concerts, and ride historical trains, and my stamp collection is still there, waiting for me when I decide to take it up again.

In fact, the best SysAdmins, at least the ones I know, are all multifaceted. We are involved in many different things, and I think that is due to our inexhaustible curiosity about pretty much everything. So if you have an insatiable curiosity about Linux and want to learn about it – regardless of your past experience or lack thereof – then this course is most definitely for you.

Who should not take this course

If you do not have a strong desire to learn about or to administer Linux systems, this course is not for you. If all you want – or need – to do is use a couple apps on a Linux computer that someone has put on your desk, this course is not for you. If you have no curiosity about what superpowers lie underneath the GUI desktop, this course is not for you.

Why this course

Someone asked me why I want to write this course. My answer is simple – I want to give back to the Linux community. I have had several amazing mentors over the span of my career and they taught me many things – things I find worth sharing with you along with much that I have learned for myself.

This course – all three volumes of it – started its existence as the slide presentations and lab projects for three Linux courses I created and taught. For a number of reasons, I do not teach those classes anymore. However, I would still like to pass on my knowledge and as many of the tips and tricks I have learned for the administration of Linux as possible. I hope that with this course I can pass on at least some of the guidance and mentoring that I was fortunate enough to have in my own career.

CHAPTER 1

Server Preparation

Objectives

In this chapter you will

- Create a new VM on which to install Fedora to use as a server, firewall, and router.

- Install the latest version of Fedora on the VM to be used as the server.

- Make a few configuration changes to ensure that the new VM will provide a suitable base to use as a server.

Overview

There are some preparatory tasks that need to be accomplished in order to perform the experiments in this third volume of *Using and Administering Linux – Zero to SysAdmin*. Most lab environments use physical machines for training purposes, but in this volume, we use at least two Linux hosts in a private network in order to enable a realistic environment for learning about being a SysAdmin.

As we have seen in the previous two volumes of this course, the use of multiple VMs to create a virtual network on a single physical host provides a safe virtual computing and network environment in which to learn by making mistakes.

In Volume 1, you created a VM in a custom virtual network and installed Fedora on it to use in the many experiments encountered in the rest of the course. We now need to create a new VM that we can use as a server for this volume of the course.

In this volume of the course, I assume that you have completed the previous two volumes. You will not be able to successfully perform the experiments in this volume if you have not completed the first two volumes. This is for two reasons. First, you will probably not have sufficient knowledge to do so, and second, the virtual network and

1

© David Both 2020
D. Both, *Using and Administering Linux: Volume 3*, https://doi.org/10.1007/978-1-4842-5485-1_1

virtual machine created in Volume 1 and changed and modified throughout Volume 2, and will not be available or configured correctly to work in this volume.

Creating the VM

We first need to create the VM we will use in the rest of this course and then make some configuration changes. Create the new VM using the specifications listed in Figure 1-1.

Item	Value
VM Name	StudentVM2
Machine folder	/Experiments
(OS) Type	Linux
Version	Fedora 64-bit
Memory size	4096MB – The memory size can be changed at any time later so long as the VM is powered off. For now this should be more than enough RAM.
File location	/Experiments
(Hard disk) File size	60GB
Hard disk file type	.vdi – The .vdi extension is the VirtualBox Disk Image file format. You could select other formats but this VDI format will be perfect for our needs.
Storage on physical hard disk	Dynamically allocated

Figure 1-1. *The specifications for the StudentVM2 virtual machine*

At this point, the basic virtual machine has been created, but we need to make a few changes to some of the configuration. Use the VirtualBox Manager **Settings** dialog for StudentVM2 to make these changes.

1. Deselect the **Floppy** disk and then move it down the **Boot Order** to below the **Hard Disk**.

2. Increase the number of **CPUs** from 1 to 2 for the StudentVM2 virtual machine.

3. If your physical host has 8G of RAM or more, increase the amount of video memory to 128MB. It is neither necessary nor recommended that you enable 2D or 3D video acceleration because it is not needed for this course.

4. Select the **Network** settings page and, in the **Adapter 1** tab, select **NAT Network** in the **Attached to:** field. Because we have created only one NAT Network, the StudentNetwork, that network will be selected for us. Click on the little blue triangle next to Advanced to view the rest of the configuration for this device. Do not change anything else on this page.

The virtual machine is now configured and ready for us to install Linux.

Installing Linux

Now install the most recent Fedora Linux Xfce version on StudentVM2. The initial configuration for both VMs is exactly the same with only one exception. The host name for the server VM, StudentVM2, should be studentvm2 in all lowercase.

EXPERIMENT 1-1

Using the VirtualBox Manager, insert the ISO image file, Fedora-Xfce-Live-x86_64-28-1.1.iso, or whatever the current version of the Xfce Live image happens to be into the StudentVM1 virtual machine's storage controller as the IDE secondary master. Then boot the VM and proceed with the installation from the Live image using the filesystem configuration shown in Figure 1-2.

Be sure to use manual filesystem configuration during the installation. If you need a bit of assistance, Volume 1, Chapter 5, of this course contains the details of how to do the complete installation, including creating the filesystems. Just remember to use the correct hostname for this second virtual machine, studentvm2.

Filesystem	Partition	Filesystem Type	Size (GB)	Label
/boot	Standard	EXT4	1.0	boot
/ (root)	LVM	EXT4	2.0	root
/usr	LVM	EXT4	15.0	usr
/home	LVM	EXT4	2.0	home
/var	LVM	EXT4	10.0	var
/tmp	LVM	EXT4	5.0	tmp
swap	swap	swap	8.0	swap
Total			43.00	

Figure 1-2. *The disk partitions – filesystems – and their sizes*

Note that we do not initially allocate all of the space on the volume group. However, be sure to create the /boot partition first and then – this is very important – after creating the first filesystem that is part of the LVM system, be sure to alter the configuration of the volume group to use the option "As large as possible" in order to include all of the remaining space on the virtual hard drive in the logical volume.

Important   Be sure to modify the volume group so that it takes up all of the remaining space on the virtual hard drive after creation of the /boot partition.

As the installation proceeds, set the root password and create a non-root user with the name of "student" and set a password for that user.

After the Fedora installation has completed, reboot StudentVM2 to verify that it comes up, runs properly, and can ping example.com and StudentVM1.

Personalization

By this time in this course, you should have enough experience to have some favorite tools that you like to use. I suggest that you take some time right now to install your favorite command line and desktop tools and personalize StudentVM2.

EXPERIMENT 1-2

As the root user on StudentVM2, configure the kernel so that it displays all kernel and startup messages. If you need some guidance with this, we did it for StudentVM1 in Volume 1, Chapter 16.

Perform any additional personalization to both the student and root accounts.

Chapter summary

You have finished preparations for performing the experiments in the rest of this course. You prepared an external USB disk drive to hold the virtual machine we will use in this course and you have created that VM. You have also made some modifications to the VM that could not be made during its initial creation, such as the network adapter settings and the number of processors allocated to the VM.

You now should have two VMs created using VirtualBox, each with Fedora Xfce installed from the Fedora Live USB drive. You have added your favorite command line tools and personalized the Linux operating system in both VMs to meet your own needs and methods.

Exercises

Perform the following exercises to complete this chapter.

1. What is the IP address of StudentVM1?

2. How was the IP address set?

CHAPTER 2

Server Configuration

Objectives

In this chapter you will learn about and perform some basic configuration on the StudentVM2 server VM including:

- Setting the hostname.

- Prepare the server to become the DHCP server for the virtual network.

- Changing the network configuration to static.

- Verifying the virtual network connection between StudentVM1 and StudentVM2, as well as between the VMs and the outside world.

Overview

In Chapter 1 of Volume 3 we created the StudentVM2 virtual machine which will become the server for our virtual network. There are some configuration items that we need to modify on the VM to further prepare it for its new role.

Network configuration

Using DHCP for network configuration in a traditional environment is good for some hosts, but not necessarily for servers. Servers in traditional environments need to set their own network configuration; relying on DHCP can cause changing IP addresses and possibly other information that might lead to the inability of other hosts to find the servers on the network. In a cloud environment the provider will assign addresses and

© David Both 2020
D. Both, *Using and Administering Linux: Volume 3*, https://doi.org/10.1007/978-1-4842-5485-1_2

you may not be able to depend upon a specific IP address. In Volume 3 of this course we will use the traditional approach in which we have control over all aspects of our environment.

The initial virtual network we have configured for this course provides a virtual router with a DHCP server. So long as we use the virtual DHCP server that is a part of the virtual router, our new server will not receive a static IP address. So we need to change the network configuration of StudentVM2 from DHCP to static. We will discuss DHCP in more detail in Chapter 3.

The desired result of our combined objectives for Chapters 2 and 3 is that our server, StudentVM2, will become the DHCP server for our new internal virtual network. One underlying reason for this is that the simple DHCP server in the virtual router is not capable of handling some of the configuration settings we will need later on. This will also lay the groundwork for installing other services on our server so that we can explore them more fully.

The virtual router provided by VirtualBox when we created StudentVM1 in Volume 1 of this course, provides us with the 10.0.2.0/24 address range by default. Now we need an "inside" virtual network for the inside clients like StudentVM1 so we must first create a new "Host" network and then a new interface card to StudentVM2. A "Host" network is one in which the hosts on the network can only connect with each other and not to the outside world.

EXPERIMENT 2-1

Use the VirtualBox Manager to create a new network.

Power down StudentVM2. Using the menu bar, open the **File ➤ Host Network Manager** dialog. Click Create to create a new Host network.

The default is to configure the adapter manually and some of the required data is already generated and placed in the appropriate locations. Figure 2-1 shows the configuration for this adapter. There is no need to change anything on this tab.

Configuration item	Value
Configure Adapter Manually	Radio button is checked
IPV4 address	192.168.56.1
IPV4 Network Mask	255.255.255.0
IP V6 Address	May auto fill when **Apply** is pressed.
IPV6 Prefix Length	May auto fill when **Apply** is pressed.

Figure 2-1. *The Host network configuration*

Be sure that the DHCP server Enable box is not checked in the network list area of the dialog. We do not want two DHCP servers on the network and this one must be disabled. We will be using vboxnet0 for this course because it is created automatically.

Figure 2-2 shows the completed dialog box, but the IPV6 data fields may be empty. If this is the case, the **Apply** button will be grayed out and we will need to use the **Close** button to finish.

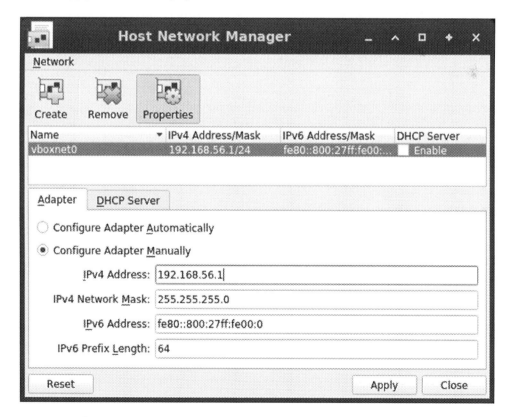

Figure 2-2. *The Host network configuration*

Click **Apply** if it is highlighted or **Close** if it is not to finish creating the new network. Now we can add the new NIC to StudentVM2 and connect it to this network.

Again, use the VirtualBox Manager. Select StudentVM2 which should be powered off. If it is not, do so now. Open the **Settings** dialog for StudentVM2 and select the **Network** tab. Click the **Adapter 2** tab and place a check mark in the **Enable Network Adapter** check box.

In the **Attached To** drop-down selection box, click **Host-only Adapter**. Because we have only one network of this type, the **vboxnet0** network is chosen by default. Click the little twistie next to **Advanced** and check out the rest of the configuration for this new NIC, including the MAC address. Verify that there is a check mark in the **Cable Connected** box.

Click the OK button to complete the addition of this new NIC.

Before we continue, we want to have a set of requirements that define the network address map for our new, internal network. We should always create requirements before starting a project of any kind. Figure 2-3 shows the range of network addresses we – well, I, actually, but you get the idea – have arbitrarily decided upon for our very simple internal network. It is typical for the router to have the "1" or other lowest IP address in the available IP address range.

Role	IP Address ranges
Router/server	192.168.56.1
Workstations	192.168.56.21 – 192.168.56.29
Guest computers	192.168.56.50 – 192.168.56.59

Figure 2-3. *The general address map for the virtual network as we want it to be when we are finished*

We have defined address ranges for workstations, servers, and even guest computers such as might be used in a flexible work environment. We will explore more about assigning workstation and guest IP addresses in Chapter 3 of this volume, "DHCP."

Before we can continue, we need to obtain some information about the NICs in our VMs.

```
                        EXPERIMENT 2-2
```

Perform this experiment as root. This experiment obtains the information we need to create our address map. Remember that the MAC addresses will be different for your VMs than they are for mine.

Power on StudentVM2. Log into StudentVM2, open a terminal session, and **su –** to root.

As the root user on StudentVM2, list the NICs installed in StudentVM2 and the associated MAC and IP addresses. Remember that your MAC addresses will be different from mine and the IP addresses may also be different.

```
[root@studentvm2 ~]# ip addr
1: lo: <LOOPBACK,UP,LOWER_UP> mtu 65536 qdisc noqueue state UNKNOWN group
default qlen 1000
    link/loopback 00:00:00:00:00:00 brd 00:00:00:00:00:00
    inet 127.0.0.1/8 scope host lo
       valid_lft forever preferred_lft forever
    inet6 ::1/128 scope host
       valid_lft forever preferred_lft forever
2: enpOs3: <BROADCAST,MULTICAST,UP,LOWER_UP> mtu 1500 qdisc fq_codel state UP
group default qlen 1000
    link/ether 08:00:27:81:ec:cc brd ff:ff:ff:ff:ff:ff
    inet 10.0.2.11/24 brd 10.0.2.255 scope global noprefixroute enpOs3
       valid_lft forever preferred_lft forever
    inet6 fe80::f8b5:5762:6eaa:cf8e/64 scope link noprefixroute
       valid_lft forever preferred_lft forever
3: enpOs8: <BROADCAST,MULTICAST,UP,LOWER_UP> mtu 1500 qdisc fq_codel state UP
group default qlen 1000
    link/ether 08:00:27:9f:67:cb brd ff:ff:ff:ff:ff:ff
    inet 192.168.56.1/24 brd 192.168.56.255 scope global noprefixroute enpOs8
       valid_lft forever preferred_lft forever
    inet6 fe80::981c:73b4:21c2:9e6d/64 scope link noprefixroute
       valid_lft forever preferred_lft forever
[root@studentvm2 ~]#
```

Remember that we don't really care much about the current IP address. We will assign IP addresses according to our own plan. What we want from this data is the MAC address that is associated with the NIC name. The MAC address for enpOs3 on my VM is 08:00:27:81:ec:cc.

11

There are three NICs listed here. The first is the local loop, lo. Interface lo stands for "local." This is an internal interface for software clients on the local host (localhost) to talk to server services on the localhost without needing to communicate over the external network. This is one of the incredibly intelligent design points of Linux (and Unix) because programs can talk to other programs through the network interfaces regardless of whether the clients and servers are on the same hosts or remote ones. This really simplifies the work of the developer. We obviously do not have anything using the lo interface, but we will later.

You already know that enp0s3 is the network connection for NIC number 1. This is the one that our VMs have been using for communicating with each other on the virtual network, as well as with the outside world through the virtual router. We will continue to use this NIC on the 10.0.2.0/24 network as the connection to the outside world.

The enp0s8 NIC is the second network adapter for any VirtualBox VM. This is the NIC we will use for our internal network.

We need to know the IP address of the default gateway router.

```
[root@studentvm2 ~]# ip route
default via 10.0.2.1 dev enp0s3 proto static metric 100
10.0.2.0/24 dev enp0s3 proto kernel scope link src 10.0.2.11 metric 100
192.168.56.0/24 dev enp0s8 proto kernel scope link src 192.168.56.1 metric
101
```

This tells us that the IP address for the default gateway to the outside world is 10.0.2.1 which is a best practice address for the default gateway.

This data allows us to fill in the MAC addresses needed for Figure 2-2. It also provides the current IP address associated with each MAC address although we really don't need the current IP addresses because we will be changing them.

VirtualBox allows up to four NICs for each virtual machine. The virtual adapters NIC names are assigned as follows. These names are assigned based on the location of the NIC adapter in the PCI device tree, whether physical or virtual. All of our VMs will have the same PCI device tree, so the adapters will have the same assignments. That is not a problem, and the adapters for one VM will not conflict with the adapters from another.

NIC 1: enp0s3

NIC 2: enp0s8

NIC 3: enp0s9

NIC 4: enp0s10

The MAC addresses must be different on each host because that is an identifier that is visible to all the other hosts on the network. Each MAC address must be unique; this is true in both the virtual and the physical worlds. The MAC addresses on your virtual NICs will therefore be different from the ones seen in these examples and experiments. Be sure to use the MAC addresses for the NICs on your own experimental configuration.

The IP addresses specified in Figure 2-4 are the ones that we ultimately want to have assigned to the hosts and not the ones currently assigned. There are many strategies for assigning IP addresses. Each organization and every SysAdmin have their own favored methods. It is common practice to set the IP address for the default gateway router to x.x.x.1. For this course, I have arbitrarily decided that servers will be assigned IP addresses in the range from 192.168.56.1 to 192.168.56.9 and that workstations will be in the address range from 192.168.56.21 to 192.168.56.29. These IP addresses will be assigned from the lowest to the highest in each group.

Hostname	Role	MAC Address	NIC Name	IP Address
Virtual Router	Router		N/A	10.0.2.1
studentvm1	Workstation	08:00:27:e1:0c:10	enp0s3	192.168.56.21
studentvm2	Server	08:00:27:81:ec:cc	enp0s3	10.0.2.11
studentvm2	Server	08:00:27:9f:67:cb	enp0s8	192.168.56.1

Figure 2-4. *The IP Address map for the server and the workstation on our internal network*

Now that we have a little bit of a plan, let's configure the network interface cards for StudentVM2. After a new installation, the network interface configuration files that are normally located in the /etc/sysconfig/network-scripts directory are absent, so the NetworkManager simply looks for a DHCP server and accepts whatever network configuration data is provided. In Chapter 3 of this volume, we will install the DHCP server package and make the StudentVM2 virtual machine into a DHCP server.

We will use the **nmcli** (NetworkManager Command Line Interface) utility to create the static network connection needed by the server. This command creates the network configuration files, and we will look at those files as we proceed through the experiments in this chapter.

> **Tip**   The **nmcli** command is complex and can be frustrating at first. This is especially true because the available man pages seem to have some discrepancies with the actual command and its options. The best documentation I have found is the RHEL 7 Networking Guide.[1]

The **nmcli** command has many sub-commands and options. We will only look at a few here, but these will allow us to configure our server with the static IP address specified in Figure 2-2.

EXPERIMENT 2-3

This experiment must be performed as root on StudentVM2. It covers configuration for hosts using static IP addresses and other typical configuration parameters. In most cases, the default configuration has been performed by DHCP in which a DHCP server provides all of the data required for network configuration of the host. We need to change that to static configuration in which we provide all of the required configuration parameters.

First open a root terminal session and make /etc/sysconfig/network-scripts the PWD. List the content of this directory which should be empty. If it is not, and you are using Fedora 29 or higher,[2] delete any files you find there.

Use the data provided in Figure 2-5 to create an interface configuration file for enp0s3.

---

[1]Red Hat, *Red Hat Enterprise Linux Networking Guide*, https://access.redhat.com/documentation/en-us/red_hat_enterprise_linux/7/html/networking_guide/sec-configuring_ip_networking_with_nmcli

[2]The requirements for this course specify Fedora 29 or higher so you should be using at least Fedora 29. Other distributions are not recommended and you may run into problems if you use them.

Config item	Option name	Value	Description
Network type	type	ethernet	This could also be various types of VPN, or bonded connections. Those options are outside the scope of this course.
Interface name	ifname	enp0s3	This is the name of the interface as displayed by the nmcli device command.
Connection name	con-name	enp0s3	This is the name of the connection that will be used in commands. It will be part of the interface configuration file name. I like to keep this name short for ease of typing. I use the NIC name to make identification easy.
IPV4 address	ipv4	10.0.2.11	The static IP V4 address we assign to this interface.
Gateway IPV4 Address	gw4	10.0.2.1	The default route through the virtual router.
IPV4 DNS servers	ipv4.dns	"10.0.2.1 8.8.8.8"	Up to three DNS server IP addresses, Be sure to use the double quotes.

Figure 2-5. *A list of the information required to configure the enp0s3 network interface*

Enter this command to configure the network interface, enp0s3. Then verify the presence and content of the new file, ifcfg-enp0s3.

```
[root@studentvm2 ~]# nmcli connection add save yes type ethernet ifname
enp0s3 con-name enp0s3 ip4 10.0.2.11/24 gw4 10.0.2.1 ipv4.dns "10.0.2.1
8.8.8.8"
Connection 'enp0s3' (5d4c3d0d-e1a3-4017-bed8-3eb0fa98883c) successfully
added.
[root@studentvm2 network-scripts]# cat ifcfg-enp0s3
TYPE=Ethernet
PROXY_METHOD=none
BROWSER_ONLY=no
BOOTPROTO=none
IPADDR=10.0.2.11
PREFIX=24
GATEWAY=10.0.2.1
DNS1=10.0.2.1
DNS2=8.8.8.8
DEFROUTE=yes
IPV4_FAILURE_FATAL=no
IPV6INIT=yes
```

```
IPV6_AUTOCONF=yes
IPV6_DEFROUTE=yes
IPV6_FAILURE_FATAL=no
IPV6_ADDR_GEN_MODE=stable-privacy
NAME=enp0s3
UUID=5d4c3d0d-e1a3-4017-bed8-3eb0fa98883c
DEVICE=enp0s3
ONBOOT=yes
```

Ping example.com to ensure that the DNS and gateway configurations are working.

The **nmcli** command below creates the interface configuration file for enp0s8 using the data provided in Figure 2-6.

Config item	Option name	Value	Description
Network type	type	ethernet	This could also be various types of VPN, or bonded connections. Those options are outside the scope of this course.
Interface name	ifname	enp0s3	This is the name of the interface as displayed by the nmcli device command.
Connection name	con-name	enp0s3	This is the name of the connection that will be used in commands. It will be part of the interface configuration file name. I like to keep this name short for ease of typing. I use the NIC name to make identification easy.
IPV4 address	ipv4	192.168.56.1	The static IP V4 address we assign to this interface.
Gateway IPV4 Address	gw4	N/A	The default route through the virtual router.
IPV4 DNS servers	ipv4.dns	N/A	Up to three DNS server IP addresses, Be sure to use the double quotes.

Figure 2-6. *A list of the information required to configure the enp0s8 network interface*

Enter this command to configure the network interface, enp0s8.

[root@studentvm2 ~]# **nmcli connection add save yes type ethernet ifname enp0s8 con-name enp0s8 ip4 192.168.56.11/24**

Now view the content of the ifcfg-enp0s8 file.

[root@studentvm2 network-scripts]# **cat ifcfg-enp0s8**

The content of the interface configuration files on your VM should be very close to that above. The UUID will definitely be different. Note that there are some IPV6 entries that were placed there by the Network Manager but that are essentially ignored.

Tip   Because the interface configuration files such as /etc/sysconfig/network-scripts/ifcfg-enp0s3 are managed by the Network Manager and the **nmcli** command, it is strongly recommended that you do not edit these files by hand. Use the **nmcli** command to make changes to them.

Now let's do a bit of testing to verify that our new configuration is working properly.

```
                        EXPERIMENT 2-4
```

This experiment must be performed as root on StudentVM2. In it we test to ensure that the configuration we have created for NIC enp0s3 is working as expected.

Use the dig or nslookup command to ensure that the DNS resolution is working properly.

```
[root@studentvm2 ~]# dig www.cnn.com

; <<>> DiG 9.11.4-P1-RedHat-9.11.4-5.P1.fc28 <<>> www.cnn.com
;; global options: +cmd
;; Got answer:
;; ->>HEADER<<- opcode: QUERY, status: NOERROR, id: 48252
;; flags: qr rd ra; QUERY: 1, ANSWER: 2, AUTHORITY: 4, ADDITIONAL: 5

;; OPT PSEUDOSECTION:
; EDNS: version: 0, flags:; udp: 4096
;; QUESTION SECTION:
;www.cnn.com.                    IN      A

;; ANSWER SECTION:
www.cnn.com.            300     IN      CNAME   turner-tls.map.fastly.net.
turner-tls.map.fastly.net. 30   IN      A       151.101.201.67

;; AUTHORITY SECTION:
fastly.net.             156515  IN      NS      ns3.fastly.net.
```

```
fastly.net.                156515  IN      NS      ns4.fastly.net.
fastly.net.                156515  IN      NS      ns1.fastly.net.
fastly.net.                156515  IN      NS      ns2.fastly.net.

;; ADDITIONAL SECTION:
ns1.fastly.net.            156515  IN      A       23.235.32.32
ns2.fastly.net.            156515  IN      A       104.156.80.32
ns3.fastly.net.            156515  IN      A       23.235.36.32
ns4.fastly.net.            156515  IN      A       104.156.84.32

;; Query time: 71 msec
;; SERVER: 192.168.56.1#53(192.168.56.1)
;; WHEN: Tue Oct 02 16:48:35 EDT 2018
;; MSG SIZE  rcvd: 231

[root@studentvm2 ~]#
```

This tells us the DNS service in the virtual router is working. You may also want to ping a host out on the Internet to verify that you have complete connectivity.

```
[root@studentvm2 ~]# ping www.example.net
PING www.example.net (93.184.216.34) 56(84) bytes of data.
64 bytes from 93.184.216.34 (93.184.216.34): icmp_seq=1 ttl=54 time=28.10 ms
64 bytes from 93.184.216.34 (93.184.216.34): icmp_seq=2 ttl=54 time=51.5 ms
64 bytes from 93.184.216.34 (93.184.216.34): icmp_seq=3 ttl=54 time=40.1 ms
64 bytes from 93.184.216.34 (93.184.216.34): icmp_seq=4 ttl=54 time=117 ms
64 bytes from 93.184.216.34 (93.184.216.34): icmp_seq=5 ttl=54 time=42.5 ms
^C
--- www.example.net ping statistics ---
5 packets transmitted, 5 received, 0% packet loss, time 211ms
rtt min/avg/max/mdev = 28.970/56.009/116.966/31.312 ms
[root@studentvm2 ~]#
```

The domain names example.com and example.net are both reserved for testing, and we can ping those without interfering with someone's production environment.

Chapter summary

We have made some configuration changes to the VM that will be used as the server in our network. We renamed it and set up a static IP configuration. This provided an opportunity to learn a bit about network configuration and use several network management commands.

We also created a network address map that can be used as a guide for assigning IP addresses as we proceed through the rest of this course. This chapter also sets the stage for configuring a DHCP service on our new server.

Exercises

1. Why is it necessary or at least a very good idea and a best practice to use static IP addressing for a server?

2. What function does a network address map serve?

3. Describe the function of the MAC address.

4. Is communication working between StudentVM1 and StudentVM2? Why?

5. How can you tell which DNS server responded to a **dig** command?

6. What command would you use to determine the DNS names, MAC addresses, and IP addresses of the other hosts on the network with which a given host such as StudentVM2 has been communicating?

7. In case the primary DNS server fails, test whether the second DNS server specified in the interface configuration file for enp0s3 on StudentVM2 is responding.

CHAPTER 3

DHCP

Objectives

In this chapter you will learn

- The purpose and functions of DHCP

- The functions of and the differences between MAC and IP addresses

- Several of the many network configuration items that DHCP can serve

- How to assign and manage static IP addresses for specific hosts based on the MAC address

Overview of DHCP

The Dynamic Host Configuration Protocol (DHCP) provides a centralized and automated method for configuring hosts when they connect to the network. This reduces the need to configure each network host individually. It is useful for portable devices such as laptops which might connect as unknown guests. DHCP offers even more advantages when used to manage static IP address assignments for known hosts using the central DHCP database.

The DHCP server uses a database of information created by the SysAdmin. This database is entirely contained in the /etc/dhcp/dhcpd.conf configuration file. Like all well-designed Linux configuration files, it is a simple ASCII plain text file. This means that it is open and knowable and that it can be examined by standard, simple text manipulation tools like **cat** and **grep** and modified by any text editor such as Emacs or Vim, or a stream editor such as **sed**.

In addition to assigning IP addresses to client hosts, DHCP can also provide host configuration information such as DNS servers, the domain name used for DNS searches, the default gateway, an NTP (Network Time Protocol) server, a server from which a network boot can be performed, and more.

© David Both 2020
D. Both, *Using and Administering Linux: Volume 3*, https://doi.org/10.1007/978-1-4842-5485-1_3

The DHCP client is always installed on Linux clients – certainly at least Red Hat–based distros and all the other distros I have tried – because of the very high probability that they will be connected to a network using DHCP and not with a static configuration.

When a host configured for DHCP is booted, or its NIC is turned up (activated), it sends a broadcast request to the network asking for a DHCP server to respond. The client and the server engage in a bit of conversation and the server sends the configuration data to the client which uses it to self-configure its network connection. Hosts may have multiple NICs connected to different networks and any or all may be configured using DHCP, or one or more of the NICs may be configured using DHCP and one or more NICS may be configured using static configuration.

Installing the DHCP server

The DHCP server is not installed by default and, like the other servers we will install during this course, we must install it ourselves.

EXPERIMENT 3-1

This experiment must be performed as root. For now, we will leave StudentVM1 turned off while we get DHCP configured and running. If it is not powered off, do so now. We will first check the installation status of DHCP and then install the DHCP server.

1. Start StudentVM2 if it is not already running.

2. After StudentVM2 has finished boot and startup, login as the student1 user, open a terminal session and **su** – to root.

3. Check to see which DHCP packages are already installed.

    ```
    [root@studentvm2 ~]# dnf list installed dhcp*
    Installed Packages
    dhcp-client.x86_64          12:4.3.6-28.fc29          @anaconda
    dhcp-common.noarch          12:4.3.6-28.fc29          @anaconda
    dhcp-libs.x86_64            12:4.3.6-28.fc29          @anaconda
    [root@studentvm2 ~]#
    ```

    This shows the DHCP client has been installed along with libraries and supporting files common to the client, server, and possibly the DHCP development packages.

4. The DHCP server is not installed, so we need to install it. a

```
[root@studentvm2 ~]# dnf install -y dhcp-server
Last metadata expiration check: 2:39:06 ago on Wed 26 Dec 2018
12:19:46 PM EST.
Dependencies resolved.
========================================================================
 Package        Arch     Version              Repository   Size
========================================================================
Installing:
 dhcp-server    x86_64   12:4.3.6-28.fc29     fedora       431 k

Transaction Summary
========================================================================
Install  1 Package

Total download size: 431 k
Installed size: 1.2 M
Downloading Packages:
dhcp-server-4.3.6-28.fc29.x86_64.rpm      120 kB/s | 431 kB     00:03
------------------------------------------------------------------------
Total                                      78 kB/s | 431 kB     00:05
Running transaction check
Transaction check succeeded.
Running transaction test
Transaction test succeeded.
Running transaction
  Preparing        :                                          1/1
  Running scriptlet: dhcp-server-12:4.3.6-28.fc29.x86_64         1/1
  Installing       : dhcp-server-12:4.3.6-28.fc29.x86_64         1/1
  Running scriptlet: dhcp-server-12:4.3.6-28.fc29.x86_64         1/1
  Verifying        : dhcp-server-12:4.3.6-28.fc29.x86_64         1/1

Installed:
  dhcp-server-12:4.3.6-28.fc29.x86_64

Complete!
[root@studentvm2 ~]#
```

That was easy and no reboot of the server, StudentVM2, is required.

Configuring the DHCP server

With the DHCP server installed, the next step is to configure the server. Having more than one DHCP server on the same network can cause problems because one would never know which DHCP server is providing the network configuration data to the client. However, a single DHCP server on one host can listen to multiple networks and provide configuration data to clients on more than one network.

It is possible for DHCP to provide DNS names for the gateway and other servers. For example, the NTP server could use the hostname of that server, such as NTP1 instead of the IP address. Most of the time this would work well, but this configuration might cause problems if the DNS name services server were to be disabled or if our own server does not exist, such as right at the moment.

The IP addresses specified in Figure 3-1 are the ones that we will assign to the hosts on our internal network. We do not need to assign the IP address for the router because that is configured by the virtual network. I have arbitrarily chosen these IP addresses and they will be used for the rest of this course.

Hostname	Role	MAC Address	NIC Name	IP Address
studentvm1	Workstation	08:00:27:e1:0c:10	enp0s3	192.168.56.21/24
studentvm2	Server	08:00:27:9f:67:cb	enp0s8	192.168.56.1/24

Figure 3-1. *The specific IP Address map for the server and the workstation on our network*

Before configuring and starting the DHCP server on StudentVM2, we will turn off the DHCP server that is part of the virtual router.

EXPERIMENT 3-2

In this experiment, we create a fairly simple configuration file, start the DHCP server, and then test it by determining that StudentVM1 receives the correct network configuration information. Be absolutely certain to use the MAC addresses for the specific hosts on your virtual network. As the non-root user on your physical host, turn off the virtual network DHCP server to prevent conflict. You need to use the command line to do this. Use the VirtualBox Manager and click the menu bar, **File ➤ Preferences** to open the preferences dialog box.

Click the **Network** tab on the left side of the Preferences dialog. Then click **StudentNetwork**.

Remove the check mark from the **Supports DHCP** check box. Note that the existing IP address leases will remain in effect until they expire, the client host NICs are turned down and then up again, or the systems are rebooted. We are not turning off the StudentNetwork, just its DHCP server. Click **OK** and then again **OK** in the Preferences dialog.

Now we can configure the DHCP server on StudentVM2.

As root, let's look at the existing dhcpd.conf file. Make /etc/dhcp the PWD and then **cat** the dhcpd.conf file to view the content. There is not much there, but it does point to an example file, /usr/share/doc/dhcp-server/dhcpd.conf.example, which you can read in order to understand the main components and syntax of the dhcpd.conf file.

The dhcpd.conf(5) man page also has some excellent descriptions of the various configuration statements that we are likely to need.

Open the dhcpd.conf file in a text editor – I prefer Vim, but use whichever editor you prefer – and we will add the statements required for our network in the steps below. Only the five lines shown in the following should exist in this file. We are going to add the lines we need as we proceed through this experiment.

```
#
# DHCP Server Configuration file.
#   see /usr/share/doc/dhcp-server/dhcpd.conf.example
#   see dhcpd.conf(5) man page
#
```

Add the following statements to the bottom of the dhcpd.conf file. This first section contains configuration items that are global – common to all subnets that DHCP is configured to provide for. In our case, we have only a single subnet, but we still place these statements in the global section because they are likely to be the same for all subnets. If they were to differ for a given subnet, placing a statement with different values in the subnet declaration will override the global declaration.

These first lines define the name of the domain, example.com, and the default domain name for DNS lookups to search when no domain is explicitly provided.

```
# option definitions common to all supported networks...
# These directives could be placed inside the subnet declaration
# if they are unique to a subnet.
```

```
option domain-name "example.com";
option domain-search "example.com";
```

This next line sets the virtual router as the domain name server (DNS). For now, be sure to use the IP address of the virtual router for your virtual network. We will change this entry in Chapter 5 when we add DNS services to our own server.

```
option domain-name-servers 10.0.2.1;
```

Now we set the default lease times in seconds

```
# All networks get the default lease times
default-lease-time 600;   # 10 minutes
max-lease-time 7200;      # 2 hours
#
```

Next add these lines, the last of which specifies that this is the authoritative DHCP server for this network.

```
# If this DHCP server is the official DHCP server for the local
# network, the authoritative directive should be uncommented.
authoritative;
```

Now we can add the declaration for our subnet. We also add a host declaration inside that subnet declaration to provide specific IP address configuration for the StudentVM1 host. Be sure to use the correct MAC address for the host studentvm1 in your setup.

```
############################################################
# This is a very basic subnet declaration.                #
############################################################
subnet 192.168.56.0 netmask 255.255.255.0 {
        # default gateway
        option routers                  192.168.56.1;
        option subnet-mask              255.255.255.0;
############################################################
# Dynamic allocation range for otherwise unknown hosts    #
############################################################
        range dynamic-bootp 192.168.56.50 192.168.56.59;
############################################################
# Host declaration in the 192.168.56.0/24 subnet.         #
############################################################
```

```
host studentvm1 {
        hardware ethernet 08:00:27:E1:0C:10;
        fixed-address 192.168.56.21;
    }
}
```

Note that the host declaration has curly braces, {}, around the configuration declarations. The curly braces for the subnet declaration also surround the host declaration because the host declarations need to be inside the subnet declaration.

Be sure to save the file which is now complete enough to test. To test the new DHCP configuration, first start the DHCP service, then configure it to start every time the server is rebooted. Lastly, verify that it is running.

```
[root@studentvm2 ~]# systemctl start dhcpd
[root@studentvm2 ~]# systemctl enable dhcpd
Created symlink /etc/systemd/system/multi-user.target.wants/dhcpd.service →
/usr/lib/systemd/system/dhcpd.service.
[root@studentvm2 ~]# systemctl status dhcpd
• dhcpd.service - DHCPv4 Server Daemon
   Loaded: loaded (/usr/lib/systemd/system/dhcpd.service; enabled; vendor
   preset: disabled)
   Active: active (running) since Thu 2019-07-18 14:45:05 EDT; 1min 36s ago
     Docs: man:dhcpd(8)
           man:dhcpd.conf(5)
 Main PID: 2334 (dhcpd)
   Status: "Dispatching packets..."
    Tasks: 1 (limit: 4696)
   Memory: 5.1M
   CGroup: /system.slice/dhcpd.service
           └─2334 /usr/sbin/dhcpd -f -cf /etc/dhcp/dhcpd.conf -user dhcpd
           -group dhcpd --no-pid

Jul 18 14:45:05 studentvm2.example.com dhcpd[2334]:
Jul 18 14:45:05 studentvm2.example.com dhcpd[2334]: No subnet declaration for
enp0s3 (10.0.2.11).
Jul 18 14:45:05 studentvm2.example.com dhcpd[2334]: ** Ignoring requests on
enp0s3.  If this is>
Jul 18 14:45:05 studentvm2.example.com dhcpd[2334]:    you want, please write
a subnet declaration
```

```
Jul 18 14:45:05 studentvm2.example.com dhcpd[2334]:    in your dhcpd.conf
file for the network s>
Jul 18 14:45:05 studentvm2.example.com dhcpd[2334]:    to which interface
enp0s3 is attached. **
Jul 18 14:45:05 studentvm2.example.com dhcpd[2334]:
Jul 18 14:45:05 studentvm2.example.com dhcpd[2334]: Sending on    Socket/
fallback/fallback-net
Jul 18 14:45:05 studentvm2.example.com dhcpd[2334]: Server starting service.
Jul 18 14:45:05 studentvm2.example.com systemd[1]: Started DHCPv4 Server
Daemon.
```

You should see no errors from the status command but you will see a number of statements indicating the DHCP daemon is listening on a specific NIC and the MAC address of the NIC. If this information is not correct, verify that the dhcpd.conf file is correct and try to restart. If there are syntactical errors in your configuration, they will show up in the status report.

If StudentVM1 is already up and running, run the following commands to turn enp0s3 down and then back up.

```
[root@studentvm1 ~]# ip link set enp0s3 down ; ip link set enp0s3 up
```

If the StudentVM1 host is not already running, start it now. Nothing further will need to be done to obtain an IP address from the newly configured DHCP server.

Login to StudentVM1, open a terminal session, and **su** **–** to root.

Run this command to verify that the network is configured with the correct IP address. Note that the syntax of this command shows only the desired NIC and not any of the others that might be installed, including the lo local device.

```
[root@studentvm1 ~]# ip addr show dev enp0s3
2: enp0s3: <BROADCAST,MULTICAST,UP,LOWER_UP> mtu 1500 qdisc fq_codel state UP
group default qlen 1000
    link/ether 08:00:27:e1:0c:10 brd ff:ff:ff:ff:ff:ff
    inet 192.168.56.21/24 brd 192.168.56.255 scope global dynamic
noprefixroute enp0s3
       valid_lft 474sec preferred_lft 474sec
```

Verify the default route on StudentVM1 is correct.

```
[root@studentvm1 ~]# ip route
default via 192.168.56.1 dev enp0s3 proto dhcp metric 100
192.168.56.0/24 dev enp0s3 proto kernel scope link src 192.168.56.21 metric 100
```

On StudentVM1, verify connectivity to the StudentVM2 server using the ping command. The -c option specifies the number of ping requests to send, in this case 2. We need to specify the IP address of the server because we do not yet have a name server on this network.

```
[root@studentvm1 ~]# ping 192.168.0.1 -c 2
PING 192.168.0.1 (192.168.0.1) 56(84) bytes of data.
64 bytes from 192.168.0.1: icmp_seq=1 ttl=64 time=0.229 ms
64 bytes from 192.168.0.1: icmp_seq=2 ttl=64 time=0.216 ms

--- 192.168.0.1 ping statistics ---
2 packets transmitted, 2 received, 0% packet loss, time 60ms
rtt min/avg/max/mdev = 0.216/0.222/0.229/0.016 ms
```

Access to the outside world from StudentVM1 will not be working because our name server is not yet up and running and StudentVM2 is not yet configured as a router.

```
[root@studentvm1 ~]# ping -c2 example.net
ping: example.net: Name or service not known
```

If the dhcpd.conf file is still open in your editor, close it now.

A reboot is not required for either the DHCP client or the server. No configuration changes were required on the client, StudentVM1, and simply turning down the NIC and bringing it back up again enabled it to obtain the configuration data from the new DHCP server.

Configuring guest hosts

Configuring the network settings for guest hosts such as laptops and other mobile devices is also possible with DHCP. This implies that we have no information such as the MAC address for these computers and that we must assign an IP address anyway.

In most cases, this usage for DHCP, despite the fact that it was the original intention for DHCP, requires a good bit of trust be afforded to the guest hosts. I personally dislike having guests on my own network, so I usually find a way to set up a second network subnet to which I relegate all guest hosts. This protects my own network and improves security because the guest hosts have no access to it.

There are times when it becomes necessary to include guest computers in a network. The use of DHCP makes that not just possible but also easy. All we need to do is introduce a short stanza into our subnet configuration.

EXPERIMENT 3-3

This experiment must be performed as root.

Insert the following lines in the subnet declaration for the 192.168.56.0/24 subnet but outside of any individual host declarations within that subnet. I added it immediately under the `option subnet-mask` line.

```
###########################################################
# Dynamic allocation range for otherwise unknown hosts    #
###########################################################
        range dynamic-bootp 192.168.56.50 192.168.56.59;
```

Restart the DHCP service to enable this change.

```
[root@studentvm2 ~]# systemctl restart dhcpd
```

Verify that there were no errors during the restart.

To test this DHCP guest allocation, create a brand new VM, StudentVM3 with a dynamically allocated 120GB hard drive and 4GB of RAM. Be sure the VM is in the StudentNetwork. Do not clone this VM from one of the other VMs we have already created. Boot to the Live USB image ISO file from which StudentVM1 was created. After the Live image boots, open a terminal session and verify that the network configuration is correct and that the IP address falls within the range specified in the declaration.

I have found that it is sometimes necessary to power off all open VMs and VirtualBox itself before restarting VirtualBox, then StudentVM2, and then the rest of the Student VMs in order to reset the VirtualBox DHCP server to off. This behavior is inconsistent and I have no current explanation for it. Just be aware that it can happen.

Perform some additional testing to ensure that network communication to the Internet is working properly.

After you have finished testing, you can power off the StudentVM3 virtual machine. Do not delete the VM you created for this test.

The dhcpd.conf file

The final dhcpd.conf file is shown in Figure 3-2.

```
#
# DHCP Server Configuration file.
#    see /usr/share/doc/dhcp-server/dhcpd.conf.example
#    see dhcpd.conf(5) man page
#
# option definitions common to all supported networks…
# These directives could be placed inside the subnet declaration
# if they are unique to a subnet.
option domain-name "example.com";
option domain-search "example.com";
option domain-name-servers 192.168.56.1, 10.0.2.1;
#
# All networks get the default lease times
default-lease-time 600; # 10 minutes
max-lease-time 7200;     # 2 hours
authoritative;
#
##############################################################
# This is a very basic subnet declaration.             #
##############################################################
subnet 192.168.56.0 netmask 255.255.255.0 {
    # default gateway
    option routers               192.168.56.1;
    option subnet-mask           255.255.255.0;
##############################################################
# Dynamic allocation range for otherwise unknown hosts     #
##############################################################
    range dynamic-bootp 192.168.56.50 192.168.56.59;
##############################################################
# Host declaration in the 192.168.56.0/24 subnet.       #
##############################################################
    host studentvm1 {
        hardware ethernet 08:00:27:E1:0C:10;
        fixed-address 192.168.56.21;
    }
}
```

Figure 3-2. *The completed dhcpd.conf file*

Chapter summary

DHCP is designed to provide network configuration data to client hosts on a network. This allows for centralization of network configuration management.

You now have a working DHCP server on StudentVM2. You have turned off the DHCP server embedded in the virtual router created for our virtual network to ensure that there are no conflicts between servers. You have tested the new DHCP server by using the StudentVM1 as a DHCP client to obtain the revised network configuration data from the new DHCP server. You have used typical Linux command line networking tools to verify that the new configuration is working properly.

A DHCP server can provide many configuration options to clients, including many required for Windows hosts that might connect to the network. This configuration data includes gateway routers, NTP servers, DNS servers, PXE boot servers, and much more. As we continue through this course, we will add configuration items for DNS and NTP servers to our DHCP configuration.

Exercises

1. What is the function of DHCP?

2. What five common configuration items are provided by DHCP to Linux hosts?

3. How many name servers can be specified?

4. Can servers and routers be specified by name as well as by IP address in the dhcpd.conf file? If so, what problems might arise?

5. Based on the content of the DHCP configuration database we have created in this chapter, what IP address would likely be served to a new VM that booted up on the network?

CHAPTER 4

Name Services

Objectives

In this chapter, you will learn:

- To describe the structure and function of Domain Name Services (DNS)

- How to test name services (DNS)

- About the Berkeley Internet Name Domain (BIND)

- How to use the client configuration files

- How to set up a caching name server

- How to configure the iptables firewall for DNS services

- How to create a primary[1] name server from a caching name server including both forward and reverse zones

- How to use several types of records commonly found in zone files

Introducing Domain Name Services

Surfing the Web is fun and easy, but think what it would be like if you had to type in the IP address of every web site you wanted to view. For example, locating a web site would look like this when you type it in – https://93.184.216.34 – which would be nearly impossible for most of us to remember. Of course, using bookmarks would help but suppose your friend tells you about a cool new web site and tells you to go to

---

[1] I prefer not to use the common contemporary terms for the primary and secondary name servers because they have deep racial and gender connotations that I find offensive.

© David Both 2020
D. Both, *Using and Administering Linux: Volume 3*, https://doi.org/10.1007/978-1-4842-5485-1_4

93.184.216.34. How would you remember that? Telling someone to go to "Opensource. com," for example, is far easier to remember than 54.204.39.132.

The Domain Name Services system provides the database to be used in the translation from human-readable hostnames, such as www.opensource.com, to IP addresses, like 54.204.39.132, so that your Internet-connected computers and other devices can access them. The primary function of the BIND software (Berkeley Internet Name Domain software) is that of a domain name resolver which utilizes that database. There are other name resolver software, but BIND is currently the most widely used DNS software on the Internet. I will use the terms name server, DNS, and resolver pretty much interchangeably throughout this chapter.

Without these name resolver services, it would be nearly impossible to surf the Web as freely and easily as we do. As humans, we tend to do better with names like Opensource.com, while computers do much better with numbers like 54.204.39.132. So we need a translation service to convert the names that are easy for us to the IP addresses that are easy for our computers.

The /etc/hosts file

In small networks, the /etc/hosts file on each host can be used as a simple local name resolver. The SysAdmin would add and manage entries in the hosts file. Maintaining copies of this file on several hosts can become very time-consuming and errors can cause much confusion and wasted time before they are found. Experiment 4-1 shows a simple /etc/hosts file. A default hosts file is always present but it would contain only the first two lines. Those two lines enable internal services and commands to translate the localhost hostname to 127.0.0.1 – this is an explicitly defined standard to enable services and commands to deal with the local host.

EXPERIMENT 4-1

This experiment must be performed as root on StudentVM1.

Make a backup copy of the /etc/hosts file and store it in /root. Try to ping studentvm2 before we change anything.

```
[root@studentvm1 ~]# ping -c2 studentvm2
ping: studentvm2: Name or service not known
[root@studentvm1 ~]#
```

This result shows that there is no resolution from the studentvm2 hostname to an IP address. Now edit the /etc/hosts file on StudentVM1 so that it looks like this:

```
127.0.0.1    localhost localhost.localdomain localhost4 localhost4.localdomain4
::1          localhost localhost.localdomain localhost6 localhost6.localdomain6

# Student hosts
192.168.56.1              router
192.168.56.1              server studentvm2
192.168.56.21             studentvm1 host1
192.168.56.22             host2
192.168.56.23             host3
192.168.56.24             host4
```

Notice that IP addresses can have multiple hostnames associated with them. Only a single host can be assigned an address so these hostnames are aliases and all point to the same host. This can be a way to maintain backward compatibility with previous naming systems, for example. We have also added some hostnames and IP addresses that are not actually present on our network.

Let's test the /etc/hosts file.

```
[root@studentvm1 ~]# ping -c2 studentvm2
PING server (192.168.56.1) 56(84) bytes of data.
64 bytes from server (192.168.56.1): icmp_seq=1 ttl=64 time=0.419 ms
64 bytes from server (192.168.56.1): icmp_seq=2 ttl=64 time=0.383 ms

--- server ping statistics ---
2 packets transmitted, 2 received, 0% packet loss, time 1058ms
rtt min/avg/max/mdev = 0.383/0.401/0.419/0.018 ms
[root@studentvm1 ~]# ping -c2 server
PING server (192.168.56.1) 56(84) bytes of data.
64 bytes from server (192.168.56.1): icmp_seq=1 ttl=64 time=0.371 ms
64 bytes from server (192.168.56.1): icmp_seq=2 ttl=64 time=0.393 ms

--- server ping statistics ---
2 packets transmitted, 2 received, 0% packet loss, time 1001ms
rtt min/avg/max/mdev = 0.371/0.382/0.393/0.011 ms
[root@studentvm1 ~]# ping -c2 router
```

```
PING router (192.168.56.1) 56(84) bytes of data.
64 bytes from router (192.168.56.1): icmp_seq=1 ttl=255 time=0.287 ms
64 bytes from router (192.168.56.1): icmp_seq=2 ttl=255 time=0.211 ms

--- router ping statistics ---
2 packets transmitted, 2 received, 0% packet loss, time 1004ms
rtt min/avg/max/mdev = 0.211/0.249/0.287/0.038 ms
[root@studentvm1 ~]#
```

Try pinging the hosts that do not exist.

In the second part of this experiment, we pinged the same host – at IP address 192.168.56.1 – using the hostnames of server and studentvm2. Both of these hostnames were correctly resolved to the IP address of 192.168.56.1.

Comment out the lines you added to /etc/hosts by prepending a # character to each line. This is necessary so that the /etc/hosts file will not contain the host resolutions we will be testing with BIND.

I used the /etc/hosts file to manage name services for my network for several years. It ultimately became too much trouble to maintain even with only the usual 8 to 12 computers I usually have operational. As a result, I converted to running my own name server to resolve both internal and external hostnames.

Most networks of any size require centralized management of this service with name services software such as BIND. BIND is called that because it was developed by the University of California Berkeley (UCB) in the early 1980s. Hosts use the Domain Name System (DNS) to locate IP addresses from the names given in software such as web browsers, email clients, SSH, FTP, and many other Internet services.

How a name search works

Let's take look at a simplified example of what happens when a name request for a web page is made by a client service on your computer. For this example, I will use www.opensource.com as the web site I want to view in my browser. I also assume that there is a local name server on the network, as is the case with my own network.

1. First, I type in the URL or select a bookmark containing that URL. In this case, the URL is www.opensource.com.

2. The browser client, whether it is Opera, Firefox, Chrome, Min, Lynx, Links, or any other browser, sends the request to the operating system.

3. The operating system first checks the /etc/hosts file to see if the hostname is there. If so, the IP address of that entry is returned to the browser. If not, we proceed to the next step. In this case, we assume that the name is not in /etc/hosts.

4. The hostname is then sent to the first name server specified in /etc/resolv.conf. In this case, the IP address of the first name server is my own internal name server. For this example, my name server does not have the IP address for www.opensource.com cached and must look further afield. So we go on to the next step.

5. The local name server sends the request to a remote name server. This can be one of two destination types, one type of which is a forwarder. A forwarder is simply another name server such as the ones at your ISP, or a public name server such as Google at 8.8.8.8 or 8.8.4.4. The other destination type is that of the top-level root name servers. The root servers don't usually respond with the desired target IP address or www.opensource.com; they respond with the authoritative name server for that domain. The authoritative name servers are the only ones that have the authority to maintain and modify the data for a domain.

6. The local name server is configured to use the root name servers so the root name server for the com. top-level domain returns the IP address of the authoritative name server for opensource.com. That IP address could be for any one of the three (at the time of this writing) name servers, ns1.redhat.com, ns2.redhat.com, or ns3.redhat.com.

7. The local name server then sends the query to the authoritative name server which returns the IP address for www.opensource.com.

8. The browser uses the IP address for www.opensource.com to send a request for a web page which is downloaded to the browser.

One of the important side effects of this name search is that the results are cached for a period of time by my local name server. That means that the next time I, or anyone on my network, wants to access Opensource.com, the IP address is probably already stored in the local cache which prevents doing another remote lookup.

The DNS database

The DNS system is dependent upon its database to perform lookups on hostnames to locate the correct IP address. The DNS database is a general-purpose distributed, hierarchical, replicated database. It also defines the style of hostname used on the Internet, properly called a fully qualified domain name (FQDN).

FQDNs consist of complete hostnames such as hornet.example.com and studentvm2.example.com. FQDNs break down into three parts.

1.   The top-level domain names (TLDNs) such as .com, .net, .biz, .org, .info, .edu, and so on provide the last segment of a FQDN. All TLDNs are managed on the root name servers. Aside from the country top-level domains such as .us, .uk, and so on, there were originally only a few main top-level domains. As of February 2017, there are 1,528 top-level domains.

2.   The second-level domain name is always immediately to the left of the top-level domain when specifying a hostname or URL. So names like redhat.com, opensource.com, getfedora.org, and example.com provide the organizational address portion of the FQDN.

3.   The third level of the FQDN is the hostname portion of the name. So the FQDN of a specific host in a network would be something like host1.example.com.

Figure 4-1 shows a simplified diagram of the DNS database hierarchy. The "top" level, which is represented by a single dot (.) has no real physical existence. It is a device for use in DNS zone file configuration to enable an explicit end-stop for domain names. A bit more on this later.

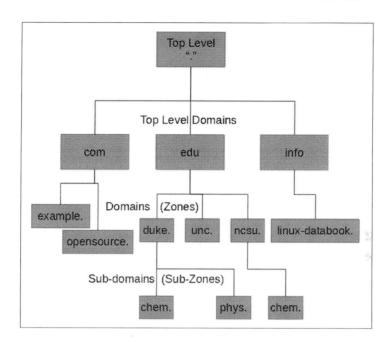

Figure 4-1. *A very simplified representation of the DNS database hierarchical structure*

The true top level consists of the root name servers. These are a limited number of servers that maintain the top-level DNS databases. The root level may contain the IP addresses for some domains and the root servers will directly provide those IP addresses where they are available. In other cases, the root servers provide the IP addresses of the authoritative server for the desired domain.

For example, assume we want to browse www.opensource.com. Our browser makes the request of the local name server which does not contain that IP address. My local name server is configured to use the root servers when an address is not found in the local cache, so it sends the request for www.opensource.com to one of the root servers. Of course, the local name server must know how to locate the root name servers so it uses the /var/named/named.ca file which contains the names and IP addresses of the root name servers. The named.ca file is also known as the hints file.

In this example, the IP address for www.opensource.com is not stored by the root servers. The root server uses its database to locate the name and IP address of the authoritative name server for www.opensource.com. The local name server queries the authoritative name server which returns the IP address of www.opensource.com. The local name server then responds to the browser's request and provides it with the IP address. The authoritative name server for Opensource.com contains the zone files for that domain.

The Internet Assigned Numbers Authority (IANA)[2] is responsible for global coordination and management of IP address and autonomous system (AS) number assignments. This organization coordinates the assignments of IP addresses to large geographic–political entities. Registries within those divisions are responsible for assigning addresses to customers such as ISPs. The IANA web site has a great deal of information that you may find useful.

The dig command is a powerful tool that can tell us a lot of information about the DNS configuration for a host. The dig command returns the actual records from the DNS database and displays the results in four main sections.

EXPERIMENT 4-2

Perform this experiment as root. Use the **dig** command to obtain DNS information about the www.opensource.com domain.

```
[root@studentvm1 ~]# dig www.opensource.com
; <<>> DiG 9.11.4-P2-RedHat-9.11.4-10.P2.fc29 <<>> www.opensource.com
;; global options: +cmd
;; Got answer:
;; ->>HEADER<<- opcode: QUERY, status: NOERROR, id: 9554
;; flags: qr rd ra; QUERY: 1, ANSWER: 2, AUTHORITY: 3, ADDITIONAL: 4

;; OPT PSEUDOSECTION:
; EDNS: version: 0, flags:; udp: 4096
;; QUESTION SECTION:
;www.opensource.com.            IN      A

;; ANSWER SECTION:
www.opensource.com.     300     IN      CNAME   opensource.com.
opensource.com.         300     IN      A       54.204.39.132

;; AUTHORITY SECTION:
opensource.com.         169682  IN      NS      ns3.redhat.com.
opensource.com.         169682  IN      NS      ns2.redhat.com.
opensource.com.         169682  IN      NS      ns1.redhat.com.

;; ADDITIONAL SECTION:
```

---

[2]Internet Assigned Numbers Authority (IANA), www.iana.org/

```
ns2.redhat.com.          169682  IN     A      209.132.183.2
ns3.redhat.com.          169682  IN     A      66.187.233.212
ns1.redhat.com.          169682  IN     A      209.132.186.218

;; Query time: 71 msec
;; SERVER: 192.168.56.1#53(192.168.56.1)
;; WHEN: Thu Dec 27 15:04:33 EST 2018
;; MSG SIZE  rcvd: 186
```

Refer to the results of this experiment as you read the descriptions of these sections.

QUESTION: The first section of specific interest in Experiment 4-1 is the QUESTION section. For our example, it states that we are looking for the A record of "www. opensource.com". Notice the dot at the end of the top-level domain name. This explicitly indicates that .com. is the final domain name component in the hostname.

ANSWER: This section shows two entries, a CNAME record and an A record. A records are the primary name resolver records, and there must be an A record which contains the IP address for each host. CNAME stands for canonical name, and this record type is an alias for the A record and points to it. It is not typical practice to use "www" as the hostname for a web server. It is common to see a CNAME record that points to the A record of the FQDN. However, that is not quite the case here. Notice that the A record for opensource.com does not have a hostname associated with it. It is possible to have a record that applies to the domain as a whole as is the case here.

AUTHORITY: The AUTHORITY section lists the authoritative name servers for the opensource.com domain. In this case, those are the Red Hat name servers. Notice that the record type is NS for these entries.

ADDITIONAL: The ADDITIONAL section lists the A records for the Red Hat name servers.

Following the ADDITIONAL section, you can find some additional interesting information, including the IP address of the server that returned the information shown in the results. In this case, it was my own internal name server.

Common DNS record types

There are a number of different DNS record types, and I want to introduce some of the more common ones here. Later in this chapter, you will create your own name server using BIND and will use many of these record types. These record types are used in the zone files that comprise the DNS database. One common field in all of these records is "IN" which specifies that these are INternet records. You can find a complete list of DNS record types at Wikipedia.[3]

I will make the assertion in this discussion that studentvm2.example.com is the BIND name server which is why its hostname appears in these records. The example. com domain is a valid domain and is used for testing purposes on the Internet. It can also be used for internal testing and we will be doing that later in this chapter. Therefore, the sample listings in the following figures will use example.com for the domain name.

SOA

SOA is the Start of Authority record.[4] It is the first record in any forward or reverse zone file, and it identifies this as the authoritative source for the domain it describes. It also specifies certain functional parameters. A typical SOA record looks like the sample here.

```
@   IN SOA  studentvm2.example.com   root.studentvm2.example.com. (
                      2018101501       ; serial
                      1D               ; refresh
                      1H               ; retry
                      1W               ; expire
                      3H )             ; minimum
```

The first line of the SOA record contains the name of the server for the zone and the zone administrator, in this case root.

The second line is a serial number. In this example, I use the date in YYYYMMDDXX format where XX is a counter for 00 to 99. The serial number in the SOA record represents the first version of this file on October 15, 2018. This format ensures that all

---

[3]Wikipedia, *List of DNS record types*, https://en.wikipedia.org/wiki/
List_of_DNS_record_types
[4]The Network Encyclopedia, *Start of Authority (SOA) record*, www.thenetworkencyclopedia.com/
entry/start-of-authority-soa-record/

changes to the serial number are incremented in a numerically sequential manner. That is important because secondary name servers only replicate from the primary server when the serial number of the zone file on the primary is greater than the serial number on the secondary. Be sure to increment the serial number when you make changes or the secondary server will not sync up with the modified data.

The rest of the SOA record consists of various times that secondary servers should perform a refresh from the primary and wait for retries if the first refresh fails. It also defines the amount of time before the zone's authoritative status expires.

Times all used to be specified in seconds, but recent versions of BIND allow other options defined with W=week, D=day, H=hour, and M=minute. Seconds are assumed if no other specifier is used.

$ORIGIN

The $ORIGIN record is like a variable assignment. The value of this variable is appended by the BIND program to any hostname in an A or PTR record that does not end in a period (.) in order to create the FQDN for that host. This makes for less typing because the zone administrator only has to type the hostname portion and not the fully qualified domain name (FQDN) for each record.

```
$ORIGIN          example.com.
```

The @ symbol is used as a shortcut for this variable and any occurrence of @ in the file is replaced by the value of $ORIGIN.

NS

The NS record specifies the authoritative name server for the zone. Note that both names in this record end with periods so that ".example.com" does not get appended to them. This record will usually point to the local host – which is also the name server – by its fully qualified domain name.

```
example.com.            IN     NS      studentvm2.example.com.
```

Note that the host, studentvm2.example.com, must also have an A record in the zone. The A record can point to the external IP address of the host or to the localhost address, 127.0.0.1.

A

The A record is the address record type that specifies the relationship between the hostname and the IP address assigned to that host. In the example below, the host studentvm2 has IP address 192.168.56.1. Note that the value of $ORIGIN is appended to the name studentvm2 because studentvm2 is not an FQDN and does not have a terminating period in this record.

```
studentvm2                      IN      A       192.168.56.1
```

The A record is the most common type of DNS database record.

AAAA

The AAAA records are used for IPv6 addresses in the DNS system. They perform exactly the same function as A records do for IPv4 addresses.

CNAME

The CNAME record is an alias for the name in the A record for a host. For example, the hostname studentvm2.example.com might serve as both the web server and the mail server. So there would be one A record and possibly two or three CNAME records as shown in the following.

```
studentvm2      IN      A       192.168.56.1
server          IN      CNAME   studentvm2
www             IN      CNAME   studentvm2
mail            IN      CNAME   studentvm2
```

It is good practice to have the A record contain the true hostname of the host. All of the other alias hostnames can be set using CNAME records. It is possible to have multiple A records, each with a different hostname, point to the same IP address, but this is not a good practice because it requires more work if the host's IP address is changed. The lazy SysAdmin types as little as possible and keeps things like configuration files as simple as possible.

Lookups with the dig command on www.example.com and mail.example.com will return the CNAME record for mail or www and the A record for server.example.com. These records contain only the hostnames with no terminating dot (.), so the domain name as defined in the $ORIGIN variable will be appended to the hostname.

PTR

The PTR records are to provide for reverse lookups. This is when you already know the IP address and need to know fully qualified hostname. For example, many mail servers do a reverse lookup on the alleged IP address of a sending mail server to verify that the name and IP address given in the email headers match. PTR records are located in reverse zone files. Reverse lookups can also be used when attempting to determine the source of suspect network packets.

Be aware that not all hosts have PTR records. Most ISPs create and manage the PTR records for home and small business accounts, so reverse lookups may not provide the needed information. For example, I use Spectrum business class for my Internet connection. I use Google Domains to manage my several external domains including both.org, linux-databook.info, and mtc-llc.net. Google Domains does allow me to create PTR records, but my ISP has already created an authoritative PTR record for my external IP address. I have not taken much time to explore whether this can be changed or not but early experiments indicate not.

MX

The MX record defines the Mail eXchanger, that is, the mail server for the domain example.com. Notice that it points to the CNAME record for the server in the example earlier. Note that both example.com names in the MX record terminate with a dot so that example.com is not appended to the names.

```
; Mail server MX record
example.com.             IN     MX     10      mail.example.com.
```

Domains may have multiple mail servers defined. The number "10" in the above MX record is a priority value. Other servers may have the same priority or different ones. The lower numbers define higher priorities. So if all mail servers have the same priority, they would be used in round-robin fashion. If they have different priorities, the mail delivery would first be attempted to the mail server with the highest priority – the lowest number – and if that mail server did not respond, delivery would be attempted to the mail server with the next highest priority.

Other records

There are other types of records that you may encounter in the DNS database. One type, the TXT records, are used to record comments about the zone or hosts in the DNS database. TXT records can also be used for DNS security. The rest of the DNS record types are outside the scope of this chapter.

Using BIND

BIND is the Berkeley Internet Name Daemon (Domain). It is used to centrally manage name services, generally in medium and large environments. It can, however, be used very successfully in smaller environments as well. Configuring BIND requires editing a number of files. The BIND configuration can be very picky about syntax, and I have found that some syntactical elements that should work apparently do not.

We will first configure a caching name server and then add the necessary configuration components to convert it into a primary name server. We will also configure the DHCP server for client-side DNS configuration.

Preparation

A caching name server cannot replace our use of /etc/hosts to resolve hostnames on the internal network. Compared to using an ISP or other public name server, however, a caching name server can improve both reliability and performance when resolving external names that are commonly used, such as www.cnn.com. I have experienced loss of DNS services from my ISP many times and have found my own name server is far more reliable than most ISPs. The best part is that setting up a caching name server is quite easy. It is also the first step in creating a primary name server that we can use for name resolution inside our own network.

EXPERIMENT 4-3

This experiment must be performed as root. Install the following BIND RPMs on the studentvm2 host: bind, bind-chroot, and bind-utils.

```
[root@studentvm2 ~]# dnf -y install bind bind-chroot bind-utils
```

To enable your StudentVM2 host to use itself as a caching name server, you must change the DNS1 line in /etc/sysconfig/network-scripts/ifcfg-enp0s3 to point to your own host. We could change /etc/resolv.conf, but that change would not be persistent through a reboot or a restart of NetworkManager. The /etc/resolv.conf file is recreated by NetworkManager every time the host is booted or NetworkManager is restarted.

Change the DNS1 line in /etc/sysconfig/network-scripts/ifcfg-enp0s3 to the following.

```
DNS1=192.168.56.1
```

Comment out the DNS2 line so that the secondary server will not be listed.

You could use the IP address of the localhost, 127.0.0.1, instead of the external IP address, but by using the external address, you know that other hosts on your network can see it as well.

```
[root@studentvm2 ~]# systemctl restart NetworkManager
[root@studentvm2 ~]# cat /etc/resolv.conf
# Generated by NetworkManager
search example.com
nameserver 192.168.56.1
[root@studentvm2 ~]#
```

We have now prepared our host so that it can be configured as a caching name server.

Setting up the caching name server

It is necessary to make a couple modifications to the /etc/named.conf file. First, add the IP address of your local student host to the "listen-on port 53" line. This enables named to listen on the external IP address of your host so that other computers can use it as a name server as well.

Note   The named.conf file is very particular about syntax and especially punctuation. Semi-colons are used to delineate the end of an entry and the end of a stanza as well as the end of a line. Be sure to add them in correctly as shown in the samples.

EXPERIMENT 4-4

This experiment must be performed as root. In this experiment, we alter the default /etc/named.conf file to create our caching name server. The lines that need to be changed are highlighted in bold. I have removed some comment lines from the version of named.conf shown here to save some space.

By default, BIND refers to the Internet's root name servers to locate the authoritative name servers for a domain. It is possible to specify other servers that are called "forwarders" to which the local instance of BIND will send requests instead of the root servers. This does increase the possibility of DNS hijacking.

Add a "forwarders" line as shown in the following. This tells your caching DNS server where to obtain IP addresses when they are not already cached locally. The IP address listed there is for the virtual router and DNS server of the virtual network. You could use your local ISP or OpenDNS or some other public name server as your forwarder.

It is not necessary to define any forwarders at all. By default, BIND will use the Internet root servers as defined in the file /var/named/named.ca to locate the authoritative name servers for domains if no forwarders are defined. However, for this part of the exercise, you will define two forwarders in /etc/named.conf. We will use the virtual router/name server of our virtual network with IP address 192.168.56.1 and one of the Google public name servers at IP address 8.8.8.8.

Comment out the IPV6 line as we are not using IPV6 in the test environment. Add the local network CIDR address to the allow-query line.

```
//
// named.conf
// Provided by Red Hat bind package to configure the ISC BIND named(8) DNS
// server as a caching only name server (as a localhost DNS resolver only).
```

```
// See /usr/share/doc/bind*/sample/ for example named configuration files.
//
//
options {
        listen-on port 53 { 127.0.0.1; 192.168.56.1; };
//      listen-on-v6 port 53 { ::1; };
        forwarders { 192.168.56.1; 8.8.8.8; };
        directory       "/var/named";
        dump-file       "/var/named/data/cache_dump.db";
        statistics-file "/var/named/data/named_stats.txt";
        memstatistics-file "/var/named/data/named_mem_stats.txt";
        secroots-file   "/var/named/data/named.secroots";
        recursing-file  "/var/named/data/named.recursing";
        allow-query     { localhost; 192.168.56.0/24; };
        recursion yes;

        dnssec-enable yes;
        dnssec-validation yes;
        dnssec-lookaside auto;

        /* Path to ISC DLV key */
        bindkeys-file "/etc/named.iscdlv.key";

        managed-keys-directory "/var/named/dynamic";
        pid-file "/run/named/named.pid";
        session-keyfile "/run/named/session.key";

        /* https://fedoraproject.org/wiki/Changes/CryptoPolicy */
        include "/etc/crypto-policies/back-ends/bind.config";
};
logging {
        channel default_debug {
                file "data/named.run";
                severity dynamic;
        };
};
zone "." IN {
        type hint;
        file "named.ca";
};
```

```
include "/etc/named.rfc1912.zones";
include "/etc/named.root.key";
```

Also add the local network address, 192.168.56.0/24, to the **allow-query** line. This line specifies the network(s) from which DNS queries will be accepted by this DNS server. Multiple networks can be specified.

Keep the named.conf file open in your editor as you will be making several changes to it during the rest of this chapter.

Configuring IPTables for DNS

The firewall on your student host currently blocks everything except SSH. The firewall must be configured to allow UDP and TCP packets inbound on your name server in order for other hosts to use it for name resolution.

We will take this opportunity to switch from firewalld to IPTables. Firewalld is a wrapper around IPTables and it can be used to create complex and flexible rules for IPTables. Firewalld is overly complex for many networks and many of the rules it creates by default are used to create a zoning structure that is simply not required in most environments. A simple IPTables firewall is just as effective and much easier to manage and understand, especially while learning about firewall rules. This falls under the tenet, "Find the Simplicity," of my book *The Linux Philosophy for SysAdmins*.[5] Simple things are easier for us as SysAdmins to manage.

We will discuss firewalls using IPTables in more detail in Chapter 6 in this volume. If you are interested in more information about firewalld, Opensource.com has an excellent article[6] to get you started.

---

[5]Both, David, *The Linux Philosophy for SysAdmins*, Apress, 2018, Chapter 18
[6]Kenlon, Seth, *Make Linux stronger with firewalls*, https://opensource.com/article/19/7/make-linux-stronger-firewalls

---
EXPERIMENT 4-5

This experiment must be performed as root on StudentVM2. We will create a simple rule set for IPTables and then we will disable firewalld and enable IPTables.

First we need to install another package, iptables-services which provides the services required to manage iptables for IPv4 and IPv6. This package was removed from the base iptables package when firewalld became the default firewall service.

```
[root@studentvm2 sysconfig]# dnf install -y iptables-services
```

Now look at the current firewalld rules. You may need to pipe the results of this command through the **less** utility in order to see all of the rules.

```
[root@studentvm2 ~]# iptables-save
```

I have not reproduced the output here because you can see for yourself how complex it is.

If the file /etc/sysconfig/iptables does not exist, create it and add the following content to it. The iptables-services package should install this file so you may only need to add the line for port 53, DNS. This is the full extent of the firewall rules we need for now.

```
# sample configuration for iptables service
# you can edit this manually or use system-config-firewall
# please do not ask us to add additional ports/services to this default
configuration
*filter
:INPUT ACCEPT [0:0]
:FORWARD ACCEPT [0:0]
:OUTPUT ACCEPT [0:0]
-A INPUT -m state --state RELATED,ESTABLISHED -j ACCEPT
-A INPUT -p icmp -j ACCEPT
-A INPUT -i lo -j ACCEPT
-A INPUT -p tcp -m state --state NEW -m tcp --dport 22 -j ACCEPT
-A INPUT -p tcp -m state --state NEW -m tcp --dport 53 -j ACCEPT
-A INPUT -j REJECT --reject-with icmp-host-prohibited
-A FORWARD -j REJECT --reject-with icmp-host-prohibited
COMMIT
```

This simple set of rules rejects all incoming packets except SSH (tcp port 22) and DNS (udp port 53) which it accepts.

Now we need to switch services. We start by turning down the network interface to ensure that black hat hackers cannot take advantage of the moments in which our server's firewall is down. Next we need to turn off and disable firewalld, turn on and enable iptables, and finally turn the network interface on again.

All of the necessary steps can be performed in a single command line program. The command shown here should be entered all on a single line. You could split it up so long as you perform the tasks in the same order.

```
[root@studentvm2 ~]# ip link set enpOs3 down ; systemctl disable firewalld
; systemctl stop firewalld ; systemctl enable iptables ; systemctl start
iptables ; ip link set enpOs3 up
Removed /etc/systemd/system/dbus-org.fedoraproject.FirewallD1.service.
Removed /etc/systemd/system/multi-user.target.wants/firewalld.service.
Created symlink /etc/systemd/system/basic.target.wants/iptables.service →
/usr/lib/systemd/system/iptables.service.
[root@studentvm2 ~]# iptables-save
# Generated by iptables-save v1.6.2 on Thu Oct 18 16:25:51 2018
*filter
:INPUT ACCEPT [0:0]
:FORWARD ACCEPT [0:0]
:OUTPUT ACCEPT [414:42571]
-A INPUT -m state --state RELATED,ESTABLISHED -j ACCEPT
-A INPUT -p icmp -j ACCEPT
-A INPUT -i lo -j ACCEPT
-A INPUT -p tcp -m state --state NEW -m tcp --dport 22 -j ACCEPT
-A INPUT -p udp -m state --state NEW -m udp --dport 53 -j ACCEPT
-A INPUT -j REJECT --reject-with icmp-host-prohibited
-A FORWARD -j REJECT --reject-with icmp-host-prohibited
COMMIT
# Completed on Thu Oct 18 16:25:51 2018
```

The firewall is much simplified and will now accept DNS queries from other hosts on our network.

Start the name service

Now we start the named service and configure the named service to start at every boot.

EXPERIMENT 4-6

As root on StudentVM2, run the following command to enable and start the named service.

```
[root@studentvm2 ~]# systemctl enable named.service ; systemctl start named.
service
```

The named resolver service is now up and ready for local testing.

To test your caching name server, use the dig command to obtain the IP address(es) for some common Internet web sites, such as CNN, Wired, and any others you like. Notice that the results should now show your host as the responding server rather than the virtual router or the Google name server.

Note that on the first attempt, the responding server might be one of the upstream resolvers because your host as client may have timed out waiting for the result from your host as DNS server. Additional attempts will be resolved from the cache of your host as DNS server.

EXPERIMENT 4-7

This experiment can be performed as either the root or student user on StudentVM2.

```
[student@studentvm2 ~]$ dig www.redhat.com
; <<>> DiG 9.11.4-P2-RedHat-9.11.4-10.P2.fc29 <<>> www.redhat.com
;; global options: +cmd
;; Got answer:
;; ->>HEADER<<- opcode: QUERY, status: NOERROR, id: 36287
;; flags: qr rd ra; QUERY: 1, ANSWER: 4, AUTHORITY: 13, ADDITIONAL: 1

;; OPT PSEUDOSECTION:
; EDNS: version: 0, flags:; udp: 4096
; COOKIE: 8ca858d91e1307d4c8fee0af5c254d28565b285017734c80 (good)
;; QUESTION SECTION:
;www.redhat.com.                          IN      A
```

```
;; ANSWER SECTION:
www.redhat.com.           1242    IN      CNAME   ds-www.redhat.com.edgekey.
net.
ds-www.redhat.com.edgekey.net. 6095 IN  CNAME   ds-www.redhat.com.edgekey.
net.globalredir.akadns.net.
ds-www.redhat.com.edgekey.net.globalredir.akadns.net. 3596 IN CNAME e3396.
dscx.akamaiedge.net.
e3396.dscx.akamaiedge.net. 16   IN      A       23.1.49.220

;; AUTHORITY SECTION:
.                         1925    IN      NS      l.root-servers.net.
.                         1925    IN      NS      d.root-servers.net.
.                         1925    IN      NS      c.root-servers.net.
.                         1925    IN      NS      j.root-servers.net.
<snip>

;; ADDITIONAL SECTION:
d.root-servers.net.       15202   IN      A       199.7.91.13
j.root-servers.net.       15202   IN      A       192.58.128.30
l.root-servers.net.       15202   IN      A       199.7.83.42
c.root-servers.net.       15202   IN      A       192.33.4.12
a.root-servers.net.       447202  IN      A       198.41.0.4
<snip>
;; Query time: 1045 msec
;; SERVER: 192.168.56.1#53(192.168.56.1)
;; WHEN: Fri Dec 28 08:12:21 EST 2018
;; MSG SIZE  rcvd: 1009
```

That is a lot of information, so I have snipped out large sections of it to save space here. Clearly, the dig command did return the correct information for CNN. The important bit of data in this result is that the responding server (located near the bottom of the output) is 192.168.56.1 which is the IP address of our new caching DNS server.

The local caching server does not respond immediately the first time a new domain name is resolved. This delay, usually a few hundred milliseconds, should be very small and is the result of having to query the forwarder for the information. After that, query times should be minimal.

This abundance of data is the result of using forwarders. This is not a problem and does not affect the results or speed of queries from application programs and utilities. The dig command is intended to provide data that can be used by a SysAdmin for use in problem determination when there is an issue of some type. You should also be aware that different servers and forwarders may produce different amounts of data in the Authority and Additional sections of the **dig** output.

Do some additional queries using both dig and nslookup to further verify the results from our server.

We are not quite finished. The caching name server is working as we expect it to, but we do need to ensure that hosts configured by DHCP services now have the correct IP address for our new name server.

Reconfiguring DHCP

This step is important so that hosts being booted on our virtual network are served the correct IP address for the name server. We do not need to turn off the name server in the virtual router, and we do not want to do that anyway because we are using it as a forwarder. Also, I have not found a way to turn off DNS services on the virtual router.

EXPERIMENT 4-8

Perform this experiment as root. In this experiment, we change the DNS server to the new one we just created. We will leave the DNS server in the virtual router as an alternative in case our primary name server fails.

On StudentVM2, change the "option domain-name-servers" line in the dhcpd.conf configuration file as follows.

```
option domain-name-servers 192.168.56.1, 10.0.2.1;
```

Now restart the DHCPD service.

```
[root@studentvm2 ~]# systemctl restart dhcpd
```

Now let's ensure that the host StudentVM1 receives the correct name server.

EXPERIMENT 4-9

Perform this experiment as root on StudentVM1. All we really need to do is bounce the network interface and check the /etc/resolv.conf file.

```
[root@studentvm1 ~]# ip link set enp0s3 down
[root@studentvm1 ~]# ip link set enp0s3 up
[root@studentvm1 ~]# cat /etc/resolv.conf
# Generated by NetworkManager
search example.com
nameserver 192.168.56.1
nameserver 10.0.2.1
```

Verify that the resolver is working.

```
[root@studentvm1 ~]# dig example.net
```

It shows the name data for example.net and it also proves that the resolver used to obtain this data is our own name server. Try some additional lookups for additional testing and verification.

Using the top-level DNS servers

We could continue to use the forwarders as the source of our DNS information. Forwarders are not a bad thing and they are very useful in many environments. The problem is that most forwarders are configured to be the DNS servers of the ISP providing the Internet connection. My personal experience is that some ISPs DNS reliability is significantly less than stellar. For a while I used public DNS servers to test them, including Google public DNS which is reliable, fast, and not censored. Some other public DNS systems are censored or redirect you to places you did not intend and subject you to things like advertisements or pages flogging domains for sale.

However, I decided years ago that I would use my own DNS server and that I would also use the top-level DNS servers rather than forwarders. One reason for this is that the top-level servers reflect database record changes much faster than down-level servers. As a SysAdmin I find this helpful when I make changes for my own domains. I also use the top-level servers as a learning experience so that I can more fully understand how to manage that environment for my networks and others.

A really good forwarder is perfectly fine, but let's now use the top-level servers.

EXPERIMENT 4-10

Perform this experiment as root. Here we comment out the forwarders line in named.conf in order to use the DNS top-level name servers. Use the double forward slash (//) to comment out the forwarders line in /etc/named.conf.

```
//        forwarders { 192.168.56.1; 8.8.8.8; };
```

Restart named on StudentVM2.

`[root@studentvm2 etc]# `**`systemctl restart named`**

Test this change on StudentVM1.

`[root@studentvm1 ~]# `**`dig www.redhat.com`**

There was a significant delay in getting the return data because of the fact we restarted the named service which flushed the cache. Additional searches on the same name will return much faster because the data is now cached. Notice the difference in the output data. Leave named.conf open in your editor because we will be making more changes to it in this chapter.

Creating a primary name server

Once a caching name server has been created, it is not too difficult to convert it into a full-fledged master name server. We need to change named.conf again and create a couple new files. We will create a domain called example.com which is a valid public domain name reserved for testing labs and classes.

The two new files we will create are the forward and reverse zone files. They will be located in the /var/named directory. Remember that this location is specified by the "directory" directive in the named.conf configuration file.

Creating the forward zone file

The forward zone files are the name database files that are used to cross-reference hostnames with their assigned IP addresses. Each zone file contains the database for a single domain. Each host has at least one A record entry in the zone file with the name of the host and its IP address. Each host may also have one or more CNAME records that provide aliases for the primary hostname.

We are going to create a simple zone file for our example.com domain. This will be our local test instance of the example.com domain and not the public instance.

EXPERIMENT 4-11

This experiment must be performed as root on studentvm2. Create a basic forward zone file, /var/named/example.com.zone and add the following content to it. We will be using lines taken almost directly from the DNS Record Type section earlier in this chapter.

```
; Authoritative data for example.com zone
;
$TTL 1D
@   IN SOA  studentvm2.example.com    root.studentvm2.example.com. (
                              2018101501    ; serial
                              1D            ; refresh
                              1H            ; retry
                              1W            ; expire
                              3H )          ; minimum

$ORIGIN         example.com.
example.com.              IN    NS     studentvm2.example.com.
router                   IN    A      192.168.56.1
studentvm2               IN    A      192.168.56.1
studentvm1               IN    A      192.168.56.21
studentvm3               IN    A      192.168.56.22
studentvm4               IN    A      192.168.56.23
```

These entries will give you a few hostnames to experiment with even though some do not exist on the virtual network. Be sure to use today's date and a sequence number for the serial number.

Adding the forward zone files to named.conf

Before your DNS server will work, however, you need to create an entry in /etc/named.conf that will point to your new zone file.

EXPERIMENT 4-12

As root on StudentVM2, add the following lines below the entry for the top-level hints zone - zone "." IN.

```
zone "example.com" IN {
        type master;
        file "example.com.zone";
};
```

Now restart the named service.

```
[root@studentvm2 named]# systemctl restart named
```

Test your name server by using the **dig** and **nslookup** commands to obtain the IP addresses for the hosts you have configured in the forward zone file. Note that the host does not have to exist on the network for the **dig** and **nslookup** commands to return an IP Address.

```
[root@studentvm2 named]# dig studentvm1.example.com

; <<>> DiG 9.11.4-P2-RedHat-9.11.4-10.P2.fc28 <<>> studentvm1.example.com
;; global options: +cmd
;; Got answer:
;; ->>HEADER<<- opcode: QUERY, status: NOERROR, id: 56892
;; flags: qr aa rd ra; QUERY: 1, ANSWER: 1, AUTHORITY: 1, ADDITIONAL: 2

;; OPT PSEUDOSECTION:
; EDNS: version: 0, flags:; udp: 4096
; COOKIE: a14b3813f15356a4fea00a975bc73bb290d8147f29624b43 (good)
;; QUESTION SECTION:
;studentvm1.example.com.             IN      A

;; ANSWER SECTION:
studentvm1.example.com. 86400   IN      A       192.168.56.21

;; AUTHORITY SECTION:
example.com.            86400   IN      NS      studentvm2.example.com.

;; ADDITIONAL SECTION:
studentvm2.example.com. 86400   IN      A       192.168.56.1

;; Query time: 0 msec
```

```
;; SERVER: 192.168.56.1#53(192.168.56.1)
;; WHEN: Wed Oct 17 09:40:02 EDT 2018
;; MSG SIZE  rcvd: 136
```

Ping the router and the studentvm1 host. Also ping some external hosts to verify that external name services are still working as expected. You can use the example.org domain for this because we have used example.com for our test domain.

Be aware that it is necessary to use the FQDN for the dig command but not for the nslookup command so long as the domain and search entries are provided in the /etc/resolv.conf file. Ping one of the hosts that does exist, such as the studentvm1 host. Notice that it is not necessary to use the FQDN for this command.

Our name server is up and responding to requests but there is more to do.

Adding CNAME records

Now we will add some CNAME records; these are like aliases. These records can be added almost anywhere after the name server (NS) line in the zone file, but I like to keep them with the A record to which they point which makes it easier to find related records. The example.com.zone file below is what yours should look like when you have finished adding the CNAME entries.

EXPERIMENT 4-13

As the root user on the name server, add the CNAME records to the forward zone file as shown below. Be sure to set ownership of the zone file to root.named and increment the serial number.

```
; Authoritative data for example.com zone
;
$TTL 1D
@   IN SOA  studentvm2.example.com   root.studentvm2.example.com. (
                                 2018122802     ; serial
                                 1D             ; refresh
                                 1H             ; retry
                                 1W             ; expire
                                 3H )           ; minimum
```

```
$ORIGIN          example.com.
example.com.     IN    NS       studentvm2.example.com.
router           IN    A        192.168.56.1
studentvm2       IN    A        192.168.56.1
server           IN    CNAME    studentvm2
studentvm1       IN    A        192.168.56.21
workstation1     IN    CNAME    studentvm1
ws1              IN    CNAME    studentvm1
wkst1            IN    CNAME    ws1
studentvm3       IN    A        192.168.56.22
studentvm4       IN    A        192.168.56.23
```

Note that some of the CNAME records ultimately point to the same host IP address for the studentvm1 host. CNAME records can be nested to as many levels as necessary, but it tends to complicate things when there are too many levels of indirection.

This time, instead of doing a complete restart of the named service, we will use the "reload" which causes the named service to reload all of its configuration files. This is usually faster than a restart and can prevent interruptions to the service. Test these CNAME entries using dig and nslookup.

```
[root@studentvm2 etc]# systemctl reload named
[root@studentvm2 etc]#
```

Be sure to perform a lookup on wkst1.example.com and examine the answer lines in the results. You should be able to see the CNAME and A record trail from the CNAME you requested to the A record. This is especially apparent when using the dig command.

```
[root@studentvm2 etc]# dig wkst1.example.com
; <<>> DiG 9.11.4-P2-RedHat-9.11.4-10.P2.fc29 <<>> wkst1.example.com
;; global options: +cmd
;; Got answer:
;; ->>HEADER<<- opcode: QUERY, status: NOERROR, id: 53034
;; flags: qr aa rd ra; QUERY: 1, ANSWER: 3, AUTHORITY: 1, ADDITIONAL: 2

;; OPT PSEUDOSECTION:
; EDNS: version: 0, flags:; udp: 4096
; COOKIE: adba4e416fff6d97d8b358455c262fdfee167f5b3d286c7b (good)
;; QUESTION SECTION:
;wkst1.example.com.               IN      A
```

```
;; ANSWER SECTION:
wkst1.example.com.          86400    IN      CNAME    ws1.example.com.
ws1.example.com.            86400    IN      CNAME    studentvm1.example.com.
studentvm1.example.com.     86400    IN      A        192.168.56.21

;; AUTHORITY SECTION:
example.com.                86400    IN      NS       studentvm2.example.com.

;; ADDITIONAL SECTION:
studentvm2.example.com.     86400    IN      A        192.168.56.1

;; Query time: 0 msec
;; SERVER: 192.168.56.1#53(192.168.56.1)
;; WHEN: Fri Dec 28 09:14:55 EST 2018
;; MSG SIZE  rcvd: 174
```

Also use the ping command with these CNAME aliases to verify that the end result is a correct ping response.

Creating the reverse zone file

A reverse zone for your domain will provide the ability to do reverse lookups. Many organizations do not do these internally, but reverse lookups can be helpful in doing problem determination. Many spam-fighting configurations such as SpamAssassin look for reverse lookups to verify valid email servers.

EXPERIMENT 4-14

Create the reverse zone file, /var/named/example.com.rev and add the following contents. Use an appropriate serial number. Be sure to set ownership of the zone file to root.named.

```
; reverse mapping for example.com zone
;
$TTL 1D
@       IN SOA  studentvm2.example.com.    root.studentvm2.example.com. (
                                        2018122801      ; serial
                                        1D              ; refresh
                                        1H              ; retry
```

```
1W                      ; expire
3H )                    ; minimum
```

```
@       IN      NS      studentvm2.example.com.
1       IN      PTR     router.example.com.
11      IN      PTR     studentvm2.example.com.
21      IN      PTR     studentvm1.example.com.
```

You could also name your reverse zone file /var/named/25.168.192.in-addr.arpa which follows older conventions. You can actually name it anything you want because you will point to it explicitly in the named.conf file, but using one of the two conventions will make it easier for others to follow your work.

The serial numbers for the named.conf file, and the forward and reverse zones do not need to be the same. It is important to remember to update the serial number of any given file every time its content is altered. This does provide a way to determine the last time a file was modified if you use the same numbering strategy that I do. It is also critical in an environment where the primary server updates secondary name servers when the primary is changed.

Add the reverse zone to named.conf

We need to add a stanza for the reverse zone file to named.conf to complete the reverse lookup function.

EXPERIMENT 4-15

Add the following stanza to the /etc/named.conf file to point to the new reverse zone. I always add the reverse zone stanza after the forward zone.

```
zone    "2.0.10.in-addr.arpa" IN {
    type master;
    file "example.com.rev";
};
```

Now reload named and test your reverse zone. The -x option specifies that we are requesting a reverse lookup. Appending .service to the service name is optional in most current Linux distros that use systemd. It was a requirement in early versions.

```
[root@studentvm2 ~]# systemctl reload named.service
[root@studentvm2 ~]# dig -x 192.168.56.21

; <<>> DiG 9.11.4-P2-RedHat-9.11.4-10.P2.fc28 <<>> -x 192.168.56.21
;; global options: +cmd
;; Got answer:
;; ->>HEADER<<- opcode: QUERY, status: NOERROR, id: 56257
;; flags: qr aa rd ra; QUERY: 1, ANSWER: 1, AUTHORITY: 1, ADDITIONAL: 2

;; OPT PSEUDOSECTION:
; EDNS: version: 0, flags:; udp: 4096
; COOKIE: 6baa8f2ab5d903b3a9d3d6575bc75a367621c5300cbc5433 (good)
;; QUESTION SECTION:
;21.2.0.10.in-addr.arpa.            IN      PTR

;; ANSWER SECTION:
21.2.0.10.in-addr.arpa. 86400   IN      PTR     studentvm1.example.com.

;; AUTHORITY SECTION:
2.0.10.in-addr.arpa.    86400   IN      NS      studentvm2.example.com.

;; ADDITIONAL SECTION:
studentvm2.example.com. 86400   IN      A       192.168.56.1

;; Query time: 0 msec
;; SERVER: 192.168.56.1#53(192.168.56.1)
;; WHEN: Wed Oct 17 11:50:14 EDT 2018
;; MSG SIZE  rcvd: 156

[root@studentvm2 named]#
```

Now let's see what the status of a working name server looks like.

```
[root@studentvm2 ~]# systemctl status named
• named.service - Berkeley Internet Name Domain (DNS)
   Loaded: loaded (/usr/lib/systemd/system/named.service; enabled; vendor
   preset: disabled)
   Active: active (running) since Fri 2018-12-28 09:06:56 EST; 37min ago
  Process: 15964 ExecStop=/bin/sh -c /usr/sbin/rndc stop > /dev/null 2>&1 ||
  /bin/kill -TER>
  Process: 16463 ExecReload=/bin/sh -c /usr/sbin/rndc reload > /dev/null 2>&1
  || /bin/kill >
```

```
 Process: 15978 ExecStart=/usr/sbin/named -u named -c ${NAMEDCONF} $OPTIONS
 (code=exited, >
 Process: 15976 ExecStartPre=/bin/bash -c if [ ! "$DISABLE_ZONE_CHECKING" ==
 "yes" ]; then>
Main PID: 15979 (named)
   Tasks: 5 (limit: 4696)
  Memory: 102.0M
  CGroup: /system.slice/named.service
          └─15979 /usr/sbin/named -u named -c /etc/named.conf

Dec 28 09:44:09 studentvm2 named[15979]: network unreachable resolving
'./DNSKEY/IN': 2001:>
Dec 28 09:44:09 studentvm2 named[15979]: network unreachable resolving
'./DNSKEY/IN': 2001:>
Dec 28 09:44:09 studentvm2 named[15979]: network unreachable resolving
'./DNSKEY/IN': 2001:>
Dec 28 09:44:09 studentvm2 named[15979]: network unreachable resolving
'./DNSKEY/IN': 2001:>
Dec 28 09:44:09 studentvm2 named[15979]: zone 2.0.10.in-addr.arpa/IN: loaded
serial 2018122>
Dec 28 09:44:09 studentvm2 named[15979]: network unreachable resolving
'./DNSKEY/IN': 2001:>
Dec 28 09:44:09 studentvm2 named[15979]: all zones loaded
Dec 28 09:44:09 studentvm2 named[15979]: running
Dec 28 09:44:10 studentvm2 named[15979]: managed-keys-zone: Key 19036 for
zone . acceptance>
Dec 28 09:44:10 studentvm2 named[15979]: managed-keys-zone: Key 20326 for
zone . acceptance
```

The lines indicating that a network is unreachable refer to the IPV6 network which we have not activated.

Perform some additional testing as you see fit to ensure that the reverse lookup is working. Be sure to test the name services from StudentVM1, too.

At this point, you have a working name server using BIND. Do not turn it off or disable it. You will use your own name server for the rest of these experiments and you will be adding some entries to it.

Chapter summary

Name services is a very important part of making the Internet easily accessible. It binds the myriad disparate hosts connected to the Internet into a cohesive unit that makes it possible to communicate with the far reaches of the planet with ease. It has a complex distributed database structure that is perhaps even unknowable in its totality, yet which can be rapidly searched by any connected device to locate the IP address of any other device that has an entry in that database.

If you are a system administrator on a network of almost any size, you will find it helpful to know how to build your own name server as we did in this chapter.

Exercises

Perform these exercises to complete this chapter.

1. Why do local networks and the Internet need name services?

2. What is the sequence of events that will take place in order to obtain the IP address for a host on our own network if we enter the command **ping router**? Assume the setup is identical to the one which we have created in this course.

3. What difference is there – if any – if we use the command **ping router.example.com**?

4. Is a reverse zone required for DNS services to work for forward lookups?

5. How is it possible for organizations to use DNS to redirect – not block – web browsing to one or more outside web sites?

6. Can a single name server provide name services for more than one domain such that it can be the authoritative name server for both example.com and example.org – for example?

CHAPTER 5

Remote Access with SSH

Objectives

In this chapter you will learn:

- How SSH works to create and maintain secure connections.

- Advanced SSH usage and techniques.

- How to use SSH for secure file transfers.

- How to use SSH to perform remote command execution.

- How to generate and use Public/Private Key Pairs (PPKP) for authentication.

- To use X-forwarding to run GUI programs on the remote host so that the windows of their GUI interface are displayed on the local host.

- An easy and elegant way to perform a centralized backup of remote hosts.

Introduction

We looked at using Secure Shell (SSH) in Volume 2, Chapter 17, of this course. We set up the SSH server and used it to connect to itself as the localhost for some simple testing.

SSH is an important mechanism for secure connections between Linux hosts. SSH is a software-based virtual private network (VPN) tool that can create a secure VPN whenever needed. It can be used to securely log in to any remote host so long as you have proper credentials, and it can be used to enhance tools such as **tar** and other backup programs like rsync so that remote hosts can be easily backed up to a local system. The scp (secure copy) program uses the SSH encrypted tunnel to copy files between a remote host and a local one.

© David Both 2020
D. Both, *Using and Administering Linux: Volume 3*, https://doi.org/10.1007/978-1-4842-5485-1_5

In this chapter, we will explore SSH in more depth and use it to communicate between two separate VM hosts. We will also use Public/Private Key Pairs for authentication that is more secure than using passwords.

The name Secure Shell is misleading. SSH is not a shell; it is a set of connection protocols that enables secure, encrypted links between two computers. An SSH login to a remote host uses the default shell of the user on the remote host. In most cases, this would be Bash, but some users prefer other shells and have designated them as their default shell. Whichever shell the use as their default will be the shell used for the SSH connection.

SSH provides three important properties:

1. It provides reliable authentication for the identities of the hosts as well as the users. It ensures that the hosts and users are who they claim to be.

2. It encrypts the communication between the hosts, including the transmission of any login ID and password or Public/Private Key Pairs (PPKP).

3. It ensures the integrity of the transmissions and can detect and notify the user if data is missing, added, or changed.

Using SSH for inter-host communications is an excellent security precaution and can prevent data that is transmitted over any part of a public network from being intercepted, blocked, or altered. As with all security tools, SSH is not the complete solution and other security precautions must also be taken. But SSH ensures secure communications can be easily accomplished.

Starting the SSH server

We started the SSH server on the StudentVM1 host in the first book of this course but we need to start it on StudentVM2, too. Any Linux host can be an SSH server, and it makes sense to do so at least some of the time in order to facilitate easy communications and the ability to work on remote hosts.

The SSH server should already be running on StudentVM1. If so, the first set of commands in Experiment 5-1 will emit errors, but nothing bad will happen. However, do be sure to complete the rest of the experiment as well.

EXPERIMENT 5-1

Start this experiment as the root user on StudentVM2. Start the SSHD server daemon and enable it so it will start on boot. The default SSHD configuration is perfect for our needs and it allows direct login by the root user; in a real-world environment, we would most likely change that so that direct root logins would be disallowed.

```
[root@studentvm2 ~]# systemctl start sshd ; systemctl enable sshd
Created symlink /etc/systemd/system/multi-user.target.wants/sshd.service →
/usr/lib/systemd/system/sshd.service.
[root@studentvm2 ~]#
```

That was easy and our StudentVM2 host is now ready for us to try out an SSH connection. In a terminal session as the student user on StudentVM1, SSH to StudentVM2.

```
[student@studentvm1 ~]$ ssh studentvm2
The authenticity of host 'studentvm2 (192.168.56.1)' can't be established.
ECDSA key fingerprint is SHA256:NDM/B5L3eRJaalex6IOUdnJsE1smOSiQNWgaI8BwcVs.
Are you sure you want to continue connecting (yes/no)? yes
Warning: Permanently added 'studentvm2,192.168.56.1' (ECDSA) to the list of
known hosts.
Password: <Enter the password for student1 on StudentVM2>
[student@studentvm2 ~]$
```

The first time an SSH connection is made to any host the authenticity message is displayed along with the fingerprint of the private key of the remote host. In a very security conscious environment, we would have already received a copy of the remote host's key fingerprint. This allows comparison so that we know we are connecting to the correct remote host. This is not the security key; it is a fingerprint that is unique to that host's private key. It is impossible to reconstruct the original private key from which the fingerprint was generated.
You must type "yes" – the full word – in order to continue the login. Then you must enter the password for the remote host.

Now let's look at the /home/student/.ssh directory. Then look at the contents of the ~/.ssh/ known_hosts file on StudentVM1. You should see the public host key for the remote host, StudentVM2. This file is created in the local host, the one we are connecting from, and not on the remote host, the one we are connecting to. Each host we connect to will have a unique signature of its own in our known_hosts file to identify it for future connections.

```
[student@studentvm1 ~]$ cat .ssh/known_hosts
studentvm2,192.168.56.1 ecdsa-sha2-nistp256
AAAAE2VjZHNhLXNoYTItbmlzdHAyNTYAAAAIbmlzdHAyNTYAAABBBMDg3AOuakzj1P14aJgeOHCR
SJpsxOAlU6fXiVRlc/RwQRvFkMblO5/t7wSFcwOG8tRSiNaktVs4dxpAoMbrT3c=
[student@studentvm1 ~]$
```

After accepting this key during the first connection to the remote host, the connections initialize a little faster because the two computers now know each other and can identify themselves via the keys.

The host keys are stored in /etc/ssh along with the SSH client and server configuration files. List the contents of that directory to view the various key files.

Now, as the root user on StudentVM1, connect to StudentvM2 and verify that connection works as well.

Type **exit** to disconnect the SSH connections. Exit from all SSH connections if there are more than just one.

Now we know that the SSH server on StudentVM2 is working as it should and can accept connections from remote hosts. But there is so much more.

How SSH works – briefly

Let's look briefly at the sequence of events that take place when an SSH connection is made between hosts.

1. Enter the **ssh studentvm2** command.

2. The local host establishes an unencrypted TCP connection to remote host.

3. The remote host sends its own public key to the local host which compares it to the one for that host in ~/.ssh/known_hosts. This authenticates the remote host.

4. The two hosts negotiate the encryption algorithm to use and start it so that all further communications are performed through the encrypted channel.

5. The local host prompts the user for their password and sends it to the remote server over the encrypted channel.

6. The remote server verifies the password is correct and permits the login to proceed.

7. The remote host launches the user's default shell – usually Bash.

If no user is specified as part of the SSH command in user@host format, the user issuing the command is assumed by SSH to be the user to connect with on the remote host.

As an alternative to using passwords, a Public/Private Key pair (PPKP) could be used. The details of this will be covered later in this chapter. The PPKP may also use an arbitrarily long optional passphrase for an additional level of security.

SSH can multiplex many different concurrent channels over the authenticated connection. This allows tunneling of login sessions and TCP forwarding so that other protocols such as Telnet and the X Window System, that are not normally encrypted can use this encrypted channel.

SSH today is normally implemented with OpenSSH[1]. Until September of 2000, SSH was encumbered with patents and other proprietary restriction, but those all expired years ago. There are still commercial versions of SSH available but there is no reason to use them on Linux. Fedora, and at least some other distributions I have tried, installs both the client and server by default and allows root access by default.

Public/Private Key Pairs

PPKPs are used to enhance security by – mostly – removing the need for passwords to initiate SSH connections to a remote host. For the user, this is more secure because it eliminates the need to memorize and the temptation to write down long but good passwords.

Each host already has a PPKP that was generated during first boot after install. As we have seen, those key host pairs are stored in the /etc/ssh directory. The host's public key is swapped at the first SSH connection during the initial handshaking protocols. These host keys are used to positively identify the hosts to each other and are used to launch the initial encryption of the connection so that the authentication sequences are secure.

---

[1]OpenSSH, www.openssh.com

How PPKPs work

Suppose that I want to send you encrypted messages that only you – and others with the public key – can read. I need to be able to encrypt it and you need to be able to decrypt it. Cryptology texts are full of ways to do this that involve various types of keys and varying levels of security. Shared keys are fine until the key is compromised. I may not know that the key we share has been compromised and will keep sending messages that can be intercepted and read by the very people I might want to keep them from.

The use of Public/Private Key Pairs resolves this problem in a very elegant and secure manner. The key (if you will pardon the pun) is that the public key is the only one that can decrypt messages encrypted by the private key, and the private key is the only one that can decrypt messages encrypted with the public key. I had to think about that for a few minutes when I first heard it.

1. Create a Public/Private Key Pair.

2. Send the public key to the remote computer which will be decrypting my messages and encrypting the reply messages back to me.

3. Encrypt messages with the private key and send then to the remote computer.

4. The encrypted message is decrypted by the remote computer using public key.

5. To respond, the remote computer encrypts the message using the public key from my host and sends it to my host.

6. The message encrypted by the public key is decrypted on the local host using the private key.

Of course, these messages are the data contained in the TCP packets sent between the computers.

There are some interesting implications from all this. First, anyone who has the public key can decrypt the messages (data packets) that I send. Therefore, I can send my one public key to many different computers and then use SSH to connect to them all using the single private key. I do not need a separate set of keys for each computer.

Another inference that we can make is that anyone with the public key can send me messages. However, only I can initiate a conversation by using the private key. If another host wishes to initiate a conversation, they must create a PPKP and send a copy of their public key to me. So someone cannot just obtain a copy of my public key and then use it to initiate encrypted connections to my host computer.

I could send my public key to the user of the host on the other end in an email, and the user at that end could then append it to their ~/.ssh/authorized_keys file. However, there is a tool that I can use to install my public key on the remote host so long as I have the password of the user account with which I want to communicate. Therefore, without the cooperation of a friendly user at the remote host, or already having my own user account and password, I cannot just push my public key across the network and login to any random remote host.

This is all very nice and secure which is, of course, the intention.

So I am limited to SSH connections to remote hosts on which I have an account and know the original password. This reduces to the student user (or the root user) having an account on both StudentVM1 and StudentVM2 and sending the public key from one host to another.

EXPERIMENT 5-2

Perform this experiment as the student user on both StudentVM1 and StudentVM2 hosts.

On the StudentVM1 host as the student user, use the following command to create a Public/Private Key Pair. The -b 2048 option generates a key that is 2048 bits in length, the minimum allowable length is 1024 bits. By default, it will generate an RSA key, but we could also specify other key types. RSA is considered to be very secure so we will use RSA. We will press **Enter** to respond to all inquiries so as to take all of the defaults.

```
[student@studentvm1 ~]$ ssh-keygen -b 2048
Generating public/private rsa key pair.
Enter file in which to save the key (/home/student/.ssh/id_rsa): <Enter>
Enter passphrase (empty for no passphrase): <Enter>
Enter same passphrase again: <Enter>
Your identification has been saved in /home/student/.ssh/id_rsa.
Your public key has been saved in /home/student/.ssh/id_rsa.pub.
The key fingerprint is:
SHA256:y/y5kKXhceb093iLg3XhOZGIqFBsEZSTXi3cdKh22fY student@studentvm1
```

```
The key's randomart image is:
+---[RSA 2048]----+
|      +=* =.o.. .|
|    . * = =.. o  |
|     + + o o   o|
|       o o o o o.|
|       S * . o o|
|       + % . . E |
|       O . + o  |
|        o o o.o.|
|          +. .ooo|
+----[SHA256]-----+
[student@studentvm1 ~]$
```

The host key's fingerprint and/or the randomart image can be used to verify the validity of a public key for the host. It cannot be used to recreate the original public or private key and it cannot be used for communication. It is used only to verify the validity of the key.

Now that we have generated our key pair, look again at the contents of the ~/.ssh directory for the student user on StudentVM1. You should see two new files: id_rsa which is the private key and id_rsa.pub which is the public key. The .pub extension kind of gives that away.

These days, it is not necessary to send our public keys via email or other off-network type of delivery. We have a nice tool for that. Do this as the student user on StudentVM1.

```
[student@studentvm1 ~]$ ssh-copy-id studentvm2
/usr/bin/ssh-copy-id: INFO: Source of key(s) to be installed: "/home/
student/.ssh/id_rsa.pub"
The authenticity of host 'studentvm2 (10.0.2.11)' can't be established.
ECDSA key fingerprint is SHA256:NDM/B5L3eRJaalex6IOUdnJsE1smOSiQNWgaI8BwcVs.
Are you sure you want to continue connecting (yes/no)? yes
/usr/bin/ssh-copy-id: INFO: attempting to log in with the new key(s), to
filter out any that are already installed
/usr/bin/ssh-copy-id: INFO: 1 key(s) remain to be installed -- if you are
prompted now it is to install the new keys
Password: <Enter password of the user on the remote host>
Running /home/student/.bashrc
Running /etc/bashrc
```

Number of key(s) added: 1

Now try logging into the machine, with: "ssh 'studentvm2'"
and check to make sure that only the key(s) you wanted were added.

As the student user on StudentVM1, open a terminal session and SSH to StudentVM2. Verify that you are logged in to the studentvm1 host.

```
[student@studentvm1 ~]$ ssh studentvm2
Files in /etc/profile.d are being run.
Running /etc/bashrc
Running /home/student/.bash_profile
Running /home/student/.bashrc
Running /etc/bashrc
```

You could do some tests on the remote host like listing files and so on. Let's copy a file from StudentVM1 to StudentVM2.

As the student user on StudentVM1, open a new terminal session if necessary. If you did the experiments in book 1 of this course, there should be several files and directories in the student user's home directory, one of which should be random.txt. If you do not have this file, create it.

```
[student@studentvm1 ~]$ dd if=/dev/urandom of=random.txt2 bs=512 count=500
500+0 records in
500+0 records out
256000 bytes (256 kB, 250 KiB) copied, 0.00304606 s, 84.0 MB/s
[student@studentvm1 ~]$ ll rand*
-rw-rw-r-- 1 student 256000 Jun 18 14:50 random.txt
```

Now we can copy this file to the remote host. We use ~ which expands to the home directory of the student user on the remote host. We could also have used "pwd" to specify the PWD which just happens to be the student user's home directory at this moment.

```
[student@studentvm1 ~]$ scp random.txt studentvm2:~
Running /home/student/.bashrc
[student@studentvm1 ~]$
```

Use the terminal session on StudentVM1 that is logged in to the student user on StudentVM2 via SSH to verify that the file has been copied to StudentVM2. There is a possibility that it has not been copied. If the random.txt file is not present in the student user's home directory on StudentVM2, it is likely the unintended consequence of the echo statements we added to various Bash configuration files. You can see that line earlier, in which it states that .bashrc is running. Even if you did not encounter this problem, be aware that disruption of the expected protocol stream by added comments like this can cause SSH and SCP to fail without an error. To fix this, locate and edit all of the Bash configuration files for root and the student user. Comment out the echo statements that indicate the name of the running scripts. Do this on both hosts:

1. ~/.bashrc

2. ~/.bash_profile

3. /etc/bashrc

4. /etc/profile

5. /etc/profile.d/myBashConfig.sh

Then try the copy again. It should work now. Be sure to verify. Now exit the SSH session from StudentVM1 to StudentVM2, if it is still open.

```
[student@studentvm2 ~]$ exit
logout
Connection to studentvm2 closed.
[student@studentvm1 ~]$
```

Create a PPKP for the root user on StudentVM1 and copy the public key to StudentVM2. Also create PPKPs for both the root and student users on the StudentVM2 host and copy them to studentVM1. This sets up a situation where users can SSH easily from one host to another.

Now, as the student user on StudentVM2, copy your public key to the student1 account on the StudentVM1 host. That account should already exist; create it if it does not. Now SSH from student on StudentVM2 to student1 on StudentVM1. Notice that the key fingerprint here matches that of the key we saw above because this is the fingerprint of the host key for the StudentVM1 host and not the fingerprint of the user key.

```
[student@studentvm2 ~]$ ssh-copy-id student1@studentvm1
/usr/bin/ssh-copy-id: INFO: Source of key(s) to be installed: "/home/
student/.ssh/id_rsa.pub"
The authenticity of host 'studentvm1 (192.168.0.181)' can't be established.
ECDSA key fingerprint is SHA256:NDM/B5L3eRJaalex6IOUdnJsE1smOSiQNWgaI8BwcVs.
Are you sure you want to continue connecting (yes/no)? yes
/usr/bin/ssh-copy-id: INFO: attempting to log in with the new key(s), to
filter out any that are already installed
/usr/bin/ssh-copy-id: INFO: 1 key(s) remain to be installed -- if you are
prompted now it is to install the new keys
student1@studentvm1's password: <Enter password for student1 on StudentVM1>

Number of key(s) added: 1

Now try logging into the machine, with:   "ssh 'student1@studentvm1'"
and check to make sure that only the key(s) you wanted were added.

[student@studentvm2 ~]$
```

Now SSH from the student account on StudentVM2 to the student1 account on StudentVM1. Run a couple simple tests to verify the host and user account ID. Then exit from the SSH connection.

```
[student@studentvm2 ~]$ ssh student1@studentvm1
Last login: Thu May 30 14:39:56 2019 from 10.0.2.11
[student1@studentvm1 ~]$ pwd
/home/student1
[student1@studentvm1 ~]$ hostname
studentvm1
[student1@studentvm1 ~]$ whoami
student1 pts/4       2019-06-20 08:12 (192.168.0.182)
[student1@studentvm1 ~]$ exit
```

Even without a passphrase, using a PPKP is more secure than a basic SSH connection using a password.

X-forwarding

We now have SSH working and tested. There is more fun stuff ahead. Let's start by running a GUI program on the remote host with the display of the program's window on the local host. Most GUI desktop systems use Wayland[2] windowing system, or the X Window System,[3] a.k.a, X, as their underlying windowing engines. X-forwarding works in either event because they both use the same protocols.

EXPERIMENT 5-3

Perform this experiment as the student user on the StudentVM1 host.

First, SSH from StudentVM1 to StudentVM2 using the -X (uppercase) option to specify the use of X-forwarding. The message regarding the Xauthority file is normal at this stage and the file will be created.

```
[student@studentvm1 ~]$ ssh -X studentvm2
Last login: Wed Jun 19 08:31:28 2019 from 10.0.2.21
/usr/bin/xauth:  file /home/student/.Xauthority does not exist
[student@studentvm2 ~]$ thunar &
[1] 2683
[student@studentvm2 ~]$
```

The result of this is shown in Figure 5-1 as a screen capture of the StudentVM1 host desktop. It shows the effects of using X-forwarding via SSH to display the Thunar file manager running on StudentVM2 on the desktop of StudentVM1. Navigate around the directory structure on StudentVM2 for a bit.

---

[2]Wikipedia, *Wayland,* https://en.wikipedia.org/wiki/Wayland_(display_server_protocol)
[3]Wikipedia, *X Window System*, https://en.wikipedia.org/wiki/X_Window_System

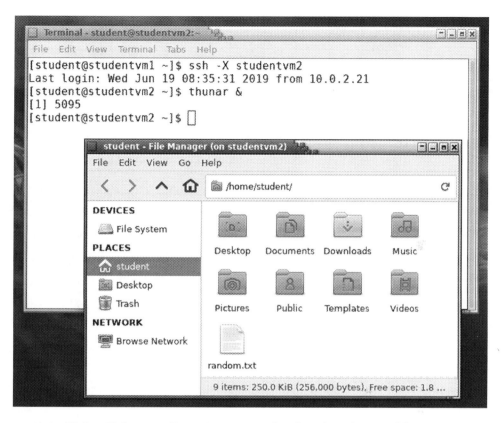

Figure 5-1. *Using X-forwarding via SSH to display the Thunar file manager running on StudentVM2 in a window on the desktop of StudentVM1*

Now install some fun and interesting Xorg programs. As root on StudentVM2, install the xorg-x11-apps package on StudentVM2 but not StudentVM1.

[root@studentvm2 ~]# **dnf -y install xorg-x11-apps**

As the student user on StudentVM2, log in to the desktop if you are not already, open a terminal session, and start the xeyes program.

[student@studentvm2 ~]$ **xeyes &**
[1] 23848
[student@studentvm2 ~]$

Now, as the student user on StudentVM1, try to start xeyes (X eyes). It fails because we did not install the xorg-x11-apps package on StudentVM1.

```
[student@studentvm1 ~]$ xeyes &
-bash: xeyes: command not found
[1]+  Exit 127                xeyes
[student@studentvm1 ~]$
```

Now, from the StudentVM1 desktop, use the SSH connection to StudentVM2 that has X-forwarding enabled. Enter the same command. Move the mouse pointer to see the eyes follow it.

The ampersand (&) after the command specifies that the command is to run in the background; that returns the terminal session to a command prompt while leaving the GUI program to run. That will not affect running the specified program like Thunar or xeyes, but if you run Thunar without the &, the terminal session does not return to a command prompt. You would need to terminate Thunar or log in remotely again to get a command line from which to launch xeyes.

Have some fun with this for a minute or two and then close down both Thunar and xeyes. The xeyes program must be moved or closed from the application bar because it has no window frame to manipulate.

This capability can be both fun and useful.

The X Window System

Because X-forwarding over SSH is a client/server type of operation, let's look at the details a little more closely.

Tip   Although some people call it X Windows or X-Windows, to be technically and legally correct, it should be called the "X Window System" or just "X".

It seems pretty clear that a standard SSH connection takes place from the client on the local host to a server on the remote host. We have, in fact, done that over the course of these experiments. But is that also true of X-forwarding over SSH?

To understand this, we need to know more about the X Window System.[4] Wikipedia has a rather old article describing the X Window System and some of its history. The short version is that the X Window System is a windowing system for Unix-like operating

---

[4]Wikipedia, *X Window System*, https://en.wikipedia.org/wiki/X_Window_System

systems such as Linux. X does not do anything other than provide the primitive graphical tools to create and manipulate windows and objects on a bit-mapped display. It does not impose any aspect of the user interface such as how it looks or how users and application programs can interact with it.

The X Window System uses a client-server model which separates the applications and their requests from the server functions that fulfill those requests. This allows X to be versatile and creates the base for X-forwarding. However, it is necessary to think about the client–server model from the perspective of the application rather than of the user, which is how we normally think of it. Let's do this thinking about the way we did it in Experiment 5-3 where we used SSH from the local host, StudentVM1, to connect to the remote host, StudentVM2, and then started applications running on StudentVM2 with the applications' windows displayed on StudentVM1.

1. We use the mouse on StudentVM1 to select a folder in Thunar.

2. Thunar running on StudentVM2 opens the folder and generates a series of graphical commands that cause the redrawing of the Thunar window. This is a client request to the X server.

3. Those commands are sent to StudentVM1 where the X server translates them into the new images in the Thunar window. This is the X server fulfilling the request from the client.

Most of the time, the server and the client are located on the same host but they can be located on different hosts as seen in the preceding experiment. This is only possible because the client and server functions are separate.

Remote commands

Although using SSH to perform remote commands may sound like logging in to a remote computer using SSH and then typing in commands on the remote Bash shell, there is a significant difference. And that little difference is what makes SSH such a powerful tool.

Let's start with a simple task like checking the contents of a directory on the remote host.

```
┌─────────────────────────────────────────────────────────────────────────┐
│                            EXPERIMENT 5-4                                  │
└─────────────────────────────────────────────────────────────────────────┘
```

Perform this experiment as the student user. Our objective is to determine the contents of the student user's home directory on the remote host.

As the student user on the StudentVM1 host, run the following command. This can only be accomplished without using a password if a PPKP is in place.

The quotes are used to delimit the command being sent to the remote host but can actually be dispensed with for simple commands like this. For more complex commands, such as we will see further along in this experiment, they are quite useful and necessary.

```
[student@studentvm1 ~]$ ssh studentvm2 "ls -l"
total 284
drwxr-xr-x. 2 student student   4096 Dec 24 08:19 Desktop
drwxr-xr-x. 2 student student   4096 Dec 22 13:15 Documents
drwxr-xr-x. 2 student student   4096 Dec 22 13:15 Downloads
drwxr-xr-x. 2 student student   4096 Dec 22 13:15 Music
drwxr-xr-x. 2 student student   4096 Dec 22 13:15 Pictures
drwxr-xr-x. 2 student student   4096 Dec 22 13:15 Public
-rw-rw-r--. 1 student student 256000 Jun 19 08:16 random.txt
drwxr-xr-x. 2 student student   4096 Dec 22 13:15 Templates
drwxr-xr-x. 2 student student   4096 Dec 22 13:15 Videos
```

Now a bit more fun with this.

```
[student@studentvm1 ~]$ ssh studentvm2 "cp random.txt textfile.txt ; ls -l"
total 536
drwxr-xr-x. 2 student student   4096 Dec 24 08:19 Desktop
drwxr-xr-x. 2 student student   4096 Dec 22 13:15 Documents
drwxr-xr-x. 2 student student   4096 Dec 22 13:15 Downloads
drwxr-xr-x. 2 student student   4096 Dec 22 13:15 Music
drwxr-xr-x. 2 student student   4096 Dec 22 13:15 Pictures
drwxr-xr-x. 2 student student   4096 Dec 22 13:15 Public
-rw-rw-r--. 1 student student 256000 Jun 19 08:16 random.txt
drwxr-xr-x. 2 student student   4096 Dec 22 13:15 Templates
-rw-rw-r--. 1 student student 256000 Jun 20 08:22 textfile.txt
drwxr-xr-x. 2 student student   4096 Dec 22 13:15 Videos
[student@studentvm1 ~]$
```

So that works as we expect. But try the same command without quotes. You will see that the remote command ends at the semicolon that the local shell uses to delimit the final command. The quotes are required so that the shell can properly send the entire command to the remote host.

Tip   Bash shell aliases such as the ll command are not available when using remote commands. So be careful when using scripts containing remote commands to not use command aliases.

Remote backups

The term "remote backups" may be a bit misleading, even with what we now know about running commands remotely. For many years, I used a script to perform backups on my main workstation and several remote hosts. I used remote commands to perform the remote backups to the local workstation.

Making backups of remote hosts is much easier than you might think. We used the **tar** command to create backups in Volume 2, Chapter 18. We will use it again for this.

EXPERIMENT 5-5

Perform this experiment as the root user on StudentVM1. We start with the simple task of creating a backup of the remote host with the resulting backup stored on the remote host. We will make a backup of /home, /root, and /etc. and store the backup tarball in /tmp.

```
[root@studentvm1 ~]# ssh studentvm2 "tar -cvf /tmp/studentvm2.tgz /home /etc
/root ; ls -l /tmp "
```

Now verify that the tarball /tmp/studentvm2.tgz contains the files we expect. But do it from StudentVM1.

Now let's look at something and try to make a bit of sense from it.

```
[root@studentvm1 ~]# ssh studentvm2 "tar -c /home /etc /root"
```

Do you see what happened? The data stream from the tar command that was executed on the remote host is sent across the SSH connection to the standard out (STDOUT) of the terminal session on the local host. So now we have the data stream from a remote host here on our local host just waiting to be piped or redirected – on our local host. Got it yet? Note where we place the closing quote in this simple command line program.

```
[root@studentvm1 ~]# ssh studentvm2 "tar -cz /home /etc /root" > /tmp/
studentvm2.tgz ; ls -l /tmp
tar: Removing leading `/' from member names
tar: Removing leading `/' from hard link targets
total 287352
-rw-r--r-- 1 root     root      104151040 Jun 17 14:47 backup.tar
-rw-r--r-- 1 root     root       33189296 Jun 17 14:52 backup.tgz
<snip>
-rw-r--r-- 1 root     root        6259259 Jun 20 08:57 studentvm2.tgz
<snip>
```

We have now used an SSH remote **tar** command to create a stream consisting of the backup data from the remote host. That data stream is sent across the SSH connection to STDOUT on the local host where it can be used with other commands through pipes or redirected to a file.

We have now performed a backup of a remote host and stored the backup file on the local host, all with a simple command line program.

Once I had created an easy and elegant method for creating backups of remote hosts using **tar** and SSH, the next step for me was to create a script that would perform that same backup on several hosts and then set up a cron job or a systemd timer to do those backups every night.

Chapter summary

SSH uses two levels of authentication, first authenticating the hosts themselves and then user authentication. It encrypts the entire session including the authentication and all of the data transmission. SSH is very secure and can be used to transmit data securely over public networks.

SSH features such as remote command execution and data stream transmission over the encrypted connection enable powerful solutions for things like backups using simple tools like **tar**. SSH also provides X-forwarding so that we can run graphical programs on the remote host with their windows on our local host.

Exercises

Perform the following exercises to complete this chapter.

1. What are the permissions on the ~/.ssh/id_rsa file? Why?

2. What are the permissions on the ~/.ssh/id_rsa.pub file? Why?

3. The StudentVM1 host should have several user accounts including one named "student1." If it does not, create that account. As the student1 user on StudentVM1, create a PPKP and copy the public key to the student (NOT student1) account on StudentVM2. SSH to the student account on the StudentVM1 host.

4. You should already have created PPKPs for both root and the student user on both hosts, StudentVM1 and StudentVM2. Copy the public key of the student user on StudentVM1 to the root account of StudentVM2. As the student user on StudentVM1, SSH to root at StudentVM2.

5. Suppose you, as the student user, have created a PPKP and copied the public key to the remote host using your password. A few days or weeks later, as is the policy, you change the password on both the local and remote hosts. Can you still login to the remote host using the PPKP?

6. Write a Bash script on StudentVM1 to back up the /home, /root, and /etc of it and to also back up /home, /root, /etc, and /var of the StudentVM2 host.

7. After you have tested the backup script from the previous exercise, create a cron job or systemd timer to run the script every morning at 2 a.m.

8. When using X-forwarding over SSH, which host is the X server?

9. When using X-forwarding over SSH, which host is the X Client?

## CHAPTER 6

Routing and Firewalls

Objectives

In this chapter you will learn

- To define the function of a router

- To configure a Linux host as a router

- To configure the router firewall to support routing functions

- To understand and create entries for a routing table

- To install Fail2Ban, a tool that can dynamically modify the firewall to block various types of attacks

Introduction

At first glance, routing and firewalls might seem to have little to do with each other, but they are very closely entwined. Both are found at network boundaries and they work together to perform routing.

Routing is the task of ensuring that packets get routed to their specified destination. Every computer attached to a network requires some type of routing instructions for network TCP/IP packets when they leave the local host. This is usually very straightforward because most network environments are very simple and there are only two options for departing packets. All packets are sent either to a device on the local network or to some remote network via a router which may also be known as the default gateway. Multiple routers may be in use on a network, but only one router can be the default gateway.

© David Both 2020

D. Both, *Using and Administering Linux: Volume 3*, https://doi.org/10.1007/978-1-4842-5485-1_6

Let's be sure to define the "local" network as the logical and usually also the physical network in which the local host resides. Logically that means the local subnet in which the host is assigned is within the range of the local subnet's IP addresses. Physically that means the host is connected to one or more switches that are also connected to the rest of the local network.

A firewall is responsible for protecting the firewall host and the internal network from network-based attacks of many kinds. Firewalls are also used to aid in router implementation by providing a mechanism to route packets from one network interface on the router host to another network interface.

In this chapter, we will look at routing on a workstation, StudentVM1, that is not used as a router. We will then convert our server, StudentVM2, into a router and change the DHCP configuration to use it as the router for the virtual network. Of course, the packets must still pass through the virtual router to get to the outside world. This is a common enough situation in many networks and we will explore that, too.

We are also going to cover installation and configuration of Fail2Ban, which is a tool for dynamically blocking IP addresses that are making attempts to crack into our systems. We did this on StudentVM1 in Volume 2, Chapter 17, but we also need to ensure that it is done on StudentVM2. It will also be a good review.

Every device on a network that will connect to another network, such as the Internet or other internal networks, needs to have its own routing table. By default, Fedora creates a routing table on every device on which it is installed.

If the network uses a static configuration, the IP address of the default gateway is defined during that configuration and is stored in the interface configuration file for the host. Fedora does not allow static configuration during the initial installation from the live image so it would need to be done later, as we did in the first book of this course. If DHCP is used to configure the host, no interface configuration file is required because the IP address of the default gateway is provided to the host at each boot.

When we created the StudentVM1 virtual machine in the first volume of this course, we eventually added an interface configuration file for the enp0s3 interface. Let's go through that here again anyway.

NIC configuration files

By default, all current release images of Fedora default to DHCP configuration. No options are provided during installation to configure any aspect of the network interface. Starting with Fedora 29, Linux hosts using DHCP for network configuration no longer require interface configuration files if all of the DHCP default configurations are sufficient.

However, nonstandard configuration of the NICs for each network connection is still accomplished with ifcfg-X files in the /etc/sysconfig/network-scripts directory. Each NIC can have an interface configuration file named ifcfg-enp0s3, or something similar, where enp0s3 is the interface name assigned by the udev daemon. Each interface configuration file is bound to a specific physical NIC. Using the **nmcli** tool (network manager command-line interface) to configure an interface creates the interface configuration file for that interface.

The current strategy is to use the contents of the interface configuration files to generate the rules. However, if an interface configuration file does not exist, plugging in a new device or connecting with a new wireless network causes udev to notify NetworkManager of the new device or wireless connection. Then, in Fedora up through release 28, NetworkManager creates the new interface configuration file. As of Fedora 29 and higher, the Network Manager only creates the connection but does not create an interface configuration file.

The udev daemon creates an entry for each NIC installed in the system in the network rules file. The Network Manager uses these entries, along with information in the interface configuration files in the /etc/sysconfig/network-scripts/ directory to initialize each NIC.

Other distributions may keep their network configuration files in the /etc/NetworkManager/system-connections directory, with the name of the network as the file name. For example, my System76 laptop uses POP!_os which is based on Ubuntu. The /etc/NetworkManager/system-connections directory on that laptop contains files for the wired network as well as each of the wireless networks I have connected with. The structure of these files is different from the ifcfg files we will explore later in this chapter, but they are in ASCII plain text format and are readable and easily understandable.

The ip command

The **ip** command is designed to replace the **ifconfig**, **arp**, and some other network-related commands, so Red Hat has published a very nice IP command cheat sheet[1] that I use frequently. The man page for the **arp** command contains the following note: "This program is obsolete. For replacement check **ip neigh**" and man page for the **ifconfig** command has a similar statement.

For now, those commands are still available and it may be years before they disappear completely.

Create an interface configuration File

Let's do a quick experiment to see why creating an interface configuration file might be a good idea for a workstation even if it uses DHCP.

EXPERIMENT 6-1

Perform this experiment as the root user on the StudentVM1 host. When we need to turn the network interface up or down, we normally use the **ifdown** or the more recent **ip** commands to do that.

First verify that enp0s3 currently has an IP address assigned.

```
[root@studentvm1 ~]# ip addr show enp0s3
2: enp0s3: <BROADCAST,MULTICAST,UP,LOWER_UP> mtu 1500 qdisc fq_codel state UP
group default qlen 1000
    link/ether 08:00:27:e1:0c:10 brd ff:ff:ff:ff:ff:ff
    inet 10.0.2.7/24 brd 10.0.2.255 scope global dynamic noprefixroute enp0s3
       valid_lft 1143sec preferred_lft 1143sec
    inet6 fe80::c33:30e7:314e:e83e/64 scope link noprefixroute
       valid_lft forever preferred_lft forever
```

Now turn enp0s3 off.

```
[root@studentvm1 ~]# ip link set enp0s3 down
```

---

[1]Red Hat, *IP Command Cheat Sheet*, https://access.redhat.com/sites/default/files/ attachments/rh_ip_command_cheatsheet_1214_jcs_print.pdf

And verify.

```
[root@studentvm1 ~]# ip addr show enpOs3
2: enpOs3: <BROADCAST,MULTICAST> mtu 1500 qdisc fq_codel state DOWN group
default qlen 1000
    link/ether 08:00:27:e1:0c:10 brd ff:ff:ff:ff:ff:ff
    inet 10.0.2.7/24 brd 10.0.2.255 scope global dynamic noprefixroute enpOs3
       valid_lft 1118sec preferred_lft 1118sec
[root@studentvm1 ~]#
```

If the link is still up and active, that is the problem, so go ahead and perform Experiment 6-2. Skip the rest of this experiment.

If the link is down, there is already an interface configuration file for enpOs3 on StudentVM1. First bring the interface back up.

```
[root@studentvm1 ~]# ip link set enpOs3 up
```

And verify.

```
[root@studentvm1 ~]# ip addr show enpOs3
```

Now move the configuration file to /tmp so it no longer exists in /etc/sysconfig/network-scripts.

```
[root@studentvm1 ~]# mv /etc/sysconfig/network-scripts/ifcfg-enpOs3 /tmp
```

Now try to turn down the enpOs3 interface. It should fail this time.

```
[root@studentvm1 ~]# ip link set enpOs3 down
```

And verify.

```
[root@studentvm1 ~]# ip addr show enpOs3
```

After some experimentation of my own, I have learned that it is not possible to turn off an active link or to turn on an inactive one unless there is an interface configuration file for it. So let's create one.

EXPERIMENT 6-2

This experiment must be performed as the root user on the StudentVM1 host.

We could actually create an interface configuration file, ifcfg-enp0s3, for this interface, using an editor like Vim, but that is actually the hard way. Instead we will use the **nmcli** (NetworkManager command-line interface) to do this. Open a terminal session and make /etc/sysconfig/network-scripts the PWD. Then list the contents. The directory should be empty.

```
[root@studentvm1 ~]# cd /etc/sysconfig/network-scripts/ ; ll
total 4
[root@studentvm1 network-scripts]#
```

The following command adds the new connection and saves the interface configuration file in /etc/sysconfig/network-scripts/. Note that it is not necessary for this to be the PWD; it just makes it easier to see the before and after, with and without the file.

```
[root@studentvm1 network-scripts]# nmcli connection add save yes type
ethernet ifname enp0s3 con-name enp0s3
Connection 'enp0s3' (9e08333c-4458-4c7e-9632-16e3afe41f93) successfully
added.
[root@studentvm1 network-scripts]# ll
total 8
-rw-r--r--  1 root root 282 May  8 16:09 ifcfg-enp0s3
[root@studentvm1 network-scripts]#
```

Now stop the enp0s3 network connection and verify that it is now down. The lack of an IP address indicates that the interface is down.

```
[root@studentvm1 network-scripts]# ip link set enp0s3 down
```

It can take a few moments for the link to go down, so if the next command still shows it as up, wait a few seconds and try it again.

```
[root@studentvm1 network-scripts]# ip addr show enp0s3
2: enp0s3: <BROADCAST,MULTICAST> mtu 1500 qdisc fq_codel state DOWN group
default qlen 1000
    link/ether 08:00:27:e1:0c:10 brd ff:ff:ff:ff:ff:ff
[root@studentvm1 network-scripts]#
```

Now bring interface enp0s3 back up again.

I find that remembering these commands is somewhat difficult because I don't use them very often. Using tab completion will always give me a hint as to what the next possible entry might be.

The interface configuration file

Now let's look at the contents of the ifcfg-enp0s3. Regardless of when you created the interface configuration file for enp0s3, it will be the same with the possible exception of the UUID.

EXPERIMENT 6-3

As root, **cat** the /etc/sysconfig/network-scripts/ifcfg-enp0s3 file.

```
[root@studentvm1 network-scripts]# cat ifcfg-enp0s3
TYPE=Ethernet
PROXY_METHOD=none
BROWSER_ONLY=no
BOOTPROTO=dhcp
DEFROUTE=yes
IPV4_FAILURE_FATAL=no
IPV6INIT=yes
IPV6_AUTOCONF=yes
IPV6_DEFROUTE=yes
IPV6_FAILURE_FATAL=no
IPV6_ADDR_GEN_MODE=stable-privacy
NAME=enp0s3
UUID=4a527023-daa4-4dfb-9775-dbe9fb00fb0b
DEVICE=enp0s3
ONBOOT=yes
```

This is a typical interface configuration file as created by the **nmcli** command. It contains the bare minimum necessary for such a file. The primary purpose for creating this file is that it allows the SysAdmin to control the interface.

Figure 6-1 lists the configuration options shown above and some common ones that aren't in that file we just created, along with some brief explanations for each. Many of the IPV6 options are similar to those of the similarly named IPV4 ones. Note that local configuration variable settings override those provided by a DHCP server.

Configuration variable	Description
TYPE	Type of network such as Ethernet or token ring.
PROXY_METHOD	Proxy configuration method. "none" means no proxy is in use.
BROWSER_ONLY	Whether a proxy configuration is for browsers only.
BOOTPROTO	Options are dhcp, bootp, none, and static.
DEFROUTE	This interface is the default route for this host to the outside world.
IPV4_FAILURE_FATAL	If this is set to "no" failure to obtain an IPV4 connection will not affect any attempt to make an IPV6 connection.
IPV6INIT	Whether to initialize IPV6 or not. The default is yes.
IPV6_AUTOCONF	Yes means use DHCP for configuration of IPV6 on this interface.
IPV6_DEFROUTE	This interface is the IPV6 default route for this host to the outside world.
IPV6_FAILURE_FATAL	If this is set to "no" failure to obtain an IPV6 connection will not affect any attempt to make an IPV4 connection.
IPV6_ADDR_GEN_MODE	Configure IPv6 Stable Privacy addressing.
NAME	The interface name, such as enp0s3.
UUID	A Universally Unique Identifier for the interface. It is created with a hash of the interface name.
DEVICE	The name of the interface to which this configuration file bound.
ONBOOT	If yes, this starts the interface at boot (really startup time). If no, the interface is not started until a user logs in at the GUI or manually starts the interface. I always set this to yes if it is not already.

Figure 6-1. *Some of the more common configuration items found in network interface configuration files*

Configuration variable	Description
HWADDR	The MAC address of the interface.
DNS1, DNS2	Up to two name servers may be specified.
USERCTL	Specifies whether non-privileged users may start and stop this interface. Options are yes/no.
IPADDR	The IP Address assigned to this NIC
BROADCAST	The broadcast address for this network such as 10.0.2.255
NETMASK	The netmask for this subnet such as 255.255.255.0
NETWORK	The network ID for this subnet such as 10.0.2.0
SEARCH	The DNS domain name to search when doing lookups on unqualified hostnames such as using studentvm1 instead of studentvm1.example.com.
GATEWAY	The network router or default gateway for this subnet, such as 10.0.2.1.
PEERDNS	The yes option indicates that /etc/resolv.conf is to be modified by inserting the DNS server entries specified by DNS1 and DNS2 options in this file. No means do not alter the resolv.conf file. Yes is the default when DHCP is specified in the BOOTPROTO line.

Figure 6-1. (*continued*)

The lines in the interface configuration files are not sequence sensitive and work just fine in any order I have ever tried. By convention, the option names are in uppercase and the values are in lowercase. Option values can be enclosed in quotes, but that is not necessary unless the value is more than a single word or number.

For more information about configuration files, the file /usr/share/doc/initscripts/sysconfig.txt contains a list of all the files that can be found in the /etc/sysconfig directory and its subdirectories. This includes the network ifcfg-<interface> files. The descriptions of each file lists all of the possible configuration variables and their possible values along with terse explanations.

Routing on a workstation

Routing packets on a workstation is usually pretty straightforward. Packets go either to another device on the local network segment or they go to a device on another network. In the latter case, the network packets must be sent to a router in order to be sent to the correct network. In many cases, there is only a single router for a network segment because the local network is only connected to a single external network.

The logic used to determine routing is simple.

1. If the destination host is on the local network, send the data directly to the destination host.

2. If the destination host is on a remote network that is reachable via a local gateway listed in the routing table, send it to the explicitly defined gateway.

3. If the destination host is on a remote network, and there is no other entry that defines a route to that host, send the data to the default gateway.

These rules mean that if all else fails because there is no match, send the packet to the default gateway.

So let's look at the simple scenario of our StudentVM1 host.

EXPERIMENT 6-4

Perform this experiment as the root user on the StudentVM1 host. Look at the current route information.

```
[root@studentvm1 ~]# ip route
default via 10.0.2.1 dev enp0s3 proto dhcp metric 100
10.0.2.0/24 dev enp0s3 proto kernel scope link src 10.0.2.21 metric 100
```

The default route set on StudentVM1 is that of the virtual router in our virtual network at the IP address of 10.0.2.1. If you recall, that is the configuration we set in the dhcpd.conf file of the DHCP server on StudentVM2.

This is a trivial and common routing configuration with only a single default gateway. It means that any packet that has a destination other than the local network, 10.0.2.0/24, will be sent to the default router from where it will be routed onward, perhaps through several more routers, to its final destination.

Network routing

The last sentence in Experiment 6-4 has some important implications. Routing to the default gateway is not usually the last router that the packets will traverse. We can trace the routes packets might take to arrive at a specific destination.

EXPERIMENT 6-5

This experiment can be performed as the student user on the StudentVM1 host. In this experiment, we will discover the list all of the routers through which packets travel to a destination and some interesting metrics pertaining to that.

My preferred tool for this is **mtr**. This tool started out as Matt's traceroute because Matt wrote it and it was designed as a dynamic replacement for the old **traceroute** tool. Because Matt no longer maintains this and someone else has taken over, it is now referred to as "my traceroute."

```
[student@studentvm1 ~]$ mtr example.org
                    My traceroute  [v0.92]
studentvm1 (10.0.2.21)                   019-06-21T14:34:52-0400
Keys:  Help    Display mode    Restart statistics    Order of fields    quit
                                    Packets                 Pings
Host                                Loss%  Snt  Last   Avg Best  Wrst  StDev
 1. router                          0.0%   11   0.3   0.3  0.3   0.3   0.0
 2. 192.168.0.254                   0.0%   11   0.5   0.6  0.5   0.7   0.1
 3. rrcs-24-199-159-57.midsouth.biz.rr.com  0.0%  11  5.5  20.8  2.9  174.6  51.1
 4. 142.254.207.205                 0.0%   11  16.2  37.7 15.3 111.1  30.8
 5. cpe-174-111-105-178.triad.res.rr.com  0.0%  11  22.1  30.5 18.4  90.1  20.1
 6. cpe-024-025-062-106.ec.res.rr.com  0.0%  10  25.2  25.2 20.0  31.6   3.5
 7. be31.chrcnctr01r.southeast.rr.com  0.0%  10  42.4  38.4 31.2  46.4   5.1
 8. bu-ether11.atlngamq46w-bcr00.tbone.rr.com  0.0%  10  42.9  41.1 32.0  45.4  4.0
 9. 152.195.80.196                  0.0%   10  41.7  36.3 29.6  41.7   3.9
10. 152.195.80.131                  0.0%   10  40.5  39.0 31.4  49.1   5.2
11. 93.184.216.34                   0.0%   10  39.2  39.2 32.1  48.2   5.4
```

This is a dynamic display and it keeps checking the route until you press **q** to quit. Because of this, **mtr** can display statistics for each hop along the way to the destination including response times and packet loss at each intermediate router along the way.

Another thing you might see for any given hop number (the sequential numbers down the left side of the display) is multiple routers indicating that the path to the remote host is not always through the same sequence of routers.

Using the -n option displays only the IP addresses of the routers. The routers shown in your results will probably be different from my results until the last few hops, as it gets closer to the target host.

```
[student@studentvm1 ~]$ mtr -n example.org
                        My traceroute  [v0.92]
studentvm1 (10.0.2.21)                                   2019-06-
21T14:38:21-0400
Keys:  Help   Display mode   Restart statistics   Order of fields   quit
                                           Packets                Pings
Host                            Loss%   Snt   Last   Avg  Best  Wrst StDev
 1. 10.0.2.1                    0.0%    25    0.3   0.3   0.2   0.4   0.1
 2. 192.168.0.254              0.0%    25    0.5   0.6   0.4   0.9   0.1
 3. 24.199.159.57              0.0%    25    3.7   6.3   2.1  13.4   3.4
 4. 142.254.207.205            0.0%    25   69.3  23.6  12.0  69.3  11.9
 5. 174.111.105.178            0.0%    25   25.3  24.0  12.6  38.9   6.5
 6. 24.25.62.106               0.0%    25   28.1  24.9  17.7  36.4   4.5
 7. 24.93.64.186               0.0%    25   30.4  43.3  26.5 161.2  29.0
 8. 66.109.6.34                8.3%    24   35.5  47.8  27.5 158.8  30.9
 9. 152.195.80.196             0.0%    24   45.7  45.7  26.1 156.3  30.5
10. 152.195.80.131             0.0%    24   37.3  56.8  27.4 238.1  50.8
11. 93.184.216.34              0.0%    24   32.3  43.0  26.4 142.0  26.9
```

Note the packet loss at hop 8. Although this could indicate a problem, it is more likely that the router is discarding unimportant packets such as ICMP if the router is heavily loaded. If you try this at another time, the packet loss will probably be zero.

If you are actually having problems connecting with a site and **mtr** indicates a high packet loss, that could be the source of the problem. The only thing to be done is to report this to your ISP.

Creating a router

Let's make a router out of the StudentVM2 host. We have previously configured our internal network to match the default defined by the virtual network router as generated by VirtualBox. Both of our hosts use the virtual router as the default gateway.

What we want to do now is to create an internal network that uses StudentVM2 as the default gateway while it, in turn, uses the virtual router as its default gateway. To do this, we need to set up a new network segment for the internal network using a different IP address range. We can select this arbitrarily, and since the current network defined by the virtual router is 10.0.2.0/24, we will create a Host-only network for this internal network and VirtualBox automatically selects the IP address range of 192.168.56.0/24. We could change this but there is really no need to do so. The use of the 192.168 address range also is different enough from the 10.0 address range to ensure that we are less likely to be confused about which network we are working with.

Our new network configuration will look like Figure 6-2. This is a very common configuration for many networks. The ISP supplies the modem/router to the outside world, and the organization maintains its own internal firewall and router to provide security and isolation from the Internet or other external network.

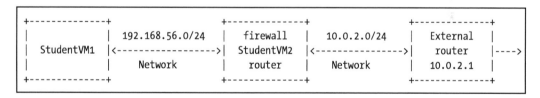

```
+--------------+                       +--------------+                   +--------------+
|              |   192.168.56.0/24     |  firewall    |   10.0.2.0/24     |   External   |
|  StudentVM1  |<--------------------->|  StudentVM2  |<----------------->|    router    |---->
|              |       Network         |   router     |     Network       |   10.0.2.1   |
+--------------+                       +--------------+                   +--------------+
```

Figure 6-2. *The new network configuration*

This means we need to "install" a second virtual network interface for StudentVM2. It also means reconfiguring both DHCP and name services on the servers already present on StudentVM2 to reflect the new network. This will take a good bit of work and it is possible to make mistakes. To make recovery easier, we will also make snapshots of both virtual machines.

Preparation

We need to do a bit of preparation before we can set up our new network. We will define a new host-only network and add the new NIC to StudentVM1. We do not need to make any changes directly to the internal configuration for StudentVM1 as it gets its network configuration from the DHCP server, but we will need to connect it to the new network using VirtualBox Manager.

EXPERIMENT 6-6

Power off both StudentVM1 and StudentVM2. We will create a new network, make one change to StudentVM1, and add a new NIC to StudentVM2.

The VirtualBox documentation contains a description of the different networking types it supports.[2] We are going to create a Host-only network that will allow us to connect the second NIC on StudentVM2 and the only NIC on StudentVM1 to it.

Create a new snapshot of both virtual machines. Add a comment to clearly identify these snapshots. I used something like, "Starting Chapter 7 before network reconfiguration." Now if we make a mess, we can easily recover by rebooting to these snapshots.

Open the VirtualBox Manager and use the menu bar to select **File ➤ Host Network Manager**. Click the **Create** icon to create a new network. Do not enable the DHCP server because StudentVM2 will perform that function for this network. Click **Close** to finish creating this virtual network. This network is named vboxnet0.

Open the VirtualBox settings for StudentVM1. Open the Network Settings page. For Adapter 1, find the **Attached to:** selection box and choose **Host-only Adapter**. The name of the vboxnet0 network will appear in the Name field because it is the only host-only network available. Click the OK button to complete this change.

Open the VirtualBox settings for StudentVM2. Open the Network Settings page. For Adapter 2, place a check in the **Enable Network Adapter** box, and then, in the **Attached to:** selection box, choose **Host-only Adapter**. Click the OK button to complete this change.

---

[2]VirtualBox UserManual, `https://download.virtualbox.org/virtualbox/6.0.8/UserManual.pdf`, 99-109

Check the /etc/hosts file for both StudentVM1 and StudentVM2 and make sure that only the first two lines are active. Delete and comment out all lines except the ones for localhost. We have already turned off the DHCP server on the virtual router so we do not need to do that at this time. We will leave StudentVM1 powered off until we have configured DHCP and DNS for the new network.

Configure the new NIC

Now that we have made the network changes in VirtualBox, we can start StudentVM2, perform some initial testing, and configure the new network interface card.

EXPERIMENT 6-7

Launch the StudentVM1 virtual machine and log in to the desktop. Perform the rest of this experiment as the root user.

We need to first verify that network adapter 1 still has connectivity to the virtual router on 10.0.2.1. Ping the router. If that is not successful, resolve any problems and try again. If it is successful, ping an external host such as www.example.org.

Verify that enpOs8 does not have an IP address assigned. The enpOs3 adapter should still have IP address 10.0.2.11 which is what we specified in the static configuration.

```
[root@studentvm2 ~]# ip addr
1: lo: <LOOPBACK,UP,LOWER_UP> mtu 65536 qdisc noqueue state UNKNOWN group
default qlen 1000
    link/loopback 00:00:00:00:00:00 brd 00:00:00:00:00:00
    inet 127.0.0.1/8 scope host lo
       valid_lft forever preferred_lft forever
    inet6 ::1/128 scope host
       valid_lft forever preferred_lft forever
2: enpOs3: <BROADCAST,MULTICAST,UP,LOWER_UP> mtu 1500 qdisc fq_codel state UP
group default qlen 1000
    link/ether 08:00:27:81:ec:cc brd ff:ff:ff:ff:ff:ff
    inet 10.0.2.11/24 brd 10.0.2.255 scope global noprefixroute enpOs3
       valid_lft forever preferred_lft forever
    inet6 fe80::f8b5:5762:6eaa:cf8e/64 scope link noprefixroute
```

```
          valid_lft forever preferred_lft forever
3: enpOs8: <BROADCAST,MULTICAST,UP,LOWER_UP> mtu 1500 qdisc fq_codel state UP
group default qlen 1000
     link/ether 08:00:27:9f:67:cb brd ff:ff:ff:ff:ff:ff
[root@studentvm2 ~]#
```

You may notice the network icon in the system tray will continue trying to connect to the network. It is attempting to obtain a configuration from DHCP for adapter 2. This will continue until we generate a static configuration.

Create a static configuration for the enpOs8 network adapter. We can specify the IP address of 192.168.56.1/24 in the command. This by itself informs the fact that this is a static connection instead of a DHCP connection.

```
[root@studentvm2 ~]# nmcli connection add save yes type ethernet ifname
enpOs8 con-name enpOs8 ip4 192.168.56.1/24
Connection 'enpOs8' (5db99e30-0544-4fd1-b060-7efa03a417db) successfully
added.
[root@studentvm2 ~]# ip addr show enpOs8
3: enpOs8: <BROADCAST,MULTICAST,UP,LOWER_UP> mtu 1500 qdisc fq_codel state UP
group default qlen 1000
     link/ether 08:00:27:9f:67:cb brd ff:ff:ff:ff:ff:ff
     inet 192.168.56.1/24 brd 192.168.56.255 scope global noprefixroute enpOs8
        valid_lft forever preferred_lft forever
     inet6 fe80::981c:73b4:21c2:9e6d/64 scope link noprefixroute
        valid_lft forever preferred_lft forever
[root@studentvm2 ~]#
```

At this point, our initial changes to StudentVM1 have all been made and tested. Both NICs are configured and connected to the network although we cannot yet do a good test of enpOs8.

Reconfiguring DHCP

The DHCP server needs to be reconfigured to provide IP addresses, gateway information, and name service data using the new IP address for StudentVM2 on the new internal network.

EXPERIMENT 6-8

Perform this experiment as the root user on StudentVM2. In it we will reconfigure the IP addresses that the DHCP server offers to the clients on the new 192.168.56.0/26 network.

First, stop the DHCP server.

```
[root@studentvm2 ~]# systemctl stop dhcpd
```

Now use Vim, or another editor if you have installed one, to edit /etc/dhcp/dhcpd.conf.

Change the file to look like the following. I have highlighted the changed data.

```
#
# DHCP Server Configuration file.
#   see /usr/share/doc/dhcp-server/dhcpd.conf.example
#   see dhcpd.conf(5) man page
#
# option definitions common to all supported networks…
# These directives could be placed inside the subnet declaration
# if they are unique to a subnet.
option domain-name "example.com";
option domain-search "example.com";
option domain-name-servers 192.168.56.1, 10.0.2.1;
#
# All networks get the default lease times
default-lease-time 600; # 10 minutes
max-lease-time 7200;    # 2 hours
#
############################################################
# This is a very basic subnet declaration.                #
############################################################
subnet 192.168.56.1 netmask 255.255.255.0 {
        # default gateway
        option routers              192.168.56.1;
        option subnet-mask          255.255.255.0;
```

```
###############################################################
# Dynamic allocation range for otherwise unknown hosts      #
###############################################################
        range dynamic-bootp 192.168.56.50 192.168.56.59;
###############################################################
# Host declaration in the 192.168.56.0/24 subnet.           #
###############################################################
        host studentvm1 {
                hardware ethernet 08:00:27:E1:0C:10;
                fixed-address 192.168.56.21;
        }
}
```

We need to use the IP address of the new NIC, and we have kept the virtual router as our secondary server. These are the name server IP addresses that other hosts within our network will be served by the DHCP server.

We also needed to change the IP addresses in the subnet declaration to reflect those of the newly created subnet on 192.168.56.0/24 and the IP address we have explicitly defined for StudentVM2.

Now restart the DHCP service. If there are errors, and I had a couple typos in my revised configuration, fix them and try again. You can see the errors with the following command. In a black on white terminal with color enabled, the error messages will be displayed in red.

```
[root@studentvm2 ~]# journalctl -xe
<snip>
-- Unit dhcpd.service has begun starting up.
Jun 22 11:03:00 studentvm2 dhcpd[2508]: Copyright 2004-2017 Internet Systems
Consortium.
Jun 22 11:03:00 studentvm2 systemd[1]: dhcpd.service: Main process exited,
code=exited, status=1/FAILU>
Jun 22 11:03:00 studentvm2 dhcpd[2508]: All rights reserved.
Jun 22 11:03:00 studentvm2 systemd[1]: dhcpd.service: Failed with result
'exit-code'.
Jun 22 11:03:00 studentvm2 dhcpd[2508]: For info, please visit https://www.
isc.org/software/dhcp/
```

Jun 22 11:03:00 studentvm2 systemd[1]: Failed to start DHCPv4 Server Daemon.

-- Subject: Unit dhcpd.service has failed

-- Defined-By: systemd

-- Support: https://lists.freedesktop.org/mailman/listinfo/systemd-devel

--

-- Unit dhcpd.service has failed.

--

-- The result is failed.

Jun 22 11:03:00 studentvm2 dhcpd[2508]: /etc/dhcp/dhcpd.conf line 27: 561 exceeds max (255) for precis>

Jun 22 11:03:00 studentvm2 dhcpd[2508]:   range dynamic-bootp 192.168.56.50 192.168.561.

Jun 22 11:03:00 studentvm2 dhcpd[2508]:   ^

Jun 22 11:03:00 studentvm2 dhcpd[2508]: bad range, address 192.168.49.59 not in subnet 192.168.56.0 ne>

Jun 22 11:03:00 studentvm2 dhcpd[2508]:

Jun 22 11:03:00 studentvm2 dhcpd[2508]: This version of ISC DHCP is based on the release available

Jun 22 11:03:00 studentvm2 dhcpd[2508]: on ftp.isc.org. Features have been added and other changes

Jun 22 11:03:00 studentvm2 dhcpd[2508]: have been made to the base software release in order to make

Jun 22 11:03:00 studentvm2 dhcpd[2508]: it work better with this distribution.

Jun 22 11:03:00 studentvm2 dhcpd[2508]:

Jun 22 11:03:00 studentvm2 dhcpd[2508]: Please report issues with this software via:

Jun 22 11:03:00 studentvm2 dhcpd[2508]: https://bugzilla.redhat.com/

Jun 22 11:03:00 studentvm2 dhcpd[2508]:

Jun 22 11:03:00 studentvm2 dhcpd[2508]: exiting.

After correcting any and all errors start the DHCP server again.

Now we can test StudentVM1 to verify that our network connection and DHCP are both working.

EXPERIMENT 6-9

Start the StudentVM1 virtual machine. Login to the desktop. You should notice right away that the network monitor in the system tray shows that the network is connected.

Perform the rest of this experiment as the student user on StudentVM1. Verify that the IP address for enp0s8 on StudentVM1 is 192.168.56.21. Then ping the server, StudentVM2, but we need to use the IP address of 192.168.56.1 instead of the hostname because we don't have name services up and running for the new network yet.

At this point, we have tested as much as we can. The new network is working as expected and both student hosts have access to it.

Reconfiguring DNS

The last thing we need to do to reconfigure our network is to reconfigure the addresses in the DNS server.

EXPERIMENT 6-10

Perform this experiment as the root user on StudentVM2. Use your preferred editor to modify the NAMED configuration files.

1. In the /etc/named.conf file, change all instances of "10.0.2" to "192.168.56".

2. Change the "Listen on" line to the IP address of NIC 2 on StudentVM2, 192.168.56.1.

3. Comment out the recursion line because we want this to be the authoritative name server for our domain.

4. Change the first line of the reverse zone stanza to "zone 56.168.192.in-addr. arpa" IN {" to reflect the new reverse zone IP address.

    Save the file and exit from Vim. This file should look like the following when the changes are complete. The modified portions have been highlighted in bold.

```
//
// named.conf
//
// Provided by Red Hat bind package to configure the ISC BIND named(8)
DNS
// server as a caching only nameserver (as a localhost DNS resolver
only).
//
// See /usr/share/doc/bind*/sample/ for example named configuration
files.
//

options {
        listen-on port 53 { 127.0.0.1; 192.168.56.1; };
//      listen-on-v6 port 53 { ::1; };
//      forwarders { 192.168.56.1; 8.8.8.8; }; // Forwarders not used
        directory       "/var/named";
        dump-file       "/var/named/data/cache_dump.db";
        statistics-file "/var/named/data/named_stats.txt";
        memstatistics-file "/var/named/data/named_mem_stats.txt";
        secroots-file   "/var/named/data/named.secroots";
        recursing-file  "/var/named/data/named.recursing";
        allow-query     { localhost; 192.168.56.0/24; };

        /*
         - If you are building an AUTHORITATIVE DNS server, do NOT
           enable recursion.
         - If you are building a RECURSIVE (caching) DNS server, you
           need to enable recursion.
         - If your recursive DNS server has a public IP address,
           you MUST enable access control to limit queries to your
           legitimate users. Failing to do so will cause your server
           to become part of large scale DNS amplification attacks.
           Implementing BCP38 within your network would greatly reduce
           such attack surface
        */
        // recursion yes;
```

```
                dnssec-enable yes;
                dnssec-validation yes;

                managed-keys-directory "/var/named/dynamic";

                pid-file "/run/named/named.pid";
                session-keyfile "/run/named/session.key";

                /* https://fedoraproject.org/wiki/Changes/CryptoPolicy */
                include "/etc/crypto-policies/back-ends/bind.config";
        };
        logging {
                channel default_debug {
                        file "data/named.run";
                        severity dynamic;
                };
        };

        zone "." IN {
                type hint;
                file "named.ca";
        };

        zone "example.com" IN {
                type master;
                file "example.com.zone";
        };

        zone    "56.168.192.in-addr.arpa" IN {
                type master;
                file "example.com.rev";
        };

        include "/etc/named.rfc1912.zones";
        include "/etc/named.root.key";
```

Save the file. I like to leave the files open in Vim so I can make changes if necessary.

Now edit the forward zone file, /var/named/example.com.zone.

1. Change the serial number to the current date and add a 2-digit sequence number at the end. It should have the format YYYYMMDDSS where SS is the sequence number, not seconds.

2. Change all instances of "10.0.2" to "192.168.56".

3. Change the IP address for StudentVM2 to 192.168.56.1.

    The file will look like this when the changes are completed.

```
; Authoritative data for example.com zone
;
TTL 1D
@   IN SOA  studentvm2.example.com   root.studentvm2.example.com.
(
                               2019162201           ; serial
                                    1D               ; refresh
                                    1H               ; retry
                                    1W               ; expire
                                    3H )             ; minimum
$ORIGIN          example.com.
example.com.          IN      NS      studentvm2.example.com.
router               IN      A       192.168.56.1
studentvm2           IN      A       192.168.56.1
server               IN      CNAME   studentvm2
studentvm1           IN      A       192.168.56.21
workstation1         IN      CNAME   studentvm1
ws1                  IN      CNAME   studentvm1
wkst1                IN      CNAME   ws1
studentvm3           IN      A       192.168.56.22
studentvm4           IN      A       192.168.56.23
testvm1              IN      A       192.168.56.50
```

We can now test the forward zone, so let's reload the named service configuration. We did not stop it so a restart or a reload is used. A reload forces the service to reread the configuration files without stopping the service.

```
[root@studentvm2 ~]# systemctl reload named
```

A lack of error messages is a good sign. If you encounter any errors, fix them and continue until there are no further errors and named is running.

Now we also need StudentVM2 to use itself as the primary name server, so change the DNS1 line in /etc/sysconfig/network-scripts to "DNS1=127.0.0.1", then restart NetworkManager to make this change effective.

```
[root@studentvm2 ~]# systemctl restart NetworkManager
```

As root on StudentVM1, use the following commands to test our new DNS configuration. We want to verify both internal and external results. Remember that our chosen internal network name is example.com.

```
[root@studentvm1 ~]# dig studentvm1.example.com
[root@studentvm1 ~]# dig studentvm2.example.com
[root@studentvm1 ~]# dig router.example.com
[root@studentvm1 ~]# dig example.org
[root@studentvm1 ~]# dig example.net
[root@studentvm1 ~]# dig www.cnn.com
```

Try to ping a remote host. This will fail because the ICMP packets cannot get to the Internet. The StudentVM2 host is not yet a router.

```
[root@studentvm1 ~]# ping example.org
```

Setting up the router

Finally, we are ready to configure the StudentVM2 host as a router. There are two things that we need to do to accomplish that and they are both easy. We need to tell the Linux kernel that it can act as a router, and we need to reconfigure the firewall so that it can route packets between the appropriate network interfaces.

Kernel configuration

Configuring the kernel to support routing is trivial. Really! We do not need to recompile the kernel and we do not even need to reboot. We only need to turn on packet forwarding which allows packets to be accepted on one network interface and sent back out on another. Keeping packet forwarding turned off when it is not required is a smart security precaution.

```
┌─────────────────────────────────────────────────────────────┐
│                      EXPERIMENT 6-11                         │
└─────────────────────────────────────────────────────────────┘
```

Perform this experiment as the root user on StudentVM2. We will turn on packet forwarding and set that up so that it is permanent.

First, let's set packet forwarding on in the /proc filesystem. We could do this with the **sysctl** command, but that would not really show you how simple and easy it really is.

Make /proc/sys/net/ipv4 the PWD. List the files in this directory. Check the current value of the file ip_forward. It should contain the number 0. To turn on packet forwarding for IPV4, overwrite the content of the ip_forward file with the number 1.

```
[root@studentvm2 ipv4]# echo 1 > ip_forward ; cat ip_forward
1
```

Testing this does not result in complete success but does show a change in the error message. Do this as root on StudentVM1. The reply indicates that StudentVM2 is now working differently. It is now a router but it is rejecting these packets because there is not an appropriate rule in the firewall.

```
[root@studentvm1 ~]# ping -c2 example.org
PING example.org (93.184.216.34) 56(84) bytes of data.

--- example.org ping statistics ---
2 packets transmitted, 0 received, 100% packet loss, time 57ms

[root@studentvm1 ~]# ping -c2 example.org
PING example.org (93.184.216.34) 56(84) bytes of data.
From _gateway (192.168.56.1) icmp_seq=1 Destination Host Prohibited
From _gateway (192.168.56.1) icmp_seq=2 Destination Host Prohibited

--- example.org ping statistics ---
2 packets transmitted, 0 received, +2 errors, 100% packet loss, time 3ms
```

We have set ip forwarding on, but it is not permanent. The value of this file will return to 0 at the next reboot. To make this change permanent, we need to add a new file to the /etc/sysctl.d/ directory.

Although the /etc/sysctl.conf file still exists, it is no longer used to set kernel parameters. Rather all kernel parameters are now set using files in /etc/sysctl.d. There is no naming convention for the files stored in this directory except that they all be prepended with a two-digit number which will define the sorted order in which the files are acted upon. Back on StudentVM2, create a new file named 98-network.conf[3] in the /etc/sysctl.d directory and add the following content to it.

```
# Controls IP packet forwarding
net.ipv4.ip_forward = 1
```

This file will now be read at each boot.

Notice that the file name contains a partial path indicating the location of the file referred to by this statement. The base path is proc/sys/ and the separators are dots (.) instead of slashes (/).

Save the new file. The default permissions are fine.

We explored the /proc filesystem in some detail in Chapter 5 of Volume 2.

Changing the firewall

The final step in creating a router on StudentVM2 is adding some new rules to the firewall. This includes creating a new table, the NAT table.

EXPERIMENT 6-12

Perform this experiment as root on StudentVM2. Edit the /etc/sysconfig/iptables file and add the lines highlighted in bold.

We add a nat table which we have not had before. This causes the firewall to perform network address translation on all packets passing from the internal network to the external network and all of the reply packets.

```
# sample configuration for iptables service
# you can edit this manually or use system-config-firewall
# please do not ask us to add additional ports/services to this default
configuration
*nat
:INPUT ACCEPT [0:0]
```

---

[3] I arbitrarily chose the number 98 for this file. The number used should be irrelevant – at least for our purposes.

```
:OUTPUT ACCEPT [0:0]
:POSTROUTING ACCEPT [0:0]
-A POSTROUTING -s 192.168.56.0/24 -j MASQUERADE
COMMIT
*filter
:INPUT ACCEPT [0:0]
:FORWARD ACCEPT [0:0]
:OUTPUT ACCEPT [0:0]
 -A INPUT -m state --state RELATED,ESTABLISHED -j ACCEPT
-A INPUT -p icmp -j ACCEPT
-A INPUT -i lo -j ACCEPT
-A INPUT -p tcp -m state --state NEW -m tcp --dport 22 -j ACCEPT
-A INPUT -p udp -m state --state NEW -m udp --dport 53 -j ACCEPT
-A INPUT -j REJECT --reject-with icmp-host-prohibited
-A FORWARD -m state --state RELATED,ESTABLISHED -j ACCEPT
-A FORWARD -i enpos8 -j ACCEPT
-A FORWARD -j REJECT --reject-with icmp-host-prohibited
COMMIT
```

Our firewall just got more complex, but it is still simpler than had we used firewalld instead of IPTables.

Understanding the rule set

IPTables rules are organized in chains. There are five predefined tables consisting of multiple chains of rules, but SysAdmins can also define their own chains. Each table has a specific purpose. We are now using the first two of these, the NAT and Filter tables.

- **Filter**: The filter table is the one chain defined in the tiny default rule set. It is used to filter packets and to discard them or accept them. This chain is the one most commonly used in very simple firewalls.

- **NAT**: The NAT table is used for Network Address Translation. Internal private addresses like the 10.0.0.0/8 addresses used by our virtual router or the 192.168.0.0/16 range are not routable through the Internet. So outbound request packets to, for example, a web site must have the return IP address of the router at the edge of the

113

internal network and the Internet. NAT substitutes the routable IP address in place of the nonroutable one for outbound packets and the nonroutable IP in place of the routable one for the return packets.

- **Mangle**: The mangle table is used to change – mangle – various portions of a packet. One example is to redefine the source IP address of the packet. Although such mangling does have legitimate uses, it can also be used by crackers to spoof the source address of packets as part of distributed denial of service (DDOS) attacks.

- **Raw**: This table would be used to configure exemptions to packet tracking rules.

- **Security**: This table would be used to implement Mandatory Access Control rules. It is generally used in conjunction with SELinux to enhance security.

In Figure 6-3, we have a breakdown of the lines in the default iptables file. We skip the comment lines which are ignored by IPTables.

IPTables Line	Description
*nat	The following rules are to be inserted into the NAT table.
:INPUT ACCEPT [0:0]	Accepts incoming packets to the NAT table. The [0:0] are counters for the numbers of transmitted and received packets for this chain. The other rules in the INPUT chain modify the default policy.
:OUTPUT ACCEPT [0:0]	This policy rule accepts all packets outbound from the NAT table. The other rules in the OUTPUT chain modify the default policy.
:POSTROUTING ACCEPT [0:0]	This policy accepts packets after other processing by the NAT table and applies post-routing rules that enable masquerading. The other rules in the POSTROUTING chain modify the default policy.
-A POSTROUTING -s 192.168.56.0/24 -j MASQUERADE	This rule makes it possible for computers on the internal network, that is a source IP address in the 192.168.56.0/24 range, to communicate with computers on the outside. Packets from the internal computers, such as StudentVM1, have a return address, the Source IP embedded. But that address is one on the internal network. This rule substitutes the external IP address of the router, for the internal IP address of StudentVM1. Then when the reply packet is sent back to our network, the router changes the destination IP address to that of the computer that sent the original packet, StudentVM1. This is called masquerading.
COMMIT	This line is not a rule. It is the last line of the NAT table and causes the previous rules for this table to be committed to the active firewall rule set.
*filter	The following rules are to be inserted into the FILTER table.
:INPUT ACCEPT [0:0]	This is a policy rule which accepts all packets on the input chain of the table. The [0:0] are counters for the numbers of transmitted and received packets for this chain. The other rules in the INPUT chain modify the default policy.
:FORWARD ACCEPT [0:0]	The forward chain is used in routers for forwarding packets to the correct network interface. This rule sets the default policy to accept.

Figure 6-3. *A description of the rules in the IPTables firewall*

IPTables Line	Description
`:OUTPUT ACCEPT [0:0]`	This policy rule accepts all packets outbound from the host. Should we desire to block outbound packets of a specific type, we can do that with the OUTPUT chain.
`-A INPUT -m state --state RELATED,ESTABLISHED -j ACCEPT`	This rule works with stateful connections. It accepts all packets after the first one has been accepted by other rules. That is packets that belong to an already established connection and that are related to an existing connection. All the rest of the rules in the INPUT chain are matched only on the first packet to initialize the connection. The rest of the packets are matched in any allowed connection are matched by this rule.
`-A INPUT -p icmp -j ACCEPT`	This entry accept all ICMP (Ping) requests thus allowing a response.
`-A INPUT -i lo -j ACCEPT`	Accepts packets from the localhost on interface lo. Without this we would not be able to SSH or Telnet to the localhost from the localhost.
`-A INPUT -p tcp -m state --state NEW -m tcp --dport 22 -j ACCEPT`	This entry accepts the first packet of a new connection on port 22, SSH. This sets up a stateful connection all further packets of which can then be accepted by rule #5.
`-A INPUT -j REJECT --reject-with icmp-host-prohibited`	This rule rejects all packets that don't match other rules. Essentially this rejects everything except ICMP and SSH packets because they have already matched other rules.
`-A FORWARD -m state --state RELATED,ESTABLISHED -j ACCEPT`	As in the INPUT chain above, this rule works with stateful connections in the FORWARD chain. It accepts all packets after the first one has been accepted by other rules. That is packets that belong to an already established connection and that are related to an existing connection. All the rest of the rules in this chain are matched only on the first packet to initialize the connection. The rest of the packets that are matched in any allowed connection are matched by this rule.
`-A FORWARD -i enp0s8 -j ACCEPT`	This rule allows all packets from the enp0s8 interface to be forwarded to the outbound network interface.
`-A FORWARD -j REJECT --reject-with icmp-host-prohibited`	This rule rejects all packets sent to the FORWARD chain of the filter table.
`COMMIT`	This line is not a rule. It is the last line of the FILTER table and causes the previous rules for this table to be committed to the active firewall rule set.

Figure 6-3. (*continued*)

So now we have a complete working router. Now we need to test it.

EXPERIMENT 6-13

Perform this experiment as the student user on StudentVM1.

Ping StudentVM2 to ensure that connection still works. It is possible to accidentally kill this one while enabling the routing function of StudentVM2.

```
[student@studentvm1 ~]# ping -c2 studentvm2
PING studentvm2.example.com (192.168.56.1) 56(84) bytes of data.
64 bytes from _gateway (192.168.56.1): icmp_seq=1 ttl=64 time=0.282 ms
64 bytes from _gateway (192.168.56.1): icmp_seq=2 ttl=64 time=0.391 ms

--- studentvm2.example.com ping statistics ---
2 packets transmitted, 2 received, 0% packet loss, time 3ms
rtt min/avg/max/mdev = 0.282/0.336/0.391/0.057 ms
```

Now check the routing to a remote host.

```
[student@studentvm1 ~]# mtr -n example.net
```

```
                          My traceroute  [v0.92]
studentvm1 (192.168.56.21)
2019-06-23T21:02:22-0400
Keys:  Help    Display mode    Restart statistics    Order of fields    quit
                                          Packets               Pings
  Host                      Loss%   Snt   Last   Avg  Best  Wrst StDev
  1. 192.168.56.1           0.0%     6    0.4   0.4   0.4   0.5   0.0
  2. 10.0.2.1               0.0%     6    0.5   0.6   0.5   0.7   0.1
  3. 192.168.0.254          0.0%     6    0.8   0.8   0.7   0.9   0.1
  4. 24.199.159.57          0.0%     6    6.8  22.5   6.0  91.5  33.9
  5. 142.254.207.205        0.0%     6   13.4  44.9  13.4  85.5  30.2
  6. 174.111.105.178        0.0%     5   22.2  33.0  13.2  79.2  26.3
  7. 24.25.62.106           0.0%     5   32.3  31.7  25.2  36.2   4.3
  8. 24.93.64.186           0.0%     5   30.4  34.1  24.9  41.8   7.3
  9. 66.109.6.34            0.0%     5   33.1  34.8  28.9  41.0   4.6
 10. 152.195.80.196         0.0%     5   49.7  44.6  33.5  49.7   6.4
 11. 152.195.80.131         0.0%     5   35.9  35.9  27.1  43.1   6.1
 12. 93.184.216.34          0.0%     5   29.0  33.2  29.0  39.9   4.2
```

117

We have now determined that our local name server is working and providing internal and external name resolution. We also see that the routing functions of StudentVM2 are working correctly.

Try using the Firefox web browser on StudentVM1 to access www.example.org.

Verify that the SSH connection from StudentVM1 to StudentVM2 is working.

Complex routing

It is possible to add more complexity to our router. We won't actually do that, but this section will explore what that looks like.

The routing table shown using the old and newer commands in Figure 6-4 is a bit more complex because it belongs to a Linux host acting as a router that connects to three networks, one of which leads to the Internet. The local networks, 192.168.0.0/24 on interface enp6s0, 192.168.10.0/24 on enp4s0, each have entries in the table, as well as the default route that leads to the rest of the world on enp2s0.

```
[root@wally1 ~]# ip route
default via 24.199.159.57 dev enp2s0 proto static metric 103
24.199.159.56/29 dev enp2s0 proto kernel scope link src 24.199.159.59 metric 103
192.168.0.0/24 dev enp6s0 proto kernel scope link src 192.168.0.254 metric 102
192.168.10.0/24 dev enp4s0 proto kernel scope link src 192.168.10.1 metric 104


[root@wally1 ~]# route -n
Kernel IP routing table
Destination     Gateway         Genmask         Flags Metric Ref  Use Iface
0.0.0.0         24.199.159.57   0.0.0.0         UG    103    0    0   enp2s0
24.199.159.56   0.0.0.0         255.255.255.248 U     103    0    0   enp2s0
192.168.0.0     0.0.0.0         255.255.255.0   U     102    0    0   enp6s0
192.168.10.0    0.0.0.0         255.255.255.0   U     104    0    0   enp4s0
[root@wally1 ~]#
```

***Figure 6-4.** A more complex routing table from my own network router*

Note that there is still only one default gateway, and that is on interface enp2s0.

Of course, it is also necessary to have appropriate rules in the firewall to allow routing.

Fail2Ban

A dynamic firewall is one that can adapt as the threats change. I needed something like this to stem the large number of attacks via SSH I had been experiencing a few years ago. After a good bit of exploring and research, I found fail2ban, an open source software which automates what I was previously doing manually.

Fail2Ban has a complex series of configurable matching rules and separate actions that can be taken when attempts are made to crack into a system. It has rules for many types of attacks that include web, email, and many other services that might have vulnerabilities. Fail2Ban works by detecting attacks and then adding a rule to the firewall that will block further attempts from that specific, single IP address for a specified and configurable amount of time. After the time has expired, it removes the blocking rule.

Let's install Fail2Ban and see how it works.

EXPERIMENT 6-14

Perform this experiment as the root user on StudentVM2. First, install Fail2Ban. This only takes a minute or so and does not require a reboot.

```
[root@studentvm2 ~]# dnf -y install fail2ban gamin
```

Fail2Ban is not started by the installation, so we will need to do so after we do a bit of configuration. Make /etc/fail2ban the PWD and list the files there. The jail.conf file is the main configuration file but it is not used for most configuration because it might get overwritten during an update. We will create a jail.local file in the same directory. Any settings defined in jail.local will override ones set in jail.conf.

Copy jail.conf to jail.local. Edit the jail.local file and delete the comment near the beginning that tells you not to modify this file. It is, after all, the one we will be modifying.

Scroll down to the line **bantime = 10m** and change that to 5 minutes. Since we have no other hosts to test from, we will test using StudentVM1. We do not want it banned for long so that we can resume experiments quickly, but this also gives us enough time to look at the IPTables rule set before the address is automatically unbanned. In the real world, I would set this to several hours so that the crackers cannot get more attempts for a long time.

Change **maxretry = 5** to 2. This is the maximum number of retries allowed after any type of failed attempt. Two retries is a good number for experimental purposes. I normally set this to three because anyone failing three tries to get into my system using SSH does not belong there.

We could also change both of these configuration options in the [sshd] filter section which would limit them to sshd while the original settings would apply to all other filters. Read the comments for the other miscellaneous options in this section of the file, and then scroll down to the [sshd] section in JAILS.

Add the highlighted line. The documentation is not clear about needing to add this line. In previous versions, the line was **enabled = false,** so it was clear that changing false to true would enable the sshd jail.

```
[sshd]

# To use more aggressive sshd modes set filter parameter "mode" in jail.
local:
# normal (default), ddos, extra or aggressive (combines all).
# See "tests/files/logs/sshd" or "filter.d/sshd.conf" for usage example and
details.
enabled = true
#mode    = normal
port     = ssh
logpath = %(sshd_log)s
backend = %(sshd_backend)s
```

Do not enable fail2ban, but start it.

```
[root@studentvm2 ~]# systemctl start fail2ban
```

From StudentVM1, ssh to StudentVM1 and login using a bad username; I used cracker which is not a valid user on StudentVM2. It takes three failed attempts to log in, not three failed passwords entries. After three failed login attempts, the following error message is displayed.

```
[student@studentvm1 ~]$ ssh cracker@studentvm2
ssh: connect to host localhost port 22: Connection refused
```

This means that the sshd jail is working. Look at the active firewall rules. Remember that these fail2ban rules are stored in memory and are not added to the /etc/sysconfig/iptables file.

On StudentVM2 list, the IPTables rule set. There is a line in the output below that rejects connections from 192.168.56.21 which is the IP address of StudentVM1. The IPTables rejection lines are removed after one minute, so if you don't see that line, force the failed logins again.

```
I have highlighted the IPTables rules that were added by Fail2Ban.

[root@studentvm2 ~]# iptables-save
# Generated by iptables-save v1.8.0 on Tue Jun 25 09:10:55 2019
*filter
 :INPUT ACCEPT [0:0]
:FORWARD ACCEPT [0:0]
:OUTPUT ACCEPT [7:1148]
:f2b-sshd - [0:0]
-A INPUT -p tcp -m multiport --dports 22 -j f2b-sshd
-A INPUT -m state --state RELATED,ESTABLISHED -j ACCEPT
-A INPUT -p icmp -j ACCEPT
-A INPUT -i lo -j ACCEPT
-A INPUT -p tcp -m state --state NEW -m tcp --dport 22 -j ACCEPT
-A INPUT -p udp -m state --state NEW -m udp --dport 53 -j ACCEPT
-A INPUT -j REJECT --reject-with icmp-host-prohibited
-A FORWARD -m state --state RELATED,ESTABLISHED -j ACCEPT
-A FORWARD -i enp0s8 -j ACCEPT
[root@studentvm2 sysconfig]# iptables-save | less
# Generated by iptables-save v1.8.0 on Tue Jun 25 09:12:10 2019
*nat
:PREROUTING ACCEPT [2560:323026]
:INPUT ACCEPT [298:20544]
:OUTPUT ACCEPT [2660:354694]
:POSTROUTING ACCEPT [2131:178008]
```

```
-A POSTROUTING -s 192.168.56.0/24 -j MASQUERADE
COMMIT
# Completed on Tue Jun 25 09:13:45 2019
# Generated by iptables-save v1.8.0 on Tue Jun 25 09:13:45 2019
*filter
:INPUT ACCEPT [0:0]
:FORWARD ACCEPT [0:0]
:OUTPUT ACCEPT [6:984]
:f2b-sshd - [0:0]
-A INPUT -p tcp -m multiport --dports 22 -j f2b-sshd
-A INPUT -m state --state RELATED,ESTABLISHED -j ACCEPT
-A INPUT -p icmp -j ACCEPT
-A INPUT -i lo -j ACCEPT
-A INPUT -p tcp -m state --state NEW -m tcp --dport 22 -j ACCEPT
-A INPUT -p udp -m state --state NEW -m udp --dport 53 -j ACCEPT
-A INPUT -j REJECT --reject-with icmp-host-prohibited
-A FORWARD -m state --state RELATED,ESTABLISHED -j ACCEPT
-A FORWARD -i enp0s8 -j ACCEPT
-A FORWARD -j REJECT --reject-with icmp-host-prohibited
-A f2b-sshd -s 192.168.56.21/32 -j REJECT --reject-with icmp-port-unreachable
-A f2b-sshd -j RETURN
COMMIT
# Completed on Tue Jun 25 09:13:45 2019
[root@studentvm2 ~]#
```

Now let's look at a couple log files on StudentVM2. In /var/log, first look at /var/log/secure. You should see a number of entries indicating failed passwords. These are the log entries checked by Fail2Ban for failures.

Look at the /var/log/fail2ban.log file. This log file shows the times that triggering entries were found in the secure log and the ban and unban actions taken to protect the system.

Be aware that the f2b-sshd chain entries do not appear in the IPTables rule set until the first time a ban is triggered. Once there, the first and last lines of the chain are not deleted, but the lines rejecting specific IP addresses are removed as they time out. It took me a bit of work to figure out this bit.

The installation of Fail2Ban installs the configuration files needed for logwatch to report on Fail2Ban activity. It is possible to create your own filters and actions for Fail2Ban but that is beyond the scope of this course.

Chapter summary

In this chapter, we converted the StudentVM2 host into a router, adding a new virtual network adapter to it, and reconfigured the internal network to a new IP address range. We modified the DHCP and DNS servers to accommodate that change.

We configured the kernel to perform IP forwarding which is the functional basis for routing. We added the NAT table and a FORWARD chain to our IPTables firewall to complete the transformation. And – of course – we tested the results.

Exercises

1. Why is a router required when connecting two networks?

2. What is the function of the default router?

3. Can there be more than one router on a network segment?

4. Can there be more than one default router on a network segment?

5. Why did we use the domain example.org instead of example.com in Experiment 6-5?

6. Before StudentVM2 is made into a router, why do DNS queries from StudentVM2 regarding external hosts, such as example.org and cnn.com, return the correct responses?

7. List the routers between your StudentVM1 host and www.apress. com. Are any of the routers dropping packets?

## CHAPTER 7

Introducing Email

Objectives

In this chapter you will learn

- How email clients and servers function to transmit email from one user to another

- How to install and configure SendMail to act as a mail transfer agent (MTA)

- To configure the firewall for email

- To configure name services to accommodate email with an MX record

- How to test email using a command line email client

- To use email headers to trace the origin and route of an email

- To configure a host to use the email server as a smart host

- To configure the aliases file to forward system level email intended for root to another email address like the student user

Introduction

Email is a ubiquitous messaging service and is available on devices ranging from work and home desktop computers to various mobile devices such as smart phones and tablets. There are two sides to email. The IMAP and POP protocols are used to receive email on your device and the SMTP protocol is used to send email from your device to and between email servers.

© David Both 2020
D. Both, *Using and Administering Linux: Volume 3*, https://doi.org/10.1007/978-1-4842-5485-1_7

Email is an asynchronous messaging protocol at the macro level. That is, if I send you an email message, you do not have to be at the receiving computer at that moment in order to receive the message. The computer does not even need to be turned on. The message is stored at the server until the computer is turned on and you retrieve it.

A typical synchronous messaging system is a face-to-face conversation or a telephone call which requires both parties to the conversation to be on the line or in the same place at the same time. Voicemail is just a corrupted version of a telephone call in which we leave messages for each other – another form of asynchronous messaging.

Email services were originally limited to users on a local Unix computer. All users of an email system had to be connected via a hardware terminal to the Unix computer. Because computers were not normally connected in any way, email systems were very localized. As slow dial-up connections became available, remote computers could be connected but only for specified and relatively short periods of time. Email messages could be stored on the sending server until the connection was made and all messages intended for the remote email server would be sent using that temporary connection. Email bound for other remote servers were held on the local server until a connection to the destination remote server was made. It is these ancient requirements that helped to define many of today's email protocols such as the ability to store messages for a period of time until the remote server is available.

Today we can send email to almost anyone on the planet, but spam is a major issue. With so many people connected to the same Internet that allows us to communicate with email, there are also those who use email for scamming the rest of us. We will discuss dealing with spam in Chapter 9 of this volume.

Definitions

Let's define a few terms before going any further.

> **Protocol** – A set of formal rules describing how to transmit data, especially across a network.
>
> **SMTP** – Simple Mail Transfer Protocol: A protocol used to transfer electronic mail between computers.
>
> **POP** – Post Office Protocol: A simple protocol designed to allow single user computers to retrieve electronic mail from a POP server. Once retrieved by the client, the email is deleted from the server.

IMAP – Internet Message Access Protocol: A protocol allowing a client to access and manipulate electronic mail messages on a server. Emails are retained on the server until explicitly deleted by the user.

MTA – Mail Transfer Agent: An agent such as Sendmail that transfers email from one host to another. These transfers may not only be between email servers but also from a sending email client to an email server.

SendMail – A very common MTA that has been around for many years.

Email data flow

Figure 7-1 is a simplified diagram of the flow of an email message from the sending client to the receiving client. Note that the sending client uses SMTP as the protocol to send the outbound email to the local email server. Let's track the progress of an email through this diagram.

1. The client adds an initial set of headers to the email to be sent. This includes the subject line, a date stamp, and the From: and To: lines.

2. The sending client uses SMTP to send the email to the local email (SMTP) server, SMTP server1, as defined in the client configuration. So, for clients in the domain example.com, their email would typically go to an email server for example.com. One common method is to identify that server as mail.example.com in the internal name services (DNS) database.

3. SMTP Server1 receives the email and adds a Received: line to the headers that lists where the email came from with IP address and host name if possible, along with a timestamp. The header entry also indicates the addressee.

4. SMTP Server1 parses the address(es) to which the email is destined.

5. SMTP Server1 uses DNS to specifically request the MX (Mail eXchanger) record for the target domain.

6. SMTP Server1 then sends the email to the receiving server, SMTP Server2, through the Internet.

7. SMTP Server2 adds another Received: line to the headers.

8. SMTP Server2 holds the email in the user's inbox until the client connects to the server to retrieve the email. Using the relatively more common and newer IMAP protocol on the receiving client, the user can view the email on SMTP Server2.

Emails remain in the inbox which is located in /var/spool/email/<username> until they are moved to another email folder or deleted. The email remains on the server until it is deleted regardless of which folder it is in.

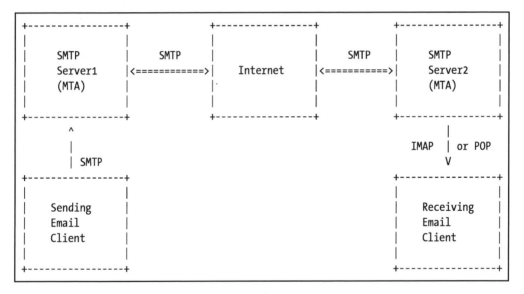

Figure 7-1. *The flow of data for email messages*

Structure of an email

The primary structure of an email message has two parts as defined in RFC 822, the headers and the message body. The headers are separated from the message body by a single blank line.

The message body can contain ASCII plain text or MIME[1] components consisting of HTML messages, images, or other types. The text body content of an email message is limited to 7-bit ASCII which is why MIME is used to attach data types based on 8-bit data.

Email headers

The email headers provide a record of the email's travels and can help us identify their true source. Each MTA adds one or more lines to the headers to record the email's passage. The email headers are normally hidden from users by the email clients, but a SysAdmin can access them to use in the task of problem determination for email delivery issues. I refer to email headers frequently for various types of problems including spam source identification, to determine where an email may have been delayed in its transit across the Internet from sender to receiver, and to use as the basis for blocking spam.

Figure 7-2 shows the headers from a test email I sent to myself from a network for which I am the SysAdmin. This email was sent from the remote host, host1, using the following command. We will use **mailx** commands like this to test our own email server later in this chapter.

```
[root@host1 ~]# echo "This is a test email" | mailx -s "Test email"
linuxgeek46@both.org
```

I have hacked some of the host names and external IP addresses in Figure 7-2 to obscure their true identities.

---

[1]MIME: Multipurpose Internet Mail Extensions are used in email messages to contain data types other than text messages. Images, HTML, and audio data are commonly embedded in email as MIME types.

```
Received: from mailserver.example.net (rrcs-96-10-0-10.se.biz.rr.com [96.10.0.10])
        by yorktown.both.org (8.15.2/8.15.2) with ESMTP id x5Q7sZwg006558
        for <linuxgeek46@both.org>; Wed, 26 Jun 2019 03:54:38 -0400
Received: from host1.example.net (host1.example.net [192.168.0.1])
        by mailserver.example.net (8.14.7/8.14.4) with ESMTP id x5Q7sZgN028979
        for <linuxgeek46@both.org>; Wed, 26 Jun 2019 03:54:35 -0400
Received: from host1.example.net (localhost [127.0.0.1])
        by host1.example.net (8.14.7/8.14.7) with ESMTP id x5Q7sZx0032630
        for <linuxgeek46@both.org>; Wed, 26 Jun 2019 03:54:35 -0400
Received: (from root@localhost)
        by host1.example.net (8.14.7/8.14.7/Submit) id x5Q7sZZ3032629
        for linuxgeek46@both.org; Wed, 26 Jun 2019 03:54:35 -0400
From: root <root@host1.example.net>
Message-Id: <201906260754.x5Q7sZZ3032629@host1.example.net>
Date: Wed, 26 Jun 2019 03:54:35 -0400
To: linuxgeek46@both.org
Subject: Test email
User-Agent: Heirloom mailx 12.5 7/5/10
MIME-Version: 1.0
Content-Type: text/plain; charset=us-ascii
Content-Transfer-Encoding: 7bit
X-Spam-Score: -40.5 () ALL_TRUSTED,USER_IN_WHITELIST
X-Spam-Status: No, score=-28.2 required=10.6 tests=BAYES_50,RDNS_DYNAMIC,USER_IN_WHITELIST
X-Spam-Status: No, score=-40.5 required=10.9 tests=ALL_TRUSTED,USER_IN_WHITELIST
X-Scanned-By: MIMEDefang 2.84 on 192.168.0.52
X-Scanned-By: MIMEDefang 2.84 on 192.168.0.75
This is a test email
```

Figure 7-2. *Typical email headers*

Let's examine these headers from bottom to top as that is the order in which they will make the most sense.

X-Spam-Score: -40.5 () ALL_TRUSTED,USER_IN_WHITELIST
X-Spam-Status: No, score=-28.2 required=10.6 tests=BAYES_50,RDNS_
DYNAMIC,USER_IN_WHITELIST
X-Spam-Status: No, score=-40.5 required=10.9 tests=ALL_TRUSTED,USER_IN_
WHITELIST
X-Scanned-By: MIMEDefang 2.84 on 192.168.0.52
X-Scanned-By: MIMEDefang 2.84 on 192.168.0.75

This series of headers were all added by MIMEdefang and SpamAssassin, the anti-spam software we will explore in Chapter 9. There are two sets of entries because the email was scanned by the outbound server and the inbound server. Email should be scanned before it is sent in order to ensure that we are not spamming others from our mail server or via an internal email client that uses our outbound mail server.

Content-Type: text/plain; charset=us-ascii
Content-Transfer-Encoding: 7bit

These two lines define the basic content type in our message. In this case, it is simple plain text, 7-bit ASCII which was the original encoding for email when it was first developed. This is the simplest form of encoding for email messages and requires no special processing like that needed for special forms like various MIME types.

Content-Type: multipart/mixed; boundary="----------=_1560989912-23914-8"

Although this line does not appear in our headers, you will see a header like this if there are multiple MIME parts in the body. The long number at the end is a boundary identifier to specify the beginning and ending of a MIME part.

MIME-Version: 1.0

This line is an indicator that the body of the email is ASCII plain text, or that there is a non-text attachment. It can also mean that the message body has multiple parts, that is, more than one type such as text and image.

This header can also mean that some other header information might be in a non-ASCII text character set. This can occur when spammers try to obfuscate the subject line in order to circumvent anti-spam filters. A typical sample of this is shown here.

```
Subject: =?utf-8?B?V2hpdGXCoEtpZG5lecKgQmVhbnPCoEJsb2NrwqBDYXJicw==?=
```

By specifying the character set utf-8 at the beginning of the subject line, the client can use that set to generate the ASCII text version of the subject so that you can read whatever nastiness they are peddling.

User-Agent: Heirloom mailx 12.5 7/5/10

The user agent is the sending email client. In this case, it is the mailx command I used to send the email. You might also see something like this which is for Thunderbird or other Mozilla-based email clients.

```
User-Agent: Mozilla/5.0 (X11; Linux x86_64; rv:52.0) Gecko/20100101
```
Subject: Test email

This is the subject line. It can contain almost anything. I have seen some users that are new to email manage to place their entire message in the subject line. I have also seen this field to be blank. This is normally a few words describing the subject of the email.

To: linuxgeek46@both.org

This is, quite obviously, the email account to which this email is addressed.

Date: Wed, 26 Jun 2019 03:54:35 -0400

This header specifies the date and time the email was sent as well as the time zone offset. In this case -0400 means GMT -4 hours or EDT.

Message-Id: <201906260754.x5Q7sZZ3032629@host1.example.net>

Every message has an ID, and this is the ID for the message from which our headers were extracted. This message ID was generated after the sending software, Fail2Ban, sent it to the local email MTA on the local host.

Each message has a different ID one every server through which it travels. This is to prevent the possibility of having a message sent from one server having the same ID as a message sent from another server. These message IDs are stored in the headers as a permanent record which enables us to locate log entries pertaining to the message in each server.

The first part of the message ID is a date and time in YYYYMMDDNNNN where NNNN is a sequence number. Many email servers are so busy that many emails can arrive at exactly the same time. The second part of the ID is the assigned ID. Message ID formats may vary between email servers that use different operating systems, but that is OK so long as we have the IDs in the headers to work with.

From: root <root@host1.example.net>

This line identifies the sending host of the email. This, like many of the other headers, can be spoofed so that it looks like it came from another email account entirely. We will explore that later in this chapter. But for this example, we can be sure that none of the headers have been tampered with.

This line is added by the mailx email client which now sends the email to the MTA on the local host.

```
Received: (from root@localhost)
    by host1.example.net (8.14.7/8.14.7/Submit) id x5Q7sZZ3032629
    for linuxgeek46@both.org; Wed, 26 Jun 2019 03:54:35 -0400
```

This header tells us that the email MTA on host1 received the email from the localhost. It might sound confusing, but so far we are still working on host1, which originated the email message. Each MTA that the email passes through always adds its own received header.

The fact that this was received from root@localhost indicates that the **mailx** email program sent this email to the MTA.

```
Received: from host1.example.net (localhost [127.0.0.1])
    by host1.example.net (8.14.7/8.14.7) with ESMTP id x5Q7sZx0032630
    for <linuxgeek46@both.org>; Wed, 26 Jun 2019 03:54:35 -0400
```

This received header was also added by host1. It indicates that the email has passed into the mail queue and that it has a new ID. At this point, host1 sends the email to the mail server in its own domain, example.net.

```
Received: from host1.example.net (host1.example.net [192.168.0.1])
    by mailserver.example.net (8.14.7/8.14.4) with ESMTP id x5Q7sZgN028979
    for <linuxgeek46@both.org>; Wed, 26 Jun 2019 03:54:35 -0400
```

This, the third received header, shows that the email was received by the email server for the example.net domain.

Note that there is no time difference within the 1 second granularity of these headers between the original date stamp placed on the email and this header. All of these time stamps so far place the date and time at Wed, 26 Jun 2019 03:54:35 -0400. So far the email has been processed on two computers.

Now the mail server for the example.com domain sends the email to the destination domain, my own both.org.

```
Received: from mailserver.example.net (rrcs-96-10-0-10.se.biz.rr.com
[96.10.0.10])
    by yorktown.both.org (8.15.2/8.15.2) with ESMTP id x5Q7sZwg006558
    for <linuxgeek46@both.org>; Wed, 26 Jun 2019 03:54:38 -0400
```

The email has now been received by my email server, yorktown.both.org. We now notice a 3-second time difference since the previous header. This is due to two factors: the time required to process the email through the spam detection software on the mailserver.example.net system and the time needed to connect with my server and to perform the handshaking and data transfer. Almost all of this time is due to the spam filtering.

Different email servers use somewhat different formats for some of the headers and they also may insert headers in different places in the stream. As we proceed through this chapter and these next chapters that also relate closely to email, I suggest that you take time to view the headers of the emails we send as part of the experiments.

SendMail on the server

Sendmail is a common email transfer agent. It has been around since 1983 and is still widely used on many email servers. There are a number of other good MTAs available, many of which are open source. Understanding SendMail – at least what we will be able to do here in this course – will provide a good basis for understanding email and mail transfer agents in general.

Although I use SendMail for my domain email server, it is also useful on a host that is not being used as the primary email server for a domain. Sendmail can be used on any host to provide an MTA to deal with emails sent to root by various system level applications and servers. If not sent to an email server, the local emails will be sent to the root user on the local host. Thus, they may never be read and acted upon. SendMail is required for each host that is intended to send its system management emails to a central mail server for further relay and distribution. When a network of hosts is configured to send all emails to the email server for the domain, that email server is called a smart host.

In the experiments below, we will install and configure SendMail as the primary mail server for our domain on StudentVM2 and we will install it on StudentVM1 to act as a transfer agent which can forward emails to the domain email server on StudentVM2. From there, these emails can be sent to any email client account.

Sendmail installation

Let's start by installing SendMail on both of our virtual machines.

EXPERIMENT 7-1

Perform this experiment as the root user on both VMs. We will install the sendmail and sendmail-cf packages on both of our virtual machines in this experiment.

StudentVM1 may already have SendMail installed. Even so, the sendmail-cf RPM must also be installed. The sendmail-cf package provides the makefiles[2] and configuration files that allow configuration and recompilation of sendmail.mc and other SendMail configuration files and databases.

We also install mailx, an email client that can be used as a text mode email client and as a command in a pipeline to send a data stream from its STDIN to the local mail transfer agent. This is a good tool for use to send emails in scripts. We can also use it from the command line to easily send test email.

Do this on both VMs.

```
# dnf -y install sendmail sendmail-cf mailx
```

This does not require a reboot.

SendMail configuration

Sendmail is already well configured by Red Hat in its distributions including Fedora. SendMail does still need a bit of additional configuration and it needs to be configured just a bit differently for the domain email server than for a system that will only send emails to the smart host.

It is only necessary to make some minor changes to the SendMail configuration itself.

---

[2]A makefile is a series of shell commands and variable statements that are used to create a finished project from a group of input files. Although we use it here with SendMail to create very complex configuration files and databases from various ASCII text input files, makefiles can also be used to compile programs using languages such as C. The makefile is the recipe that combines all of the input ingredients into the final product.

EXPERIMENT 7-2

Perform this experiment as root on StudentVM2. We will make StudentVM1 into the domain mail server by configuring SendMail. For the moment, we will concentrate on sending email from our server although this first change is for inbound email.

Use a text editor to make the changes to the configuration files.

In order to receive email from any remote computer on your virtual network, you will need to comment out the following line in /etc/mail/sendmail.mc. This line forces SendMail to listen for email only on the internal lo localhost interface. We want SendMail to listen on the external interface, emnp0s8, as well.

```
DAEMON_OPTIONS(`Port=smtp,Addr=127.0.0.1, Name=MTA')dnl
```

Prepend "dnl" to the above line in order to "comment it out." SendMail will now listen for inbound emails on all network interfaces.

```
dnl DAEMON_OPTIONS(`Port=smtp,Addr=127.0.0.1, Name=MTA')dnl
```

In the M4 language used in sendmail.mc, dnl means "delete through newline," which further translates into something meaningful as "ignore the rest of this line." It is an instruction for the specialized compiler used by SendMail.

Add the following lines to the /etc/mail/local-host-names file. This will tell SendMail to accept email addressed to this domain as well as the specified hosts which are all aliases for the mail server.

```
example.com
studentvm2.example.com
mail.example.com
```

Add the following line to the access database file, /etc/mail/access. This allows hosts on the 192.168.56.0/24 network to relay email through this mail server. By limiting the IP addresses to those of our network, spammers are unable to use our mail server to relay spam for them. Without this limitation, we would be running an "open relay" and the IP address of our server would be blocked by many legitimate email systems.

```
192.168.56               RELAY
```

Now, with /etc/mail as the PWD, run the **make** command. The **make** command runs the instructions required to convert the various text configuration files we have modified into the database files in the proper formats needed by SendMail.

make

Verify that the timestamps for the *.db files that correspond to the altered files have been changed.

In a separate terminal session as the root user, tail the /var/log/maillog file. This will inform us of any SendMail activity including startup information and any errors that might occur. This terminal session should be placed somewhere it can be seen on the desktop while you work in the other session to make changes and start and stop SendMail.

```
[root@studentvm2 ~]# cd /var/log/ ; tail -f maillog
```

Start SendMail, enable it to restart on boot, and verify the results.

```
# systemctl start sendmail
```

That took a long time. Too long in fact. Figuring this one out was pretty easy because you should find some error messages in the maillog file like I did.

```
Jun 27 11:56:36 studentvm2 sendmail[6078]: My unqualified host name
(studentvm2) unknown; sleeping for retry
```

This error occurs because we set the virtual machines's host name without using the fully qualified domain name (FQDN).

What?! You did not think I would divulge all of my secrets at once, did you? I learned a lot about configuring SendMail from the many mistakes I made while doing so the first several times I did it. It took me hours to work my way through some of these problems even using search engines. So my intent here is to give you a feel for SendMail, not just *what* we need to do but also the *why* of it.

So let's set the system's hostname, and this time we will include the FQDN.

```
[root@studentvm2 mail]# hostnamectl
   Static hostname: studentvm2
        Icon name: computer-vm
          Chassis: vm
       Machine ID: b62e5e58cdf74e0e967b39bc94328d81
```

```
        Boot ID: 7ae8d2bbbfaf44a6b1dd8082321d2f81
  Virtualization: oracle
 Operating System: Fedora 29 (Twenty Nine)
      CPE OS Name: cpe:/o:fedoraproject:fedora:29
           Kernel: Linux 5.1.9-200.fc29.x86_64
     Architecture: x86-64
[root@studentvm2 mail]# hostnamectl set-hostname studentvm2.example.com
[root@studentvm2 mail]# hostnamectl
   Static hostname: studentvm2.example.com
<snip>
```

Also check the /etc/hostname file which is where the hostname is stored. We could have changed the host name in that file but activating it would require a reboot. Using the **hostnamectl** command does all of that for us.

Now restart SendMail.

```
# systemctl restart sendmail
```

You should notice immediately that the command only took a very short time. You should also see an informational message on the screen following the maillog but no errors.

It is time to test our server. Let's first test from StudentVM2 in order to verify that it is working because we have not yet fixed the firewall to let other hosts send email through this server. We will use the **mailx** command to test for us. As the student user on StuidentVM2, enter the following command. The -s option of the mailx command sets the subject text – in double quotes – of the email.

```
[student@studentvm2 ~]$ echo "Hello world" | mailx -s "Test mail 1 from
StudentVM2" student@example.com
```

You should also see four log entries added to the maillog file. The last one should have a status of Sent.

Let's use the mailx command in its role as an interactive email client to view our email. In another session as the student user, start **mailx**. You may have some emails in this student account but probably not.

```
[student@studentvm2 ~]$ mailx
Heirloom Mail version 12.5 7/5/10.  Type ? for help.
"/var/spool/mail/student": 1 message 1 new
```

```
>N  1 Student User          Thu Jun 27 12:34  21/895    "Test mail 1 from
StudentVM2"
&
```

The ampersand (&) is the command prompt for the **mailx** email client interface. Just hit the Enter key to start looking at the email messages starting with the first one.

```
& <Enter>
Message  1:
From student@studentvm2.example.com  Thu Jun 27 12:34:50 2019
Return-Path: <student@studentvm2.example.com>
From: Student User <student@studentvm2.example.com>
Date: Thu, 27 Jun 2019 12:34:48 -0400
To: student@example.com
Subject: Test mail 1 from StudentVM2
User-Agent: Heirloom mailx 12.5 7/5/10
Content-Type: text/plain; charset=us-ascii
Status: RO

Hello world

&
```

Do not delete this email. That worked and you could use **q<Enter>** to quit from **mailx,** but let's just leave it open because we will be using it a bit more.

Notice that there are very few headers because the message was delivered by the email server on the local host, StudentVM2. It is time to send an email message to the outside world. For this, you will need an external email account that you can access from wherever you are taking this course. A computer, mobile phone, or tablet that you have configured to access your real-world email account would work. If you do not have one of these, you will be able to determine the success of sending these emails from the maillog. This is what SysAdmins and especially email administrators need to do in real life anyway.

As the student user on StudentVM2, do the following. Substitute your own external email instead of mine. Remember, these commands are all on a single line unless otherwise noted.

```
[student@studentvm2 ~]$ echo "Hello world" | mailx -s "Test mail 2 from
StudentVM2" linuxgeek46@both.org
```

But don't be fooled by the last line of the latest set of log entries. It does say "Sent" but check the To: address. Read through this list of log entries and see if you can figure out what happened before continuing below my sample log entries. I have separated the outbound log entries from the inbound ones with an empty line to make it a bit easier.

```
Jun 27 13:02:17 studentvm2 sendmail[6565]: x5RH2HBh006565: from=student,
size=245, class=0, nrcpts=1, msgid=<201906271702.x5RH2HBh006565@studentvm2.
example.com>, relay=student@localhost
Jun 27 13:02:18 studentvm2 sendmail[6565]: STARTTLS=client,
relay=[127.0.0.1], version=TLSv1.3, verify=FAIL, cipher=TLS_AES_256_GCM_
SHA384, bits=256/256
Jun 27 13:02:18 studentvm2 sendmail[6572]: STARTTLS=server, relay=localhost
[127.0.0.1], version=TLSv1.3, verify=NOT, cipher=TLS_AES_256_GCM_SHA384,
bits=256/256
Jun 27 13:02:18 studentvm2 sendmail[6572]: x5RH2IT4006572: from=<student@
studentvm2.example.com>, size=524, class=0, nrcpts=1, msgid=<201906271702.
x5RH2HBh006565@studentvm2.example.com>, proto=ESMTPS, daemon=MTA,
relay=localhost [127.0.0.1]
Jun 27 13:02:19 studentvm2 sendmail[6565]: x5RH2HBh006565: to=linuxgeek46@
both.org, ctladdr=student (1000/1000), delay=00:00:02, xdelay=00:00:01,
mailer=relay, pri=30245, relay=[127.0.0.1] [127.0.0.1], dsn=2.0.0, stat=Sent
(x5RH2IT4006572 Message accepted for delivery)

Jun 27 13:02:19 studentvm2 sendmail[6574]: x5RH2IT4006572: to=<linuxgeek46@
both.org>, ctladdr=<student@studentvm2.example.com> (1000/1000),
delay=00:00:01, xdelay=00:00:00, mailer=esmtp, pri=120524, relay=mail.both.
org. [24.199.159.59], dsn=5.1.8, stat=User unknown
Jun 27 13:02:19 studentvm2 sendmail[6574]: x5RH2IT4006572: x5RH2JT3006574:
DSN: User unknown
Jun 27 13:02:20 studentvm2 sendmail[6574]: x5RH2JT3006574: to=<student@
studentvm2.example.com>, delay=00:00:01, xdelay=00:00:00, mailer=local,
pri=31843, dsn=2.0.0, stat=Sent
```

So, did you figure it out? It took me a long time at first, so let me explain it. The first set of five log entries from Jun 27 13:02:17 through Jun 27 13:02:19 are from the outbound interaction with the remote email server. In my case, this was the email server for the both.org domain. The last log entry for this series shows that the message was accepted by the remote server.

However, starting almost immediately, the next set of log entries shows that the mail server for both.org has sent us a notification via the connection that we initiated to send the mail in the first place, that the user is unknown. The final line is the indication that our email server sent an email to the sender indicating that this was the case.

As the student user in the already open mailx session, press **h** to refresh and view the headers of any new emails. You should see a new entry, message number 2. Type 2 and view the new message.

```
& h
    1 Student User           Thu Jun 27 12:34  22/906    "Test mail 1 from
    StudentVM2"
>   2 Mail Delivery Subsys   Thu Jun 27 13:11  73/2862   "Returned mail: see
    transcript fo"
& 2
Message  2:
From MAILER-DAEMON@studentvm2.example.com  Thu Jun 27 13:11:29 2019
Return-Path: <MAILER-DAEMON@studentvm2.example.com>
Date: Thu, 27 Jun 2019 13:11:28 -0400
From: Mail Delivery Subsystem <MAILER-DAEMON@studentvm2.example.com>
To: <student@studentvm2.example.com>
Content-Type: multipart/report; report-type=delivery-status;
    boundary="x5RHBSk3006610.1561655488/studentvm2.example.com"
Subject: Returned mail: see transcript for details
Auto-Submitted: auto-generated (failure)
Status: RO

Part 1:

The original message was received at Thu, 27 Jun 2019 13:11:27 -0400
from localhost [127.0.0.1]

    ----- The following addresses had permanent fatal errors -----
<linuxgeek46@both.org>
    (reason: 553 5.1.8 <linuxgeek46@both.org>... Domain of sender address
    student@studentvm2.example.com does not exist)
```

```
    ----- Transcript of session follows -----
... while talking to mail.both.org.:
>>> DATA
<<< 553 5.1.8 <linuxgeek46@both.org>... Domain of sender address
student@studentvm2.example.com does not exist
550 5.1.1 <linuxgeek46@both.org>... User unknown
<<< 503 5.0.0 Need RCPT (recipient)

Part 2:
Content-Type: message/delivery-status

Part 3:
Content-Type: message/rfc822

From student@studentvm2.example.com Thu Jun 27 13:11:27 2019
Return-Path: <student@studentvm2.example.com>
From: Student User <student@studentvm2.example.com>
Date: Thu, 27 Jun 2019 13:11:25 -0400
To: linuxgeek46@both.org
Subject: Test mail 2 from StudentVM2
User-Agent: Heirloom mailx 12.5 7/5/10
Content-Type: text/plain; charset=us-ascii

Hello world
&
```

Note the 553 message that says, "Domain of sender address student@studentvm2.example.
com does not exist)." Do you see the problem now? The domain for this email is not really a
domain; it is a host name studentvm2.example.com. It includes the domain name. I ran into
this problem, too, the first couple times I set up an email server. It is an unintended side effect
of specifying the hostname of our server with the FQDN.

The reason for this failure is that the Internet name servers, not the ones in our own network,
do not have any domains named <hostname>.example.com. They do have example.com. The
remote mail server, in my case, mail.both.org, checks to see that DNS has an IP address for
the domain name in the From: header of the email message. If studentvm2.example.com does
not exist, the mail server rejects the email.

However, we do have some good news. Our server is definitely talking to the remote server or we would not be getting this type of error message. The other good news is that this, too, is easily correctable. Down near the bottom of the sendmail.cf file there are three lines we need to change so that SendMail will change the domain from host.example.com to just example. com. Change the highlighted lines:

```
dnl # The following example makes mail from this host and any additional
dnl # specified domains appear to be sent from mydomain.com
dnl #
dnl MASQUERADE_AS(`mydomain.com')dnl
dnl #
dnl # masquerade not just the headers, but the envelope as well
dnl #
dnl FEATURE(masquerade_envelope)dnl
dnl #
dnl # masquerade not just @mydomainalias.com, but @*.mydomainalias.com as
well
dnl #
dnl FEATURE(masquerade_entire_domain)dnl
```

To this:

```
dnl # The following example makes mail from this host and any additional
dnl # specified domains appear to be sent from mydomain.com
dnl #
MASQUERADE_AS(`example.com')dnl
dnl #
dnl # masquerade not just the headers, but the envelope as well
dnl #
FEATURE(masquerade_envelope)dnl
dnl #
dnl # masquerade not just @mydomainalias.com, but @*.mydomainalias.com as
well
dnl #
FEATURE(masquerade_entire_domain)dnl
```

These lines now masquerade hostnames like studentvm1.example.com and studentvm2. example.com to a true, two-part domain name, example.com.

With /etc/mail as the PWD, make and restart SendMail.

make ; systemctl restart sendmail

Now send the email to your real-world email account. The log should show a successful delivery with no entries to indicate a return error message. Check your external email account to verify the successful receipt of the test email.

This is the source of the email as viewed on my real mail client.

```
Received: from studentvm2.example.com (wally1.both.org [192.168.0.254])
    by yorktown.both.org (8.15.2/8.15.2) with ESMTP id x5RKTGa1030600
    for <linuxgeek46@both.org>; Thu, 27 Jun 2019 16:29:16 -0400
Received: from studentvm2.example.com (localhost [127.0.0.1])
    by studentvm2.example.com (8.15.2/8.15.2) with ESMTPS id x5RKTFBw007324
    (version=TLSv1.3 cipher=TLS_AES_256_GCM_SHA384 bits=256 verify=NOT)
    for <linuxgeek46@both.org>; Thu, 27 Jun 2019 16:29:15 -0400
Received: (from student@localhost)
    by studentvm2.example.com (8.15.2/8.15.2/Submit) id x5RKTE1h007323
    for linuxgeek46@both.org; Thu, 27 Jun 2019 16:29:14 -0400
From: Student User <student@example.com>
Message-Id: <201906272029.x5RKTE1h007323@studentvm2.example.com>
Date: Thu, 27 Jun 2019 16:29:14 -0400
To: linuxgeek46@both.org
Subject: Test mail 3 from StudentVM2
User-Agent: Heirloom mailx 12.5 7/5/10
MIME-Version: 1.0
Content-Type: text/plain; charset=us-ascii
Content-Transfer-Encoding: 7bit
X-Spam-Status: No, score=-0.5 required=10.6 tests=ALL_TRUSTED,BAYES_50
X-Scanned-By: MIMEDefang 2.84 on 192.168.0.52

Hello world
```

Now enable sendmail to restart on boot, and verify the results.

systemctl enable sendmail ; systemctl status sendmail

Our email server is now capable of sending emails to external, real-world mail servers so long as the email originates from a local account.

Firewall and DNS configuration

Now that our email server can send emails, we need it to also receive emails. Let us start with using it as a "smart host" so that it accepts email from other hosts on our network and can pass them on to the external world. We also want to set up a CNAME record for mail.example.com and a Mail eXchanger (MX) record that explicitly defines the mail server for a domain no matter its given hostname.

EXPERIMENT 7-3

Perform this Experiment as root on StudentVM2. We will configure both DNS and the firewall.

Let's start with DNS. Edit the DNS forward lookup database file, /var/named/example.com. zone. Edit this file and add the following lines to it. You can add them at the bottom of the file, or wherever your own organizational desires decide, so long as they are placed after the Origin line. Be sure to change the serial number to the current date and time using the format YYYYMMDDHHMMSS, where SS is a sequence number and not seconds.

```
mail                    IN    CNAME   studentvm2
example.org.            IN    MX      10      mail.example.org.
```

My file looks like this after making these changes as shown highlighted in bold.

```
; Authoritative data for example.com zone
;
$TTL 1D
@   IN SOA  studentvm2.example.com   root.studentvm2.example.com. (
                                      2019062701    ; serial
                                      1D            ; refresh
                                      1H            ; retry
                                      1W            ; expire
                                      3H )          ; minimum

$ORIGIN         example.com.
example.com.          IN    NS      studentvm2.example.com.
router                IN    A       192.168.56.1
studentvm2            IN    A       192.168.56.1
server                IN    CNAME   studentvm2
mail                  IN    CNAME   studentvm2
```

```
studentvm1              IN      A       192.168.56.21
workstation1            IN      CNAME   studentvm1
ws1                     IN      CNAME   studentvm1
wkst1                   IN      CNAME   ws1
studentvm3              IN      A       192.168.56.22
studentvm4              IN      A       192.168.56.23
testvm1                 IN      A       192.168.56.50

; Mail server MX record
example.org.            IN      MX      10      mail.example.org.
```

Restart name services.

systemctl restart named

We need to add a rule to the firewall to allow access on port 25, SMTP. Edit /etc/sysconfig/
iptables and add the highlighted line to the existing filter table.

```
*nat
:INPUT ACCEPT [0:0]
:OUTPUT ACCEPT [0:0]
:POSTROUTING ACCEPT [0:0]
-A POSTROUTING -s 192.168.56.0/24 -j MASQUERADE
COMMIT
*filter
:INPUT ACCEPT [0:0]
:FORWARD ACCEPT [0:0]
:OUTPUT ACCEPT [0:0]
-A INPUT -m state --state RELATED,ESTABLISHED -j ACCEPT
-A INPUT -p icmp -j ACCEPT
-A INPUT -i lo -j ACCEPT
-A INPUT -p tcp -m state --state NEW -m tcp --dport 22 -j ACCEPT
-A INPUT -p tcp -m state --state NEW -m tcp --dport 25 -j ACCEPT
-A INPUT -p udp -m state --state NEW -m udp --dport 53 -j ACCEPT
-A INPUT -j REJECT --reject-with icmp-host-prohibited
-A FORWARD -m state --state RELATED,ESTABLISHED -j ACCEPT
-A FORWARD -i enp0s8 -j ACCEPT
-A FORWARD -j REJECT --reject-with icmp-host-prohibited
COMMIT
```

Make /etc/sysconfig the PWD, load the new rule set, and verify the new rule is active.

iptables-restore iptables ; iptables-save

The email server is now ready to accept emails from hosts inside our virtual network.

SendMail on the client

Now we can configure SendMail on the StudentVM1 client host. We already installed it
in Experiment 7-1.

EXPERIMENT 7-4

Perform this experiment starting as root on StudentVM1. We will configure this host to use
StudentVM2, the domain mail server, as the smart host. Start by using the FQDN for the
hostname.

hostnamectl set-hostname studentvm1.example.com

Edit /etc/mail/sendmail.mc and change the following line:

dnl define(`SMART_HOST', `smtp.your.provider')dnl

To:

define(`SMART_HOST', `mail.example.com')dnl

We also need to set up email domain masquerading on StudentVM1 as we did on StudentVM2.
Near the bottom of the sendmail.cf file, there are the three lines we need to change so that
SendMail will change the domain from host.example.com to just example.com. Change the
highlighted lines:

```
dnl # The following example makes mail from this host and any additional
dnl # specified domains appear to be sent from mydomain.com
dnl #
dnl MASQUERADE_AS(`mydomain.com')dnl
dnl #
dnl # masquerade not just the headers, but the envelope as well
dnl #
dnl FEATURE(masquerade_envelope)dnl
```

dnl #

dnl # masquerade not just @mydomainalias.com, but @*.mydomainalias.com as well

dnl #

dnl FEATURE(masquerade_entire_domain)dnl

To this:

dnl # The following example makes mail from this host and any additional

dnl # specified domains appear to be sent from mydomain.com

dnl #

MASQUERADE_AS(`example.com')dnl

dnl #

dnl # masquerade not just the headers, but the envelope as well

dnl #

FEATURE(masquerade_envelope)dnl

dnl #

dnl # masquerade not just @mydomainalias.com, but @*.mydomainalias.com as well

dnl #

FEATURE(masquerade_entire_domain)dnl

With /etc/mail as the PWD, make and restart SendMail.

 # make ; systemctl restart sendmail

Enable SendMail it to start on boot, and check its status to ensure that it started correctly.

 # systemctl enable sendmail ; systemctl status sendmail

Now let's test our configuration. On StudentVM1, open a terminal window as root and use it to **tail -f /var/log/maillog**. Do the same thing on StudentVM2. On StudentVM1, enter the following command and watch the log files. You may see some log entries indicating deliveries of LogWatch notifications to root@studentvm1.example.com. This is normal and I had about 30 days' worth.

As root on StudentVM1, enter the following to send an email.

 # echo "Hello world from StudentVM1" | mailx -s "Test email 1" student@example.com

You should first see some log messages on StudentVM1 indicating that its own instance of SendMail has received the message and various steps in processing it. A moment or so later, you should also see some messages in the log for StudentVM2 indicating it has received the email and is processing it.

Now, as the student user on StudentVM2, use **mailx** to view the email. It should look something like this:

```
From student@studentvm1.example.com  Sat Jun 29 09:06:35 2019
Return-Path: <student@studentvm1.example.com>
From: Student User <student@studentvm1.example.com>
Date: Sat, 29 Jun 2019 09:06:30 -0400
To: student@example.com
Subject: Test email 1
User-Agent: Heirloom mailx 12.5 7/5/10
Content-Type: text/plain; charset=us-ascii
Status: RO

Hello world from StudentVM1
```

We now know that our email server is working and that it is being used as the smart host by StudentVM1. Let's send our message a bit further afield. This time we send the email to an external email account.

Keep following the log files on both hosts. On StudentVM1, send the following message. Please use your own external email account rather than mine, which I use for illustrative purposes.

 # echo "Hello world from StudentVM1" | mailx -s "Test email 3 from StudentVM1" linuxgeek46@both.org

Here is the source of the message I received on my own email system.

```
Received: from studentvm2.example.com (wally1.both.org [192.168.0.254])
    by yorktown.both.org (8.15.2/8.15.2) with ESMTP id x5TDaORu011406
    for <linuxgeek46@both.org>; Sat, 29 Jun 2019 09:36:00 -0400
Received: from studentvm1.example.com ([192.168.56.21])
    by studentvm2.example.com (8.15.2/8.15.2) with ESMTPS id x5TDaOB9004335
    (version=TLSv1.3 cipher=TLS_AES_256_GCM_SHA384 bits=256 verify=NOT)
    for <linuxgeek46@both.org>; Sat, 29 Jun 2019 09:36:00 -0400
Received: from studentvm1.example.com (localhost [127.0.0.1])
    by studentvm1.example.com (8.15.2/8.15.2) with ESMTPS id x5TDZxp8011175
```

```
     (version=TLSv1.3 cipher=TLS_AES_256_GCM_SHA384 bits=256 verify=NOT)
     for <linuxgeek46@both.org>; Sat, 29 Jun 2019 09:35:59 -0400
Received: (from root@localhost)
     by studentvm1.example.com (8.15.2/8.15.2/Submit) id x5TDZw6c011174
     for linuxgeek46@both.org; Sat, 29 Jun 2019 09:35:58 -0400
From: Student User <student@example.com>
Message-Id: <201906291335.x5TDZw6c011174@studentvm1.example.com>
Date: Sat, 29 Jun 2019 09:35:58 -0400
To: linuxgeek46@both.org
Subject: Test email 3 from StudentVM1
User-Agent: Heirloom mailx 12.5 7/5/10
MIME-Version: 1.0
Content-Type: text/plain; charset=us-ascii
Content-Transfer-Encoding: 7bit
X-Spam-Status: No, score=-26.2 required=10.6 tests=BAYES_50,RDNS_NONE,USER_
IN_WHITELIST
X-Scanned-By: MIMEDefang 2.84 on 192.168.0.52

Hello world from StudentVM1
```

Trace the route of the email through the various hosts using the headers and the mail logs on the virtual hosts.

We now have a working email system with a server and a simple client. Note that with the setup we currently have, the student user needs to login to the StudentVM2 host to retrieve email using **mailx**. We will discuss email clients and the server requirements to support them in more detail in Chapter 8 of this volume.

SMTP – The protocol

SMTP – Simple Mail Transfer Protocol – is an ASCII plain text conversation used to transfer email between servers and from a sending email client to a server and is defined in RFC821. SMTP uses TCP port 25. The SMTP protocol is well defined in the Internet RFCs so it is an open standard. SMTP servers are known as mail transfer agents (MTAs) because their function is to transfer email messages between one another.

Let's watch this conversation.

```
EXPERIMENT 7-5
```

As the student user on StudentVM1, send an email using the -v option of the **mailx** command. The SMTP protocol commands are shown with preceding **>>>** characters. These lines are highlighted to enhance their visibility. The responses from the mail server are not highlighted and begin with message ID numbers.

We send the email from the terminal session.

[student@studentvm1 ~]$ **echo "This is a test email." | mailx -v -s "Test email from StudentVM1" student@example.com**

The **mailx** session connects to the MTA on the local host which responds with the 220 message.

```
student@example.com... Connecting to [127.0.0.1] via relay...
220 studentvm1.example.com ESMTP Sendmail 8.15.2/8.15.2; Sat, 29 Jun 2019
12:38:30 -0400
```

The MTA on StudentVM1 sends this line which is "hello – I am studentvm1.example.com." The mail server on StudentVM2 responds with its side of the greeting and a list of features it supports.

>>> EHLO studentvm1.example.com
```
250-studentvm1.example.com Hello localhost [127.0.0.1], pleased to meet you
250-ENHANCEDSTATUSCODES
250-PIPELINING
250-8BITMIME
250-SIZE
250-DSN
250-ETRN
250-AUTH GSSAPI DIGEST-MD5 CRAM-MD5
250-STARTTLS
250-DELIVERBY
250 HELP
```

The local MTA has determined that TLS is supported and tells the remote MTA to start the TLS handshaking. TLS is an encryption protocol that is configured and enabled by default in current releases of Fedora and other Linux distributions. TLS ensures that the connection between the two MTAs is encrypted and that the data can be sent between them without being read by a casual observer to the conversation.

>>> STARTTLS

```
220 2.0.0 Ready to start TLS
```

We restart the conversation now that TLS is active.

>>> EHLO studentvm1.example.com

```
250-studentvm1.example.com Hello localhost [127.0.0.1], pleased to meet you
250-ENHANCEDSTATUSCODES
250-PIPELINING
250-8BITMIME
250-SIZE
250-DSN
250-ETRN
250-AUTH GSSAPI DIGEST-MD5 CRAM-MD5
250-DELIVERBY
250 HELP
```

The local MTA tells the remote MTA who the mail is from and a bit about it. The remote MTA responds by saying that the sender is OK. That means the sending domain has not been blocked by the remote MTA.

>>> MAIL From:<student@studentvm1.example.com> SIZE=253 AUTH=student@ studentvm1.example.com

```
250 2.1.0 <student@studentvm1.example.com>... Sender ok
```

The local MTA tells the remote MTA who the email is addressed to.

>>> RCPT To:<student@example.com>

We tell the remote MTA that we are ready to send the data which consists of the body of the email. The remote MTA returns a message that implies the recipient of the email has a valid mailbox on the server and that it is not full or otherwise blocked. It also sends a response of 354 which indicates that the local MTA can begin sending the body of the email.

>>> DATA

```
250 2.1.5 <student@example.com>... Recipient ok
354 Enter mail, end with "." on a line by itself
```

Sending the dot (.) on a line by itself to the remote MTA indicates that this is the end of the email. The remote MTA returns the message ID that it has assigned to the email and that the message was accepted by the remote MTA. It also indicates it is ready to close the connection from its end.

```
>>> .
250 2.0.0 x5TGcUtk013404 Message accepted for delivery
student@example.com... Sent (x5TGcUtk013404 Message accepted for delivery)
Closing connection to [127.0.0.1]
```

The local MTA sends QUIT to close the connection. The local MTA responds with a message to indicate that it is closing the connection.

```
>>> QUIT
221 2.0.0 studentvm1.example.com closing connection
```

SMTP return messages[3] fall into the following categories shown in Figure 7-3.

Code	Class	Description
1xx	Informational	The request was received by the server and the process that sent the message is continuing.
2xx	Successful	The server understood and accepted the request sent from the client or other server.
3xx	Redirection	Some additional action needs to be taken by the server to complete the client's request.
4xx	Client Error	The request from the client cannot be completed due to an error such as incorrect syntax.
5xx	Server Error	The SMTP server is unable to complete the client's request despite the fact that it appears to be a valid request with correct syntax.

Figure 7-3. *The SMTP return code classifications*

---

[3]Wikipedia, *List of SMTP Server Return Codes*, https://en.wikipedia.org/wiki/
List_of_SMTP_server_return_codes

Sometimes these messages, especially when they are error codes, are embedded in a returned email rejection. Other times the only way to see them is to use a tool like **mailx** and to observe the conversation for yourself.

Email-only accounts

Although the student user is a valid user in our experimental environment, it is a login account. Email servers need to be secure so that the owners of email accounts are unable to actually log in to the server. This is accomplished by creating nologin accounts for email-only users.

EXPERIMENT 7-6

As the root user on the server, StudentVM1, add an account with the username of email1 that can only be used as an email account. The -s option is used to specify the special nologin shell.

```
[root@studentvm2 ~]# useradd -c "Email only account" -s /sbin/nologin email1
[root@studentvm2 ~]# passwd email1
Changing password for user email1.
New password: <Enter the password>
BAD PASSWORD: The password is shorter than 8 characters
Retype new password: <Enter the password again>
passwd: all authentication tokens updated successfully.
```

Create a password for this account. The password is used when an email client attempts to retrieve email from this account while the nologin shell prevents a login as a Linux user. Test to verify that you cannot login with this new account by attempting to do so as the user email1 using a virtual console.

As the user student, still on StudentVM1, send an email to the user email1.

```
[student@studentvm1 ~]$ echo "Test email to email1 email only account." |
mailx -v -s "Test email" email1@example.com
```

You cannot login as user email1 so you must retrieve this email with mailx a bit differently. Because root can do anything, you will have to issue the following command as root. You would get an error if you tried to do it as a non-root user.

```
[root@studentvm2 ~]# mailx -u email1
Heirloom Mail version 12.5 7/5/10.  Type ? for help.
"/var/mail/email1": 1 message 1 new
>N  1 Student User         Sat Jun 29 21:10  25/1128  "Test email"
& 1
Message  1:
From student@example.com  Sat Jun 29 21:10:57 2019
Return-Path: <student@example.com>
From: Student User <student@example.com>
Date: Sat, 29 Jun 2019 21:10:51 -0400
To: email1@example.com
Subject: Test email
User-Agent: Heirloom mailx 12.5 7/5/10
Content-Type: text/plain; charset=us-ascii
Status: R

Test email to email1 email only account.

&
```

Who gets email for root?

Many system level services can send email to root@localhost to notify the root user of the completion of an **at** job, for example, the daily LogWatch report, and more, depending upon the specific tools and their configuration. These emails can get missed and ignored on many hosts that the SysAdmin does not login to frequently. Even with only a few hosts to login to each day, I found it a chore to do so just to check root's emails.

I found an easy way to fix that now that our internal StudentVM1 host can use StudentVM2 as a smart host. I use the /etc/aliases file to send the email to my personal email address.

The /etc/aliases file contains aliases for the system users that defines who gets email sent to them. Many system services have user accounts associated and some of those services send email notifications to root or to another user. Web sites also have nonspecific email accounts such as abuse@example.com or webmaster@example.com. So if someone sends an email to abuse@example.com, the aliases file tells SendMail to route that email to root. This email ends up in root's local mailbox on the local host. If that is not what you want, and it usually is not, we need to change the /etc/aliases file.

I like to get email that is addressed to root sent to me at one of my regular email accounts so that I will be sure to get it. This allows me to keep track of notifications that might indicate a problem of some sort.

EXPERIMENT 7-7

Start this experiment as the root user on StudentVM1. We will change a few things to send notifications intended for root to the student user instead.

First, copy the current version of the /etc/aliases file to /tmp for a short-term backup. Then open /etc/aliases with a text editor. Study the entries and notice that some like the ftp entry send emails to root, while further down, four other entries, ftpadm, ftpadmin, ftp-adm, and ftp-admin, all redirect email to ftp.

Down at the bottom of the file is a line that is commented out. It is an example of how to forward root's email to another user.

```
#root:          marc
```

Below that, place the following line and save the file.

```
root:           student@example.com
```

Now run the **newaliases** command without any options or arguments to activate your changes.

```
[root@studentvm1 etc]# newaliases
/etc/aliases: 77 aliases, longest 19 bytes, 794 bytes total
```

As root on StudentVM1, send a test email to ftp without the FQDN. Verify that the email has been delivered to the user student on StudentVM1.

```
[root@studentvm1 etc]# echo "Test of /etc/aliases" | mailx -v -s "Test email for aliases" ftp
```

Now make the same change to the aliases file on StudentVM2 and test it with emails sent to root or one of the other aliases like ftp.

By making this one change in the aliases file, I do not need to change the default email address in many different services.

Things to remember

There are some things to remember about email.

It is not instant

One of the most common misconceptions that end users have about email is that it is instant. It is not. Email may get held up at one of the MTAs for various reasons. Heavy traffic can delay emails and anything marked as bulk in one of the headers will be placed at the bottom of the queue and only sent when all emails with higher precedence have been sent. Any email without a precedence header is considered to be normal. Bulk email is sent from listservs and may have many addressees at any one domain.

I had one situation when working in a government organization where a PHB tried to ream me out and threatened me with some sort of disciplinary action because an email he sent did not get to the people in his building immediately upon being sent. The email he sent was to warn of an imminent tornado which was, in fact, bearing down on that part of the city at the time. But the email was sent to a list, and between being bulk mail as well as having hundreds of recipients in an email system that received more than 20,000,000 (yes 20 million) emails per day, it took some time to process the delivery of all those emails.

And, as we have mentioned before, one must be sitting at their computer with the email client up and running and watching for new emails to come in for this asynchronous communication system to be effective. Email is just not an appropriate communication method for that type of imminent danger.

There is no delivery guarantee

Another problem is the misconception that email will always get delivered. It won't. Many email systems drop emails that don't conform to their anti-spam or bulk mail policies. They may reject emails for many reasons and there is nothing that we on the sending end can do about it. Sure, we can call or email the designated contact for the domain, but in most cases, they ignore this type of complaint.

Emails also get dropped when routers become overburdened and start dropping packets. In this case, the sending server may try to send the email again, but there is still no guarantee of its ultimate delivery.

Chapter summary

In this chapter, we have learned to use SendMail as an SMTP mail transfer agent. We have configured SendMail to be our mail server as well as to forward internal emails from our own network hosts to the mail server as a smart host. We have used the **mailx** email client on both hosts to retrieve and send emails. We have also added an MX record and a supporting record to our DNS server and added a rule to the firewall on the server to allow incoming SMTP packets on port 25.

Although we cannot receive email from the outside world on our email server, be assured that it would work. Once it can receive email from internal network hosts, and with configuration of SendMail to listen on the appropriate external network interface, we would also be able to receive emails from outside domains.

There is more to be done to make this into a fully functioning email system, but we are well on the way.

Exercises

Perform these exercises to complete this chapter:

1. Where are emails located in your inbox stored? Be specific with the host and the complete directory path.

2. Why do we need to masquerade the email sending addresses?

3. What TCP port does SMTP use?

4. Why does email on our virtual network get sent to our own instance of example.com and not to the outside world instance?

5. When sending email to an alias like www on StudentVM1, what is the To: address when the email arrives in the student email account on StudentVM2?

6. How does an email only account differ from a regular Linux user account?

7. What other things can you think of that we need to do to make our email server more functional and more secure?

CHAPTER 8

Email Clients

Objectives

In this chapter you will learn

- More about using the **mailx** email client

- To install and configure the IMAP server which allows remote email clients to access email on the server

- To install and configure Thunderbird for a graphical email client

- To use OpenSSL to generate a self-signed ID certificate suitable for testing

- To configure Thunderbird to use the self-signed certificate with the STARTTLS authentication protocol

- To use network analysis tools like **ss** and **nmap** to look for network connections related to email

- To use those network tools to look for other ports that should not be open

Introduction

In Chapter 7 of this volume, we created an email server for our virtual domain, example. com. We installed SendMail and the tools needed to modify and recompile the SendMail configuration. We also installed and learned some basic usage for the **mailx** email client. Mailx is a powerful ASCII plain text email client that has two interfaces. It can be used with Standard I/O (STDIO) as part of a command pipeline to send email from shell scripts or command line programs. It can also be used as an interactive text mode user

D. Both, *Using and Administering Linux: Volume 3*, https://doi.org/10.1007/978-1-4842-5485-1_8

interface that uses keyboard commands to perform tasks like reading and deleting email, composing and sending new emails, and much more.

In this chapter, we will explore **mailx** in a bit more detail. We will also look at the GUI email client, Thunderbird. We will install and configure the IMAP email access protocol on the server which will enable Thunderbird to access emails on the server from remote clients. We will also create a self-signed certificate[1] and use it to enable IMAP[2] over Transport Layer Security (TLS).[3] Certificates may also be referred to as certs.

More mailx

Although the **mailx** client and its predecessor, **mail**, have been around since the early days of Unix, it still has a place in today's Linux environment. We have already seen in Chapter 7 how useful the **mailx** utility can be in testing email servers and mail transfer agents (MTAs).

Much of the utility of the **mailx** program comes from its flexible interface. We have already used it as part of a pipeline to send output from one utility to an email address. This makes it a powerful tool for the SysAdmin when installing or repairing email systems. Now we want to explore the use of mailx as an ASCII text email client from which we can send and retrieve emails.

As an email client, **mailx** has some major limitations that make it unsuitable for the average user – it is typically run as a text mode tool on the email server itself. It is not intended to run on a local host to access email on a remote server. The user must use SSH to log in to the email server in order to access their email so that the email users must have a login account on the server and not the safer nologin account. This can be a security issue but we won't consider that here.

That said, **mailx** does have extensions that will allow it to connect to an IMAP server. We will get to IMAP later in this chapter but will not use **mailx** with IMAP.

---

[1]Wikipedia, *Self-Signed Certificate*, https://en.wikipedia.org/wiki/Self-signed_certificate
[2]Wikipedia, *Internet Message Access Protocol*, https://en.wikipedia.org/wiki/Internet_Message_Access_Protocol
[3]Wikipedia, *TLS*, https://en.wikipedia.org/wiki/Transport_Layer_Security

EXPERIMENT 8-1

Start this experiment as the student user on StudentVM1. This experiment is an exploration of mailx as a basic email client.

As the student user on StudentVM1, SSH to StudentVM2. Start the interactive user interface (UI) of **mailx**, and then enter a question mark to get help. Note that the ampersand (&) is the command prompt for **mailx**.

```
[student@studentvm2 ~]$ mailx
Heirloom Mail version 12.5 7/5/10.  Type ? for help.
"/var/spool/mail/student": 6 messages 3 unread
     1 Student User          Sat Jun 29 12:38  26/1140  "Test email from
     StudentVM1"
     2 Student User          Sun Jun 30 08:59  26/1130  "Test email for
     aliases"
     3 Student User          Sun Jun 30 09:06  26/1130  "Test email for
     aliases"
>U   4 Student User          Sun Jun 30 09:10  26/1132  "Test email for
aliases"
 U   5 Student User          Sun Jun 30 12:45  26/1147  "Test email for
aliases"
 U   6 logwatch@example.com  Mon Jul  1 03:44  62/2610  "Logwatch for
studentvm1.example.com (Lin"
& ?
                mailx commands
type <message list>            type messages
next                           goto and type next message
from <message list>            give head lines of messages
headers                        print out active message headers
delete <message list>          delete messages
undelete <message list>        undelete messages
save <message list> folder     append messages to folder and mark as saved
copy <message list> folder     append messages to folder without marking them
write <message list> file      append message texts to file, save attachments
```

preserve <message list>	keep incoming messages in mailbox even if saved
Reply <message list>	reply to message senders
reply <message list>	reply to message senders and all recipients
mail addresses	mail to specific recipients
file folder	change to another folder
quit	quit and apply changes to folder
xit	quit and discard changes made to folder
!	shell escape
cd <directory>	chdir to directory or home if none given
list	list names of all available commands

A <message list> consists of integers, ranges of same, or other criteria
separated by spaces. If omitted, mailx uses the last message typed.
&

As we have already discovered, many commands can be invoked with just its first letter.
Note that "R" and "r" are different commands. Now enter **l** (lowercase l – el) to list all of the
available commands. You can always view the help and list of commands if you get stuck.

In addition to using **mailx** to send a STDIN data stream as an email, we can also invoke email
from the command line. There is no option to create and send an email from within the **mailx**
text interface. Let's exit from the **mailx** user interface and then send an email to ourselves.

```
[student@studentvm2 ~]$ mailx student@example.com
Subject: Testing mailx
This email is a test of using mailx to send email.
EOT
[student@studentvm2 ~]$
```

After entering the **mailx** command, it prompts you for the subject. After entering that, you get
an empty line and you can simply start typing your message. When you have finished entering
the message, use the Ctrl-D (EOT or End Of Text) to tell **mailx** to send the message.

Now view the message in the interactive interface.

Although mailx is a powerful and flexible tool for the SysAdmin, it leaves a great deal
to be desired with respect to the normal email experience we expect today.

IMAP

Once email has been delivered to the server, you must retrieve it from the mail spool file in order to read it. Email can be retrieved from remote servers using the IMAP protocol. IMAP was designed explicitly to allow users to access all of their emails from multiple devices running an email client. This was originally conceived as multiple computers but in this Internet age encompasses, all types of connected devices.

IMAP is a much better tool to use for multiple devices than the old and much simpler post office protocol (POP). Clients connecting to an email server using POP download all of the messages to the local host and delete them from the server. Thus, those messages that have already been downloaded cannot be viewed by any of the other devices. For this reason, we will cover only IMAP in this course.

Configuring IMAP on the server

It is necessary to install a program that can deal with remote connections using IMAP. There are several, but in this class, we will install the University of Washington IMAP package. UW IMAP provides both POP and IMAP; it is simple to install and there is little configuration required. It is also necessary to install a wrapper program to control the IMAP program. The Xinetd package provides TCP Wrappers around many programs that do not run as daemons, such as Telnet, IMAP, and POP. You should have already installed Xinetd on StudentVM1 in Chapter 17 in Volume 2 of this course but have not done so yet on StudentVM2.

EXPERIMENT 8-2

Perform this experiment as the root user on StudentVM2. Install the following programs.

```
[root@studentvm2 ~]# dnf -y install uw-imap uw-imap-utils xinetd
```

There is only a bit of configuration to do. You must enable IMAP and start Xinetd. Edit the /etc/xinetd.d/imap file and change the line that says "**disable = yes**" to "**disable = no**" to enable IMAP. Then start the Xinetd service and configure it to start upon reboot.

```
[root@studentvm2 ~]# systemctl start xinetd.service ; systemctl enable
xinetd.service
```

Verify that IMAP is configured and running with the following two commands.

[root@studentvm2 xinetd.d]# **systemctl status xinetd**
• xinetd.service - Xinetd A Powerful Replacement For Inetd
    Loaded: loaded (/usr/lib/systemd/system/xinetd.service; enabled; vendor
    preset: enabled)
    Active: active (running) since Mon 2019-07-01 15:25:43 EDT; 51s ago
      Docs: man:xinetd
            man:xinetd.conf
            man:xinetd.log
  Main PID: 14417 (xinetd)
     Tasks: 1 (limit: 4696)
    Memory: 896.0K
    CGroup: /system.slice/xinetd.service
            └─14417 /usr/sbin/xinetd -stayalive -pidfile /var/run/xinetd.pid

Jul 01 15:25:43 studentvm2.example.com xinetd[14417]: removing echo
Jul 01 15:25:43 studentvm2.example.com xinetd[14417]: removing imaps
Jul 01 15:25:43 studentvm2.example.com xinetd[14417]: removing pop2
Jul 01 15:25:43 studentvm2.example.com xinetd[14417]: removing pop3
Jul 01 15:25:43 studentvm2.example.com xinetd[14417]: removing pop3s
Jul 01 15:25:43 studentvm2.example.com xinetd[14417]: removing tcpmux
Jul 01 15:25:43 studentvm2.example.com xinetd[14417]: removing time
Jul 01 15:25:43 studentvm2.example.com xinetd[14417]: removing time
Jul 01 15:25:43 studentvm2.example.com xinetd[14417]: xinetd Version 2.3.15
started with loadavg labeled-net>
Jul 01 15:25:43 studentvm2.example.com xinetd[14417]: Started working: 1
available service
[root@studentvm2 xinetd.d]# **chkconfig --list**

Note: This output shows SysV services only and does not include native
      systemd services. SysV configuration data might be overridden by native
      systemd configuration.

      If you want to list systemd services use 'systemctl list-unit-files'.
      To see services enabled on particular target use
      'systemctl list-dependencies [target]'.

livesys   0:off 1:off 2:off 3:on 4:on 5:on 6:off
livesys-late   0:off 1:off 2:off 3:on 4:on 5:on 6:off

```
xinetd based services:
    chargen-dgram:      off
    chargen-stream:     off
    daytime-dgram:      off
    daytime-stream:     off
    discard-dgram:      off
    discard-stream:     off
    echo-dgram:         off
    echo-stream:        off
    imap:               on
    imaps:              off
    ipop2:              off
    ipop3:              off
    pop3s:              off
    tcpmux-server:      off
    time-dgram:         off
    time-stream:        off
[root@studentvm2 xinetd.d]#
```

Add the following line to the IPTables filter table in /etc/sysconfig/iptables to allow IMAP on port 143. Be sure to load the revised rule set.

```
-A INPUT -p tcp -m state --state NEW -m tcp --dport 143 -j ACCEPT
```

Do a quick test using telnet to see if IMAP is working and accepting connections. You can do this as root or the student user.

```
[root@studentvm1 ~]# telnet localhost 143
Trying ::1...
Connected to localhost.
Escape character is '^]'.
* OK [CAPABILITY IMAP4REV1 I18NLEVEL=1 LITERAL+ SASL-IR LOGIN-REFERRALS
STARTTLS] localhost IMAP4rev1 2007f.404 at Mon, 19 Nov 2012 13:18:58 -0500
(EST)
a0001 login student <Student password>
a0001 OK [CAPABILITY IMAP4REV1 I18NLEVEL=1 LITERAL+ IDLE UIDPLUS
NAMESPACE CHILDREN MAILBOX-REFERRALS BINARY UNSELECT ESEARCH WITHIN SCAN
SORT THREAD=REFERENCES THREAD=ORDEREDSUBJECT MULTIAPPEND] User student
authenticated
a0002 logout
```

```
* BYE studentvm1.example.com IMAP4rev1 server terminating connection
a0002 OK LOGOUT completed
Connection closed by foreign host.
```

Note that you must use the "a000x" sequence numbers or your commands will not work. Try the same test from StudentVM1 on the virtual network.

Our IMAP server is now working.

Notice our use of Telnet to connect with the IMAP server for testing. This is only possible because the standard Internet protocols such as SMTP, IMAP, and others use ASCII plain text commands and responses. That makes it easy for us to simulate a connection from a client. We could have done the same thing with SMTP to actually send an email because it, too, uses ASCII plain text protocols.

Thunderbird

Thunderbird is only one of many email clients that are available for Linux. It is freely available for all platforms and is becoming very popular. It is my current GUI email client of choice. The Xfce version of Fedora that we installed contains the Claws GUI email client, but we will install and configure Thunderbird because it is so widespread.

EXPERIMENT 8-3

Start this experiment as the root user on StudentVM1. Use dnf to install Thunderbird on your student host.

[root@studentvm1 ~]# **dnf -y install thunderbird**
Perform the rest of this experiment as the student user on StudentVM1.

Launch Thunderbird from the **Applications ➤ Internet** menu. The first time you start Thunderbird, it will take a relatively long time – about 25 seconds on my VM. This is so that it can create the configuration directory and default configuration files. It then displays the "Set Up an Existing Email Account" dialog window as seen in Figure 8-1.

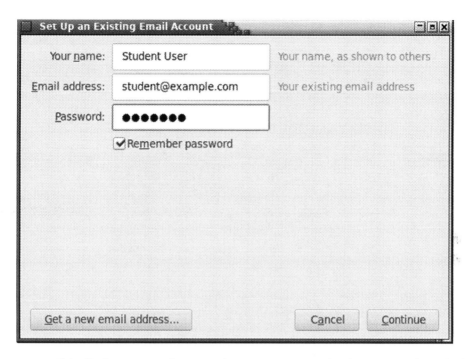

Figure 8-1. *This dialog starts the Email account setup the first time Thunderbird is launched*

Use the information in Figure 8-2 to set up an IMAP email account using the Thunderbird email client.

Field name	Value
Your (Account) name	Student User
Email address	student@example.com
Password	The password for the student user on StudentVM2, the server. The login password of the Linux account is the Email login password.
Remember password	Check the box.

Figure 8-2. *Email configuration settings for the first page of Thunderbird email account configuration*

After entering the data on this first dialog window, press the **Continue** button. Thunderbird will query the server by doing an MX lookup of the example.com domain. It then queries the server to determine the connection parameters. If the server responds appropriately, as it does for us, the rest of the configuration is performed automatically and the results are displayed as shown in Figure 8-3.

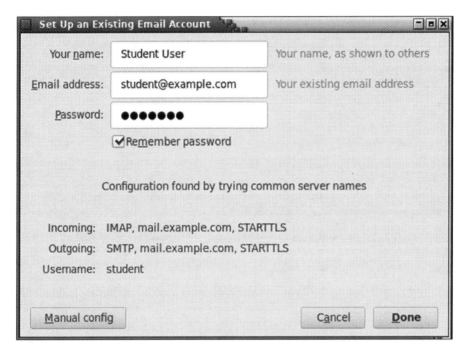

Figure 8-3. *Thunderbird has queried the email server and obtained the required connection data*

Now click the Done button to complete the configuration.

Well, things do not always work as one should be able to expect, do they? I received an error message indicating that the username or password is wrong. Having been through this many times, I already know that the configuration for authentication with the server is the most likely cause of this problem.

Click the **Manual Config** button. The dialog window seen in Figure 8-4 shows the problem. We have not configured Kerberos, an authentication protocol for computer networks, as our authentication method.

Figure 8-4. *The Manual Configuration dialog shows the problem because the configuration utility assumes that we are using Kerberos for authentication when we are not*

For now, to prevent getting too sidetracked, we will resolve this problem the easy way so that we can get email up and running. In the SSL (Secure Socket Layer) column, select **None** for both IMAP (inbound) and SMTP (outbound). In the Authentication column, select **Normal password** for IMAP and **No authentication** for SMTP. Press **Done**. You will receive a red warning dialog. Place a check in the **I understand the risks** box and click the **Done** button, and then click **Done** again.

Thunderbird will connect to the server, authenticate for the IMAP connection, and download any emails that already exist in the inbox. Click the Inbox and look at the emails there, as at least a few should be present. Notice that there is no Sent mail folder.

For a bit of additional testing, send a test email to student@example.com – yourself – and also to your external email address. The Send folder is created when the email is sent. Your instance of Thunderbird should look very similar to that shown in Figure 8-5.

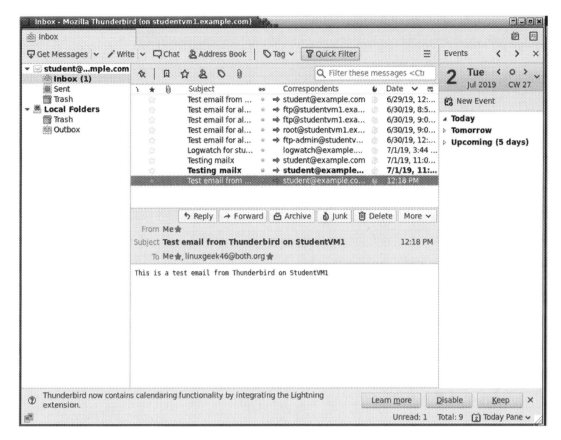

Figure 8-5. *Thunderbird after initial basic configuration with downloaded email*

Adding authentication

Email is insecure – period. No matter what we do on our servers and clients, once an email leaves our network, we must consider it to be readable by everyone on the Internet which amounts to nearly the entire world. Many politicians and white-collar criminals have found this out the hard way. No matter that we have configured TLS to provide some encryption between our SMTP server and other SMTP servers, most SMTP servers have not implemented this security mechanism. As a result, most SMTP servers talk to each other in unencrypted plain text.

Another problem I have encountered when traveling is that I do not have an email account for the local ISPs for outbound SMTP. This is usually an attempt by the ISP to block spam sent directly from infected hosts on their networks. This means that I cannot send email from those networks without some sort of circumvention. I can use my own email server as the outbound SMTP server, but that means it is accessible to spammers as an open relay.

There are a couple things we can do to improve security and help prevent the use of our mail servers as open relays. For example, the use of authentication will allow a laptop to use our own email server as a relay while preventing others from using it the same way.

It is possible to use a number of different forms of authentication so that mobile users can authenticate with their own email server in order to allow relaying. It took me a lot of work to figure this out. Using authentication so that we can connect both SMTP and IMAP to our own email server allows us to send email from anywhere even if we don't have an email account on the local ISP.

SMTP already uses STARTTLS for authentication and encryption as we found in Chapter 7 of this volume. So we do not need to do anything else for that except to configure it in the Thunderbird client.

Certificates

Certificates are the key, if you will pardon the pun, to enabling authentication and encryption. These certificates provide a verifiable identity for the server and are also used to provide the encryption key for the connections.

ID certificates are sold by a number of recognized certificate authorities (CAs) such as Verisign, Symantec, DigiCert, GeoTrust, RapidSSL, and others. Let's Encrypt[4] provides a free and open certificate authority that is backed by many well-known and respected sponsors and donors. For our purposes, a self-signed certificate is perfect.

IMAP authentication

Adding authentication and encryption to IMAP is easy because we already have most of the necessary parts in place. The IMAP protocol does not include authentication or encryption, but the IMAPS protocol does. TLS is also available just as we used for SMTP in Chapter 7 and is relatively easy to set up so we will use that.

---

[4]Home page for Let's Encrypt, `https://letsencrypt.org/`

EXPERIMENT 8-4

Start this experiment as root on StudentVM2. We will enable IMAPS, restart the Xinetd service, and add a rule to the firewall for IMAPS.

The Xinetd package that we previously installed contains the IMAPS configuration file and placed it in /etc/xinetd.d. In StudentVM2, edit /etc/xinetd.d/imaps. Change the line:

disable   = yes

to:

disable   = no
Restart Xinetd.

Generate a self-signed certificate for IMAP. The openssl program can be used to create a certificate that we can use with IMAPS like the one that was created for SMTP TLS. Enter the requested data as shown in bold. Do this as root in root's home directory.

```
[root@studentvm2 ~]# openssl req -new -x509 -nodes -out imapd.pem -keyout
imapd.pem
Generating a RSA private key
....................+++++
.......................................+++++
writing new private key to 'imapd.pem'
-----
You are about to be asked to enter information that will be incorporated
into your certificate request.
What you are about to enter is what is called a Distinguished Name or a DN.
There are quite a few fields but you can leave some blank
For some fields there will be a default value,
If you enter '.', the field will be left blank.
-----
Country Name (2 letter code) [XX]:<Your country abbreviation. I used US.>
State or Province Name (full name) []:<Your state abbreviation. I used NC>
Locality Name (eg, city) [Default City]:<Your city, I used Raleigh.>
Organization Name (eg, company) [Default Company Ltd]:<Organization name. I
used LinuxGeek46.>
Organizational Unit Name (eg, section) []:<Press Enter>
```

Common Name (eg, your name or your server's hostname) []:**studentvm2.example.com**
Email Address []:**root@example.com**

Verify that the file was created

```
[root@studentvm2 ~]# ll
total 60
-rw-------. 1 root root  2118 Dec 22  2018 anaconda-ks.cfg
-rw-r--r--. 1 root root   469 Apr 21 21:40 ifcfg-enp0s3
-rw-------. 1 root root  3123 Jul  4 17:58 imapd.pem
-rw-r--r--. 1 root root  2196 Dec 22  2018 initial-setup-ks.cfg
-rw-r--r--. 1 root root    10 Jun 19 07:20 testfile.txt
[root@studentvm2 ~]#
```

Copy the imapd.pem file to the /etc/ssl/certs directory. You should also view the content of the certificate with a paging tool like **less**.

For a real-world server, we would use the openSSL tool to generate a certification signing request and send it to a public certification authority (CA) and receive a signed certificate from them that verifies the identity of our server. A self-signed certificate like we just created is fine for a closed environment like we have in our virtual network, used inside an organization where no outsiders will be accessing the server and in other types of testing environments. Self-signed certificates should never be used on a server that allows public access.

A search on "certificate authorities list" will result in links to a good number of public CAs, many of which charge a fee for certificates. There are also some "open" and free CAs that you can find by searching, "free certificate authority."

Let's Encrypt[5] is a free certificate authority that is a collaborative project with the Linux Foundation. It is sponsored by Mozilla, Akamai, SiteGround, Cisco, Facebook, and many more organizations. It offers free SSL Certificates.

Now let's configure Thunderbird. As the student user on StudentVM1, use the Menu bar to open **Edit ➤ Account Settings**. Click **Server Settings**. In the Security Settings section, choose **STARTTLS** and **Normal password**. Port 143 is used for the IMAP TLS connection. The result should look like that shown in Figure 8-6.

---

[5]Let's Encrypt, https://letsencrypt.org/

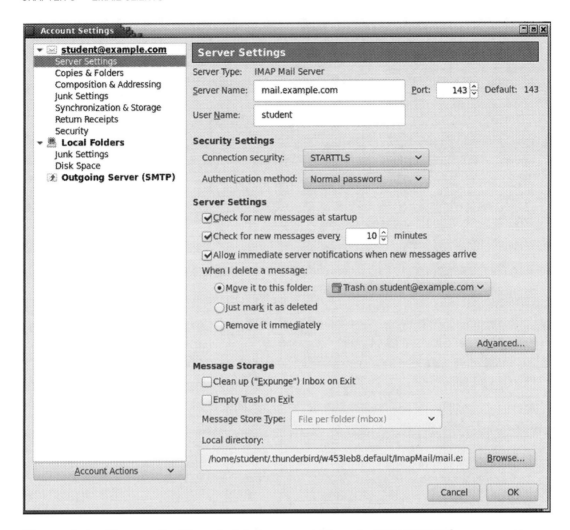

Figure 8-6. *Change the Thunderbird server settings to STARTTLS for connection security and TLS certificate for the authentication method*

Click the **OK** button to complete this configuration.

Testing is easy. Send yourself an email to student@example.com. You should receive the email within a few moments, but if it does not show up fairly, quickly click the **Get Messages** button on the Thunderbird icon bar. If you get an error, the configuration is not correct. If you have performed the configuration tasks correctly, you should receive no errors.

Be sure to view the log files and the email headers to familiarize yourself with how they might – or might not – differ from emails sent prior to adding IMAP over TLS.

Now we have IMAPS set up for authentication and encryption which enables us to obtain email from remote locations in a reasonably secure manner. The way we have done this is not completely secure because the password is transmitted as ASCII plain text and is not encrypted. However, the data connection itself is encrypted.

More about ports

We have been talking about network ports quite a bit in this course. A TCP or UDP port is not a physical port like the physical connection port on a network interface card (NIC). These are all logical ports that are defined by a number and which we humans usually refer to by the protocol assigned to that port.

We have seen that port 22 is for SSH, port 23 for Telnet, 25 for SMTP, etc. The standard and commonly recognized port assignments are defined in the file /etc/services. If you ever see a port number or name that you don't recognize, you can start your research with that file.

Although we could have discussed network ports in several places before this, it makes more sense to do so now that we have more ports open in our firewall and more services listening on various ports. This is more meaningful here and it applies to email-related ports as well.

An open port on a computer is one that some service is listening on for connections. However even an open port can be blocked by the host's firewall. This is why the services we are adding to our server need to have their respective ports added to the firewall for them to work.

Let's look at the open ports on our server. As with many things in Linux, there are multiple tools we can apply to this task.

EXPERIMENT 8-5

Perform this experiment as the root user on StudentVM2. In it we look at four tools that enable us to explore network connections and the ports they use.

Let's start with netstat which has been around for many years and is now deprecated. It is still useful because many SysAdmins already know it and use it but may soon be gone. Start with a simple look at the open ports on our server.

```
[root@studentvm2 ~]# netstat -a
Active Internet connections (servers and established)
Proto Recv-Q Send-Q Local Address           Foreign Address         State
tcp        0      0 studentvm2.examp:domain 0.0.0.0:*               LISTEN
tcp        0      0 localhost:domain        0.0.0.0:*               LISTEN
tcp        0      0 0.0.0.0:ssh             0.0.0.0:*               LISTEN
tcp        0      0 0.0.0.0:smtp            0.0.0.0:*               LISTEN
tcp        0      0 localhost:rndc          0.0.0.0:*               LISTEN
tcp        0      0 studentvm2.example:imap
192.168.56.21:38372     ESTABLISHED
tcp        0      0 studentvm2.example:imap
192.168.56.21:38310     ESTABLISHED
tcp        0      0 studentvm2.example:imap
192.168.56.21:38334     ESTABLISHED
tcp6       0      0 [::]:imap               [::]:*                  LISTEN
tcp6       0      0 [::]:domain             [::]:*                  LISTEN
tcp6       0      0 [::]:ssh                [::]:*                  LISTEN
tcp6       0      0 localhost:rndc          [::]:*                  LISTEN
tcp6       0      0 [::]:imaps              [::]:*                  LISTEN
udp        0      0 0.0.0.0:53826           0.0.0.0:*
udp        0      0 0.0.0.0:mdns            0.0.0.0:*
udp        0      0 studentvm2.examp:domain 0.0.0.0:*
udp        0      0 localhost:domain        0.0.0.0:*
udp        0      0 0.0.0.0:bootps          0.0.0.0:*
udp        0      0 localhost:323           0.0.0.0:*
udp6       0      0 [::]:mdns               [::]:*
udp6       0      0 [::]:domain             [::]:*
udp6       0      0 localhost:323           [::]:*
udp6       0      0 [::]:51664              [::]:*
```

```
raw          0        0 0.0.0.0:icmp              0.0.0.0:*                    7
raw6         0        0 [::]:ipv6-icmp            [::]:*                       7
raw6         0        0 [::]:ipv6-icmp            [::]:*                       7
Active UNIX domain sockets (servers and established)
Proto RefCnt Flags       Type      State       I-Node   Path
unix  2      [ ACC ]     STREAM    LISTENING   29386    @/tmp/.ICE-
unix/1466
unix  2      [ ACC ]     STREAM    LISTENING   29828    /tmp/.esd-1000/
socket
unix  2      [ ACC ]     STREAM    LISTENING   16648    /run/lvm/lvmetad.
socket
unix  2      [ ACC ]     STREAM    LISTENING   29339    /tmp/ssh-
MycgW2NgxAFd/agent.1254
unix  2      [ ACC ]     STREAM    LISTENING   29387    /tmp/.ICE-
unix/1466
unix  2      [ ACC ]     STREAM    LISTENING   22540    /run/gssproxy.sock
unix  2      [ ACC ]     STREAM    LISTENING   22539    /var/lib/gssproxy/
default.sock
unix  2      [ ACC ]     STREAM    LISTENING   22775    /var/lib/sss/
pipes/private/sbus-monitor
unix  2      [ ACC ]     STREAM    LISTENING   21865    @irqbalance874.
sock
unix  2      [ ACC ]     STREAM    LISTENING   15357    @/org/kernel/
linux/storage/multipathd
<snip>
```

This command with -a shows all network ports that are open and listening, IPV[460], UDP, TCP, as well as all open sockets for applications and services that are communicating with other internal processes and not with other hosts.

Let's trim this down and to look only at TCP (-t), UDP (-u), and all listening and established connections within those other two filters.

```
[root@studentvm2 ~]# netstat -tua
Active Internet connections (servers and established)
Proto Recv-Q Send-Q Local Address         Foreign Address        State
tcp        0      0 studentvm2.examp:domain 0.0.0.0:*             LISTEN
tcp        0      0 localhost:domain        0.0.0.0:*             LISTEN
tcp        0      0 0.0.0.0:ssh             0.0.0.0:*             LISTEN
```

```
tcp        0        0 0.0.0.0:smtp              0.0.0.0:*              LISTEN
tcp        0        0 localhost:rndc            0.0.0.0:*              LISTEN
tcp        0        0 studentvm2.example:imap
192.168.56.21:38372       ESTABLISHED
tcp        0        0 studentvm2.example:imap
192.168.56.21:38310       ESTABLISHED
tcp        0        0 studentvm2.example:imap
192.168.56.21:38334       ESTABLISHED
tcp6       0        0 [::]:imap                 [::]:*                LISTEN
tcp6       0        0 [::]:domain               [::]:*                LISTEN
tcp6       0        0 [::]:ssh                  [::]:*                LISTEN
tcp6       0        0 localhost:rndc            [::]:*                LISTEN
tcp6       0        0 [::]:imaps                [::]:*                LISTEN
udp        0        0 0.0.0.0:53826             0.0.0.0:*
udp        0        0 0.0.0.0:mdns              0.0.0.0:*
udp        0        0 studentvm2.examp:domain 0.0.0.0:*
udp        0        0 localhost:domain          0.0.0.0:*
udp        0        0 0.0.0.0:bootps            0.0.0.0:*
udp        0        0 localhost:323             0.0.0.0:*
udp6       0        0 [::]:mdns                 [::]:*
udp6       0        0 [::]:domain               [::]:*
udp6       0        0 localhost:323             [::]:*
udp6       0        0 [::]:51664                [::]:*
```

Now display only those ports listening on IPV4.

```
[root@studentvm2 ~]# netstat -tua4
Active Internet connections (servers and established)
Proto Recv-Q Send-Q Local Address           Foreign Address         State
tcp        0        0 studentvm2.examp:domain 0.0.0.0:*              LISTEN
tcp        0        0 localhost:domain          0.0.0.0:*            LISTEN
tcp        0        0 0.0.0.0:ssh               0.0.0.0:*            LISTEN
tcp        0        0 0.0.0.0:smtp              0.0.0.0:*            LISTEN
tcp        0        0 localhost:rndc            0.0.0.0:*            LISTEN
tcp        0        0 studentvm2.example:imap
192.168.56.21:38372       ESTABLISHED
tcp        0        0 studentvm2.example:imap
192.168.56.21:38310       ESTABLISHED
```

```
tcp         0         0 studentvm2.example:imap
192.168.56.21:38334        ESTABLISHED
udp         0         0 0.0.0.0:53826            0.0.0.0:*
udp         0         0 0.0.0.0:mdns             0.0.0.0:*
udp         0         0 studentvm2.examp:domain 0.0.0.0:*
udp         0         0 localhost:domain         0.0.0.0:*
udp         0         0 0.0.0.0:bootps           0.0.0.0:*
udp         0         0 localhost:323            0.0.0.0:*
```

The **ss** utility has replaced the **netstat** command, but the available options are much the same. Let's see what results we get from that.

```
[root@studentvm2 ~]# ss -tua
Netid  State    Recv-Q  Send-Q    Local Address:Port      Peer Address:Port
udp    UNCONN   0       0         0.0.0.0:53826           0.0.0.0:*
udp    UNCONN   0       0         0.0.0.0:mdns            0.0.0.0:*
udp    UNCONN   0       0         192.168.56.1:domain     0.0.0.0:*
udp    UNCONN   0       0         127.0.0.1:domain        0.0.0.0:*
udp    UNCONN   0       0         0.0.0.0:bootps          0.0.0.0:*
udp    UNCONN   0       0         127.0.0.1:323           0.0.0.0:*
tcp    LISTEN   0       10        192.168.56.1:domain     0.0.0.0:*
tcp    LISTEN   0       10        127.0.0.1:domain        0.0.0.0:*
tcp    LISTEN   0       128       0.0.0.0:ssh             0.0.0.0:*
tcp    LISTEN   0       10        0.0.0.0:smtp            0.0.0.0:*
tcp    LISTEN   0       128       127.0.0.1:rndc          0.0.0.0:*
tcp    ESTAB    0       0         192.168.56.1:imap       192.168.56.21:38372
tcp    ESTAB    0       0         192.168.56.1:imap       192.168.56.21:38310
tcp    ESTAB    0       0         192.168.56.1:imap       192.168.56.21:38334
```

It appears from this that the new ss command can be used in place of the netstat command with similar options. The results show the same data although a bit different column and row orders. This might affect existing scripts that parse this data.

Now try this one.

```
[root@studentvm2 ~]# ss -atu4
Netid  State    Recv-Q  Send-Q  Local Address:Port     Peer Address:Port
udp    UNCONN   0       0       0.0.0.0:53826          0.0.0.0:*
udp    UNCONN   0       0       0.0.0.0:mdns           0.0.0.0:*
udp    UNCONN   0       0       192.168.56.1:domain    0.0.0.0:*
udp    UNCONN   0       0       127.0.0.1:domain       0.0.0.0:*
udp    UNCONN   0       0       0.0.0.0:bootps         0.0.0.0:*
udp    UNCONN   0       0       127.0.0.1:323          0.0.0.0:*
tcp    LISTEN   0       10      192.168.56.1:domain    0.0.0.0:*
tcp    LISTEN   0       10      127.0.0.1:domain       0.0.0.0:*
tcp    LISTEN   0       128     0.0.0.0:ssh            0.0.0.0:*
tcp    LISTEN   0       10      0.0.0.0:smtp           0.0.0.0:*
tcp    LISTEN   0       128     127.0.0.1:rndc         0.0.0.0:*
tcp    ESTAB    0       0       192.168.56.1:50590     192.168.56.21:ssh
tcp    ESTAB    0       0       192.168.56.1:imap      192.168.56.21:38372
tcp    ESTAB    0       0       192.168.56.1:imap      192.168.56.21:38310
tcp    ESTAB    0       0       192.168.56.1:imap      192.168.56.21:38334
tcp    ESTAB    0       0       192.168.56.1:ssh       192.168.56.21:40168
```

Note the peer address port numbers on the established connections which are very high. When any service connects to a remote host, the outbound port number is a high random one. This source port can be different for each connection and usually is. The destination port is the one that is assigned and standardized.

There are three IMAP connections from 192.168.56.21, studentvm1, from three different ports to studentvm2 at 192.168.56.1 on port 143. This also illustrates that multiple connections can be made to the same port. There are two SSH connections in this result, one inbound and one outbound.

What results do you get with the following command?

```
[root@studentvm2 ~]# ss -antu4
```

Do you remember the many times I have mentioned that "everything is a file?" Good, because network connections are files, too. The **lsof** (list open files) utility will show us that. Although intended primarily for listing the files in a specific filesystem that are open and thus allowing us to locate and close them in order to unmount a filesystem, it can also work with network connections.

Let's take a quick look at lsof and its use with regular files and filesystems. First, try unmounting the /home filesystem.

```
[root@studentvm2 ~]# umount /home
umount: /home: target is busy.
```

Now list all of the open files in the /home filesystem.

```
[root@studentvm2 ~]# lsof /home | less
COMMAND     PID    USER    FD   TYPE DEVICE SIZE/OFF NODE NAME
imapd       936 student    cwd    DIR 253,3     4096   12 /home/student
ssh        1204 student    cwd    DIR 253,3     4096   12 /home/student
pulseaudi  1238 student    mem    REG 253,3    45056   23 /home/student/.
config/pulse/b62e5e58cdf74e0e967b39bc94328d81-card-database.tdb
pulseaudi  1238 student    mem    REG 253,3    12288   22 /home/student/.
config/pulse/b62e5e58cdf74e0e967b39bc94328d81-stream-volumes.tdb
pulseaudi  1238 student    mem    REG 253,3    12288   21 /home/student/.
config/pulse/b62e5e58cdf74e0e967b39bc94328d81-device-volumes.tdb
pulseaudi  1238 student    10u    REG 253,3    12288   21 /home/student/.
config/pulse/b62e5e58cdf74e0e967b39bc94328d81-device-volumes.tdb
pulseaudi  1238 student    11u    REG 253,3    12288   22 /home/student/.
config/pulse/b62e5e58cdf74e0e967b39bc94328d81-stream-volumes.tdb
pulseaudi  1238 student    12u    REG 253,3    45056   23 /home/student/.
config/pulse/b62e5e58cdf74e0e967b39bc94328d81-card-database.tdb
dbus-daem  1242 student    cwd    DIR 253,3     4096   12 /home/student
sh         1254 student    cwd    DIR 253,3     4096   12 /home/student
sh         1254 student     2w    REG 253,3     2200   36 /home/student/.
xsession-errors
imsetting  1325 student    cwd    DIR 253,3     4096   12 /home/student
gvfsd      1328 student    cwd    DIR 253,3     4096   12 /home/student
xfconfd    1335 student    cwd    DIR 253,3     4096   12 /home/student
<snip>
```

This was a very long list on my VM, and you should have a fairly long list, too. Just being logged in opens a number of files.

Now on to network connections. The following command lists network connections. I have reduced the font size of the output to make it a little more organized.

```
[root@studentvm2 ~]# lsof -i
COMMAND      PID     USER    FD    TYPE DEVICE SIZE/OFF NODE NAME
avahi-dae    858     avahi   15u   IPv4  22281      0t0  UDP *:mdns
avahi-dae    858     avahi   16u   IPv6  22282      0t0  UDP *:mdns
avahi-dae    858     avahi   17u   IPv4  22283      0t0  UDP *:53826
avahi-dae    858     avahi   18u   IPv6  22284      0t0  UDP *:51664
chronyd      915     chrony  6u    IPv4  21416      0t0  UDP localhost:323
chronyd      915     chrony  7u    IPv6  21417      0t0  UDP localhost:323
imapd        936  student   0u    IPv4 280506      0t0  TCP studentvm2.example.
com:imap->192.168.56.21:38372 (ESTABLISHED)
imapd        936  student   1u    IPv4 280506      0t0  TCP studentvm2.example.
com:imap->192.168.56.21:38372 (ESTABLISHED)
sshd         964     root    4u    IPv4  22514      0t0  TCP *:ssh (LISTEN)
sshd         964     root    6u    IPv6  22516      0t0  TCP *:ssh (LISTEN)
dhcpd       1094     dhcpd   10u   IPv4  25593      0t0  UDP *:bootps
sshd        1139     root    5u    IPv4 281551      0t0  TCP studentvm2.example.
com:ssh->192.168.56.21:40168 (ESTABLISHED)
sshd        1152     root    5u    IPv4 281551      0t0  TCP studentvm2.example.
com:ssh->192.168.56.21:40168 (ESTABLISHED)
ssh         1204  student   5u    IPv4 283915      0t0  TCP studentvm2.example.
com:50590->192.168.56.21:ssh (ESTABLISHED)
named       2269     named   21u   IPv6  37221      0t0  TCP *:domain (LISTEN)
named       2269     named   22u   IPv4  37225      0t0  TCP localhost:domain
(LISTEN)
named       2269     named   23u   IPv4  37227      0t0  TCP studentvm2.example.
com:domain (LISTEN)
named       2269     named   24u   IPv4  37230      0t0  TCP localhost:rndc
(LISTEN)
named       2269     named   25u   IPv6  37231      0t0  TCP localhost:rndc
(LISTEN)
named       2269     named   512u  IPv6  37219      0t0  UDP *:domain
named       2269     named   513u  IPv4  37224      0t0  UDP localhost:domain
named       2269     named   514u  IPv4  37226      0t0  UDP studentvm2.example.
com:domain
```

```
xinetd      21749      root      5u   IPv6 186294       0t0   TCP *:imap (LISTEN)
xinetd      21749      root      6u   IPv6 186295       0t0   TCP *:imaps (LISTEN)
sendmail    26853      root      6u   IPv4 229788       0t0   TCP *:smtp (LISTEN)
imapd       31774 student       0u   IPv4 270554       0t0   TCP studentvm2.example.
com:imap->192.168.56.21:38310 (ESTABLISHED)
imapd       31774 student       1u   IPv4 270554       0t0   TCP studentvm2.example.
com:imap->192.168.56.21:38310 (ESTABLISHED)
imapd       32384 student       0u   IPv4 274289       0t0   TCP studentvm2.example.
com:imap->192.168.56.21:38334 (ESTABLISHED)
imapd       32384 student       1u   IPv4 274289       0t0   TCP studentvm2.example.
com:imap->192.168.56.21:38334 (ESTABLISHED)
```

The **nmap** utility is used to scan and map open network ports on a host, local or remote, not just those on which a service is actually listening. Because **nmap** can scan remote hosts, it is used by security specialists to test the vulnerability of hosts that are network connected. It can also be used by crackers to locate those same vulnerabilities with the intent to force access to the systems. I strongly suggest you not use **nmap** to scan systems that do not belong to you. Many organizations look for such scanning attacks and will react very aggressively to protect their networks.

We start as root on StudentVM2. Install **nmap** because it is not already installed.

```
[root@studentvm2 ~]# dnf install nmap
```

I suggest reading the DESCRIPTION section of the **nmap** man page before continuing.

Note   The nmap utility will take a significant amount of time to perform its task of probing both local and remote hosts for open network ports. From 94 minutes in one instance to 19 hours when scanning StudentVM1 from StudentVM2. Your virtual environment will be different so the times you experience will also be different.

Do not terminate or skip these parts of this experiment because there is much to be learned. However, you may continue on with the rest of this chapter and beyond while you allow these tests to run.

The **nmap** utility works quite differently from the other tools we have seen. Where the other tools use data from the /proc filesystem, **nmap** actively tries to connect to all potential network ports on the target computer. Because of this, nmap can take a significant amount of time to scan a host, about 94 minutes on my StudentVM2 host.

```
[root@studentvm2 ~]# nmap -n -PN -sT -sU -p- localhost
Starting Nmap 7.70 ( https://nmap.org ) at 2019-07-06 09:24 EDT
Nmap scan report for localhost (127.0.0.1)
Host is up (0.00042s latency).
Other addresses for localhost (not scanned): ::1
Not shown: 131059 closed ports
PORT        STATE          SERVICE
22/tcp      open           ssh
25/tcp      open           smtp
53/tcp      open           domain
143/tcp     open           imap
953/tcp     open           rndc
993/tcp     open           imaps
53/udp      open           domain
67/udp      open|filtered dhcps
323/udp     open|filtered unknown
5353/udp    open|filtered zeroconf
53826/udp   open|filtered unknown
```

Nmap done: 1 IP address (1 host up) scanned in 5634.56 seconds

Now let's run this same command from StudentVM2 against StudentVM1.

But let's watch nmap as it works. As root on StudentVM1 start **tcpdump**.

```
[root@studentvm1 ~]# tcpdump -n
```

As the root user on StudentVM2, run the following command. This will take a long time – nearly 19 hours in my virtual network.

```
[root@studentvm2 ~]# nmap -n -PN -sT -sU -p- studentvm1
```

You will be able to observe a continuous sequence of probes against the network interface of StudentVM1.

Now try these same commands as root on StudentVM1 and compare the results from StudentVM2.

It is fine to let these commands continue to run while you finish this chapter and proceed on with the next chapters in this course.

Experiment 8-5 shows us some diverse tools that we can use to test the network vulnerability of our hosts. Finding open ports that should not be open or that are valid in some situations but which are not needed for a specific environment should trigger some research. Why are these ports open and what happens if I use the firewall to block them and disable the services behind them?

One thing this does tell us is that IMAP and IMAPS are both open. We only need IMAP because we are using TLS so IMAPS could be disabled and the firewall rule that allows external access from IMAPS can be removed from the firewall.

Other considerations

You should be aware that different email clients have some unique configuration requirements that will be different from Thunderbird. For example, some clients do not support certain types of encryption. If you have problems configuring those clients, refer to the web pages and other documentation for those clients and ensure that the server is configured to support their unique requirements.

Chapter summary

This chapter explored the mailx client a bit more. Although it is a powerful tool for the SysAdmin, it leaves a lot to be desired for most users and even for us SysAdmins for daily email use. It does make an excellent tool for testing.

We installed Thunderbird, one of the popular email clients, and used it to test various configurations of our email server. This included with and without authentication using TLS.

We also used some tools that enable us to view open network ports, network connections, and to determine whether some actions should be taken to lock down unused network ports. We used the **nmap** tool to probe the localhost and a remote host on our virtual network for vulnerabilities.

Exercises

Perform the following exercises to complete this chapter.

1. What unique capability makes mailx an ideal tool for the SysAdmin who works with and supports email systems?

2. What limitations does mailx have that make it a poor choice for most of today's email users?

3. Where are the email inboxes for email users located?

4. From StudentVM1, use Telnet and SMTP to send an email from StudentVM2.

5. Where are email folders other than the Inbox stored?

6. What other methods could be used to create an encrypted TLS connection between the local email client such as Thunderbird on StudentVM1 and the remote email server on StudentVM2?

7. Disable IMAPS and remove the firewall rule that allows external access from IMAPS.

8. Based on nmap scans of both StudentVM1 and StudentVM2, did you find unused but open ports that could be closed down?

CHAPTER 9

Combating Spam

Objectives

In this chapter, you will learn

- How to use SpamAssassin to identify spam email using a set of scoring rules

- How to create and modify SpamAssassin rules

- How to hack MIMEDefang to classify spam depending upon its spam score

- How to use Procmail to sort spam and other emails into mail folders

Introduction

Email is a powerful and useful tool and – despite other, newer types of communication such as texts and social media – email retains a prime place in the communications strategies of most organizations and individuals. Email is not the oldest form of digital communication, having been preceded by tools such as the telegraph and teletype, but it has been around since the early years of Unix. Email is a well-defined tool and is available not just on computers but on nearly every connected device such including mobile phones and tablets.

Email is also used as a tool by spammers and the distributors of malware. Spammers use email to defraud recipients of huge amounts of money each year, to steal IDs, and to peddle knock-off or nonexistent wares. Some crackers send emails with attached malware that they try to entice users into installing to their own detriment.

All of this criminal and disruptive spam requires some method for dealing with it. I use three open source programs to do this and it has reduced my need to read or even to glance at offensive or undesirable material in order to identify and classify incoming email.

© David Both 2020
D. Both, *Using and Administering Linux: Volume 3*, https://doi.org/10.1007/978-1-4842-5485-1_9

The problem

I like to sort incoming email into a couple folders besides the inbox. Spam is always filed into the spam folder, and I leave it there for a couple days so I can look at it later in case someone sends something that I want to receive but that got marked as spam because I have not whitelisted them. Some of the incoming ham (good) email from a couple other sources is also sorted into other folders. The rest does get filed into the inbox by default.

So a quick word about terminology before going any further. Sorting is the process of classifying email and storing it in an appropriate folder. Filters like SpamAssassin classify the email. MIMEDefang uses that classification to mark it as spam by adding a text string to the subject line. That classification allows other software to file the email into the designated folders. It is this last bit of software that I was looking for – the one that does the filing.

I had several email filters set up in Thunderbird, my client of choice and the best GUI client I have found for my personal needs. I also had set up some email filters for my wife on her computer. When we travel, or use our handheld devices, those filters would not always work because Thunderbird – or any other email client with filters – must be running in order to perform their filtering tasks. If I have my laptop with me, I can set that up to do the filtering, but that means I have to maintain multiple sets of filters.

I also ran into a technical problem that I wanted to fix. Client-side email filtering relies on scanning messages after they are deposited in the inbox. For some unknown reason, this has resulted in situations where the client does not always delete (expunge) the moved messages from the Inbox. This may be an issue with Thunderbird or it may be a problem with my configuration of Thunderbird. I have worked on this problem for years with no success, even through multiple complete reinstallations of Fedora and Thunderbird.

I have my own email server and Spam is a major problem for me. I have several email addresses I use, some of which I have had for a couple decades so they have become major spam magnets. In fact, I get at a minimum of 300 spam emails per day. The record was just over 2,500 spam emails in a single day. I currently get between 800 and 1,200 spam emails per day, and the numbers keep increasing.

So I needed a method for filing emails, that is, sorting it into appropriate folders, that is server-based rather than client-based. This would solve a number of issues. I would no longer need to leave an email client running on my home workstation just to perform filtering.

It would prevent the need to delete or expunge messages – especially the spam – from our inboxes. And it would require filter configuration in just one location, the server.

But why?

By now, after two full chapters on email and just starting another one, you are probably asking yourself, "Why do I want to put myself through all of this aggravation just to have an email server? Why not just use Gmail or the email service provided by my ISP?" This is an excellent question because I ask it of myself on occasion.

When I decided that I wanted to become a Unix and Linux SysAdmin, I understood that I needed to learn about all aspects of system administration. I needed to deal with clients, but especially with servers of all types. Despite the fact that it takes a lot of work to set up, configure, and maintain a series of servers, like the ones we cover in this volume of *Using and Administering Linux – Zero to SysAdmin,* I learn best with hands-on. Working with these servers and the clients that use them on a daily basis enabled me to learn so much more than I would have otherwise.

I believe that most of us who are truly well-suited for the role of SysAdmin are the same way. Not everyone but many of us.

But even if we learn best in other ways, we always need a laboratory in which to perform our experiments and to learn to use and support hardware and software of all kinds. I have learned enough by doing this in my own home network that I have landed some amazing jobs and currently write prolifically about Linux.

Oh – and because it is fun![1]

My email server

Having grown up with SendMail as the de facto email server in more than one of my jobs, I started using it for my own email server as soon as I switched permanently from OS/2 to Red Hat Linux 5 in about 1997. I have used it as my mail transfer agent (MTA) since then for both business and personal use.

---

[1]DataBook for Linux, *The real reason we use Linux,* www.linux-databook.info/?page_id=5042

> **Note**   I am not sure why Wikipedia refers to SendMail as a "message" transfer
> agent. All my other references use "mail" transfer agent. The Talk tab of the
> Wikipedia page has a bit of discussion about this which generated even more
> confusion for me.

I was already using SpamAssassin and MIMEDefang together to score and mark
incoming emails as spam, placing a known string in the subject, "###SPAM###", so that I
can identify and sort spam both as a human and with software. I use UW IMAP for client
access to emails, but that is not a factor in server-side filtering and sorting.

Yes, I use a lot of old-school software for the server side of email, but it is well
known, well documented, it works well, and I understand how to make it do the things
I need it to do. Understanding this old but still extensively used software is the key to
understanding many of the more recent incarnations of email software. This software
enables us to understand the protocols and requirements for any software that is used to
perform these tasks. Current versions of Fedora provide all of these tools as packages in
their standard repositories.

Project requirements

Having a well-defined set of requirements before starting a project is imperative, so
based on the description of the problem, I created five simple requirements for this
project.

1. Sort incoming spam emails into the spam folder on the server side
   using the identifying text that is already being added to the subject
   line by MIMEDefang.

2. Sort other incoming emails into designated folders.

3. Circumvent problems with moved messages not being deleted or
   expunged from the Inbox.

4. Keep the SpamAssassin and MIMEDefang software that I was
   already using.

5. Any new software would have to be easy to install and configure.

This set of objectives meant that I would therefore need to be using a sorting program that would integrate well with the parts I already have.

Procmail

After extensive research, I settled on the venerable Procmail.[2] I know – more old stuff – and allegedly unsupported these days, too. But it does what I need it to do and is known to work well with the software I am already using. It is stable and has no known serious bugs. It can be configured for use at the system level as well as at the individual user level.

Red Hat and RH-based distributions such as CentOS and Fedora use Procmail as the default mail delivery agent (MDA) for SendMail, so it does not even need to be installed because it is already there. The MDA delivers email to users' mailboxes on the local host so it can also be known as the LDA or Local Delivery Agent.

My email server runs Fedora, so this is a real no-brainer. I will use Procmail. Besides, Red Hat is now supporting Procmail no matter what else you might read on the Internet, and several recent patches have been included in the most recent version. We can check the change log for Procmail to verify this.

EXPERIMENT 9-1

Perform this experiment as the root user on StudentVM2.

```
[root@yorktown mail]# dnf list procmail
Last metadata expiration check: 0:05:37 ago on Sun 07 Jul 2019 09:39:50 PM EDT.
Installed Packages
procmail.x86_64                    3.22-50.fc30                    @fedora
[root@yorktown mail]# rpm -q --changelog procmail | less
* Sat Feb 02 2019 Fedora Release Engineering <releng@fedoraproject.org> -
3.22-50
- Rebuilt for https://fedoraproject.org/wiki/Fedora_30_Mass_Rebuild

* Thu Dec 06 2018 Jaroslav Škarvada <jskarvad@redhat.com> - 3.22-49
- Fixed issues found by Coverity Scan
```

---

[2]RHEL 7 Deployment Guide, *Procmail*, https://access.redhat.com/documentation/en-us/
red_hat_enterprise_linux/7/html/system_administrators_guide/s1-email-mda

```
* Fri Jul 20 2018 Jaroslav Škarvada <jskarvad@redhat.com> - 3.22-48
- Fixed FTBFS by adding gcc requirement
  Resolves: rhbz#1606850
<snip>
```

I have shortened the output data, but you can see that there are several issues that have been fixed since 2017 including one security patch.

The results of Experiment 9-1 also show that we should not always believe everything we read on the Internet, including Wikipedia. We should also explore the sources of statements we encounter online and look for ourselves at the original data – in this case the Procmail RPM package.

In addition to delivering email, Procmail can be used to filter and sort it. Procmail rules – known as recipes – can be used to identify spam and delete or sort it into a designated mail folder. Other recipes can identify and sort other mail as well such as sorting emails from specific email accounts or organizations into particular folders. Procmail can be used for many other things besides sorting email into designated folders, such as automated forwarding, duplication, and much more. In this chapter, we will confine our use of it to identifying spam and sorting it into the Spam folder.

How it works

A complete discussion of the configuration SpamAssassin, MIMEDefang, and Procmail is beyond the scope of this chapter, in part because there are so many ways of implementing anti-spam solutions using these three programs. This chapter will be limited to the configuration I used to integrate these three packages to implement my own solution.

Processing of incoming email begins with SendMail. SendMail calls MIMEDefang as part of the normal email processing. MIMEDefang uses SpamAssassin as a subroutine. MIMEDefang sends email to SpamAssassin and receives the spam score as a return code.

SpamAssassin uses its default set of rules and scores, as well as any located in the local.cf file, to evaluate each email and generate a total score. We can modify the scores for existing rules, add your own rules, and create white- and blacklists that can assist you in adapting the rules and scoring to the needs of your own installation. The /etc/mail/spamassassin/local.cf file is used for all of this and it can grow quite large; mine is just over 70KB at this writing and still growing.

It is important to understand that when SpamAssassin scans an email, it checks every rule, both its default rules and local rule sets that are created and maintained by the SysAdmin or email administrator. For each rule that matches, the score defined for that rule is added to the total score for that email. This is not a "one and done" type of scan; the email is checked against every rule.

SpamAssassin can be run as standalone software in some applications, however, in this environment, SpamAssassin is not run as a daemon, it is called by MIMEDefang. After the spam score for the email is returned to it, MIMEDefang calls the /etc/email/mimedefang-filter program which can perform any of several actions on the email. This program can add headers to the email, modify the subject, or just discard the email.

MIMEDefang is programmed in Perl, so it is easy to hack. I have hacked the last major portion of the code in /etc/mail/mimedefang-filter to provide a filtering breakdown with a little more granularity than it does by default. This code adds specified text to the subject line of the emails as a means to identify how likely this particular email is to be spam.

Preparation

Although I had already installed MIMEDefang and SpamAssassin on my email server prior to using Procmail for email sorting, our server, StudentVM2, does not have those tools installed. So we need to install them.

EXPERIMENT 9-2

Perform this experiment as the root user on StudentVM2. We will install MIMEDefang and SpamAssassin.

```
[root@studentvm2 ~]# dnf -y install mimedefang spamassassin
```

Note that despite the fact that Perl is already installed on our VMs, this command results in the installation of about 30 additional Perl packages that are required for MIMEDefang.

Verify that there are now some mimedefang* files and a spamassassin directory in /etc/mail.

Configuration

We need to configure MIMEDefang in order to have it add the text we need to the subject line and we also need to set up some SpamAssassin rules that we can intentionally trigger with our test emails so that they will be marked as spam. We also need to configure SendMail to call MIMEDefang as part of its normal mail processing tasks.

Configuring SendMail

SendMail must call MIMEDefang in order to start the spam-filtering process. It does this by calling the MIMEDefang mail filter. The term "mail filter" is generally shortened to "milter."

We enable the MIMEDefang mail filter by inserting one line into our sendmail.cf configuration file.

EXPERIMENT 9-3

Perform this experiment as the root user on StudentVM2. Edit the sendmail.mc file and insert the following lines. I placed them just after the EXPOSED_USER line.

```
dnl ##################################################################dnl
dnl # The following line causes sendmail to use the MIMEdefang milter. dnl
INPUT_MAIL_FILTER(`mimedefang', `S=unix:/var/spool/MIMEDefang/mimedefang.sock,
T=S:5m;R:5m')dnl
dnl ##################################################################dnl
```

Ensure that /etc/mail is the PWD and run the **make** command.

`[root@studentvm2 mail]# ` **make**

Test to verify that we have not broken anything. Use tail -f to follow the maillog file on StudentVM2 and send an email from the student user StudentVM1 to the student@example. com account and your external email account. Ensure that there are no errors in the maillog file and that the email is delivered to the addressees.

Refer to Chapter 8 of the *SpamAssassin*[3] book for more information about using MIMEDefang with SendMail and SpamAssassin.

Hacking mimedefang-filter

Let's hack mimedefang-filter and have it add the text *"####SPAM####"* to emails with high enough spam scores to be considered spam. This is easy even if you don't know Perl[4] because I will show you exactly what to do.

EXPERIMENT 9-4

Perform this experiment as the root user on StudentVM2. In a later experiment in this chapter, we are going to modify one line of the mimedefang-filter Perl program but make a backup copy first and then examine the code we want to change.

After making a backup of the mimedefang-filter program, open it with the Vim editor. The code reproduced below is near the end of the mimedefang-filter file, starting around line 263 for version 2.84.

```
# Spam checks if SpamAssassin is installed
if ($Features{"SpamAssassin"}) {
    if (-s "./INPUTMSG" < 100*1024) {
        # Only scan messages smaller than 100kB.  Larger messages
        # are extremely unlikely to be spam, and SpamAssassin is
        # dreadfully slow on very large messages.
        my($hits, $req, $names, $report) = spam_assassin_check();
        my($score);
        if ($hits < 40) {
            $score = "*" x int($hits);
```

---

[3]Schwartz, Alan, *SpamAssassin: A Practical Guide to Configuration, Customization, and Integration*, [PACT] Publishing, ISBN1-904811-12-4. This book also contains information about MIMEDefang and Procmail.

[4]I strongly suggest that you learn at least some Perl basics because it is a very powerful string processing language. Many programmers today use Python, Ruby, and other languages and that is fine, but I find Perl to still be relevant and quite useful for system administration. Perl uses a C-like syntax so if you already program in C, Perl should seem familiar and be fairly easy to learn.

```
        } else {
            $score = "*" x 40;
        }
        # We add a header which looks like this:
        # X-Spam-Score: 6.8 (******) NAME_OF_TEST,NAME_OF_TEST
        # The number of asterisks in parens is the integer part
        # of the spam score clamped to a maximum of 40.
        # MUA filters can easily be written to trigger on a
        # minimum number of asterisks...
        if ($hits >= $req) {
            action_change_header("X-Spam-Score", "$hits ($score) $names");
            md_graphdefang_log('spam', $hits, $RelayAddr);

            # If you find the SA report useful, add it, I guess...
            action_add_part($entity, "text/plain", "-suggest",
                            "$report\n",
                            "SpamAssassinReport.txt", "inline");
        } else {
            # Delete any existing X-Spam-Score header?
            action_delete_header("X-Spam-Score");
        }
    }
}
```

The first two non-comment lines begin with "my" and are used to create local copies of certain variables that may be used in this code segment. The $hits variable is a numeric value that represents the spam score of the email.

The first if-else structure uses the Perl "x" operator to create a string that consists of a number of asterisks (*) equal to the integer number of the spam score. For example, a spam score of 7 would result in a string of 7 asterisks "*******" which results in a bar graph of the spam score. The first part of this if statement does this so long as the value of the $hits variable is less than 40. The "else" part of the logic simply creates a string of 40 asterisks if the value of $hits is 40 or more.

The second if-else statement takes some defined actions. If $hits is larger than the $req (required) variable, a header named X-Spam-Score is added with the following structure:

```
numeric spam score ($hits), the string of asterisks, test names (hits) that
comprise the score
```

The line **md_graphdefang_log('spam', $hits, $RelayAddr);** adds an entry to a log file in the /var/log directory if we uncomment a line earlier in this file.

The final statement in this "if" section appends a SpamAssassin report to the email as an inline attachment. I find this report makes it easy to do problem determination when issues arise with SpamAssassin and its scoring.

If the $hits variable is less than $req, any existing spam score headers are deleted. Since emails may be scanned by multiple mail servers, this prevents spam scores from other servers from looking like we think this is spam. The $req variable defines the score at or above which an email is considered to be spam. The default is 5. To change this value, you must change the following entry in the /etc/mail/sa-mimedefang.cf configuration file.

```
required_hits          5
```

Over years of working with MIMEDefang and SpamAssassin, I have decided that I do not like the default actions taken to mark this as spam. The bar graph is not visible to the end user, and although it could be used by Procmail to determine how to sort the spam, I wanted something in the subject line where the recipient could see it and decide what to do with the message. I created a set of actions that works better for me and enable me to see spam info more quickly.

In this experiment, we change both sets of actions – the actions taken when an email is determined to be spam and those taken when it is not. That completely revised section of code is shown here. Replace the original section in your mimedefang-filter with the following code.

```
if ($hits >= $req) {
    action_add_header("X-Spam-Status", "Spam, score=$hits required=$req
    tests=$names");
    action_change_header("Subject", "####SPAM#### ($hits) $Subject");
    action_add_part($entity, "text/plain", "-suggest", "$report\n",
    "SpamAssassinReport.txt", "inline");
# action_discard();
} else {
    action_add_header("X-Spam-Status", "Spam, score=$hits required=$req
    tests=$names");
    action_change_header("Subject", "####NOT SPAM#### ($hits) $Subject");
    action_add_part($entity, "text/plain", "-suggest", "$report\n",
    "SpamAssassinReport.txt", "inline");
```

```
    # Delete any existing X-Spam-Score header?
    # action_delete_header("X-Spam-Score");
}
```

This revised code adds the X-Spam-Status header, prepends the "####SPAM####" string and the number of hits to the subject line, and attaches the SpamAssassin report to the end of the email message. It also does this for non-spam emails except that the message prepended to the subject is a bit different and says "####NOT SPAM####." We do it this way in this experiment so that we can see that our spam detector is working even if the emails are not spam.

In a real-world environment, I do add the X-Spam-Status line to the headers on non-spam messages (ham), but I do not normally add anything to the subject line or append the SpamAssassin report to the message.

Note that this revision of the code does not delete existing headers.

Many users tend to freak out when they see that SpamAssassin report and the subject line with "####SPAM####" in it. As a result, I only add the report when I am trying to determine the source of a problem, such as a rule that is not working. The report allows me to easily see what is in the headers, but includes more information such as the exact score added by each rule. Also, if a user forwards an email to me, the report stays attached to the email but the original headers are deleted so they would be useless at that point.

Now we can start and enable MIMEDefang and restart SendMail. Note that SendMail must always be restarted after starting or restarting MIMEDefang. I wrote a little shell script to stop both services and then restart them in the correct sequence because I automate everything. It does not matter in which order they are stopped but they must be started MIMEDefang first and then SendMail. This is because MIMEDefang opens a socket that SendMail must find and also connect to. The socket is their communication channel.

```
[root@studentvm2 ~]# systemctl start mimedefang ; systemctl enable mimedefang
Created symlink /etc/systemd/system/multi-user.target.wants/mimedefang.
service → /usr/lib/systemd/system/mimedefang.service.
Created symlink /etc/systemd/system/multi-user.target.wants/mimedefang-
multiplexor.service → /usr/lib/systemd/system/mimedefang-multiplexor.
service.
[root@studentvm2 ~]#
```

Restart SendMail.

```
[root@studentvm2 ~]# systemctl restart sendmail
```

Test this as the student user on StudentVM1, and send an email to student@example.com. When the email shows up in the Thunderbird inbox, view the email source. You could also use mailx as the student user on StudentVM2 to view the email which always shows the headers.

```
Return-Path: <student@example.com>
Received: from studentvm1.example.com ([192.168.56.21])
    by studentvm2.example.com (8.15.2/8.15.2) with ESMTP id x691SGdO016816;
    Mon, 8 Jul 2019 21:28:16 -0400
From: Student User <student@example.com>
Subject: ####NOT SPAM#### (-1) Test of SpamAssassin and MIMEDefang
To: student@example.com, linuxgeek46@both.org
Message-ID: <77e93abb-2761-56f9-775f-9011a8ca5692@example.com>
Date: Mon, 8 Jul 2019 21:28:16 -0400
User-Agent: Mozilla/5.0 (X11; Linux x86_64; rv:60.0) Gecko/20100101
 Thunderbird/60.7.0
MIME-Version: 1.0
Content-Type: multipart/mixed; boundary="-----------=_1562635701-16772-0"
Content-Language: en-US
X-Spam-Status: Spam, score=-1 required=5 tests=ALL_TRUSTED
X-Scanned-By: MIMEDefang 2.84 on 192.168.56.1

This is a multi-part message in MIME format...

------------=_1562635701-16772-0
Content-Type: text/plain; charset=utf-8; format=flowed
Content-Transfer-Encoding: 7bit
Content-Language: en-US

Hello world!

------------=_1562635701-16772-0
Content-Type: text/plain; name="SpamAssassinReport.txt"
Content-Disposition: inline; filename="SpamAssassinReport.txt"
Content-Transfer-Encoding: 7bit
```

Spam detection software, running on the system "studentvm2.example.com", has NOT identified this incoming email as spam. The original message has been attached to this so you can view it or label similar future email. If you have any questions, see @@CONTACT_ADDRESS@@ for details.

Content preview: Hello world!

Content analysis details: (-1.0 points, 5.0 required)

```
 pts rule name            description
---- -------------------- --------------------------------------------------
-1.0 ALL_TRUSTED          Passed through trusted hosts only via SMTP

------------=_1562635701-16772-0--
```

Now we need to find a way to test for true spam. SpamAssassin has provisions for this. In a terminal session as root on StudentVM2, make /usr/share/doc/spamassassin the PWD and list the contents. You will find, among other files, two text files that we can use to test with, sample-nonspam.txt, and sample-spam.txt. Use the test mode of the spamassassin command to test this.

```
[root@studentvm2 spamassassin]# spamassassin --test-mode < sample-spam.txt
X-Spam-Checker-Version: SpamAssassin 3.4.2 (2018-09-13) on
        studentvm2.example.com
X-Spam-Flag: YES
X-Spam-Level: **************************************************
X-Spam-Status: Yes, score=1000.0 required=5.0 tests=GTUBE,NO_RECEIVED,
        NO_RELAYS autolearn=no autolearn_force=no version=3.4.2
X-Spam-Report:
        * -0.0 NO_RELAYS Informational: message was not relayed via SMTP
        * 1000 GTUBE BODY: Generic Test for Unsolicited Bulk Email
        * -0.0 NO_RECEIVED Informational: message has no Received headers
Subject: [SPAM] Test spam mail (GTUBE)
Message-ID: <GTUBE1.1010101@example.net>
Date: Wed, 23 Jul 2003 23:30:00 +0200
From: Sender <sender@example.net>
To: Recipient <recipient@example.net>
Precedence: junk
MIME-Version: 1.0
```

Content-Type: text/plain; charset=us-ascii
Content-Transfer-Encoding: 7bit
X-Spam-Prev-Subject: Test spam mail (GTUBE)

This is the GTUBE, the
        Generic
        Test for
        Unsolicited
        Bulk
        Email

If your spam filter supports it, the GTUBE provides a test by which you can verify that the filter is installed correctly and is detecting incoming spam. You can send yourself a test mail containing the following string of characters (in upper case and with no white spaces and line breaks):

XJS*C4JDBQADN1.NSBN3*2IDNEN*GTUBE-STANDARD-ANTI-UBE-TEST-EMAIL*C.34X

You should send this test mail from an account outside of your network.

Spam detection software, running on the system "studentvm2.example.com", has identified this incoming email as possible spam. The original message has been attached to this so you can view it or label similar future email. If you have any questions, see @@CONTACT_ADDRESS@@ for details.

Content preview: This is the GTUBE, the Generic Test for Unsolicited Bulk Email
   If your spam filter supports it, the GTUBE provides a test by which you can
   verify that the filter is installed correctly and is detecting incoming spam.
   You can send yourself a test mail containing t [...]

Content analysis details: (1000.0 points, 5.0 required)

 pts rule name   description
 ---- -------------------- --
 -0.0 NO_RELAYS   Informational: message was not relayed via SMTP
 1000 GTUBE   BODY: Generic Test for Unsolicited Bulk Email
 -0.0 NO_RECEIVED   Informational: message has no Received headers

(END)

This method tests SpamAssassin and MIMEDefang but not the full path a real email would take through the MTAs and the email never appears in our inbox. So we can also test using the mailx command so that the email goes to our inbox.

[root@studentvm2 spamassassin]# **cat sample-spam.txt | mailx -s "Test spam"
student@example.com**

Open the email as the student user on StudentVM2 in the **mailx** client. Examine the email and view the added headers and the attached SpamAssassin report.

We can see that our anti-spam configuration is working as it should.

The subject line of the now contains the string "####SPAM####" or "####NOT SPAM####" but without the quotes, and the spam score, that is, the variable $hits. Having a known string in the subject line of spam makes further filtering easy.

The modified email is returned to SendMail for further processing.

Setting up a mail folder

We have not yet set up a folder on the server to contain the email folders like Spam and others we might want to create for the student user. We want to store all of our email folders in a subdirectory of the account's home directory to prevent our email client from accessing other files and folders in the account's home directory.

Whether a login or non-login account, the email client will see all files in the home directory as a possible email folder. We want to prevent that so we create a folder called "Mail" to use as the main email location in which the folders created by the email client, such as Thunderbird, are located.

EXPERIMENT 9-5

Start this experiment as the root user on StudentVM2. We do this because most email accounts will be no-login accounts so root normally does this.

Ensure that the home directory for the student user is the PWD. Create a directory, /home/student/Mail, and set the user and group ownership both to student.

Move the Sent and Trash files into the Mail directory.

Now, as the student user on StudentVM1, open the Thunderbird **Edit ➤ Account Settings**, and select **Server Settings**. Click the **Advanced** button to open the **Advanced Account Settings** dialog. In the field for **IMAP server directory**, type **Mail**. Click **OK** to close the dialog and **OK** to close the Account Settings.

On the main Thunderbird window, right-click the student@example.com account – the top-level folder where it says student@example.com and not any of the sub-folders – and choose **New Folder**. Type "Spam" (without the quotes) in the **Name** field and click the **Create Folder** button. The new folder should appear in the list of folders along with Sent and Trash.

Configuring Procmail

The last thing that SendMail does is call Procmail to act as the MDA. Procmail then checks the home directory of the user to which the email is addressed for the existence of a ~/.procmailrc file. If one does not exist, Procmail deposits the email into the user's inbox in /var/spool/mail. What happens when the ~/.procmailrc file does exist is the topic of this section.

What we need Procmail to do is to use the text now added to the subject line to look at the email before it gets placed in the Inbox and to route it to a different folder which we will call, naturally enough, "Spam."

Procmail uses global and user-level configuration files. The global /etc/procmailrc file and individual user ~/.procmailrc files must be created. The structure of the files is the same, but the global file operates on all incoming email while the local files can be configured for each individual user. I do not use a global file so all of the sorting is done on the user level. My .procmailrc file is shown in Experiment 9-6 and is simple.

Note that the ~/.procmailrc file must be located in the home directory of the email account on the email server. It does not go in the home directory on individual client workstations. Because most email accounts are not login accounts, they use the nologin program as the default shell. Therefore, the admin will need to create and maintain these files. The other option is to change to a login shell such as BASH and set passwords so that knowledgeable users can login to their email accounts on the server and maintain their ~/.procmailrc files.

Each recipe starts with :0 (yes, that is a zero) on the first line and contains a total of three lines. The second line starts with * and contains a conditional statement consisting of a regular expression (regex) that Procmail compares to each line in the incoming email. If there is a match, Procmail sorts the email into the folder specified by the third line. The use of the ^ symbol denotes the beginning of the line when making the comparison.

EXPERIMENT 9-6

Perform this experiment as the root user on StudentVM2. We are going to create a .procmailrc file for the student user.

Use a text editor to create a new /home/student/.procmailrc file and add the following content.

```
###############################################################################
# .procmailrc file for student@example.com                                   #
#                                                                            #
# Rules are run sequentially - first match wins                              #
# It is not necessary to reboot or to restart email. Changes take place as   #
# soon as the file is saved.                                                 #
#                                                                            #
###############################################################################
# Set the environment
PATH=/usr/sbin:/usr/bin
MAILDIR=$HOME/Mail   #location of your mailboxes
DEFAULT=/var/spool/mail/student

# Send Spam to the spam mailbox
:0
* ^Subject:.*####SPAM####
$MAILDIR/Spam

# sorts all remaining messages into the default inbox
:0
* .*
$DEFAULT
###############################################################################
```

The first recipe in my .procmailrc file sorts the spam identified in the subject line by MIMEDefang into my spam folder. Procmail ignores case, so there is no need to create recipes that look for various combinations of upper- and lowercase. The second and last recipe sorts all email that does not match another recipe into the default folder, usually the Inbox.

Having the .procmailrc file in my home directory does not cause Procmail to filter my mail. I have to add one more file, the ~/.forward file, which tells Procmail to filter all of my incoming email. Create the /home/student/.forward file and add the following content.

```
# .forward file
# process all incoming mail through procmail - see .procmailrc for the filter
rules.
|/usr/bin/procmail
```

Ensure that both of these new files have ownership of student.student. It is not necessary to restart either SendMail or MIMEDefang when creating or modifying the Procmail configuration files.

To test all of these changes, return to StudentVM2 as the root user and from a root terminal session send some test emails, both ham and spam. Make sure that /usr/share/doc/ spamassassin is the PWD and then issue these commands.

```
[root@studentvm2 spamassassin]# cat sample-nonspam.txt | mailx -s "Test
nonspam" student@example.com
[root@studentvm2 spamassassin]# cat sample-spam.txt | mailx -s "Test spam"
student@example.com
```

The non-spam email should be sorted to the Inbox and the spam email sorted to the Spam folder. Except that did not happen. So I looked in /var/log/maillog and found the entries below.

```
Jul 10 07:10:33 studentvm2 sendmail[3930]: x6ABAU7d003928: x6ABAX7c003930:
DSN: Service unavailable
Jul 10 07:10:33 studentvm2 smrsh[3932]: uid 1000: attempt to use "procmail"
(stat failed)
```

The problem here is that, as I did on my own mail server, I missed one step. It is easy to miss because I found the true answer in only one place.

We need to add a symbolic link in the /etc/smrsh directory. Smrsh stands for "SendMail restricted shell," which is a reasonably Secure Shell in which SendMail can run scripts and which will help prevent crackers from exploiting SendMail for their own purposes.

Create the link, /etc/smrsh/procmail using the following commands.

```
[root@studentvm2 ~]# cd /etc/smrsh ; ln -s /usr/bin/procmail procmail ; ll
total 0
lrwxrwxrwx. 1 root root 17 Jul 10 07:15 procmail -> /usr/bin/procmail
```

Now perform the test again by sending the spam and non-spam email messages again. Now they should go into the correct folders.

We could have created both of these files as the student user on StudentVM2 but, in most environments, regular users will not have login access to the server.

Reports of Procmail's demise

Having done many Internet searches while researching this chapter, I found a number of results dating from 2001 through about 2013 that declare Procmail to be dead. They point for evidence at the no longer working web pages, missing source code, and a short article on Wikipedia that does no more than declare Procmail to be dead and provides links to more recent replacements.

However, all Red Hat, Fedora, and CentOS distributions install Procmail as the MDA for SendMail. The Red Hat, Fedora, and CentOS repositories all have the source RPMs for Procmail, and the source code is also on GITHub. Red Hat documentation for CentOS contains some decent documentation for Procmail.[5]

Considering the continued use of Procmail by Red Hat, I have no problem with using this mature software that does its job silently and without fanfare.

Creating SpamAssassin rules

Now that we have a working solution, what happens when we start getting spam that does not match any rules or for which the matched rules do not add up to a high enough score to make the cut as spam? We can adjust the default scores and write new rules using the /etc/mail/spamassassin/local.cf file.

---

[5]Red Hat, *Red Hat Linux 8.0 The Official Red Hat Linux Reference*, www-uxsup.csx.cam.ac.uk/pub/doc/redhat/redhat8/rhl-rg-en-80.pdf

The files located in /usr/share/spamassassin that begin with two-digit numbers are configuration files that define rules for specific types of spam. When SpamAssassin matches a rule in one of these files, it then searches for a score in the 72_scores.cf file. These files should not be altered.

There are also two files in /usr/share/spamassassin that we can use as templates or starting points for local configuration. These files make it easy for us to configure SpamAssassin by adding rules and changing scores so that we don't need to change the default configuration files. The default files can be replaced during an update and cause our changes to them to be overwritten.

The local.cf file, of which there is already a copy in /etc/mail/spamassassin, is used to create local rules, alter the scores of existing default rules, and set whitelist and blacklist entries.

The user_prefs.template can be used by individual users to override the default preferences. This file would need to be copied to the user's home directory and renamed to user_prefs. For example, a user might wish to specify a higher required_score to ensure that some emails with somewhat higher spam scores than the default of 5 be allowed through as ham. This would also be the file in which users would add whitelist and blacklist entries, create their own rules, and change scores. In most modern installations, end users will not be knowledgeable enough, or not have login access to the email server, to perform these tasks so it would fall to the SysAdmin to make those changes for them.

Before we make any changes, we need to look at the default rule set which should never be changed in any way.

EXPERIMENT 9-7

Begin this experiment as the root user on StudentVM2. If you do not already have a root terminal session open on the desktop and following /var/log/maillog, do so now with this command.

```
[root@studentvm2 ~]# tail -f /var/log/maillog
```

In another root terminal session, make /usr/share/spamassassin the PWD. List the files in that directory. The files you see there are used for local configuration or, as in the case of the files that begin with "V", are version-specific configuration. We need only concern ourselves with the local.cf file to specify our local configuration changes.

We start by changing the score for a rule that we know the spam test email already matches. As the student user on StudentVM2 make /usr/share/doc/spamassassin the PWD and send this email.

```
[student@studentvm2 spamassassin]$ cat sample-spam.txt | mailx -s "Test email" student@example.com
```

As the student user on StudentVM1, open Thunderbird, if it is not already, and look in the Spam folder for the new email. Select the spam email that was just received and scroll down to the SpamAssassin attachment. You will see that this email matched the GTUBE[6] rule which gave the email a score of 1000 which is high enough that even the best non-spam rules, such as ALL_TRUSTED and many more, could not overcome this score to make it look like non-spam.

Let's change this number just to see how a score change works. As root on StudentVM2, edit /etc/mail/spamassassin/local.cf and add the following line.

```
score          GTUBE   600
```

Save the local.cf file but do not exit the editor because we will be making some additional changes to the local.cf file. Stop both SendMail and MIMEDefang and then start them MIMEDefang first and then SendMail.

```
[root@studentvm2 ~]# systemctl stop sendmail ; systemctl stop mimedefang ; systemctl start mimedefang ; systemctl start sendmail
```

I wrote a little script to do this on my own mail server and you can too, if you like. I experiment with this a lot and make changes to the local.cf so a script with a short name can save a lot of typing. At any rate, here are the commands you need. It does not matter in which order you stop the services.

Now send the following email message as the student user on StudentVM2, where the number in the subject is in the form YYYYMMDDHHMM for easy identification.

```
[student@studentvm2 spamassassin]$ cat sample-spam.txt | mailx -s "Test email 201907220828" student@example.com
```

Be sure to check the log file messages and then look at the email using Thunderbird on StudentVM1. If necessary, scroll down and look at the SpamAssassin report which shows the scores. The score for GTUBE should be 600.

---

[6]The GTUBE rule is a special rule used for testing with the SpamAssassin test emails and should never be matched by a real email.

Now let's add a new rule to local.cf. It takes three lines to create a new rule. The first line defines the location of the search such as the header or body of the message and a Perl REGEX to define a specific line such as the subject and the pattern to be matched. Each line also contains an identifier that is typically in uppercase.

The second line is a description of the rule that will be printed in the SpamAssassin report. And the third line contains the score that is applied to the message when the rule is matched. I also add a comment as a bit of explanation and a separator to make a long list of rules easier to read. And I have a very long list.

I get a lot of spam email that has something about "back taxes" in the body of the message. It can take a long time to scan the body of a message especially if the body is large so I try to have as few rules that scan the body as possible.

Add the following three lines below the score modification that we previously added to local.cf.

```
# Back Taxes
body            BACK_TAXES          /back taxes/i
describe        BACK_TAXES          Contains "back taxes" in the body
score           BACK_TAXES          6.0
```

The regular expression **/back taxes/i** looks for the text "back taxes" and the trailing "**i**" tells Perl to ignore the case so that any combination of upper- and lowercase will match.

Restart the MIMEDefang and SendMail services in the correct order and send the following email as the student user on StudentVM2. Be careful because it is different and now has our trigger text in the body.

[student@studentvm2 spamassassin]$ **echo "Let us save your back taxes." | mailx -s "Test email 201907220910" student@example.com**

View the message and its source using Thunderbird. The message source looks like this on my host. It should be very similar on yours. Notice the X-Spam-Status line and the SpamAssassin report.

```
Received: from studentvm2.example.com (localhost [127.0.0.1])
    by studentvm2.example.com (8.15.2/8.15.2) with ESMTPS id x6MDANK6003406
    (version=TLSv1.3 cipher=TLS_AES_256_GCM_SHA384 bits=256 verify=NOT)
    for <student@example.com>; Mon, 22 Jul 2019 09:10:23 -0400
Received: (from student@localhost)
    by studentvm2.example.com (8.15.2/8.15.2/Submit) id x6MDAMSG003405
    for student@example.com; Mon, 22 Jul 2019 09:10:22 -0400
```

```
From: Student User <student@example.com>
Message-Id: <201907221310.x6MDAMSG003405@studentvm2.example.com>
Date: Mon, 22 Jul 2019 09:10:22 -0400
To: student@example.com
Subject: ####SPAM#### (5) Test email 201907220910
User-Agent: Heirloom mailx 12.5 7/5/10
MIME-Version: 1.0
Content-Type: multipart/mixed; boundary="-----------=_1563801023-3364-0"
X-Spam-Status: Spam, score=5 required=5 tests=ALL_TRUSTED,BACK_TAXES
X-Scanned-By: MIMEDefang 2.84 on 192.168.56.1

This is a multi-part message in MIME format...

------------=_1563801023-3364-0
Content-Type: text/plain; charset=utf-8
Content-Transfer-Encoding: 8bit

â€œLet us save your back taxes.â€

------------=_1563801023-3364-0
Content-Type: text/plain; name="SpamAssassinReport.txt"
Content-Disposition: inline; filename="SpamAssassinReport.txt"
Content-Transfer-Encoding: quoted-printable

Spam detection software, running on the system "studentvm2.example.com",
has identified this incoming email as possible spam.  The original
message has been attached to this so you can view it or label
similar future email.  If you have any questions, see
@@CONTACT_ADDRESS@@ for details.

Content preview:  =E2=80=9CLet us save your back taxes.=E2=80=9D=20

Content analysis details:  (5.0 points, 5.0 required)

 pts rule name                description
---- -------------------- -------------------------------------------------=
---
-1.0 ALL_TRUSTED          Passed through trusted hosts only via SMTP
 6.0 BACK_TAXES           BODY: Contains "back taxes" in the body

------------=_1563801023-3364-0--
```

Send an email that does not contain "back taxes" in the body to verify that this rule would not match. Also, send some emails with various upper- and lowercase combinations of "back taxes" to ensure that they do match.

Now add a rule that checks for the text string "XXX" in the subject line and adds 15 points to ensure that it gets counted as spam. The Perl regular expression uses =~ to specify that the subject "contains" the search pattern. So "I have XXX for you" would be a match.

```
# XXX
header          XXX           Subject =~ /XXX/i
describe        XXX           Contains "XXX" in the subject line
score           XXX           15.0
```

Restart the SendMail and MIMEDefang services in the proper sequence and test this new rule.

We want to ensure that email from certain domains such as example.com, both.org, and opensource.com are allowed through regardless of their other spam scores. We can also blacklist a domain like spammer.com.

Add the following lines to the local.cf file and restart the services.

```
whitelist_from  *@example.com
whitelist_from  linuxgeek46@both.org
whitelist_from  *@opensource.com
blacklist_from  *@spammer.com              # Misc spammer
```

The * character is a metacharacter that matches all characters to the left of the @ sign in the email address. Entries using this metacharacter as we have here match all email accounts from the specified domain. I have specified a whitelist for only my own email from my personal both.org domain. Other accounts from both.org will not be whitelisted. That does not mean that they will be automatically considered spam because they would still need a score of at least +5.

We can only test this with the example.com domain by sending another email to ourselves. Send the following email as the student user on StudentVM1.

```
[student@studentvm1 ~]$ echo "This is a test email" | mailx -s "Test email"
student@example.com
```

Additional resources

There are few really good resources for someone who needs to create an email system from nothing. My intent in the chapters about and pertaining to email in this course was to at least partially fill that gap. Chapters 7, 8, and 9 of this volume of the course provide enough information to get started with a reasonably well-constructed email server that can grow to absorb the workloads of a small to medium-sized organization.

As part of my research for this course – these chapters dealing with email, spam, and malware in particular – I discovered the book *Pro Open Source Mail – Building an Enterprise Mail Solution*[7] by Curtis Smith. That book is the one I wish I had when I first started my own email server. In many ways, Smith takes the same path as I did and ends up with most of the same software. The only significant difference is his choice of Dovecot as his IMAP server whereas we use UW-IMAP. The author of that book also goes into much more detail than I have in this course. I highly recommend *Pro Open Source Mail* despite the fact that it is somewhat older because it presents a complete, integrated solution rather than just one part as do most books.

Chapter summary

Although we could have used Procmail by itself for spam filtering and sorting, I think SpamAssassin does a better job of scoring because it does not rely on a single rule to match, but rather the aggregate score from all of the rules, as well as scores from Bayesian filtering.

Procmail works very well when matches can be made very explicit with known strings such as the ones that I have configured MIMEDefang to place in the subject line. I think Procmail works better as a final sorting stage in the spam-filtering process than as a complete solution all by itself. Of course, I know that many admins have made complete spam-filtering solutions using nothing more than Procmail.

Now that I have server-side filtering, I am somewhat less limited in my choice of email clients because I no longer need a client that performs filtering and sorting. Nor do I have a need to leave an email client running all the time to perform that filtering and sorting.

---

[7]Smith, Curtis, *Pro Open Source Mail – Building an Enterprise Mail Solution*, Apress, 2006, ISBN 978-1-4302-1173-0

Exercises

Perform the following exercises to complete this chapter.

1. Add and test a SpamAssassin rule that adds two points when it matches the text "free money" in the subject line. Name the rule FREE_MONEY_1. Send an email to student@example.com from StudentVM1 that contains that phrase. View the SpamAssassin report to verify that the new rule is working.

2. Use the Thunderbird email client to add a new folder and name it FreeMoney. Then add a new rule to the Procmail file that matches any emails with the string FREE_MONEY_1 in the X-Spam-Status header and sorts them into the new folder. Test.

3. Locate the file in which the default scores for whitelists and blacklists are stored. What rule name is used when a user account is whitelisted?

4. What is the score added to a user that is whitelisted?

5. Why must MIMEDefang be started (or restarted) before SendMail?

## CHAPTER 10

Apache Web Server

Objectives

In this chapter you will learn

- How to install and configure the Apache web server

- How to create simple static web pages

- How to use multiple programming languages to generate dynamic web content

Introduction

Apache is arguably the most common web server on the Internet. It is well understood, mature, and reliable. It is very configurable and flexible as you will see in this and later experiments. Apache is also free open source software that is provided under the Apache License 2.0.

Apache is an HTTP server that is available on Linux, other Unix-like operating system, and Windows. HTTP stands for HyperText Transfer protocol and is a text-based protocol that uses TCP for its transport layer. HTTPD is the HTTP daemon which runs on the server and responds to requests to serve a web page.

Although the name may seem strange, it is easily explained. Developed by Rob McCool – yes, really – at the National Center for Supercomputing Application, it was the most common HTTP server on the Internet in 1995. Some of the web masters that were using it had created many of their own plug-in extensions and bug fixes because further development had stalled. Some of those people collaborated to add these extensions and fixes to the original code in the form of patches. There were many of these patches so it was quite natural for the web master hackers to call it "a patchy web server."

© David Both 2020
D. Both, *Using and Administering Linux: Volume 3*, https://doi.org/10.1007/978-1-4842-5485-1_10

You can find documentation, support, security information, mailing lists, downloads and more at The Apache HTTP Server Project.[1]

In this chapter, we will install Apache and explore its use as a simple web server. In the following chapters, we will explore its use as the basis for more complex tools such as the WordPress content management system (CMS) to produce complex yet easily manageable web sites.

Installing Apache

Apache is very easy to install with a single command.

EXPERIMENT 10-1

Perform this experiment as the root user on StudentVM2. Install the Apache web server with the following command.

`[root@studentvm2 ~]#` **`dnf -y install httpd`**

It takes only a few moments to install the HTTPD package and several dependencies.

You may also wish to install the httpd-tools and httpd-manual packages, but they are not necessary for these experiments.

Testing Apache

No initial configuration changes are required. The default configuration works just fine without modification.

---

[1]The Apache Server Project, `https://httpd.apache.org/`

```
                           EXPERIMENT 10-2
```

Perform this experiment as the root user on StudentVM2.

Start Apache with the following command.

```
[root@studentvm2 ~]# systemctl start httpd
```

You should also enable Apache to ensure that it starts on boot.

```
[root@studentvm2 ~]# systemctl enable httpd
```

Verify that the Apache web server is running with the following command.

```
[root@studentvm2 ~]# systemctl status httpd
• httpd.service - The Apache HTTP Server
   Loaded: loaded (/usr/lib/systemd/system/httpd.service; enabled; vendor
   preset: disabled)
   Active: active (running) since Wed 2019-07-24 15:52:42 EDT; 17s ago
     Docs: man:httpd.service(8)
 Main PID: 7147 (httpd)
   Status: "Running, listening on: port 80"
    Tasks: 213 (limit: 4696)
   Memory: 15.2M
   CGroup: /system.slice/httpd.service
           ├─7147 /usr/sbin/httpd -DFOREGROUND
           ├─7148 /usr/sbin/httpd -DFOREGROUND
           ├─7149 /usr/sbin/httpd -DFOREGROUND
           ├─7150 /usr/sbin/httpd -DFOREGROUND
           └─7151 /usr/sbin/httpd -DFOREGROUND

Jul 24 15:52:42 studentvm2.example.com systemd[1]: Starting The Apache HTTP
Server...
Jul 24 15:52:42 studentvm2.example.com httpd[7147]: Server configured,
listening on: port 80
Jul 24 15:52:42 studentvm2.example.com systemd[1]: Started The Apache HTTP
Server.
```

You can test Apache by starting a Web Browser and type **localhost** in the URL field. Because no index.html or other index file is located in /var/www/html, the test page shown in Figure 10-1 is displayed.

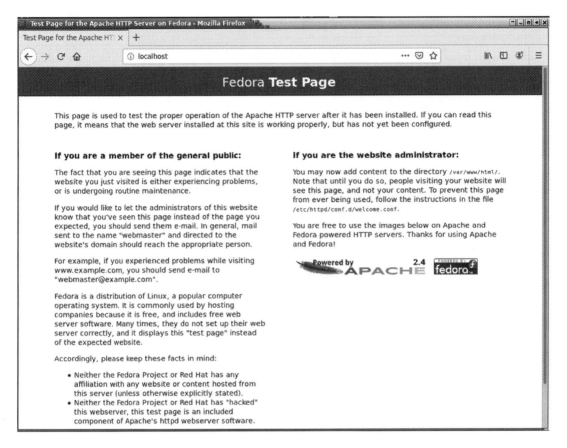

Figure 10-1. *The Fedora Test Page displayed in the browser shows that our Apache web server is working properly*

You can also install text only browsers to use for testing from the CLI. The ones I use are links and lynx.

It is necessary to add a line to the iptables firewall in order to allow inbound traffic on port 80. Add the following line on the Filter table INPUT section of /etc/sysconfig/iptables.

```
-A INPUT -p tcp -m state --state NEW -m tcp --dport 80 -j ACCEPT
```

Load the new rules.

```
[root@studentvm2 ~]# cd /etc/sysconfig/ ; iptables-restore iptables
```

To test that external hosts can access our new web site, open a browser on StudentVM1 and enter http://studentvm2.example.com/ in the URL field. The test page should be displayed.

That was easy.

Creating a simple index file

Our web server is up and running, so now we need some content. An index file is the "home page" for any web site. There are different types of index files and we will explore a few in this section.

It is easy to create a very simple index file for your web site. This can act as the starting point for a more complex site, or it can just be a placeholder until a more complex site can be built using tools such as Drupal or WordPress. We will use WordPress in Chapter 11 of this volume to create a professional-looking web site. For now, we will look at creating some simple static and dynamic web pages.

EXPERIMENT 10-3

Perform this experiment as the root user on StudentVM2. In this experiment, we will create a simple index file and then embellish it just a bit.

First make /var/www the PWD. Then change the ownership to apache.apache.

```
[root@studentvm2 www]# chown -R apache.apache *
```

Make /var/www/html the PWD. Create the index.html file and add the content "Hello World" to it – without the quotes. Ensure that the ownership of the new file is apache.apache and change it if it is not.

On either StudentVM1 or StudentVM2 – or both – refresh the web browser. The result of using an index file is shown in Figure 10-2.

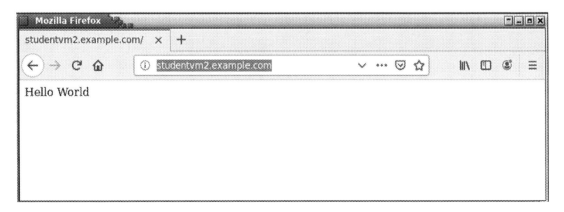

Figure 10-2. *Using a simple index file for our web site*

Note that our index.html file has no HTML (HyperText Markup Language) in it at all. It is just ASCII plain text. Because the formatting performed by the browser is based upon the HTML markup, a long document would be run together with no regard for paragraphs or spacing of any kind. So let's add a bit of HTML to pretty it up.

Edit the index.html file and add HTML tags so that it looks like the following. The <h1> tag starts a first level header and </h1> tag ends it. Many tags start a format such as headers, bold (a.k.a strong), italic, and more, and they end with a tag.

```
<h1>Hello World!</h1>
```

Save the file and refresh the browser. You should see a result identical to Figure 10-3.

Figure 10-3. *The result of using some minimal HTML tags*

Some browsers will not know how to handle this minimal HTML, so we would need more to make a complete and universally compatible web page. Edit your index.html file to have the following content.

```
<!DOCTYPE HTML PUBLIC "-//w3c//DD HTML 4.0//EN">
<html>
<head>
<title>Student Web Page</title>
</head>
<body>
<h1>Hello World!</h1>
<hr>
Welcome to my world.<p>
Student
</body>
</html>
```

This is pretty much the minimum requirements for an HTML document that conforms to W3C HTML standards.

The first line defines this as an HTML document conforming to the W3C[2] standards for HTML 4.0. The second line defines the start of the HTML document. The <head> tag defines the heading section of the document which contains only a <title> tag. The title is what appears in the browser title bar and tab for this web site. The <hr> tag generates a horizontal rule – bar – to use as a separator. The <p> tag defines the start of a paragraph. It can be used without the corresponding </p> tag as I have here in this simple web document, but it is better if you do use it to mark the end of each paragraph.

You can create this document without the enclosing <html>, <body>, and <head> tags, but it will work best with all browsers if you use all of those tags.

Now refresh the browser and see that your page looks like that in Figure 10-4.

Figure 10-4. *We have now generated a complete static web page*

As you can see, creating a simple web page is quite easy.

Adding DNS

Most web sites are accessed using the form "www.domain.com", so let's do that for our domain.

---

[2]World Wide Web Consortium

EXPERIMENT 10-4

Perform this experiment as the root user on StudentVM2. Add the following entry to your DNS zone file for www.example.com.

```
www              IN     A       192.168.56.1
```

Restart the named service.

Type www.example.com in the URL field of your browser and press **Enter** to verify that this new DNS entry for our web server works.

Using Telnet to test the web site

Another way to test your Apache web server is with Telnet. Telnet is a terribly insecure tool to use for a remote terminal session but is a great way to test many services. The only reason this is so is that these services, such as SMTP, as you saw in an earlier lab project, HTTPD, and many more, use plain text data protocols which are easy to read and interact with directly.

EXPERIMENT 10-5

Perform this experiment as the student user on StudentVM1.

```
[student@studentvm1 ~]$ telnet www.example.com 80
Trying 192.168.56.1...
Connected to www.example.com.
Escape character is '^]'.
GET /index.html HTTP/1.1<Enter>
Host: www.example.com<Enter>
<Enter>
HTTP/1.1 200 OK
Date: Thu, 25 Jul 2019 14:22:21 GMT
Server: Apache/2.4.39 (Fedora)
Last-Modified: Thu, 25 Jul 2019 13:41:13 GMT
ETag: "b9-58e819452ee58"
```

```
Accept-Ranges: bytes
Content-Length: 185
Content-Type: text/html; charset=UTF-8

<!DOCTYPE HTML PUBLIC "-//w3c//DD HTML 4.0//EN">
<html>
<head>
<title>Student Web Page</title>
</head>
<body>
<h1>Hello World!</h1>
<hr>
Welcome to my world.<p>
Student
</body>
</html>
Connection closed by foreign host.
[student@studentvm1 ~]$
```

The data sent as a result of your GET request should be the exact contents of the index.html file. It is the function of the web browser to interpret the HTML data protocols and generate a nicely formatted web page.

Good practice configuration

There is one bit of configuration that is always good practice to follow. By default, the "Listen" directive tells Apache to listen for incoming HTTP requests on port 80. In the event your host is multi-homed, that is, it has more than one active NIC or multiple IP addresses bound to a single NIC, Apache would bind to all IP addresses by default. This is probably not the desired behavior. It is good practice to use the Listen directive to specify the IP address on which Apache should listen.

For our server, we will limit access to the internal network. In a real-world environment, we would allow access to the outside world via the Internet as well.

EXPERIMENT 10-6

Perform this experiment as the root user on StudentVM2.

Edit the /etc/httpd/conf/httpd.conf file and change the "Listen" line to the following.

```
Listen 192.168.56.1:80
```

Restart httpd and refresh the browser on StudentVM1 to test your web site.

Virtual hosts

Apache provides the capability to host multiple web sites on a single Linux host by using the Name Virtual Hosts feature of Apache. I host multiple web sites on my own personal web server and it is easy.

Remember in Experiment 10-5 where we used Telnet to test the server? After the GET statement, we also entered the name of the host from which we were requesting the web page. This is part of the HTTP protocol and it can be used to differentiate between different virtual servers hosted on a single Linux computer. It means that we can set up our second web site using a different virtual host name and use that name to request web pages.

The experiments in this section guide you through the process of creating a second web site.

Configuring the primary virtual host

Before adding a second web site, we need to convert the existing one to a Name Virtual Host and test it.

EXPERIMENT 10-7

Perform this experiment as the root user on StudentVM2.

Start by commenting out all stanzas in /etc/httpd/conf/httpd.conf that contain a reference to /var/www. All of these stanzas will be recreated in the name virtual host stanzas. This includes the single DocumentRoot statement at about line number 119.

Change the name of the directory that contains the primary web site to positively identify it, from /var/www to /var/www1. Then create the following virtual host stanza at the end of the current httpd.conf file. Be sure to comment out all lines in the <Directory "/var/www"> stanza at about line 124 and the <Directory "/var/www/html"> stanza that starts at about line 131. It is not necessary to comment out the lines that are already comments.

```
####################################################################
# Configure for name based virtual hosting. The individual web
# site stanzas are located below.
####################################################################
# The primary website
<VirtualHost 192.168.56.1:80>
    ServerName www1.example.com
    ServerAlias www1.example.com
    DocumentRoot "/var/www1/html"
    ErrorLog "logs/error_log"
    ServerAdmin student@example.com
    <Directory "/var/www1/html">
        Options Indexes FollowSymLinks
        AllowOverride None
        Require all granted
    </Directory>
</VirtualHost>
```

Change the DNS record for www to www1.

```
www1            IN      A       192.168.56.1
```

Reload the configuration files for HTTPD and named, and verify that there are no errors.

```
[root@studentvm2 html]# systemctl reload httpd ; systemctl reload named
[root@studentvm2 named]# systemctl status httpd ; systemctl status named
```

Test the web site with your browser. Now edit the /var/www1/html/index.html file and make the changes indicated in bold.

```
<!DOCTYPE HTML PUBLIC "-//w3c//DD HTML 4.0//EN">
<html>
<head>
<title>Primary Web Page</title>
</head>
<body>
<h1>Hello World!</h1>
<hr>
Welcome to my world.<p>
Primary web site
</body>
</html>
```

It is not necessary to restart the HTTPD server service when web page content is changed. Test the web site by refreshing the browser, and the changed line should now be displayed.

Configuring the second virtual host

Adding the second virtual host is easy. We will copy the data for the new host from the existing one and then make any necessary changes.

EXPERIMENT 10-8

Perform this experiment as the root user on StudentVM2.

First change the PWD to /var. Copy the original web site data to a new directory to form the basis of the second web site. The -r option copies the directory structure and data recursively. The -p option preserves ownership and permissions.

```
[root@studentvm2 var]# cp -rp www1/ www2
```

Verify the ownership of the copied files and directories is apache.apache. Edit the file /var/www2/http/index.html as shown below to differentiate it from the original web site.

```
<!DOCTYPE HTML PUBLIC "-//w3c//DD HTML 4.0//EN">
<html>
<head>
<title>Second Web Page</title>
</head>
<body>
<h1>Hello World!</h1>
<hr>
Welcome to my world.<p>
This is the second web site
</body>
</html>
```

Add a new DNS entry for this second web site. We could also do this with a CNAME record instead of an A record.

```
www1                      IN      A       192.168.56.1
www2                      IN      A       192.168.56.1
```

Reload the configuration for named.

Create a new Name Virtual Host stanza below the first one. Change the data to look like that below for the second web site. Because the data is so similar, you can copy the stanza for the first and make any required alterations.

```
# The secondary website
<VirtualHost 192.168.56.1:80>
    ServerName www2.example.com
    ServerAlias www2example.com
    DocumentRoot "/var/www2/html"
    ErrorLog "logs/error_log"
    ServerAdmin student@example.com
    <Directory "/var/www2/html">
        Options Indexes FollowSymLinks
        AllowOverride None
        Require all granted
    </Directory>
</VirtualHost>
```

Test both web sites to be sure that they are both working correctly.

Using CGI scripts

CGI scripts allows creation simple or complex interactive programs that can be run to provide a dynamic web page. A dynamic web page can change based on input, calculations, current conditions in the server, and so on.

CGI stands for Common Gateway Interface.[3] CGI is a protocol specification that defines how a web server should pass a request to an application program and then receive the data from the program so that it may be passed back to the requesting web browser. There are many languages that can be used for CGI scripts. The language you choose for any project should be based upon the needs of the project. We will look at two languages, Perl and BASH. Other popular CGI languages are PHP and Python.

Using Perl

Perl is a very popular language for CGI scripts. Its primary strength is that it is a very powerful language for the manipulation of text. It also does maths better than Bash.

EXPERIMENT 10-9

Perform this experiment as the root user on StudentVM2.

We need to add some lines to the first Virtual Host stanza in httpd.conf. We need to define the ScriptAlias which specifies the location for CGI scripts. We also need to provide access for all to that directory, just like the access we specified for the html directory.

```
ScriptAlias /cgi-bin/ "/var/www1/cgi-bin/"
```

The Name Virtual Host stanza for the primary web site should now look like this. The new lines are highlighted in bold.

```
# The primary website
<VirtualHost 192.168.56.1:80>
    ServerName www1.example.com
    ServerAlias www1.example.com
    DocumentRoot "/var/www1/html"
```

---

[3]Wikipedia, *Common Gateway Interface*, https://en.wikipedia.org/wiki/Common_Gateway_Interface

```
ScriptAlias /cgi-bin/ "/var/www1/cgi-bin/"
ErrorLog "logs/error_log"
ServerAdmin student@example.com
<Directory "/var/www1/html">
    Options Indexes FollowSymLinks
    AllowOverride None
    Require all granted
</Directory>
<Directory "/var/www1/cgi-bin">
    Options Indexes FollowSymLinks
    AllowOverride None
    Require all granted
</Directory>
</VirtualHost>
```

Add the following Perl script to /var/www1/cgi-bin/index.cgi. Set the ownership to apache.
apache and permissions to 755 because it must be executable.

```
#!/usr/bin/perl
print "Content-type: text/html\n\n";
print "<html><body>\n";
print "<h1>Hello World</h1>\n";
print "Using Perl<p>\n";
print "</body></html>\n";
```

Run this program from the CLI and view the results.

```
[root@studentvm2 cgi-bin]# ./index.cgi
Content-type: text/html

<html><body>
<h1>Hello World</h1>
Using Perl<p>
</body></html>
[root@studentvm2 cgi-bin]#
```

This is correct because we want the execution of this program to send the HTML code to the
requesting browser. On StudentyVM1, view the URL www1.example.com/cgi-bin/index.cgi in
your browser. Your result should be identical to that shown in Figure 10-5.

Figure 10-5. *Using a Perl CGI script to produce a web page*

The above CGI program is still basically static because it always displays the same output. Add the following lines to your CGI program immediately after the "Hello World" line. The Perl "system" command executes the commands following it in a system shell, and returns the result to the program. In this case, we simply grep the current RAM usage out of the results from the free command.

```
system "free | grep Mem";
print "\n\n";
```

Now refresh the browser and view the results. You should see an additional line that displays the system memory statistics. Refresh the browser a couple more times and notice that the memory usage should change occasionally.

Using BASH

BASH is probably the simplest language of all for use in CGI scripts. Its primary strengths for CGI programming are that all SysAdmins should know it and it has direct access to all of the standard GNU utilities and system programs.

EXPERIMENT 10-10

Perform this experiment as the root user on StudentVM2.

Copy the existing index.cgi to Perl.index.cgi. Replace the content of the index.cgi with the following content.

```
#!/bin/bash
echo "Content-type: text/html"
echo ""
echo '<html>'
echo '<head>'
echo '<meta http-equiv="Content-Type" content="text/html; charset=UTF-8">'
echo '<title>Hello World</title>'
echo '</head>'
echo '<body>'
echo '<h1>Hello World</h1><p>'
echo 'Using BASH<p>'
free | grep Mem
echo '</body>'
echo '</html>'
exit 0
```

Test this code by running it from the command line. It will produce HTML output. Refresh the browser on StudentVM1.

Redirecting the web page to CGI

All this CGI is very nice, but people don't usually type the full URL to your CGI page. They will type the domain name and hit the Enter key. We need to add one more line to the httpd.conf file in the VirtualHost stanza for the primary web site.

```
┌─────────────────────────────────────────────────────────────────────┐
│                        EXPERIMENT 10-11                             │
└─────────────────────────────────────────────────────────────────────┘
```

Perform this experiment as the root user on StudentVM2.

Add the highlighted line to the primary web site Named Virtual Host stanza. The entire
VirtualHost stanza now looks like this. The DirectoryIndex statement defines the possible
names and locations of the index files.

```
# The primary website
<VirtualHost 192.168.56.1:80>
    ServerName www1.example.com
    ServerAlias www1.example.com
    DocumentRoot "/var/www1/html"
    DirectoryIndex index.html index.txt /cgi-bin/index.cgi
    ScriptAlias /cgi-bin/ "/var/www1/cgi-bin/"
    ErrorLog "logs/error_log"
    ServerAdmin student@example.com
    <Directory "/var/www1/html">
        Options Indexes FollowSymLinks
        AllowOverride None
        Require all granted
    </Directory>
    <Directory "/var/www1/cgi-bin">
        Options Indexes FollowSymLinks
        AllowOverride None
        Require all granted
    </Directory>
</VirtualHost>
```

Rename the /var/www1/html/index.html file to Old.index.html so that it will no longer
match the DirectoryIndex definition of an index file. Note that the search sequence in the
DirectoryIndex statement is left to right, so rearranging that sequence so that the/cgi-bin/
index.cgi is first would work also. However, there may be side effects of doing it that way that
should be considered before doing so in a production environment.

Now type www.example.com in the URL line of your browser. The result should take you to the
CGI script which will display the current memory usage.

Refreshing the page automatically

Now that we have a page that gives us memory statistics, we do not want to manually refresh the page. We can do that with a statement in our CGI script.

EXPERIMENT 10-12

Perform this experiment as the root user on StudentVM2.

Replace the existing "meta" line with the following one which points to the index.cgi file and contains a refresh instruction. The content=1 statement specifies a one second refresh interval.

```
echo '<meta http-equiv="Refresh" content=1;URL=http://www1.example.com/
cgi-bin/index.cgi>'
```

Change the refresh rate to 5 seconds. Note that this change takes effect immediately.

Chapter summary

In this chapter, we created a simple static web page with minimal content and no HTML formatting. From there, we used HTML to create progressively more complex static content. We also created a second web site hosted on the same VM. After a bit of testing with static content, we moved on to creating dynamic pages with Bash and Perl CGI scripts.

This is a very simple example of serving up two web sites with a single instance of the Apache httpd server. Configuration of the virtual hosts becomes a bit more complex when other factors are considered.

For example, you may have some CGI scripts you want to use for one or both of these web sites. You would create directories for the CGI programs in /var/www. One might be /var/www/cgi-bin and the other might be /var/www/cgi-bin2 to be consistent with the html directory naming. It would then be necessary to add configuration directives to the virtual host stanzas in order to specify the directory location for the CGI scripts. Each web site could also have directories from which files could be downloaded and that would also require entries in the appropriate virtual host stanza.

The Apache web site has some very good documentation at https://httpd.apache.org/docs/2.4/ that describes some other methods for managing multiple web sites as well as configuration options ranging from performance tuning to security.

Exercises

Perform the following exercises to complete this chapter.

1. Describe the difference between a static web page and a dynamic one.

2. List at least five popular programming languages that are used to generate dynamic web pages.

3. What limitations might prevent a program language from being used with CGI?

4. What does CGI enable web sites to do?

5. Add some code to the CGI script that will display the current CPU usage on the web page in addition to the memory usage.

CHAPTER 11

WordPress

Objectives

In this chapter, you will learn

- To install PHP and MariaDB – requirements for WordPress

- To create a MariaDB database for WordPress to use for a web site

- To do the WordPress 5-minute installation

- To use the WordPress Dashboard to make administrative changes and to add new posts and pages to the site

- To change the WordPress theme for the web site to alter its look and feel

Introduction

In the previous chapter, we installed the Apache HTTPD web server and configured it to serve two web sites – one static and one dynamic. Dynamic web sites are important for businesses and other organizations that have a need to constantly change the information on their web sites.

The manual methods we used in Chapter 10 are slow. They force the user to be knowledgeable about the tools used to create and manage web pages in a way that detracts from fully engaging with the content. There is a better way. WordPress is one of a number of higher-level tools that allow users to create web pages and news feed posts using a GUI interface that works much like a word processor.

WordPress is a powerful, highly extensible combination of web publishing, blogging, and Content Management Software (CMS). It takes only a few minutes to install and can get a good-looking, complex web site up and running very quickly.

© David Both 2020
D. Both, *Using and Administering Linux: Volume 3*, https://doi.org/10.1007/978-1-4842-5485-1_11

There are many other open source options available for building a web site. I use WordPress in this chapter because it is one of the easier to install and configure and it is very popular. It is also the one I use to build and manage all of my own web sites.

In this chapter, we will convert one of the virtual hosts to WordPress and create a minimal web site. This is not a chapter about using WordPress, so it only goes as far as getting a basic site up and running and then adding a blog post or two.

Install PHP and MariaDB

WordPress is written in PHP[1], an open source hypertext preprocessing language specifically designed for use in web applications. PHP stands for yet another recursive algorithmic name, "PHP: Hypertext Preprocessor." PHP is a server-side language in which PHP code is embedded in HTML web pages. The PHP code is executed on the server and the resultant HTML is sent to the client along with the surrounding HTML.

MariaDB is a fork of the MySQL project which was subsumed by Oracle. It is an open source SQL database used by WordPress to store all of the data for a web site. We also need to install the php-mysqlnd extension module.

These tools are not installed by default, so we need to install them.

EXPERIMENT 11-1

Perform this experiment as the root user on StudentVM2. Install the required PHP and MariaDB tools.

[root@studentvm2 ~]# **dnf -y install php php-mysqlnd mariadb mariadb-server mariadb-server-utils**

Restart the HTTPD service to enable Apache to integrate with PHP and to enable the MySQL (MariaDB) plug-in.

---

[1]PHP website, www.php.net/

236

Install WordPress

WordPress is available from the Fedora repository, but in the past, it has been multiple releases behind that on the WordPress web site. So, for this experiment, you will download and install WordPress from the WordPress web site. This is also a good introduction to installing software that won't have a nicely prepackaged version for Fedora – or whatever other distribution you might be using.

The code for WordPress is located at www.wordpress.org. Documentation for installation is located at codex.wordpress.org/Installing_WordPress. You should view the WordPress installation documentation while doing this experiment, but everything you need need is here in this experiment.

EXPERIMENT 11-2

Perform this experiment as root on StudentVM2.

Verify that the index.html file in the /var/www1/html directory has been deleted or at least renamed. It would be OK to delete it because it will not be needed again.

Download the latest tarball from the WordPress site into the /tmp directory.

```
[root@studentvm2 ~]# cd /tmp ; wget http://wordpress.org/latest.tar.gz
```

Extract the content of the tarball. The files are extracted to the ./wordpress directory which is created during the process.

```
[root@studentvm2 tmp]# tar -xzvf latest.tar.gz
```

Make /tmp/wordpress the PWD. Copy the files from the wordpress directory to the /var/www1/ html directory. The -R option copies the files recursively so that all files in all subdirectories are copied.

```
[root@studentvm2 wordpress]# cp -R * /var/www1/html/
```

Make /var/www1/ the PWD and change the ownership of the files to apache.apache. Verify that the files are in the correct location and have the new ownership.

```
[root@studentvm2 wordpress]# cd /var/www1 ; chown -R apache.apache *
```

Enable MariaDB so it will start on boot, and then start it now. You also need to restart Apache to enable the MySQL plug-in.

[root@studentvm2 ~]# **systemctl start mariadb ; systemctl enable mariadb ;**
systemctl restart httpd.service

Verify that MariaDB is up and running.

[root@studentvm2 ~]# **systemctl status mariadb**
[root@studentvm2 ~]# systemctl status mariadb
• mariadb.service - MariaDB 10.3 database server
   Loaded: loaded (/usr/lib/systemd/system/mariadb.service; enabled; vendor
   preset: disabled)
   Active: active (running) since Sat 2019-07-27 13:24:57 EDT; 1h 19min ago
    Docs: man:mysqld(8)
         https://mariadb.com/kb/en/library/systemd/
 Main PID: 27183 (mysqld)
   Status: "Taking your SQL requests now..."
    Tasks: 30 (limit: 4696)
   Memory: 73.2M
   CGroup: /system.slice/mariadb.service
        └─27183 /usr/libexec/mysqld --basedir=/usr

Jul 27 13:24:56 studentvm2.example.com mysql-prepare-db-dir[27082]: Please
report any problems at http://maria>
Jul 27 13:24:56 studentvm2.example.com mysql-prepare-db-dir[27082]: The
latest information about MariaDB is av>
Jul 27 13:24:56 studentvm2.example.com mysql-prepare-db-dir[27082]: You can
find additional information about >
Jul 27 13:24:56 studentvm2.example.com mysql-prepare-db-dir[27082]: http://
dev.mysql.com
Jul 27 13:24:56 studentvm2.example.com mysql-prepare-db-dir[27082]: Consider
joining MariaDB's strong and vibr>
Jul 27 13:24:56 studentvm2.example.com mysql-prepare-db-dir[27082]: https://
mariadb.org/get-involved/
Jul 27 13:24:57 studentvm2.example.com mysqld[27183]: 2019-07-27 13:24:57 0
[Note] /usr/libexec/mysqld (mysqld>
Jul 27 13:24:57 studentvm2.example.com mysqld[27183]: 2019-07-27 13:24:57 0
[Warning] Could not increase numbe>
Jul 27 13:24:57 studentvm2.example.com mysqld[27183]: 2019-07-27 13:24:57 0
[Warning] Changed limits: max_open>
Jul 27 13:24:57 studentvm2.example.com systemd[1]: Started MariaDB 10.3
database server.

No password is required by default, so we will set a root password using the **mysqladmin** utility.

```
[root@studentvm2 ~]# mysqladmin -u root password <Your Password>
```

Now login to the MariaDB CLI to test the new password. Your results should look like those below.

```
[root@studentvm2 ~]# mysql -u root -p
Enter password: <Enter your password>
Welcome to the MariaDB monitor.  Commands end with ; or \g.
Your MariaDB connection id is 10
Server version: 10.3.12-MariaDB MariaDB Server

Copyright (c) 2000, 2018, Oracle, MariaDB Corporation Ab and others.

Type 'help;' or '\h' for help. Type '\c' to clear the current input statement.

MariaDB [(none)]>
```

This last line is the MariaDB command prompt.

HTTPD configuration

Due to the fact that Apache has not been configured for the index file used by WordPress, index.php, we need to add that to the VirtualHost stanza for the primary web site. This ensures that Apache uses the correct index file for the WordPress web site.

```
                        EXPERIMENT 11-3
```

Perform this experiment as root on StudentVM2.

Edit the httpd.conf file. In the VirtualHost stanza for the www1 web site, change the DirectoryIndex line from:

```
DirectoryIndex index.html index.txt /cgi-bin/index.cgi
```

to

```
DirectoryIndex index.php index.html index.txt /cgi-bin/index.cgi
```

Restart or reload Apache to activate the changes.

Creating the WordPress Database

At this stage, some basic databases required by MariaDB have been created, but we have created none for the WordPress web site. In this experiment, we will look at the existing databases and create the ones required for WordPress.

EXPERIMENT 11-4

Perform this experiment as root on StudentVM2.

Use the following command to view the basic databases required by MariaDB. Be sure to add the semicolon (;) to the end of each command.

```
MariaDB [(none)]> show databases;
+--------------------+
| Database           |
+--------------------+
| information_schema |
| mysql              |
| performance_schema |
+--------------------+
3 rows in set (0.001 sec)

MariaDB [(none)]>
```

Now we can create the database for the web site we want to build and grant privileges to the root user (the MariaDB root user, not the Linux root user) to all tables in the new database.

```
MariaDB [(none)]> create database www1;
Query OK, 1 row affected (0.000 sec)

MariaDB [(none)]> grant all privileges on www1.* to "root"@"studentvm1"
identified by "<type the password here>";
Query OK, 0 rows affected (0.001 sec)

MariaDB [(none)]> flush privileges;
Query OK, 0 rows affected (0.000 sec)
```

Now check the new database. The MariaDB user interface has some command-line editing capabilities, so you can just use the up-arrow key to scroll back to the **show databases** command.

```
MariaDB [(none)]> show databases;
+--------------------+
| Database           |
+--------------------+
| information_schema |
| mysql              |
| performance_schema |
| www1               |
+--------------------+
4 rows in set (0.000 sec)
```

This completes all of the MariaDB configuration that is required to create a WordPress web site.

These are all of the SQL commands that you will ever need to know when creating a MariaDB database for WordPress. However, I have taken some time to learn a bit more for myself, and we will do a little more a bit later in this chapter. So do not log out of MariaDB. We will explore it a little further later in this lab project.

Configuring WordPress

We are now ready to configure WordPress itself. We will set up a configuration file and then run an administrative program from the web browser to complete the web site setup.

```
┌─────────────────────────────────────────────────────────────────┐
│                       EXPERIMENT 11-5                           │
└─────────────────────────────────────────────────────────────────┘
```

Perform this experiment as root on StudentVM2.

Change the PWD to /var/www1/html/. Copy the file wp-config-sample.php to wp-config. php. Copying the file leaves the original in case the copied file gets badly hosed. Change the ownership of wp-config.php to apache.apache.

Open wp-config.php in vi for editing. Change some of the lines in the file so that they look like those in the portions of the file shown below. The specific lines to be changed are in bold.

```
// ** MySQL settings - You can get this info from your web host ** //
/** The name of the database for WordPress */
define('DB_NAME', 'www1');
```

```
/** MySQL database username */
define('DB_USER', 'root');

/** MySQL database password */
define('DB_PASSWORD', '<Your password goes here>');

. . .

/**
 * WordPress Database Table prefix.
 *
 * You can have multiple installations in one database if you give each a
 unique
 * prefix. Only numbers, letters, and underscores please!
 */
$table_prefix  = 'www1_';

. . .

/** Absolute path to the WordPress directory. */
if ( !defined('ABSPATH') )
        define('ABSPATH', dirname(__FILE__) . '/var/www1/html/');
```

Save the file and exit from the editor.

Open a browser or a new tab in an existing browser instance on StudentVM2 and enter the following line in the URL field.

```
http://www1.example.com/wp-admin/install.php
```

This opens the initial WordPress web site language configuration page. The default is usually correct for your location, but ensure that you select the correct locale. English (United States) was correct for me. Press the **Continue** button.

Fill in or choose the entries as shown in Figure 11-1.Student

Field	Value
Site Title	Student Web Site
Username	student – This is the user ID that will be used to login to the administrative pages of the web site.
Password	Enter a password for the WordPress Administration page.
Your E-mail	student@example.com - Your student email account.

Figure 11-1. *WordPress configuration settings*

Then click the Install WordPress button to complete the setup. This may take a few minutes depending upon the specs of your VM. There is no progress indicator so be patient.

At the end of the process, you will be presented with a login page. Let's take a look at the web site before we change anything. In a new tab of your browser, type in the web site URL, www1.example.com and press **Enter**.

You will see the WordPress web site home page with the default theme. The default theme changes each year so your web site may look different from this one. It is a good thing that themes are easy to change because the default ones are pretty bland. This one seems to suck more than most – at least to me. We will change the theme as part of this chapter.

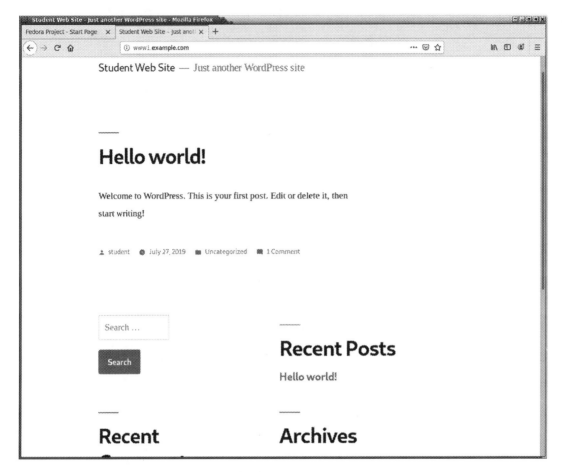

Figure 11-2. *The default WordPress home page. It may look different for you because the default theme changes each year*

Administering WordPress

WordPress is easy to administer, both in terms of creation and maintenance of content, the management of the look and feel of the site, and the ability to obtain traffic metrics. In Experiment 11-6, we take a very brief look at administering WordPress.

EXPERIMENT 11-6

Perform this experiment as the student user on StudentVM1.

We are doing this from StudentVM1 to illustrate that administration of a WordPress web site can be performed from any host that has network or Internet access to the web site. This is one good reason to use strong passwords and to not use the default Admin account.

Open a browser on StudentVM1 if one is not already open and go to URL, http://www1. example.com. Scroll down to the **Meta** section of the page and click **Log in**. Type in the username of student, enter the password, and click the **Log In** button. The WordPress Dashboard, from which all administrative activities can be performed, is shown in Figure 11-2.

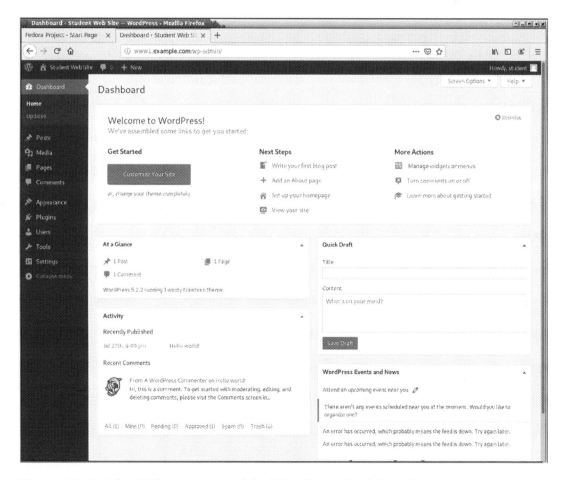

Figure 11-3. *The Welcome page of the WordPress Dashboard*

The WordPress Dashboard provides you with lists of things to do to get started customizing your web site, and the next steps that will enable you to add pages and posts to the site. Skip all that, click **Dismiss** (upper right of the welcome screen), and look at the dashboard itself on the left side of the screen.

Hover over **Users**, and then click **All Users**. Here you can manage users including adding and deleting them. Users can have roles. Since you are the admin you might not want anyone else to have that role so you would give them lesser roles.

Now hover over **Appearance** and click **Customize**. Here we can do things like change the theme which is what provides your web site with its personality. Click **Themes**, select one of the other themes, and click the **Live Preview** button to see what that theme would look like. I chose the 2017 theme, but it might not be available when you do this experiment. Just pick one and see how it changes the look and feel of your web site.

Once you have chosen one of the available themes, click the **Activate and Publish** button. Open another tab on your browser and go to the web site to see how it looks.

If none of the themes listed meet your needs, it is easy to download more from a very large selection of free ones. In the **Previewing themes** menu item, click **Change**, and then click WordPress.org themes. This opens up a list of many themes that are available for download. Scan through them and pick one or two that interest you and then click the **Install & Preview** button. This will install the theme and preview it so that you can decide whether you want to publish it. Experiment with themes for a few minutes just to get a feel for what can be done.

If you have an interest in learning more about WordPress, there is some good online help available at `https://wordpress.org/support/category/basic-usage/`. Because our objective here is to install it and get it running, we have mostly fulfilled our need as SysAdmins.

Updating WordPress

The last thing we need to know about WordPress is how to update it. This is easy and mostly takes care of itself.

When you log in to the dashboard, it will inform you when there are updates available. You can go to the updates page, click the available updates, and install them. It usually takes only a few minutes to do the updates. WordPress will go into maintenance mode during a portion of updates for WordPress itself, the active theme, and any active plug-ins.

If you create an account at WordPress.org, you can choose for updates to be installed automatically.

Exploring MariaDB

The WordPress configuration procedure created the tables for the database and there is now some content. So take a few minutes to explore the MySQL database.

EXPERIMENT 11-7

Perform this experiment as root on StudentVM2.

It is only possible to work with a given database when it is the "current" one, somewhat like the present working directory. This is called "connecting" with the database. Connect to the www1 database with the command **use www1;** and MariaDB will display a message that says, "Database changed."

```
MariaDB [(none)]> use www1;
Reading table information for completion of table and column names
You can turn off this feature to get a quicker startup with -A

Database changed
MariaDB [www1]>
```

Now list the tables in the database. The results should look like these.

```
MariaDB [www1]> show tables;
+-------------------------+
| Tables_in_www1          |
+-------------------------+
| www1_commentmeta        |
| www1_comments           |
| www1_links              |
| www1_options            |
| www1_postmeta           |
| www1_posts              |
| www1_term_relationships |
| www1_term_taxonomy      |
```

```
| www1_termmeta          |
| www1_terms             |
| www1_usermeta          |
| www1_users             |
+------------------------+
12 rows in set (0.001 sec)

MariaDB [www1]>
```

We can see that the WordPress installation procedure has created the tables in this database.

To explore the individual tables, you can use the **describe** command. This example shows the fields in the www1_posts table, along with their attributes.

```
MariaDB [www1]> describe www1_posts;
```

Field	Type	Null	Key	Default	Extra
ID	bigint(20) unsigned	NO	PRI	NULL	auto_increment
post_author	bigint(20) unsigned	NO	MUL	0	
post_date	datetime	NO		0000-00-00 00:00:00	
post_date_gmt	datetime	NO		0000-00-00 00:00:00	
post_content	longtext	NO		NULL	
post_title	text	NO		NULL	
post_excerpt	text	NO		NULL	
post_status	varchar(20)	NO		publish	
comment_status	varchar(20)	NO		open	
ping_status	varchar(20)	NO		open	
post_password	varchar(255)	NO			
post_name	varchar(200)	NO	MUL		
to_ping	text	NO		NULL	
pinged	text	NO		NULL	
post_modified	datetime	NO		0000-00-00 00:00:00	
post_modified_gmt	datetime	NO		0000-00-00 00:00:00	
post_content_filtered	longtext	NO		NULL	
post_parent	bigint(20) unsigned	NO	MUL	0	
guid	varchar(255)	NO			
menu_order	int(11)	NO		0	
post_type	varchar(20)	NO	MUL	post	
post_mime_type	varchar(100)	NO			
comment_count	bigint(20)	NO		0	

```
23 rows in set (0.001 sec)

MariaDB [www1]>
```

Use the following command to display the post_title rows of the database.

```
MariaDB [www1]> select post_title from www1_posts;
+----------------+
| post_title     |
+----------------+
| Hello world!   |
| Sample Page    |
| Privacy Policy |
| Auto Draft     |
+----------------+
4 rows in set (0.000 sec)

MariaDB [www1]>
```

Use the **exit** command to exit the MariaDB user interface.

This chapter is neither a course on web page design and creation nor one on MariaDB, so that is as far as we will go here. However, you now have at least a small bit of knowledge about using MariaDB and enough to get you started with WordPress.

Chapter summary

WordPress is a powerful and reliable tool for creating content-based web sites. It is one of the easiest ways to create and maintain a web site I have ever used. Despite that, the WordPress 5-minute installation is not really just 5 minutes – at least not for me. I do it seldom and so need to look up the steps each time. Reading the directions every time I do the installation takes some time, and I always take more than five minutes – but not much more.

If you plan to work on web sites using WordPress, spend some time learning to use it and to add posts and pages. My personal web sites www.both.org and www.linux-databook.info/ both use WordPress. I have also used it for some of my customers.

Exercises

Perform the following exercises to complete this chapter.

1. What happens if a new index.html file with a bit of plain ASCII text or HTML content is placed in the /var/www1/html directory?

2. What might you use the effect in #1 for?

3. Why did we use the download from the WordPress web site rather than the Fedora version of WordPress?

CHAPTER 12

Mailing Lists

Objectives

In this chapter, you will learn

- To install and configure the MailMan email listserv

- To create a simple mailing list

- To configure some general mailing list attributes to make the list more usable and secure

- To manage user subscriptions

- Why some listserv email get rejected by large services such as AOL, EarthLink, and Gmail

- To configure lists to circumvent the rejection problems caused by some large email services

Introduction

Mailing lists are important in many environments. They provide a single administrative point for lists rather than depending upon everyone maintaining their own local copy of an email list. MailMan is an excellent open source tool that is used for mailing lists. Of course, there are others, but once again it is free, has many useful features, and is quite configurable and fairly easy to install and use.

MailMan integrates with both your MTA for email services and the web server for administrative functions. Of course, all of the administrative tasks can be performed from the command line as well.

© David Both 2020

D. Both, *Using and Administering Linux: Volume 3*, https://doi.org/10.1007/978-1-4842-5485-1_12

Installing MailMan

Mailman installation is simple. Most Red Hat–based Linux distributions have recent versions and Fedora usually has the most current in its repository.

MailMan is written in Python, another powerful language. Because Python is not installed by default, it will be installed as a dependency when we install MailMan.

EXPERIMENT 12-1

Perform this experiment as the root user on StudentVM2. Install Mailman with the following command.

```
[root@studentvm2 ~]# dnf -y install mailman
```

This also installs Python as a dependency because it is not installed by default.

Integrating MailMan with Apache

Using the Fedora package for MailMan ensures that the vast majority of configuration is performed for you. The mailman user account and group are added, the files are all installed, and integration with SendMail using SMRSH[1] is done. There are only a couple remaining tasks. We need to ensure that all permissions are set properly and integrate the MailMan web interface with our Apache web server.

EXPERIMENT 12-2

Perform this experiment as the root user on StudentVM2.

Change the PWD to /usr/lib/mailman/bin and run the following command until it reports no errors. The -f option tells it to fix any problems it encounters. You will probably see one error as I did.

```
[root@studentvm2 ~]# cd /usr/lib/mailman/bin
[root@studentvm2 bin]# ./check_perms -f
/usr/lib/mailman/bin/mailman-update-cfg bad group (has: root, expected
mailman) (fixing)
```

---

[1]SMRSH is the SendMail Restricted Shell which we first encountered on Chapter 9 of this volume.

```
Problems found: 1
Re-run as mailman (or root) with -f flag to fix
[root@studentvm2 bin]# ./check_perms -f
No problems found
[root@studentvm2 bin]#
```

The Fedora installation places a file named mailman.conf in the /etc/httpd/conf.d directory where it will be automatically read – along with other configuration files located there – by the HTTPD service as it starts up. There is an "include" line in the httpd.conf file that causes all of the files in this directory to be read into the configuration as the service starts.

Reload the HTTPD service.

```
[root@studentvm2 ~]# systemctl reload httpd.service
```

You should take some time to examine the short /etc/httpd/conf.d/mailman.conf file to understand what it is doing. You should be able to interpret it by now.

Site mailing list

MailMan needs an internal site-wide mailing list created in order to work. This list is not one that will ever be used to send email by a user. It is used by MailMan to send email notifications, such as the monthly password reminders, to users.

EXPERIMENT 12-3

Perform this experiment as the root user on StudentVM2.

The first list we need to create is the "mailman" list. This list is used by MailMan to send monthly notifications and other administrative emails. Make /usr/lib/mailman/bin the PWD. List the contents of this directory to view the administrative programs to which you have access.

Now create the mailman list. The list owner's email address should be student@example.com.

```
[root@studentvm2 bin]# ./newlist mailman
Enter the email of the person running the list: student@example.com
Initial mailman password: <Enter list password>
To finish creating your mailing list, you must edit your /etc/aliases (or
equivalent) file by adding the following lines, and possibly running the
`newaliases' program:
```

```
## mailman mailing list
mailman:                "|/usr/lib/mailman/mail/mailman post mailman"
mailman-admin:          "|/usr/lib/mailman/mail/mailman admin mailman"
mailman-bounces:        "|/usr/lib/mailman/mail/mailman bounces mailman"
mailman-confirm:        "|/usr/lib/mailman/mail/mailman confirm mailman"
mailman-join:           "|/usr/lib/mailman/mail/mailman join mailman"
mailman-leave:          "|/usr/lib/mailman/mail/mailman leave mailman"
mailman-owner:          "|/usr/lib/mailman/mail/mailman owner mailman"
mailman-request:        "|/usr/lib/mailman/mail/mailman request mailman"
mailman-subscribe:      "|/usr/lib/mailman/mail/mailman subscribe mailman"
mailman-unsubscribe:    "|/usr/lib/mailman/mail/mailman unsubscribe mailman"

Hit enter to notify mailman owner... <Enter>

[root@studentvm2 bin]#
```

As root, copy the data from the "##" line through the "unsubscribe" line and paste it into the end of the /etc/aliases file. Then run the **newalaises** command with no options to regenerate the aliases database file. No changes need to be made to the "mailman" mailing list and you should not add users to it.

Now we can start the MailMan service. It will not start until the site-wide mailing list has been created.

```
[root@studentvm2 ~]# systemctl start mailman
[root@studentvm2 ~]# systemctl status mailman
• mailman.service - GNU Mailing List Manager
  Loaded: loaded (/usr/lib/systemd/system/mailman.service; enabled; vendor
  preset: disabled)
  Active: active (running) since Mon 2019-07-29 21:12:13 EDT; 2s ago
 Process: 21386 ExecStart=/usr/lib/mailman/bin/mailmanctl -s start
 (code=exited, status=0/SUCCESS)
 Process: 21385 ExecStartPre=/bin/chmod 660 /var/log/mailman/error
 (code=exited, status=0/SUCCESS)
 Process: 21384 ExecStartPre=/bin/chown mailman:mailman /var/log/mailman/
 error (code=exited, status=0/SUCCESS)
 Process: 21383 ExecStartPre=/bin/touch /var/log/mailman/error (code=exited,
 status=0/SUCCESS)
```

Process: 21382 ExecStartPre=/usr/bin/install -m644 -o root -g root /usr/
lib/mailman/cron/crontab.in /etc/cron.d/m>
Process: 21381 ExecStartPre=/usr/lib/mailman/bin/mailman-update-cfg
(code=exited, status=0/SUCCESS)
Main PID: 21387 (mailmanctl)
    Tasks: 9 (limit: 4696)
   Memory: 97.9M
   CGroup: /system.slice/mailman.service
           ├─21387 /usr/bin/python2 /usr/lib/mailman/bin/mailmanctl -s start
           ├─21388 /usr/bin/python2 /usr/lib/mailman/bin/qrunner
           --runner=ArchRunner:0:1 -s
           ├─21389 /usr/bin/python2 /usr/lib/mailman/bin/qrunner
           --runner=BounceRunner:0:1 -s
           ├─21390 /usr/bin/python2 /usr/lib/mailman/bin/qrunner
           --runner=CommandRunner:0:1 -s
           ├─21391 /usr/bin/python2 /usr/lib/mailman/bin/qrunner
           --runner=IncomingRunner:0:1 -s
           ├─21392 /usr/bin/python2 /usr/lib/mailman/bin/qrunner
           --runner=NewsRunner:0:1 -s
           ├─21393 /usr/bin/python2 /usr/lib/mailman/bin/qrunner
           --runner=OutgoingRunner:0:1 -s
           ├─21394 /usr/bin/python2 /usr/lib/mailman/bin/qrunner
           --runner=VirginRunner:0:1 -s
           └─21395 /usr/bin/python2 /usr/lib/mailman/bin/qrunner
           --runner=RetryRunner:0:1 -s

Jul 29 21:12:12 studentvm2.example.com systemd[1]: Starting GNU Mailing List
Manager...
Jul 29 21:12:13 studentvm2.example.com mailmanctl[21386]: Starting Mailman's
master qrunner.
Jul 29 21:12:13 studentvm2.example.com systemd[1]: Started GNU Mailing List
Manager.
[root@studentvm2 ~]#

Enable the MailMan service so that it starts on boot.

[root@studentvm2 ~]# **systemctl enable mailman.service**

MailMan is now ready for us to create a "real" list.

Create a mailing list

The next list will be a "real" one that we can use for testing. The steps are the same as creating the site mailing list but using a different list name.

EXPERIMENT 12-4

Perform this experiment as the root user on StudentVM2. Create a list named "Testlist" using similar steps to those shown above.

Make /usr/lib/mailman/bin the PWD. Then perform the following steps.

```
[root@studentvm2 bin]# ./newlist Testlist
Enter the email of the person running the list: student@example.com
Initial testlist password: <Enter list password>
To finish creating your mailing list, you must edit your /etc/aliases (or
equivalent) file by adding the following lines, and possibly running the
`newaliases' program:

## testlist mailing list
testlist:               "|/usr/lib/mailman/mail/mailman post testlist"
testlist-admin:         "|/usr/lib/mailman/mail/mailman admin testlist"
testlist-bounces:       "|/usr/lib/mailman/mail/mailman bounces testlist"
testlist-confirm:       "|/usr/lib/mailman/mail/mailman confirm testlist"
testlist-join:          "|/usr/lib/mailman/mail/mailman join testlist"
testlist-leave:         "|/usr/lib/mailman/mail/mailman leave testlist"
testlist-owner:         "|/usr/lib/mailman/mail/mailman owner testlist"
testlist-request:       "|/usr/lib/mailman/mail/mailman request testlist"
testlist-subscribe:     "|/usr/lib/mailman/mail/mailman subscribe testlist"
testlist-unsubscribe:   "|/usr/lib/mailman/mail/mailman unsubscribe testlist"

Hit enter to notify testlist owner...<Enter>

[root@studentvm2 bin]#
```

Copy the data from the "##" line through the "unsubscribe" line and paste it in at the end of the /etc/aliases file. Then run the **newalaises** command with no options to regenerate the aliases database file.

There is no need to restart MailMan or any other services when creating new lists.

Configuring the new list

If configuration changes need to be made to new lists, they can be most easily configured using the web interface. There is a file that defines default configuration parameters for new lists and we will get to that soon. For now, let's look at manual configuration via the web interface.

EXPERIMENT 12-5

Perform this experiment as the student user on StudentVM1. We could do this from StudentVM2, but this part can be done from anywhere with a web browser and network access to the server.

Open a web browser or a new tab and enter the URL **www1.example.com/mailman/admin/** which will display a page with a welcome message but no lists displayed.

We can use the URL for a specific list, so enter the following: **www1.example.com/mailman/admin/testlist**. This URL is the mail administrator page for the Testlist on our MailMan web site. We will soon configure our list so that it will be displayed in the list of advertised lists.

On the **General Options** page, add a terse phrase to identify the list in the field by that name. It can be anything you want, but one suggestion would be "Test list."

In the introductory description field, enter some text that says something like, "A list for testing MailMan." Also enter this same text in the field for the new subscriber welcome message.

There are a few options that I always want set on lists that I create. Set the following items and take a bit of time to look around each of the configuration pages to see what is there.

Scroll down the **General Options** page and check the boxes, **Conceal members address** and **Acknowledge members posting**.

Concealing the address just makes it look like, "member at example.com" so that the address will be harder to decipher by page scrapers looking for email addresses to spam. And most lists will want to send an acknowledgment of a posting, especially if members do not receive their own postings. Most users I have worked with want to get both the acknowledgment and the posting itself.

In the **Hostname this list prefers for email** field, remove the actual hostname so that only the example.com domain name is left.

Scroll down to the bottom of this first page and click the **Submit Your Changes** button.

Now go to the **Privacy options** page. Click the radio button, **Confirm and Approve**. This means that new users who subscribe themselves will get an email requesting that they confirm their desire to join the list. This can prevent "friends" from signing you up for a list you don't want to be subscribed to. And the "Approve" part means that the list administrator must approve all subscription requests. Also on this page, there may be times when you do not want even other members of the list to see the rest of the subscribers; you may wish to check the radio button for **List admin only**.

Scroll to the bottom of this page and click the **Submit Your Changes** button. I assume that you will remember to click the **Submit Your Changes** button after changing anything on the configuration web pages.

On the **Archiving options** page, it is a good practice to make the archives private unless there is a specific reason to allow them to be indexed by Google and other web bots.

Now go to the **Membership Management ➤ Mass Subscription** page and add at least two members to the list. One should be student@example.com. Another should be an email address you have access to outside the classroom lab. Use the format "Student User <student@example.net>" including the <> characters. Each user should receive an email that verifies they have been added to the list.

After submitting your changes, the page refreshes and lists the successful – or unsuccessful – results.

As the user student, view the confirmation emails sent by MailMan. Then send an email to the list to verify that it gets through. Check the archive to verify that the message you sent is archived.

You may notice that SpamAssassin is still altering the subject line and attaching a report to the emails that are not spam. You can safely comment out the lines that do that in the mimedefang-filter program.

Changing list defaults

You can change the defaults for future lists. Changing these defaults does not change any currently existing lists. The master configuration file for your MailMan site is /usr/lib/mailman/Mailman/Defaults.py, but you should not change that file. Change the file /etc/mailman/mm_cfg.py instead.

EXPERIMENT 12-6

Perform this experiment as the root user on StudentVM2. Take a quick look through the mm_cfg.py file. Let's change one of the defaults for an item we changed manually for the previous list. Note that some, like the description fields, can and should not have a default value.

The values we want to change are not in the mm_cfg.py file, so we will need to find them in the Defaults.py file and copy the line to mm_cfg.py and change the value there. If we change them in the Defaults.py file, our changes may be overwritten but future updates.

Use less to open the Defaults.py file and search for "subscribe". This word appears several places in the comments, but we are looking for the DEFAULT_SUBSCRIBE_POLICY so that we can change it. Read the text for SUBSCRIBE_POLICY. Copy the entire SUBSCRIBE_POLICY section to the end of the mm_cfg.py file and change the value of DEFAULT_SUBSCRIBE_POLICY from 1 to 3.

```
# SUBSCRIBE POLICY
# 0 - open list (only when ALLOW_OPEN_SUBSCRIBE is set to 1) **
# 1 - confirmation required for subscribes
# 2 - admin approval required for subscribes
# 3 - both confirmation and admin approval required
#
# ** please do not choose option 0 if you are not allowing open
# subscribes (next variable)
DEFAULT_SUBSCRIBE_POLICY = 3
```

Now copy the following section from Defaults.py file, paste it at the end of mm_cfg.py, and change the value of VIRTUAL_HOST_OVERVIEW from On to No.

```
# When set to Yes, the listinfo and admin overviews of lists on the machine
# will be confined to only those lists whose web_page_url configuration
option
```

```
# host is included within the URL by which the page is visited - only those
# "on the virtual host".  When set to No, all advertised (i.e. public) lists
# are included in the overview.
VIRTUAL_HOST_OVERVIEW = No
```

This will now allow the list of lists to be viewed at the administrative URL, www1.example. com/mailman/admin/. Note that none of the changes to the mm_cfg.py file require a restart of MailMan. Verify that the TestList is now visible at that URL.

To test the policy change, create a new list named Test2. Refresh the main list page and select the new Test2 list. Log in with the site or list password and verify that the policy setting is now "confirm and approve."

Add the email address for the student user to this new list and send an email to the list to test it.

The user interface

So far we have talked about the administrative interface of MailMan, but users also have an interface. This interface is shown in a link at the bottom of every email sent from the list, including the monthly password reminder if configured and the initial welcome email message.

The MailMan user interface in Figure 12-1 allows users to request a subscription, unsubscribe, change their password, and edit their options. They can also view the list of subscribers to a list, assuming that the list is configured to allow that.

In Figure 12-1, I am subscribing as LinuxGeek46@both.org. Depending upon the mailing list configuration, the list administrator may need to approve the request and an email might also be sent to the subscriber to verify that they want to subscribe. This verification step helps to prevent people from subscribing others to lists to which they don't want to belong.

Testlist -- A list for testing MailMan.

English (USA)

About Testlist

A list for testing MailMan.

To see the collection of prior postings to the list, visit the Testlist Archives. (*The current archive is only available to the list members.*)

Using Testlist

To post a message to all the list members, send email to testlist@example.com.

You can subscribe to the list, or change your existing subscription, in the sections below.

Subscribing to Testlist

Subscribe to Testlist by filling out the following form. You will be sent email requesting confirmation, to prevent others from gratuitously subscribing you. Once confirmation is received, your request will be held for approval by the list moderator. You will be notified of the moderator's decision by email. This is also a private list, which means that the list of members is not available to non-members.

Your email address:	LinuxGeek46@both.org
Your name (optional):	

You may enter a privacy password below. This provides only mild security, but should prevent others from messing with your subscription. **Do not use a valuable password** as it will occasionally be emailed back to you in cleartext.

If you choose not to enter a password, one will be automatically generated for you, and it will be sent to you once you've confirmed your subscription. You can always request a mail-back of your password when you edit your personal options. Once a month, your password will be emailed to you as a reminder.

Pick a password:	•••••••
Reenter password to confirm:	•••••••
Which language do you prefer to display your messages?	English (USA)
Would you like to receive list mail batched in a daily digest?	⦿ No ◯ Yes

Subscribe

Testlist Subscribers

(*The subscribers list is only available to the list members.*)

Enter your address and password to visit the subscribers list:

Address: LinuxGeek46@both.org   Password: [   ]   Visit Subscriber List

To unsubscribe from Testlist, get a password reminder, or change your subscription options enter your subscription email address:

[   ]   Unsubscribe or edit options

If you leave the field blank, you will be prompted for your email address

Testlist list run by testlist-owner at example.com
Testlist administrative interface (requires authorization)
Overview of all example.com mailing lists

python powered

version 2.1.29

Figure 12-1. *The MailMan user interface allows users to subscribe to the list, unsubscribe, change their password, edit their options, and view the list of subscribers to a list*

EXPERIMENT 12-7

Using the web-based user interface for MailMan, subscribe to the list, TestList, we just created in Experiment 12-5.

Then, as the list administrator, ensure that it is configured so that users can view the list of subscribers. As the user you just subscribed, view the subscriber list.

Rejections from large email services

Many large email services, such as AOL, Yahoo, Gmail, EarthLink, att.net, Spectrum, and more, are flooded with huge amounts of spam every day. Much of the spam is from mailing lists, or at least exhibits some of the attributes of email from a mailing list. Junk like joke/recipe/meme/word/quote/etc/etc, of the day, floods these services. If not controlled, those services would eventually bog down and collapse under the onslaught.

To combat spam in general and that from lists in particular, these services have instituted some interesting but obstructive countermeasures. Much of the time these measures do not affect MailMan lists but sometimes the email services apparently adjust the threshold at which a message from a list is considered to be spam. This is similar to what we can do with SpamAssassin.

The problem is that many messages from listservs of all kinds, even valid messages, are rejected or just dropped without any type of notification to the sender or recipient. This can occur particularly with messages sent by users with a sending email address domain belonging to one of the large mail services to a listserv that has a different domain and then message recipients with the same large email domain as the sender.

The large ISPs are trying to block spam which can look like it originated with them. Here is what happens if the sender domain of the email user is the same as the recipient domain, but the email was actually sent by a listserv with a different domain. The ISP has filters in place that compare the original sender's domain with the domain the email was resent from – the listserv. If they are different – which they always would be with a listserv – the logic applied is that any email from the original sender domain that is sent to a recipient in the same domain should never come from a mail server that does not belong to us. So it is labeled as spam and dropped or a return rejection message is sent.

MailMan has devised methods for encapsulating messages, but they are not perfect, and different combinations work best with different ISPs.

EXPERIMENT 12-8

Perform this experiment as the student user. If there is not already a browser tab open to the MailMan admin page for the Testlist list, do so now.

On the General Options page for Testlist, scroll down to the field that begins, **Replace the From: header address**, and click the **Munge From** radio button. Click **Submit Your Changes** at the bottom of the page.

Now go to **Privacy options ➤ Sender filters**. In the field **Action to take when anyone posts to the list from a domain with a DMARC Reject/Quarantine Policy,** choose **Munge From** radio button and click **Submit Your Changes** at the bottom of the page.

This pair of changes seems to work well most of the time.

Despite the fact that the changes made in Experiment 12-8 work well a good part of the time, the email services change things, and so list messages are once again rejected. There are other things that can be done, and the MailMan developers are constantly working to keep up with changes.

When I first started using MailMan many years ago, I joined their user's list.[2] MailMan administrators can discuss problems and get help on this list. One of the most common discussion topics is about various ISPs blocking email from lists. The best options for circumventing these issues are usually found here.

Documentation

The GNU web site contains complete documentation[3] for MailMan. This includes an installation manual, a list administration manual, and even a manual for list users. There are also discussion lists that you can join for interaction with other MailMan users and administrators.

Note that most of the work required to install and configure MailMan has already been performed by the MailMan RPM we installed from the Fedora repository. Because of this, the documentation becomes more of a theoretical reference than a help.

---

[2]GNU MailMan mailing lists, www.gnu.org/software/mailman/contact.html#the-community
[3]GNU MailMan documentation, www.gnu.org/software/mailman/docs.html

Chapter summary

In this chapter, you have installed the MailMan listserv software and integrated it with both SendMail and Apache. You have created the required site list and two usable lists and sent some emails to the lists. You have also learned how to configure default settings that will apply to newly created lists and to deal with certain types of rejections of emails from a list by some of the large ISPs.

Exercises

Perform the following exercises to complete this chapter.

1. Where does MailMan place its web server configuration data?

2. Where is the CGI file for MailMan located?

3. Create a new list. Name it whatever you choose. Verify that the defaults are set according to the changes you made on the mm_cfg.py file.

4. Add a couple members to this newest list and send an email to the list.

5. Find some volunteers who have AOL, RoadRunner, Time Warner, Spectrum, or one of the other large ISPs to help you with this one. Create a list with those people, but do not set the **Munge from** options on the list. Send them messages via the list to determine if the emails are being dropped or rejected. If some emails are being rejected, set the **Munge from** options and test again. This could be quite time-consuming, so don't spend too much time with it.

CHAPTER 13

File Sharing

Objectives

In this chapter, you will learn

- To describe file sharing and some of its uses

- To define NFS, FTP, FTPS, SFTP, VSFTP, and SAMBA

- How to install and configure an SFTPS

- How to install and configure an NFS server to share files to Linux and Unix hosts

- How to install and configure a SAMBA server to share files to Windows and Linux hosts

- To use Midnight Commander as a multi-protocol file sharing client

Introduction

Sharing files has always been one of the main features of networks. Although networks today can do so much more, file sharing[1] is still a staple of many networks. The idea is to make files that would otherwise be inaccessible to anyone else but the creator, available on some sort of central server so that others – those people we choose – can also access the same files.

Does this sound familiar? It should, especially if you use a service like Google Drive, DropBox, OneDrive, or any of several others.

Apress, the publisher of this series of books, has a Google Drive set up for all three books, each with several folders such as First Draft, Ready for Technical Edit, Author review, and more. When I finish a chapter, I upload to the First Draft folder. Later, after it

---

[1]Wikipedia, *File Sharing*, https://en.wikipedia.org/wiki/File_sharing

D. Both, *Using and Administering Linux: Volume 3*, https://doi.org/10.1007/978-1-4842-5485-1_13

has been reviewed by my development and technical editors, I download the annotated chapter file from the Ready for Author Review folder and make my revisions. Eventually the chapters go to the Ready for Production folder from where they are downloaded for processing into the production files that will be used to print this book or to create an ebook of it.

Of course, we are scattered around the world. I am in Raleigh, North Carolina; Klaatu, my Technical Editor, is in New Zealand; Nancy Chen, my Development Editor, is in New York City; Louise Corrigan, my Senior Editor, is in London, UK; production is in India and the Philippines; and so on. Yet we all have instant access to the same newly uploaded or revised files. This is a very well-defined workflow designed around shared folders and the files they contain. It is based on the simple concept of sharing files between hosts on a network.

Many organizations have a need to share files and find using their own servers to do so a better option. After all, the saying, "The cloud is just someone else's computer," is true. Using someone else's computers on the Internet – regardless of what the marketing department names it – places the responsibility for the security and integrity of your data firmly on someone else's network and their security precautions – none of which you have control over and for which you will be unable to get a detailed technical description.

There are many ways to share files such as NFS, HTTP, SAMBA, and FTP, or FTPS (Secure FTP), and VSFTP (Very Secure FTP). Although SCP (Secure CoPy), which is part of SSH which we covered in Chapter 5 of this volume, can be used for secure file transfers, it is not a file sharing tool. If you have SSH access to a remote computer, you can transfer any files to which you have access between those computers.

The Fedora online documentation[2] contains information in the System Administration Guide about SAMBA, FTP, and VSFTP.

File sharing use cases

OK, so file sharing is an obvious thing to do in our highly connected world, but what does that mean? There are different reasons to share files – use cases – and different tools work best for each. Let's look at some of these use cases and the tools best suited for each. We will then explore some of those tools as we proceed through the rest of this chapter.

---

[2]Fedora Project, Documentation web site, `https://docs.fedoraproject.org/en-US/docs/`

- **Downloading files** – This type of transaction is one way downloading only. For example, the ISO image files you downloaded from the Fedora download site and the files you can download from the Apress GitHub web site that are a part of this course. Files can be stored on hosts within the local network or on the Internet.

  File downloads can use several protocols, including FTP, FTP over SSL/TLS (FTPS), and SSH File Transfer Protocol (SFTP). Tools like FTP (File Transfer Protocol), SFTP (Simple File Transfer Protocol), wget, and even your web browser can be used to download files. Graphical tools like FileZilla can also be used to download files using many protocols. We will look at FTP and HTTP for downloading files from a central location.

- **Shared access** – This type of sharing tends to be about sharing local network access to files for reference purposes. For example, we may all need access to an organizational email and telephone directory. We can open the file for reading and obtain the information we need from the document. We will use NFS (Network File System) and SAMBA for this type of access. Tools like FTP, the SAMBA client, and SSH File Transfer Protocol (SFTP) can be used to download files for local access.

  In this type of use case, files are usually updated by one person working with a local copy of the file and then uploaded or transferred to the directory from which it will be downloaded or viewed.

- **Simple collaboration** – In this type of use case, one user at a time can access the file in its shared location to make changes to it. We can use tools such as NFS (Network File System) and SAMBA for this type of access.

- **Team collaboration** – Working on the same shared files – sometimes simultaneously – can be a powerful collaborative tool. Google Drive is an example of this type of sharing. We will not be setting up this type of collaborative file sharing in this course, but there are many commercial tools[3] available that can facilitate collaboration like this.

---

[3]Mashable.com, `https://mashable.com/2014/03/06/file-sharing-tools/`

Preparation

We will need to create a place that we can use to share files from during many of these experiments. So we need to do a little preparation. All FTP services including VSFTP use the /var/ftp directory, and we will add files to that directory after we install VSFTP in Experiment 13-2.

EXPERIMENT 13-1

Perform this experiment as the root user on StudentVM2. In this experiment, we create a directory named "/var/shared" for a mount point and a small logical volume to mount there to contain the data.

We now create a new filesystem and mountpoint. Start by creating a new filesystem to export. Remember that NFS can only export complete filesystems. We intentionally left some space unallocated in the volume group fedora_studentvm1 when we initially installed Linux. We will use a bit of that space to create our NFS share. Verify the total amount of space left on the volume group.

```
[root@studentvm2 ~]# vgs
  VG                 #PV #LV #SN Attr   VSize   VFree
  fedora_studentvm1    1   6   0 wz--n- <59.00g <21.00g
[root@studentvm2 ~]#
```

The remaining 21GB is more than enough space to create the new logical volume. Create a new LV with a size of 1GB and a name of shared.

```
[root@studentvm2 ~]# lvcreate -L 1G fedora_studentvm1 -n shared
Create the filesystem.
```

```
[root@studentvm2 ~]# mkfs -t ext4 /dev/mapper/fedora_studentvm1-shared
mke2fs 1.44.6 (5-Mar-2019)
Creating filesystem with 262144 4k blocks and 65536 inodes
Filesystem UUID: dba1207b-c36e-468b-82d8-666231143ef6
Superblock backups stored on blocks:
        32768, 98304, 163840, 229376
```

```
Allocating group tables: done
Writing inode tables: done
Creating journal (8192 blocks): done
Writing superblocks and filesystem accounting information: done
```

Add a label to the filesystem.

[root@studentvm2 ~]# **e2label /dev/mapper/fedora_studentvm1-shared shared**

Create the mountpoint.

[root@studentvm2 ~]# **mkdir /var/shared**

Add the following line to rge end of the /etc/fstab file.

```
LABEL=shared    /var/shared    ext4    defaults    0 0
```

Mount the filesystem.

[root@studentvm2 etc]# **mount /var/shared/**

Copy some files into the new filesystem or create a few files. You just want something in the filesystem so you can see them when the filesystem is accessed by a remote host. I copied some files from the root directory and created some text files with a bit of content. Only a couple dozen or so will be needed. I used the following CLI program to do that.

```
[root@studentvm2 shared]# cd /var/shared ; I=0 ; for I in `seq -w 1 25` ; do
echo "This is file $I" > file-$I.txt ; done ; ll
total 188
-rw------- 1 root root  2118 Aug  1 21:11 anaconda-ks.cfg
-rw-r--r-- 1 root root 39514 Aug  1 21:11 Chapter-36.tgz
-rw-r--r-- 1 root root    16 Aug  7 16:35 file-01.txt
-rw-r--r-- 1 root root    16 Aug  7 16:35 file-02.txt
-rw-r--r-- 1 root root    16 Aug  7 16:35 file-03.txt
-rw-r--r-- 1 root root    16 Aug  7 16:35 file-04.txt
-rw-r--r-- 1 root root    16 Aug  7 16:35 file-05.txt
-rw-r--r-- 1 root root    16 Aug  7 16:35 file-06.txt
-rw-r--r-- 1 root root    16 Aug  7 16:35 file-07.txt
-rw-r--r-- 1 root root    16 Aug  7 16:35 file-08.txt
```

```
-rw-r--r-- 1 root root     16 Aug  7 16:35 file-09.txt
-rw-r--r-- 1 root root     16 Aug  7 16:35 file-10.txt
-rw-r--r-- 1 root root     16 Aug  7 16:35 file-11.txt
-rw-r--r-- 1 root root     16 Aug  7 16:35 file-12.txt
-rw-r--r-- 1 root root     16 Aug  7 16:35 file-13.txt
-rw-r--r-- 1 root root     16 Aug  7 16:35 file-14.txt
-rw-r--r-- 1 root root     16 Aug  7 16:35 file-15.txt
-rw-r--r-- 1 root root     16 Aug  7 16:35 file-16.txt
-rw-r--r-- 1 root root     16 Aug  7 16:35 file-17.txt
-rw-r--r-- 1 root root     16 Aug  7 16:35 file-18.txt
-rw-r--r-- 1 root root     16 Aug  7 16:35 file-19.txt
-rw-r--r-- 1 root root     16 Aug  7 16:35 file-20.txt
-rw-r--r-- 1 root root     16 Aug  7 16:35 file-21.txt
-rw-r--r-- 1 root root     16 Aug  7 16:35 file-22.txt
-rw-r--r-- 1 root root     16 Aug  7 16:35 file-23.txt
-rw-r--r-- 1 root root     16 Aug  7 16:35 file-24.txt
-rw-r--r-- 1 root root     16 Aug  7 16:35 file-25.txt
-rw-r--r-- 1 root root    469 Aug  1 21:11 ifcfg-enp0s3
-rw-r--r-- 1 root root    370 Aug  1 21:11 ifcfg-enp0s3.bak
-rw-r--r-- 1 root root    340 Aug  1 21:11 ifcfg-enp0s8.bak
-rw------- 1 root root   3123 Aug  1 21:11 imapd.pem
-rw-r--r-- 1 root root   2196 Aug  1 21:11 initial-setup-ks.cfg
drwx------ 2 root root  16384 Aug  1 21:05 lost+found
-rwxr-x--- 1 root root    272 Aug  1 21:11 restartmail
-rw-r--r-- 1 root root     10 Aug  1 21:11 testfile.txt
[root@studentvm2 shared]#
```

We will use this directory and its contents for several experiments using different file sharing tools.

As a last bit of preparation, open a root terminal session on StudentVM1 and use **tcpdump** to monitor the data stream on enp0s3. Place the terminal session in a place on the desktop where it can be seen while performing the rest of these experiments. Be sure to monitor the data stream in this terminal session.

FTP and FTPS

FTP (File Transfer Protocol)[4] is an old and insecure method for sharing files. This lack of security is because the data transfer stream is not encrypted and so any data transferred may be easily read if intercepted. Because of its lack of security, FTP has been upgraded with a newer, secure version, FTPS.[5] FTPS merely adds a security layer over FTP and is called FTP over SSL (Secure Socket Layer). With FTPS, one can do the same things as with FTP but in a more secure manner.

Fedora does provide an FTP server written in Java. This is not the historical Washington University FTP server, wu-ftpd. Fedora does not provide either a recent version of the wu-ftpd server or a version of an FTPS server, so we will not cover those.

VSFTP

Fedora does provide version 3.0.3 of the VSFTP (Very Secure FTP)[6] server for Fedora 29 and 30. This is the most recent version as of July 2015. VSFTP is the primary FTP server provided with current Fedora releases although it is not installed by default. VSFTP, like other FTP services, provides the ability for FTP clients to download files from a server. It is not a collaboration service.

VSFTP is more secure because it provides encryption using SSL and it provides significant protection from privilege escalation. Developed from scratch by Chris Evans with security in mind, VSFTP minimizes the use of elevated privileges and uses unprivileged threads for most tasks. You can read the details at the web site in footnote 6.

VSFTP scales up very nicely compared to other FTP servers. One user quoted on the VSFTP web site says that they have a single VSFTP server running and that over a 24-hour period served 2.6 TeraBytes of data with more than 1,500 concurrent users at times. VSFTP, like other FTP servers, does allow anonymous downloads as well as logged in FTP users with passwords.

Installation and preparation of VSFTP

So let's install and configure VSFTP.

---

[4]Wikipedia, *File Transfer Protocol*, https://en.wikipedia.org/wiki/File_Transfer_Protocol
[5]Wikipedia, FTPS, https://en.wikipedia.org/wiki/FTPS
[6]VSFTP Web site, https://security.appspot.com/vsftpd.html

EXPERIMENT 13-2

Perform this experiment as the root user on StudentVM2. In this experiment, we will share the files in /var/shared using VSFTP. First we install VSFTP.

```
[root@studentvm2 ~]# dnf -y install vsftpd
```

For now, turn off iptables on StudentVM2. This is so we can configure and test VSFTP without the firewall getting in the way. FTP servers of all types have special needs for firewalls. Taking this out of the equation for now simplifies our initial setup and configuration.

The files served by any FTP server are located in /var/ftp. The /var/ftp/pub directory is for files served to anonymous users. These directories were created during the installation of VSFTP so all we need to do is add some files.

```
[root@studentvm2 ~]# cd /var/ftp ; I=0 ; for I in `seq -w 1 25` ; do echo
"This is file $I" > FTP-file-$I.txt ; done ; ll
total 104
-rw-r--r-- 1 root root   16 Aug  7 21:14 FTP-file-01.txt
-rw-r--r-- 1 root root   16 Aug  7 21:14 FTP-file-02.txt
-rw-r--r-- 1 root root   16 Aug  7 21:14 FTP-file-03.txt
-rw-r--r-- 1 root root   16 Aug  7 21:14 FTP-file-04.txt
-rw-r--r-- 1 root root   16 Aug  7 21:14 FTP-file-05.txt
-rw-r--r-- 1 root root   16 Aug  7 21:14 FTP-file-06.txt
-rw-r--r-- 1 root root   16 Aug  7 21:14 FTP-file-07.txt
-rw-r--r-- 1 root root   16 Aug  7 21:14 FTP-file-08.txt
-rw-r--r-- 1 root root   16 Aug  7 21:14 FTP-file-09.txt
-rw-r--r-- 1 root root   16 Aug  7 21:14 FTP-file-10.txt
-rw-r--r-- 1 root root   16 Aug  7 21:14 FTP-file-11.txt
-rw-r--r-- 1 root root   16 Aug  7 21:14 FTP-file-12.txt
-rw-r--r-- 1 root root   16 Aug  7 21:14 FTP-file-13.txt
-rw-r--r-- 1 root root   16 Aug  7 21:14 FTP-file-14.txt
-rw-r--r-- 1 root root   16 Aug  7 21:14 FTP-file-15.txt
-rw-r--r-- 1 root root   16 Aug  7 21:14 FTP-file-16.txt
-rw-r--r-- 1 root root   16 Aug  7 21:14 FTP-file-17.txt
-rw-r--r-- 1 root root   16 Aug  7 21:14 FTP-file-18.txt
-rw-r--r-- 1 root root   16 Aug  7 21:14 FTP-file-19.txt
-rw-r--r-- 1 root root   16 Aug  7 21:14 FTP-file-20.txt
-rw-r--r-- 1 root root   16 Aug  7 21:14 FTP-file-21.txt
```

```
-rw-r--r-- 1 root root    16 Aug  7 21:14 FTP-file-22.txt
-rw-r--r-- 1 root root    16 Aug  7 21:14 FTP-file-23.txt
-rw-r--r-- 1 root root    16 Aug  7 21:14 FTP-file-24.txt
-rw-r--r-- 1 root root    16 Aug  7 21:14 FTP-file-25.txt
drwxr-xr-x 2 root root 4096 Jul 25  2018 pub
[root@studentvm2 ftp]#
```

VSFTP is configured using the file, /etc/vsftpd/vsftpd.conf. This file is well commented, so I suggest you read it to understand what can be configured with it.

The default configuration is designed to listen to IPV6 only,[7] but it will work for us on IPV4 with only a couple changes. Near the bottom of the file, locate and change **listen=NO** to **listen=YES**. This allows vsftp to listen on IPv4. Then turn off IPv6 by changing **listen_ipv6=YES** to **listen_ipv6=NO**.

Start the vsftpd service and verify the result.

```
[root@studentvm2 ftp]# systemctl start vsftpd
[root@studentvm2 ftp]# systemctl status vsftpd
• vsftpd.service - Vsftpd ftp daemon
   Loaded: loaded (/usr/lib/systemd/system/vsftpd.service; disabled; vendor
   preset: disabled)
   Active: active (running) since Wed 2019-08-07 21:28:45 EDT; 8s ago
  Process: 13362 ExecStart=/usr/sbin/vsftpd /etc/vsftpd/vsftpd.conf
  (code=exited, status=0/SUCCESS)
 Main PID: 13363 (vsftpd)
    Tasks: 1 (limit: 4696)
   Memory: 496.0K
   CGroup: /system.slice/vsftpd.service
           └─13363 /usr/sbin/vsftpd /etc/vsftpd/vsftpd.conf

Aug 07 21:28:45 studentvm2.example.com systemd[1]: Starting Vsftpd ftp
daemon...
Aug 07 21:28:45 studentvm2.example.com systemd[1]: Started Vsftpd ftp daemon.
[root@studentvm2 ftp]#
```

---

[7]My interpretation of the comments surrounding the listen= and listen_ipv6= config items is that the default settings should cause VSFTP to listen on both IPV4 and IPV6. That is either incorrect or I have misunderstood. In any event, use the settings I described earlier to enable IPV4 connectivity for VSFTP.

The FTP client

Now that the server is configured, we can install the FTP client on StudentVM1 and then test file downloads. When doing downloads, the files are downloaded to the PWD that was in effect when you started the FTP client, unless you specify a different download directory.

EXPERIMENT 13-3

As root on StudentVM1, install the ftp client.

```
[root@studentvm1 ~]$ dnf -y install ftp
```

No configuration is required for the client, so we can go right to our first test. Because we are the student user on StudentVM1 and there is also a student user on StudentVM2, we can use that account for our FTP login.

```
[student@studentvm1 ~]$ ftp studentvm2
Connected to studentvm2 (192.168.56.1).
220 (vsFTPd 3.0.3)
Name (studentvm2:student): <Press Enter>
331 Please specify the password.
Password:<Enter password>
230 Login successful.
Remote system type is UNIX.
Using binary mode to transfer files.
```

Help is available if you need it.

```
ftp> help
Commands may be abbreviated.  Commands are:

!          debug        mdir      sendport    site
$          dir          mget      put         size
account    disconnect   mkdir     pwd         status
append     exit         mls       quit        struct
ascii      form         mode      quote       system
bell       get          modtime   recv        sunique
binary     glob         mput      reget       tenex
bye        hash         newer     rstatus     tick
```

case	help	nmap	rhelp	trace
cd	idle	nlist	rename	type
cdup	image	ntrans	reset	user
chmod	lcd	open	restart	umask
close	ls	prompt	rmdir	verbose
cr	macdef	passive	runique	?
delete	mdelete	proxy	send	

```
ftp> help ls
ls        list contents of remote directory
ftp> help get
get       receive file
ftp>
```

Now list the files in the remote directory.

```
ftp> ls
227 Entering Passive Mode (192,168,56,1,226,161).
150 Here comes the directory listing.
drwxr-xr-x    2 1000      1000         4096 Dec 24   2018 Desktop
drwxr-xr-x    2 1000      1000         4096 Dec 22   2018 Documents
drwxr-xr-x    2 1000      1000         4096 Dec 22   2018 Downloads
drwxr-xr-x    2 1000      1000         4096 Aug 02 12:11 Mail
drwxr-xr-x    2 1000      1000         4096 Dec 22   2018 Music
drwxr-xr-x    2 1000      1000         4096 Dec 22   2018 Pictures
drwxr-xr-x    2 1000      1000         4096 Dec 22   2018 Public
drwxr-xr-x    2 1000      1000         4096 Dec 22   2018 Templates
drwxr-xr-x    2 1000      1000         4096 Dec 22   2018 Videos
-rw-------    1 1000      1000            2 Jul 01 15:01 dead.letter
-rw-rw-r--    1 1000      1000       256000 Jun 19 12:16 random.txt
-rw-rw-r--    1 1000      1000       256000 Jun 20 12:26 textfile.txt
226 Directory send OK.
```

This is a listing of the home directory for the student user on the remote host, StudentVM2. This is the default action when doing a login on a remote host. For now, let's just go with this and download a file to our account on StudentVM2.

If you have been doing all of the experiments in this course, there should be a file named random.txt in the student home directory of StudentVM2. Download that file – or another one if you do not have random.txt.

```
ftp> get random.txt
local: random.txt remote: random.txt
227 Entering Passive Mode (192,168,56,1,33,129).
150 Opening BINARY mode data connection for random.txt (256000 bytes).
226 Transfer complete.
256000 bytes received in 0.0413 secs (6193.45 Kbytes/sec)
```

Verify that the file was downloaded as the student user on StudentVM1.

```
[student@studentvm1 ~]$ ll
total 1504
drwxrwxr-x  2 student student   4096 Mar  2 08:21 chapter25
drwxrwxr-x  2 student student   4096 Mar 21 15:27 chapter26
<snip>
-rw-rw-r--  1 student student 256000 Aug  8 12:16 random.txt
<snip>
drwxr-xr-x. 2 student student   4096 Dec 22  2018 Videos
[student@studentvm1 ~]$
```

We now know that the VSFTP server is working, but we still have a few bits to work out.

Firewall configuration for FTP

We still need to reactivate our firewall and configure it to allow FTP services through it.

Before we do that, let's look at how FTP protocols work in order to understand the problem it generates for configuring the firewall. FTP has two modes that can be used for file transfer: active and passive. These two modes work a bit differently, and the difference is important to SysAdmins and the configuration of the firewall. The web site Slacksite.com[8] has an excellent explanation of active vs. passive FTP connections and the issues had by each. The Fedora documentation[9] has a good explanation of VSFTP and other file sharing tools.

---

[8]Slacksite.com, *Active FTP vs. Passive FTP, a Definitive Explanation*, https://slacksite.com/other/ftp.html

[9]Fedora 30 Documentation, *System Administrators Guide, File and Print Servers*, https://docs.fedoraproject.org/en-US/fedora/f30/system-administrators-guide/servers/File_and_Print_Servers/

Active mode

The active mode of FTP is the one which causes problems. This short description will help illustrate why that is the case.

1. The FTP client initiates a connection to the server from a randomly selected, high-numbered, unprivileged[10] TCP port – we will use port number 1547 for this explanation – to the destination port number 21 on the server. Port 1547 is the control port for the client, and port 21 is the server's FTP control port. The client sends the command **port 1547** to the server to indicate the number of the control port.

2. The server acknowledges this by sending an ACK reply to the client from port 21 to port 1547.

3. The server now initiates a data connection from its port 20 to port 1548 on the client. The protocol always assumes that the data port is one higher than the control port. This step is the cause of the problem because the server initiates a connection to the client.

4. If the server can reach port 1548 and initiate the connection, the client sends an ACK to the server.

Remember the following lines from the filter table in our firewall rules?

```
-A INPUT -m state --state RELATED,ESTABLISHED -j ACCEPT
<snip>
-A INPUT -j REJECT --reject-with icmp-host-prohibited
```

These two lines work together to prevent connections from the outside world being made to the local host – whether server or client. If any other host attempts to open a connection to our client host, StudentVM1, the first line of the INPUT chain will not be matched so the rest of the rules in the INPUT chain are checked. Because no rule matches port 1548, the last rule in this chain rejects the attempted connection. This is why we get "No route to host" error messages, as you will see in the next experiment.

---

[10]Privileged ports are numbered from 0 to 1023 and are assigned to specific services. Ports with higher numbers are unprivileged and can be used for almost anything. However, some of these higher ports have specific services that have been used by long practice and convention and which have become de facto standards. Check the /etc/services file for specific assignments.

The ports that the client can use for the command and data connections are randomly selected from the range 1024 to 65536. This means we would need to open up all of those ports which creates a severe vulnerability and opens our host up to attack.

Passive mode

In passive mode, FTP works a bit differently as client initiates all of the connections. This means that the "state related, established" rule in our firewall would have a record of the connection and allow the server's response packet through. We can also specify a much-limited range of non-privileged ports for use by FTP when making the data connections.

Let's see how that works. For this illustration, let's assume that ports 65000 through 65534 are to be used for FTP. We will configure this in the next experiment.

1. The FTP client initiates a connection to the server from a randomly selected, high-numbered, unprivileged TCP port within the specified range – we will use port number 4048 for this explanation – to the destination port number 21 on the server. Port 4048 is the control port for the client, and port 21 is the server's FTP control port. The client sends the **PASV** (passive) command to the server. Note that the control port number does not need to be within the defined range and the client would not know that range in any event.

2. The server acknowledges this by sending an ACK reply to the client from port 21 to port 4048. The reply from the server contains the number of the data port from the defined range so that the client will know where to listen for the data stream. We will use port 65248 for the data connection.

3. The client now initiates a data connection from its port 4049, the data port, to port 65248 on the server.

4. If the client can reach port 65248 and initiate the connection, the server sends an ACK to the client and the data transfer can begin.

If the server is expected to handle very large amounts of FTP traffic, the size of the range of ports defined on the VSFTP server will need to be much larger than we have defined here. The key is that we can control this range and create firewall rules on the server to accommodate this.

Setting the firewall rules

Now that we know that the client establishes both the control and data connections to the FTP server, we can create a much more restrictive set of firewall rules. This is aided by the fact that we can control the range of ports used by the server to which send the data.

EXPERIMENT 13-4

We need to configure our firewall for FTP, and this gets a bit complex because of the way that the FTP protocols work.

In active mode, VSFTP uses the standard TCP ports for FTP, 20 and 21, but we are using passive mode which only requires port 21 on the privileged port range. We need to open our firewall to those two ports. Port 20 is for data transfer and port 21 is for command transfer. As root on StudentVM2, add entries for that in the firewall.

Now try an FTP session.

```
[student@studentvm1 ~]$ ftp studentvm2
Connected to studentvm2 (192.168.56.1).
220 (vsFTPd 3.0.3)
Name (studentvm2:student): <Enter>
331 Please specify the password.
Password:<Password>
230 Login successful.
Remote system type is UNIX.
Using binary mode to transfer files.
ftp> ls
227 Entering Passive Mode (192,168,56,1,177,55).
ftp: connect: No route to host
ftp> bye
221 Goodbye.
[student@studentvm1 ~]$
```

But there is still a problem because we get an error with this. The "No route to host" error indicates a firewall problem. The reason for this, as we have seen, is that the FTP protocol uses random high TCP ports as part of its connection and we need to open a wide range of ports on the server, StudentVM2, in order to allow these communication channels.

We can solve this in part by limiting the range of high-numbered ports in the vsftpd.conf file. Add the following lines to the end of that file. Then restart VSFTPD.

```
# Added to limit passive port ranges for better firewall control.
pasv_min_port=65000
pasv_max_port=65534
```

The second part of the solution is to add the following line to the INPUT chain of the Filter table in the iptables file. You can also delete the rule to allow port 20 because that is not needed in passive mode. Restore the iptables rules.

```
# FTP High ports
-A INPUT -p tcp -m state --state NEW -m tcp --dport 65000:65534 -j ACCEPT
```

As the student user on StudentVM1, use FTP to connect to StudentVM2 again. Use the **ls** command to verify that the FTP connection is now working as it should.

Statefulness prevents crackers from accessing our server through the high-numbered open ports. If the client has not initiated the connection to the FTP server, and some random host from the Internet attempts to initiate a connection to our server, even on those now open ports, it will be unable to do so. This is because our server did not initiate the connection and there is no record of a connection so this new connection attempt is rejected.

Anonymous FTP access

When logged in to a remote host using a valid account, such as student, the user has access to every directory and file on that host that they would if logged in locally. This is a major security issue if we were to give out accounts to just anyone. We need a way to limit FTP access.

Anonymous FTP access is the tool that can help with that. This is the type of access most of us are familiar with when we download files from a remote FTP server. It is called anonymous because anyone accessing the share files can do so without a unique account on the server. All that is required to access an anonymous FTP site is a generic username. Most FTP servers use "anonymous" or "ftp" for the username. No password is required. But this also opens up our public FTP directory to access by everyone on the Internet.

EXPERIMENT 13-5

We need to alter the vsftpd.conf file to allow anonymous FTP access.

As root on StudentVM2, edit vsftpd.conf. Find the statement **anonymous_enable=NO** and change it to **anonymous_enable=YES**. Then restart the VSFTPD service.

As the student user on StudentVM1, test the result by entering "anonymous" as the user account in the Name field. When prompted for the password, just press the **Enter** key.

```
[student@studentvm1 ~]$ ftp studentvm2
Connected to studentvm2 (192.168.56.1).
220 (vsFTPd 3.0.3)
Name (studentvm2:student): anonymous
331 Please specify the password.
Password:<Enter>
230 Login successful.
Remote system type is UNIX.
Using binary mode to transfer files.
ftp> ls
227 Entering Passive Mode (192,168,56,1,254,134).
150 Here comes the directory listing.
-rw-r--r--    1 65534    65534          16 Aug 08 01:14 FTP-file-01.txt
-rw-r--r--    1 65534    65534          16 Aug 08 01:14 FTP-file-02.txt
-rw-r--r--    1 65534    65534          16 Aug 08 01:14 FTP-file-03.txt
-rw-r--r--    1 65534    65534          16 Aug 08 01:14 FTP-file-04.txt
<snip>
-rw-r--r--    1 65534    65534          16 Aug 08 01:14 FTP-file-24.txt
-rw-r--r--    1 65534    65534          16 Aug 08 01:14 FTP-file-25.txt
drwxr-xr-x    2 65534    65534        4096 Jul 25  2018 pub
226 Directory send OK.
ftp>
```

Notice that the VSFTP server logs us into the /var/ftp directory. Download one of the files from there and verify that it was transferred to your PWD.

Close the FTP connection.

Securing VSFTP with encryption

The final bit of security we can use with VSFTP is to encrypt the data while it is being transferred. For this, we need to create a certificate that can be used with FTP. We have already created a certificate for email and this will be similar.

EXPERIMENT 13-6

Start this experiment as the root user on StudentVM2.

Generate a self-signed certificate for IMAP. The openssl program can be used to create a certificate that we can use with FTP like the ones that we created in Chapter 8 of this volume for SMTP and IMAP. Enter the requested data as shown in bold. Do this as root in root's home directory. This command does not specify a time limit for the certificate so it never expires.

```
[root@studentvm2 ~]# openssl req -x509 -nodes -newkey rsa:2048 -keyout /etc/
ssl/private/vsftpd.key -out /etc/ssl/certs/vsftpd.crt
.................................................................................
.........................................................................+++++
........................+++++
writing new private key to 'vsftpd.key'
-----
You are about to be asked to enter information that will be incorporated
into your certificate request.
What you are about to enter is what is called a Distinguished Name or a DN.
There are quite a few fields but you can leave some blank
For some fields there will be a default value,
If you enter '.', the field will be left blank.
-----
Country Name (2 letter code) [XX]:US
State or Province Name (full name) []:North Carolina
Locality Name (eg, city) [Default City]:Raleigh
Organization Name (eg, company) [Default Company Ltd]:<Enter>
Organizational Unit Name (eg, section) []:<Enter>
Common Name (eg, your name or your server's hostname) []:studentvm2.example.com
Email Address []:student@example.com
```

This command places the key file and the certificate in the correct locations. Edit the vsftpd. conf file and add the following lines at the bottom. My comments are intended to describe the function of each line but are not required to be in the csftpd.conf file. I like to keep them there so I can refresh my memory later, if need be.

```
# Configuration statements required for data encryption
# Defines the location of the certification file
rsa_cert_file=/etc/ssl/certs/vsftpd.crt
# Defines the location of the key file for the certification
rsa_private_key_file=/etc/ssl/private/vsftpd.key
# Enables SSL support
ssl_enable=YES
# We will not allow SSL used for anonymous users.
# Since this is usually the general public, what would be the point?
allow_anon_ssl=NO
# Local data connections will always use SSL.
force_local_data_ssl=YES
# Local logins will always use SSL. This is for the control port.
force_local_logins_ssl=YES
# Strong encryption with fewer vulnerabilities using TLS version 1.
ssl_tlsv1=YES
# Not secure enough so we won't use SSL versions or 3.
ssl_sslv2=NO
ssl_sslv3=NO
# Improves security by helping prevent man-in-the-middle attacks.
# May cause connections to drop out so set to NO if that occurs.
require_ssl_reuse=YES
# Requires stronger encryption.
ssl_ciphers=HIGH
```

Restart the vsftpd service. First log into an FTP session from StudentVM1 as an anonymous user that should work. Now log in as the student user and see what happens.

```
[student@studentvm1 ~]$ ftp studentvm2
Connected to studentvm2 (192.168.56.1).
220 (vsFTPd 3.0.3)
Name (studentvm2:student): <Enter>
530 Non-anonymous sessions must use encryption.
```

```
Login failed.
421 Service not available, remote server has closed connection
ftp>
```

But the command line FTP client does not support encryption. So is this encryption useless from the command line? Just wait.

Leave the VSFTP server running because we will use it in another experiment later in this chapter.

We now have the server set up to support encryption. The problem is that the Linux command-line ftp program does not support encryption. This means that using the FTP client from the command line is still not secure. This is one of the issues with FTP. There is a command line solution that we will explore later in this chapter.

NFS

The Network File System (NFS) was created by Sun Microsystems to share disk resources and the files they contain among many hosts. NFS is based upon the version of the RPC[11] (Remote Procedure Call) protocol developed by Sun.

One advantage of NFS as a means to share files is that the client hosts can mount the shares in the same way as they would any local filesystem. This means that files do not need to be downloaded; they can be accessed directly on the server by file managers and modified remotely by application programs. This is simple collaboration in that only a single user at a time should modify the file, although it may be simultaneously viewed by multiple users. NFS does not provide a locking mechanism to prevent multiple users from simultaneously editing files and overwriting each other's changes.

This section guides you through the tasks of exporting a filesystem and mounting an NFS remote filesystem.

NFS server

The NFS server is designed to share filesystems of the host acting as a server to a network so that NFS clients can mount the shared filesystems and access the files contained in them. The question of where in the filesystem structure to place filesystems that are to

---

[11]Wikipedia, *Remote Procedure Call*, https://en.wikipedia.org/wiki/Remote_procedure_call

be exported has different answers. Some SysAdmins place them at the root (/) of the filesystem, while others add them to a mount point in /var. For these experiments, we will place them in /var.

EXPERIMENT 13-7

Perform this experiment as the root user on StudentVM2. We first need to verify that some packages are installed. Check with the **dnf list** command.

```
[root@studentvm2 ~]# dnf list rpcbind nfs-utils
Last metadata expiration check: 0:00:25 ago on Thu 01 Aug 2019 03:24:12 PM
EDT.
Installed Packages
nfs-utils.x86_64          1:2.3.3-1.rc2.fc29                    @updates
rpcbind.x86_64            1.2.5-0.fc29                         @anaconda
```

The results on my VM show that these packages are already installed. If not, do so now.

Configure the /etc/exports file which is empty by default. It is only necessary to add one line for each filesystem to be exported. Add the following lines to export the /shared filesystem.

```
# Exports file for studentvm1
/var/shared              *(rw,sync,all_squash)
```

The rw option means to share it as read/write; the sync option means that the directory should be synced after changes are made and before other read requests are fulfilled. This helps to ensure that the most recent version of altered or new files are available as soon as the changes are made. The all_squash option changes the shared versions of files to the anonymous user ownership of nobody.nobody. The ownership in the shared directory on the server does not change, only the apparent ownership at the client end.

Restart and enable the RPC services and NFS.

```
[root@studentvm2 etc]# for I in rpcbind nfs-server ; do systemctl enable
$I.service ; systemctl start $I.service ; done
Created symlink /etc/systemd/system/multi-user.target.wants/rpcbind.service
→ /usr/lib/systemd/system/rpcbind.service.
Created symlink /etc/systemd/system/multi-user.target.wants/nfs-server.
service → /usr/lib/systemd/system/nfs-server.service.
```

And export the defined filesystem. The a option means to export all configured directories, and the v option means verbose so that we can see the result.

```
[root@studentvm2 etc]# exportfs -av
exporting *:/var/shared
[root@studentvm2 etc]#
```

Now verify that the filesystem has been shared and can be seen locally. The e option means to show the host's list of exported directories.

```
[root@studentvm2 etc]# showmount -e localhost
Export list for localhost:
/var/shared *
[root@studentvm2 etc]#
```

Now do the same as root on StudentVM1. You will receive an error.

```
[root@studentvm1 ~]# showmount -e studentvm2
clnt_create: RPC: Unable to receive
[root@studentvm1 ~]#
```

We must add firewall rules to allow other hosts to access the NFS share. NFS can use many ports, so we need to know which ones are being used. Use the following command on StudentVM2 to determine the ports being used by NFS and the related RPC services.

```
[root@studentvm2 etc]# rpcinfo -p
   program vers proto   port  service
    100000    4   tcp    111  portmapper
    100000    3   tcp    111  portmapper
    100000    2   tcp    111  portmapper
    100000    4   udp    111  portmapper
    100000    3   udp    111  portmapper
    100000    2   udp    111  portmapper
    100024    1   udp  57516  status
    100024    1   tcp  58993  status
    100005    1   udp  20048  mountd
    100005    1   tcp  20048  mountd
    100005    2   udp  20048  mountd
    100005    2   tcp  20048  mountd
```

```
100005    3    udp   20048   mountd
100005    3    tcp   20048   mountd
100003    3    tcp    2049   nfs
100003    4    tcp    2049   nfs
100227    3    tcp    2049   nfs_acl
100021    1    udp   46887   nlockmgr
100021    3    udp   46887   nlockmgr
100021    4    udp   46887   nlockmgr
100021    1    tcp   32933   nlockmgr
100021    3    tcp   32933   nlockmgr
100021    4    tcp   32933   nlockmgr
[root@studentvm2 etc]#
```

Note that the status ports are likely to change when the server reboots. You should be prepared for that in a production environment.

Add the necessary lines to your IPTables rule set to allow NFS and RPC access to your studentvm1 host. All of these rules are for RPC and NFS-related ports. Be sure you add IPTables rules for both TCP and UDP protocols where required.

You could add the firewall rules by entering them individually; however, we won't do it that way because there is a much easier way, especially since we can create a simple command line program that gives a list of the ports used by RPC and NFS. By looking at the preceding list, you can see that both TCP and UDP protocols are used on every required port. Let's look at the list of unique ports.

```
[root@studentvm2 etc]# rpcinfo -p | awk '{print $4}' | grep -v port | uniq |
sort -n
111
2049
20048
43099
47354
57516
58993
[root@studentvm2 etc]#
```

The following command line program will generate the rules we need to add to our firewall, but it will not change the running rule set. We could do that but then we would have to save the active rule set to the /etc/sysconfig/iptables file. That would overwrite any comment lines we might have added to the saved rule set. We will generate the new rules to STDOUT, save them as a separate file, import them into the iptables file, and then use **iptables-restore** to "restore" the iptables file into the active rule set.

You could enter the CLI program all on one line, but that would be a very long line. Entering it on separate lines makes it easier to read and understand.

Pressing the Enter key after the "**; do**" in the first line tells the Bash shell that there are more lines to come. The greater than sign (**>**) prompts you for the next line of input. Press the **Enter** key after each line and you will be prompted for another line. No part of the command line program is executed until the terminating **done** statement is entered. At that time, the entire CLI program is run.

We use the **uniq** command to ensure that only one rule is added per port and protocol. Make the root home directory the PWD.

```
[root@studentvm2 ~]# for I in `rpcinfo -p | awk '{print $4}' | grep -v port |
uniq | sort -n`;do
> echo "-A INPUT -p tcp -m state --state NEW -m tcp --dport $I -j ACCEPT" >>
new-rules
> echo "-A INPUT -p udp -m state --state NEW -m udp --dport $I -j ACCEPT" >>
new-rules
> done
[root@studentvm2 ~]# cat new-rules
-A INPUT -p tcp -m state --state NEW -m tcp --dport 111 -j ACCEPT
-A INPUT -p udp -m state --state NEW -m udp --dport 111 -j ACCEPT
-A INPUT -p tcp -m state --state NEW -m tcp --dport 2049 -j ACCEPT
-A INPUT -p udp -m state --state NEW -m udp --dport 2049 -j ACCEPT
-A INPUT -p tcp -m state --state NEW -m tcp --dport 20048 -j ACCEPT
-A INPUT -p udp -m state --state NEW -m udp --dport 20048 -j ACCEPT
-A INPUT -p tcp -m state --state NEW -m tcp --dport 43099 -j ACCEPT
-A INPUT -p udp -m state --state NEW -m udp --dport 43099 -j ACCEPT
-A INPUT -p tcp -m state --state NEW -m tcp --dport 47354 -j ACCEPT
-A INPUT -p udp -m state --state NEW -m udp --dport 47354 -j ACCEPT
-A INPUT -p tcp -m state --state NEW -m tcp --dport 57516 -j ACCEPT
-A INPUT -p udp -m state --state NEW -m udp --dport 57516 -j ACCEPT
```

```
-A INPUT -p tcp -m state --state NEW -m tcp --dport 58993 -j ACCEPT
-A INPUT -p udp -m state --state NEW -m udp --dport 58993 -j ACCEPT
[root@studentvm2 ~]#
```

Now that we have a new rule set, let's edit /etc/sysconfig/iptables and insert them in an appropriate location. Open /etc/sysconfig/iptables in Vim and place the cursor on the line immediately before the following line:

```
-A INPUT -j REJECT --reject-with icmp-host-prohibited
```

Ensure you are in command mode. Now we will use the (r)ead command to insert the new-rules file after the line on which the cursor resides. Enter the following Vim command.

:r /root/new-rules

Save the revised iptables file which should now look like this. Note that I have a couple rules I was testing commented out because I did not need them but wanted to maintain them in the file for reference. These types of things are why we are adding these rules into the file rather than inserting them directly into the active rule set and then saving that rule set. That would overwrite any of our comments.

```
# sample configuration for iptables service
# you can edit this manually or use system-config-firewall
# please do not ask us to add additional ports/services to this default
configuration
*nat
:INPUT ACCEPT [0:0]
:OUTPUT ACCEPT [0:0]
:POSTROUTING ACCEPT [0:0]
-A POSTROUTING -s 192.168.56.0/24 -j MASQUERADE
COMMIT
*filter
:INPUT ACCEPT [0:0]
:FORWARD ACCEPT [0:0]
:OUTPUT ACCEPT [0:0]
-A INPUT -m state --state RELATED,ESTABLISHED -j ACCEPT
-A INPUT -p icmp -j ACCEPT
-A INPUT -i lo -j ACCEPT
-A INPUT -p tcp -m state --state NEW -m tcp --dport 22 -j ACCEPT
-A INPUT -p tcp -m state --state NEW -m tcp --dport 25 -j ACCEPT
```

```
-A INPUT -p udp -m state --state NEW -m udp --dport 53 -j ACCEPT
-A INPUT -p tcp -m state --state NEW -m tcp --dport 80 -j ACCEPT
-A INPUT -p tcp -m state --state NEW -m tcp --dport 143 -j ACCEPT
# -A INPUT -p tcp -m state --state NEW -m tcp --dport 587 -j ACCEPT
# -A INPUT -p tcp -m state --state NEW -m tcp --dport 993 -j ACCEPT
-A INPUT -p tcp -m state --state NEW -m tcp --dport 111 -j ACCEPT
-A INPUT -p udp -m state --state NEW -m udp --dport 111 -j ACCEPT
-A INPUT -p tcp -m state --state NEW -m tcp --dport 2049 -j ACCEPT
-A INPUT -p udp -m state --state NEW -m udp --dport 2049 -j ACCEPT
-A INPUT -p tcp -m state --state NEW -m tcp --dport 20048 -j ACCEPT
-A INPUT -p udp -m state --state NEW -m udp --dport 20048 -j ACCEPT
-A INPUT -p tcp -m state --state NEW -m tcp --dport 43099 -j ACCEPT
-A INPUT -p udp -m state --state NEW -m udp --dport 43099 -j ACCEPT
-A INPUT -p tcp -m state --state NEW -m tcp --dport 47354 -j ACCEPT
-A INPUT -p udp -m state --state NEW -m udp --dport 47354 -j ACCEPT
-A INPUT -p tcp -m state --state NEW -m tcp --dport 57516 -j ACCEPT
-A INPUT -p udp -m state --state NEW -m udp --dport 57516 -j ACCEPT
-A INPUT -p tcp -m state --state NEW -m tcp --dport 58993 -j ACCEPT
-A INPUT -p udp -m state --state NEW -m udp --dport 58993 -j ACCEPT
-A INPUT -j REJECT --reject-with icmp-host-prohibited
-A FORWARD -m state --state RELATED,ESTABLISHED -j ACCEPT
-A FORWARD -i enpOs8 -j ACCEPT
-A FORWARD -j REJECT --reject-with icmp-host-prohibited
COMMIT
```

Now activate the new rule set. As root, make /etc/sysconfig the PWD and use the following command.

```
[root@studentvm2 sysconfig]# iptables-restore iptables
```

Verify that the new rules are in place and active.

```
[root@studentvm2 sysconfig]# iptables-save
```

The NFS server is now properly configured.

NFS client

Now we can connect to the NFS share from the client, StudentVM1.

EXPERIMENT 13-8

Mounting a remote NFS filesystem is easy. Now let's test whether StudentVM1 can see the shared directory. Do this as root on StudentVM1.

```
[root@studentvm1 ~]# showmount -e studentvm2
Export list for studentvm2:
/var/shared *
[root@studentvm1 ~]#
```

As root on StudentVM1, mount the remote export on the /mnt mount point with the following command. The t option is used to specify that this is an NFS4 filesystem that is being mounted. All recent versions of Fedora use NFS4 which is a more secure and flexible version than NFS3.

```
[root@studentvm1 ~]# mount -t nfs4 studentvm2:/var/shared /mnt
[root@studentvm1 ~]# ll /mnt
total 88
-rw-------  1 root root  2118 Aug  1 21:11 anaconda-ks.cfg
-rw-r--r--  1 root root 39514 Aug  1 21:11 Chapter-36.tgz
-rw-r--r--  1 root root   469 Aug  1 21:11 ifcfg-enp0s3
-rw-r--r--  1 root root   370 Aug  1 21:11 ifcfg-enp0s3.bak
-rw-r--r--  1 root root   340 Aug  1 21:11 ifcfg-enp0s8.bak
-rw-------  1 root root  3123 Aug  1 21:11 imapd.pem
-rw-r--r--  1 root root  2196 Aug  1 21:11 initial-setup-ks.cfg
drwx------  2 root root 16384 Aug  1 21:05 lost+found
-rwxr-x---  1 root root   272 Aug  1 21:11 restartmail
-rw-r--r--  1 root root    10 Aug  1 21:11 testfile.txt
[root@studentvm1 ~]#
```

Use the **mount** command on StudentVM1 to verify that the remote filesystem has been mounted. List the contents of /mnt to verify that the files are there as they should be.

Unmount the NFS. Create a mount point (directory) called /shared. Add the following line to the end of the /etc/fstab file.

```
studentvm2:/var/shared /shared        nfs4       defaults          0 0
```

Mount the NFS export and verify that the mount occurred correctly.

```
[root@studentvm1 ~]# mount /shared
[root@studentvm1 ~]# ll /shared
total 88
-rw-------  1 root root  2118 Aug  1 21:11 anaconda-ks.cfg
-rw-r--r--  1 root root 39514 Aug  1 21:11 Chapter-36.tgz
-rw-r--r--  1 root root   469 Aug  1 21:11 ifcfg-enpOs3
-rw-r--r--  1 root root   370 Aug  1 21:11 ifcfg-enpOs3.bak
-rw-r--r--  1 root root   340 Aug  1 21:11 ifcfg-enpOs8.bak
-rw-------  1 root root  3123 Aug  1 21:11 imapd.pem
-rw-r--r--  1 root root  2196 Aug  1 21:11 initial-setup-ks.cfg
drwx------  2 root root 16384 Aug  1 21:05 lost+found
-rwxr-x---  1 root root   272 Aug  1 21:11 restartmail
-rw-r--r--  1 root root    10 Aug  1 21:11 testfile.txt
[root@studentvm1 ~]#
```

Unmount the /shared directory.

Cleanup

Let's do a little cleanup before we move on to SAMBA.

EXPERIMENT 13-9

Perform this experiment as root.

Unmount the NFS on all hosts where it has been mounted. On your studentvm2 host, run the command **exportfs -uav** to unexport all exported filesystems. Unmount /shared on your studentvm2 host.

Stop the RPC and NFS services. We did not enable them, so they should not start on boot.

This completes cleanup of NFS.

SAMBA

The Samba[12] file sharing service provides a way to share files located on a Linux server with Windows systems. SAMBA is based on the Server Message Block (SMB) protocols. Originally developed by IBM, Microsoft used SMB as the primary protocol in their networking services. SMB is now known as Common Internet File System (CIFS).

SAMBA is the Linux implementation of the CIFS protocol. CIFS provides multiuser remote access and file locking to prevent multiple users from simultaneously altering the file and overwriting previous changes.

We will create a scenario in which we want to use SAMBA to share some files with Windows computers. Of course, Linux systems can also be SAMBA clients so that will make our testing easy since we do not have Windows computer from which to test in our virtual network.

EXPERIMENT 13-10

Start this experiment as root on StudentVM2. First install the required Samba packages. The Samba client should be already installed, it was on my VM, but this will ensure that it is, in addition to installing the SAMBA server.

```
[root@studentvm2 ~]# dnf -y install samba samba-client
```

Create a directory /acs which will be the shared directory. Create or copy a few files into the /acs directory so that they can be shared. I copied some files from my /root directory, which will be different from the ones in your root directory, and then generated a few additional text files using a Bash program. But not too many – no more than a dozen more files would be good.

Make /etc/samba the PWD. The smb.conf.example file contains comments and examples describing how to configure SAMBA to share various resources such as public and private directories, printers, and home directories. Read through this file to get an idea what is possible with SAMBA.

However, the smb.conf file is the one to which we need to add our shared directory. The smb.conf file is a minimal version of smb.conf.example. It has a few starter samples, but we should start our configuration file from scratch. Create a new, empty smb.conf and add the following lines.

---

[12]Wikipedia, *SAMBA*, https://en.wikipedia.org/wiki/Samba_(software)

```
# See smb.conf.example for a more detailed config file or
# read the smb.conf manpage.
# Run 'testparm' to verify the config is correct after
# you modified it.

    workgroup = WORKGROUP
    security = user

    passdb backend = tdbsam

# A publicly accessible directory for ACS files that is read/write
[ACS]
    comment = ACS Directory
    path = /acs
    public = yes
    writable = yes
    printable = no
    browseable = yes
```

Save the smb.conf file but do not exit from the editor. In another terminal session as root, test the syntax of the smb.conf file. It is not necessary to make /etc/samba the PWD.

[root@studentvm2 ~]# **testparm**
rlimit_max: increasing rlimit_max (1024) to minimum Windows limit (16384)
Registered MSG_REQ_POOL_USAGE
Registered MSG_REQ_DMALLOC_MARK and LOG_CHANGED
Load smb config files from /etc/samba/smb.conf
rlimit_max: increasing rlimit_max (1024) to minimum Windows limit (16384)
Processing section "[ACS]"
Loaded services file OK.
Server role: ROLE_STANDALONE

Press enter to see a dump of your service definitions**<Enter>**

```
# Global parameters
        server string = Samba Server Version %v
        workgroup = WORKGROUP
        idmap config * : backend = tdb
```

```
[ACS]
        comment = ACS Directory
        guest ok = Yes
        path = /acs
        read only = No
[root@studentvm2 ~]#
```

We need to open the firewall for Samba. Add rules to the firewall INPUT chain of the filter table that will allow the following TCP ports through the firewall. We do not need to add the UDP ports.

- 137

- 138

- 139

- 445

I suggest doing this by adding the rules in the iptables file and then "restoring" the revised file.

Although it is not required in a Linux environment, the NETBIOS name service is required for SAMBA to fully function in a Windows or mixed Linux and Windows environment. So start both the smb and nmb services.

```
[root@studentvm2 ~]# systemctl start smb ; systemctl start nmb
```

You should also ensure that these services start on boot in a production environment, but it is not required for this experiment.

Create a user ID and password for the user "student" using the **pdbedit** command. Use "lockout" for the password.

```
[root@studentvm2 ~]# pdbedit -a student
new password:<Enter password>
retype new password:<Enter password>
Unix username:        student
NT username:
Account Flags:        [U           ]
User SID:             S-1-5-21-1995892852-683670545-3750803719-1000
Primary Group SID:    S-1-5-21-1995892852-683670545-3750803719-513
Full Name:            Student User
Home Directory:       \\studentvm2\student
HomeDir Drive:
```

```
Logon Script:
Profile Path:           \\studentvm2\student\profile
Domain:                 STUDENTVM2
Account desc:
Workstations:
Munged dial:
Logon time:             0
Logoff time:            Wed, 06 Feb 2036 10:06:39 EST
Kickoff time:           Wed, 06 Feb 2036 10:06:39 EST
Password last set:      Tue, 06 Aug 2019 09:02:13 EDT
Password can change:    Tue, 06 Aug 2019 09:02:13 EDT
Password must change:   never
Last bad password    :  0
Bad password count   :  0
Logon hours          :  FFFFFFFFFFFFFFFFFFFFFFFFFFFFFFFFFFFFFFFFFF
[root@studentvm2 ~]#
```

Now we can perform a quick test of our SAMBA share. As the user student on StudentVM2,
use the **smbclient** command to display the shares on the localhost.

```
[student@studentvm2 ~]$ smbclient -L localhost
Unable to initialize messaging context
Enter WORKGROUP\student's password: <Enter password>

    Sharename       Type        Comment
    ---------       ----        -------
    ACS             Disk        ACS Directory
    IPC$            IPC         IPC Service (Samba 4.9.11)
Reconnecting with SMB1 for workgroup listing.

    Server              Comment
    ---------           -------

    Workgroup           Master
    ---------           -------
    WORKGROUP           STUDENTVM2
[student@studentvm2 ~]$
```

We now have the basics working.

Now that SAMBA is working, let's make a few additions to the smb.conf file. Our basic installation has caused SAMBA to use the local hosts hostname for the workgroup name and that may be incorrect. We may want to use the name of an existing workgroup or create one with a more meaningful name. We can add that information and also add some additional security to our SAMBA installation.

```
┌─────────────────────────────────────────────────────────────────────┐
│                        EXPERIMENT 13-11                              │
└─────────────────────────────────────────────────────────────────────┘
```

Perform this experiment as root on StudentVM2. Copy the following lines from smb.conf. example to the smb.conf file and place it above the ACS stanza.

```
        workgroup = MYGROUP
        server string = Samba Server Version %v

;       netbios name = MYSERVER

;       interfaces = lo eth0 192.168.12.2/24 192.168.13.2/24
;       hosts allow = 127. 192.168.12. 192.168.13.
```

Make the changes highlighted below in this listing which shows the entire file.

```
# See smb.conf.example for a more detailed config file or
# read the smb.conf manpage.
# Run 'testparm' to verify the config is correct after
# you modified it.
```

[global]
```
        workgroup = TESTGROUP
        server string = StudentVM1 - Samba Server Version %v

;       netbios name = MYSERVER

        interfaces = lo enp0s8 192.168.56.1/24
;       hosts allow = 127. 192.168.12. 192.168.13.
```

```
# A publicly accessible directory for ACS files that is read/write
[ACS]
        comment = ACS Directory
        path = /acs
        public = yes
        writable = yes
        printable = no
        browseable = yes
```

We have renamed the workgroup and added a bit more information to the server string. We also added the [global] stanza identifier to positively identify the global section of the file. Lastly, we specified the internal network interface on which SAMBA should listen. This enhances security by limiting the sources from which SAMBA clients can connect. We could also limit connections to specific hosts.

Now check the smb.conf file again.

```
[root@studentvm2 ~]# testparm
rlimit_max: increasing rlimit_max (1024) to minimum Windows limit (16384)
Registered MSG_REQ_POOL_USAGE
Registered MSG_REQ_DMALLOC_MARK and LOG_CHANGED
Load smb config files from /etc/samba/smb.conf
rlimit_max: increasing rlimit_max (1024) to minimum Windows limit (16384)
Processing section "[ACS]"
Loaded services file OK.
Server role: ROLE_STANDALONE
```

Press enter to see a dump of your service definitions**<Enter>**

```
# Global parameters
[global]
        interfaces = lo enp0s8 192.168.56.1/24
        server string = StudentVM1 - Samba Server Version %v
        workgroup = TESTGROUP
        idmap config * : backend = tdb

[ACS]
        comment = ACS Directory
        guest ok = Yes
        path = /acs
        read only = No
[root@studentvm2 ~]#
```

We must restart the smb service or the change to the workgroup name will not take effect, so do that. Now let's do another quick test as the student user.

```
[student@studentvm2 ~]$ smbclient -L localhost
Unable to initialize messaging context
```

```
Enter TESTGROUP\student's password:

    Sharename      Type    Comment
    ---------      ----    -------
    ACS            Disk    ACS Directory
    IPC$           IPC     IPC Service (StudentVM1 - Samba Server Version 4.9.11)
```

Reconnecting with SMB1 for workgroup listing.

```
    Server                 Comment
    ---------              -------

    Workgroup              Master
    ---------              -------
    TESTGROUP              STUDENTVM2
[student@studentvm2 ~]$
```

This looks good, but there is an error that I ran into and I suspect that you did, too. Internet searches discovered many references to this and similar errors but I never found a solution to it. This does not seem to affect the remaining experiments, so you can safely ignore this message.

Using the SAMBA client

Linux has a SAMBA client that allows us to connect with a Linux server using SAMBA to share directories, as well as providing client access to Windows systems that have shared directories.

EXPERIMENT 13-12

As the user student on the StudentVM1 host, make your home directory (~) the PWD. Then log in to the remote share on your student host. The -U option specifies the user ID under which we log in.

```
[student@studentvm1 /]# smbclient //studentvm2/acs -U student
Enter SAMBA\student's password: <Enter password>
Try "help" to get a list of possible commands.
smb: \>
```

Issue **dir**, the Windows equivalent of an **ls** command, to view a listing of the files you placed in the shared directory.

```
smb: \> dir
```

.	D	0	Tue Aug	6	15:25:18	2019
..	D	0	Tue Aug	6	07:59:56	2019
file0.txt	N	15	Tue Aug	6	15:25:18	2019
file10.txt	N	16	Tue Aug	6	15:25:18	2019
file5.txt	N	15	Tue Aug	6	15:25:18	2019
file11.txt	N	16	Tue Aug	6	15:25:18	2019
file13.txt	N	16	Tue Aug	6	15:25:18	2019
file14.txt	N	16	Tue Aug	6	15:25:18	2019
file12.txt	N	16	Tue Aug	6	15:25:18	2019
file6.txt	N	15	Tue Aug	6	15:25:18	2019
imapd.pem	N	3123	Tue Aug	6	15:15:07	2019
new-rules	N	946	Tue Aug	6	15:15:07	2019
testfile.txt	N	10	Tue Aug	6	15:15:07	2019
ifcfg-enp0s8.bak	N	340	Tue Aug	6	15:15:07	2019
ifcfg-enp0s3.bak	N	370	Tue Aug	6	15:15:07	2019
file1.txt	N	15	Tue Aug	6	15:25:18	2019
file3.txt	N	15	Tue Aug	6	15:25:18	2019
file8.txt	N	15	Tue Aug	6	15:25:18	2019
restartmail	N	272	Tue Aug	6	15:15:07	2019
file9.txt	N	15	Tue Aug	6	15:25:18	2019
file7.txt	N	15	Tue Aug	6	15:25:18	2019
ifcfg-enp0s3	N	469	Tue Aug	6	15:15:07	2019
file2.txt	N	15	Tue Aug	6	15:25:18	2019
anaconda-ks.cfg	N	2118	Tue Aug	6	15:15:07	2019
file4.txt	N	15	Tue Aug	6	15:25:18	2019
initial-setup-ks.cfg	N	2196	Tue Aug	6	15:15:07	2019
Chapter-36.tgz	N	39514	Tue Aug	6	15:15:07	2019

```
          1998672 blocks of size 1024. 1833760 blocks available
smb: \>
```

We have a number of commands available in this remote SAMBA session. Use the **help** command to view them and **help <commandname>** to get more information about the individual commands.

Download one of the files from the remote shared directory. Don't exit from this session yet.

```
smb: \> get file4.txt
getting file \file4.txt of size 15 as file4.txt (4.9 KiloBytes/sec) (average
4.9 KiloBytes/sec)
smb: \>
```

In another terminal session as the student user on StudentVM1, list the contents of the home directory. The file you downloaded should be there.

Using the smbclient in this way is much like using FTP. We have a view into a shared directory and the files it contains and we can perform a few operations including a download. We also have the ability to mount a SAMBA share on a mount point. This gives us much more flexible functionality because the shared directory becomes part of the filesystem.

EXPERIMENT 13-13

Start this experiment as the root user on StudentVM1. Verify that the cifs-utils package is installed. If it is not, install it now.

Using the same mount command we use for mounting any other filesystem, mount the /acs share on /mnt. The list the content.

```
[root@studentvm1 ~]# mount -t cifs //studentvm2/acs /mnt
Password for root@//studentvm2/acs:  *******
[root@studentvm1 ~]# ll /mnt
total 25600
-rwxr-xr-x 1 root root  2118 Aug  6 15:15 anaconda-ks.cfg
-rwxr-xr-x 1 root root 39514 Aug  6 15:15 Chapter-36.tgz
-rwxr-xr-x 1 root root    15 Aug  6 15:25 file0.txt
-rwxr-xr-x 1 root root    16 Aug  6 15:25 file10.txt
-rwxr-xr-x 1 root root    16 Aug  6 15:25 file11.txt
-rwxr-xr-x 1 root root    16 Aug  6 15:25 file12.txt
-rwxr-xr-x 1 root root    16 Aug  6 15:25 file13.txt
-rwxr-xr-x 1 root root    16 Aug  6 15:25 file14.txt
-rwxr-xr-x 1 root root    15 Aug  6 15:25 file1.txt
-rwxr-xr-x 1 root root    15 Aug  6 15:25 file2.txt
```

```
-rwxr-xr-x 1 root root     15 Aug  6 15:25 file3.txt
-rwxr-xr-x 1 root root     15 Aug  6 15:25 file4.txt
-rwxr-xr-x 1 root root     15 Aug  6 15:25 file5.txt
-rwxr-xr-x 1 root root     15 Aug  6 15:25 file6.txt
-rwxr-xr-x 1 root root     15 Aug  6 15:25 file7.txt
-rwxr-xr-x 1 root root     15 Aug  6 15:25 file8.txt
-rwxr-xr-x 1 root root     15 Aug  6 15:25 file9.txt
-rwxr-xr-x 1 root root    469 Aug  6 15:15 ifcfg-enp0s3
-rwxr-xr-x 1 root root    370 Aug  6 15:15 ifcfg-enp0s3.bak
-rwxr-xr-x 1 root root    340 Aug  6 15:15 ifcfg-enp0s8.bak
-rwxr-xr-x 1 root root   3123 Aug  6 15:15 imapd.pem
-rwxr-xr-x 1 root root   2196 Aug  6 15:15 initial-setup-ks.cfg
-rwxr-xr-x 1 root root    946 Aug  6 15:15 new-rules
-rwxr-xr-x 1 root root    272 Aug  6 15:15 restartmail
-rwxr-xr-x 1 root root     10 Aug  6 15:15 testfile.txt
[root@studentvm1 ~]#
```

Edit one of the files you created in an earlier experiment. This illustrates that the mounted SAMBA share works just as any other mounted filesystem.

We could have created a new mount point and added it to the fstab file, but this works just as well for our current purposes. Leave SAMBA running for the next experiment.

Midnight Commander

We have already explored the use of Midnight Commander as a file manager. It is also an excellent client for FTP, SFTP, SMB (CIFS), and SSH. It can be used with those protocols to connect to remote hosts in one panel and to copy files from and between the remote and local hosts. It can be used to display the content of remote files and to delete them.

SSH is a powerful tool, and when used in conjunction with a file manager like Midnight Commander (MC), the pair can be used as a simple and easy file sharing system using a protocol called FISH. The advantage of this is that it uses tools we have already installed and requires no additional configuration.

This is also the most secure method I know for sharing files. The login or key-based authentication sequence is encrypted as are all data transfers. This is not just the default configuration; it is the only way in which SSH works. There is not a choice about using authentication and beginning to end encryption so it cannot be bypassed.

The FISH protocol was developed by Pavel Machek in 1998 specifically for Midnight Commander. FISH stands for "Files transferred over Shell protocol." However, MC also connects with servers using FTP, SFTP, and SAMBA, so it is very versatile. I have found it needs no special configuration, unlike some other clients.

EXPERIMENT 13-14

Perform this experiment as the student user on StudentVM1. In this experiment, we will connect to the server using various file sharing protocols.

In a terminal session as the student user on StudentVM1, launch Midnight Commander. Press **F9** and then the arrow keys until the **Right** panel menu is highlighted. Then use the down arrow key to highlight **FTP link …** as shown in Figure 13-1. Press the **Enter** key to initiate the connection.

```
   Left     File    Command    Options    Right
+<- ~ ----------------------------------.+---------------------------------+-----------------.[^]>+
|.n         Name        | Size  |Modify t| File listing             |   | Size  |Modify time |
|/..                    |UP--DIR|May 30 0| Quick view        C-x q| |UP--DIR|May 30 08:41|
|/.cache                |   4096|Aug 10 1| Info              C-x i| |   4096|Aug 10 12:23|
|/.config               |   4096|Aug 10 1| Tree                   | |   4096|Aug 10 13:11|
|/.cups                 |   4096|Mar 17 2|------------------------| |   4096|Mar 17 22:15|
|/.esmtp_queue          |   4096|May  2 1| Listing format...      | |   4096|May  2 15:10|
|/.fvwm                 |   4096|Mar 14 1| Sort order...          | |   4096|Mar 14 16:00|
|/.gnupg                |   4096|Dec 22  | Filter...              | |   4096|Dec 22  2018|
|/.local                |   4096|Dec 22  | Encoding...       M-e  | |   4096|Dec 22  2018|
|/.mozilla              |   4096|May 10 1|------------------------| |   4096|May 10 11:28|
|/.putty                |   4096|Aug 10 1| FTP link...            | |   4096|Aug 10 13:03|
|/.ssh                  |   4096|Jun 28 2| Shell link...          | |   4096|Jun 28 22:04|
|/.thunderbird          |   4096|Jul  2 1| SFTP link...           | |   4096|Jul  2 11:49|
|/Desktop               |   4096|Dec 24  | SMB link...            | |   4096|Dec 24  2018|
|/Documents             |   4096|Jul  2 1| Panelize               | |   4096|Jul  2 10:43|
|/Downloads             |   4096|Jun  4 1|------------------------| |   4096|Jun  4 13:59|
|/Music                 |   4096|Dec 22  | Rescan            C-r  | |   4096|Dec 22  2018|
|/Pictures              |   4096|Dec 22 +------------------------+ |   4096|Dec 22  2018|
|/Public                |   4096|Dec 22  2018||/Public              |   4096|Dec 22  2018|
|/Templates             |   4096|Dec 22  2018||/Templates           |   4096|Dec 22  2018|
|/Videos                |   4096|Dec 22  2018||/Videos              |   4096|Dec 22  2018|
|/chapter25             |   4096|Mar  2 08:21||/chapter25           |   4096|Mar  2 08:21|
|/chapter26             |   4096|Mar 21 15:27||/chapter26           |   4096|Mar 21 15:27|
|/chapter28             | 167936|Apr 10 08:23||/chapter28           | 167936|Apr 10 08:23|
|/testdir               |   4096|Apr  2 12:45||/testdir             |   4096|Apr  2 12:45|
|/testdir1              |   4096|Dec 30  2018||/testdir1            |   4096|Dec 30  2018|
|/testdir6              |   4096|Dec 30  2018||/testdir6            |   4096|Dec 30  2018|
|/testdir7              | 663552|Feb 21 14:12||/testdir7            | 663552|Feb 21 14:12|
|/tmp                   |   4096|Jun 22 13:25||/tmp                 |   4096|Jun 22 13:25|
| .ICEauthority         |  12444|Aug 10 21:41|| .ICEauthority       |  12444|Aug 10 21:41|
| .Xauthority           |     56|Jan 30  2019|| .Xauthority         |     56|Jan 30  2019|
| .bash_history         |  28285|Aug 10 14:36|| .bash_history       |  28285|Aug 10 14:36|
| .bash_logout          |     18|Oct  8  2018|| .bash_logout        |     18|Oct  8  2018|
| .bash_profile         |    186|Jun 21 08:44|| .bash_profile       |    186|Jun 21 08:44|
|----------------------------------------||-----------------------------------------|
|UP--DIR                                 ||UP--DIR                                  |
+----------------------- 3585M/3968M (90%) -++----------------------- 3585M/3968M (90%) -+
Hint: Want your plain shell? Press C-o, and get back to MC with C-o again.
[student@studentvm1 ~]$                                                      [^]
  1Help    2Menu    3View    4Edit    5Copy    6RenMov 7Mkdir  8Delete 9PullDn 10Quit
```

Figure 13-1. *Select the FTP link to connect with the VSFTP server in standard FTP mode*

Type **studentvm2** in the FTP to machine filed, as shown in Figure 13-2, and press the **Enter** key.

```
|/Documents        +------------- FTP to machine --------------+  |   4096|Jul  2 10:43|
|/Downloads        | Enter machine name (F1 for details):     |  |   4096|Jun  4 13:59|
|/Music            | studentvm2                          [^]  |  |   4096|Dec 22  2018|
|/Pictures         |------------------------------------------|  |   4096|Dec 22  2018|
|/Public           |        [< OK >] [ Cancel ]               |  |   4096|Dec 22  2018|
|/Templates        +------------------------------------------+  |   4096|Dec 22  2018|
```

Figure 13-2. *Using Midnight Commander to access a remote host with FTP*

Figure 13-3 shows Midnight Commander with the student user's home directory on StudentVM1, the local host, in the left panel, and the anonymous FTP connection to StudentVM2 in the right panel.

```
 Left      File    Command    Options     Right
+<- ~ -------------------------------.[^]>++<- ftp://studentvm2/ ------------------.[^]>+
|.n        Name        | Size  |Modify time ||.n         Name        | Size  |Modify time |
|/..                   |UP--DIR|May 30 08:41||/..                   |UP--DIR|Aug 10 14:36|
|/.cache               |   4096|Aug 10 12:23||/pub                  |   4096|Jul 25  2018|
|/.config              |   4096|Aug 10 13:11|| FTP-file-01.txt      |     16|Aug  8 01:14|
|/.cups                |   4096|Mar 17 22:15|| FTP-file-02.txt      |     16|Aug  8 01:14|
|/.esmtp_queue         |   4096|May  2 15:10|| FTP-file-03.txt      |     16|Aug  8 01:14|
|/.fvwm                |   4096|Mar 14 16:00|| FTP-file-04.txt      |     16|Aug  8 01:14|
|/.gnupg               |   4096|Dec 22  2018|| FTP-file-05.txt      |     16|Aug  8 01:14|
|/.local               |   4096|Dec 22  2018|| FTP-file-06.txt      |     16|Aug  8 01:14|
|/.mozilla             |   4096|May 10 11:28|| FTP-file-07.txt      |     16|Aug  8 01:14|
|/.putty               |   4096|Aug 10 13:03|| FTP-file-08.txt      |     16|Aug  8 01:14|
|/.ssh                 |   4096|Jun 28 22:04|| FTP-file-09.txt      |     16|Aug  8 01:14|
|/.thunderbird         |   4096|Jul  2 11:49|| FTP-file-10.txt      |     16|Aug  8 01:14|
|/Desktop              |   4096|Dec 24  2018|| FTP-file-11.txt      |     16|Aug  8 01:14|
|/Documents            |   4096|Jul  2 10:43|| FTP-file-12.txt      |     16|Aug  8 01:14|
|/Downloads            |   4096|Jun  4 13:59|| FTP-file-13.txt      |     16|Aug  8 01:14|
|/Music                |   4096|Dec 22  2018|| FTP-file-14.txt      |     16|Aug  8 01:14|
|/Pictures             |   4096|Dec 22  2018|| FTP-file-15.txt      |     16|Aug  8 01:14|
|/Public               |   4096|Dec 22  2018|| FTP-file-16.txt      |     16|Aug  8 01:14|
|/Templates            |   4096|Dec 22  2018|| FTP-file-17.txt      |     16|Aug  8 01:14|
|/Videos               |   4096|Dec 22  2018|| FTP-file-18.txt      |     16|Aug  8 01:14|
|/chapter25            |   4096|Mar  2 08:21|| FTP-file-19.txt      |     16|Aug  8 01:14|
|/chapter26            |   4096|Mar 21 15:27|| FTP-file-20.txt      |     16|Aug  8 01:14|
|/chapter28            | 167936|Apr 10 08:23|| FTP-file-21.txt      |     16|Aug  8 01:14|
|/testdir              |   4096|Apr  2 12:45|| FTP-file-22.txt      |     16|Aug  8 01:14|
|/testdir1             |   4096|Dec 30  2018|| FTP-file-23.txt      |     16|Aug  8 01:14|
|/testdir6             |   4096|Dec 30  2018|| FTP-file-24.txt      |     16|Aug  8 01:14|
|/testdir7             | 663552|Feb 21 14:12|| FTP-file-25.txt      |     16|Aug  8 01:14|
|/tmp                  |   4096|Jun 22 13:25||                      |       |            |
| .ICEauthority        |  12444|Aug 10 21:41||                      |       |            |
| .Xauthority          |     56|Jan 30  2019||                      |       |            |
| .bash_history        |  28285|Aug 10 14:36||                      |       |            |
| .bash_logout         |     18|Oct  8  2018||                      |       |            |
| .bash_profile        |    186|Jun 21 08:44||                      |       |            |
|--------------------------------------------||------------------------------------------|
|UP--DIR                                     ||UP--DIR                                   |
+----------------------- 3585M/3968M (90%) -++------------------------------------------+
Hint: The homepage of GNU Midnight Commander: http://www.midnight-commander.org/
[student@studentvm1 ~]$                                                            [^]
 1Help    2Menu    3View    4Edit    5Copy    6RenMov  7Mkdir  8Delete 9PullDn 10Quit
```

Figure 13-3. *The student user's home directory on the local host is in the left panel, and the anonymous FTP directory on StudentVM2 is shown in the right panel of Midnight Commander*

Copy files between the directories. Can you do it from the local host to the server?

To exit the connection to the server, enter the **cd** command. This takes you back to the student user's home directory on the local host.

Now use the SFTP menu item to connect to the server. The only difference in making the connection is that you need to enter the password for the student user on the server. The connection is then opened with the root directory (/) as the PWD. Make /var/shared the PWD. We are not entering this directory using NFS, but rather SFTP.

Experiment with this SFTP environment for a bit. Download a file or two to your home directory. Then try uploading files to various directories on the server, such as /var/shared, your home directory, and the /acs directory. When finished, you can again use the **cd** command with no arguments to exit from the remote connection.

Now connect to the server using the **Shell link** option. Use this link to perform the same tasks as with the previous links.

Midnight Commander and SAMBA

Despite the fact that MC looks like it should support connected to SAMBA shares – the man page and the MC Help facility both say it can be done and how – I cannot get it to work. This is true even when the **smbclient** command works properly as in Experiment 13-12.

After some extensive Internet searches, I found that there is a bug[13] reported on this problem and that fixes are to be included in a "future" release. So we will skip any testing of MC with SAMBA shares.

Apache web server

We can also download files using the Apache web server we created in Chapter 10. This requires only a little additional work and no changes to the Apache configuration. Apache is like FTP, a tool for downloading files. It does not provide any collaborative functionality.

---

[13]https://midnight-commander.org/ticket/3938

EXPERIMENT 13-15

In this experiment, we will add some files to the Apache download directory and test the results. As the root user on StudentVM2 ensure that Apache, httpd, is running. If not, start it.

In the /var/www2/html directory, create a new directory, downloads, if it does not already exist. Then set the ownership to apache.apache. Make the new downloads directory the PWD and copy or create some new files for content. I used the following command line program to create a few files.

```
[root@studentvm2 downloads]# for I in `seq -w 0 45` ; do echo "This is file for web download $I" > file-$I.txt ; done
```

As the student user on StudentVM1, open Firefox and navigate to www2.example.com/downloads. The web page should look like that in Figure 13-4. You can click the field names to change the sort although it won't make much difference since the files are all the same size and created at the same time. However, if you click the Name field a couple times, it reverses the direction of the sort. You might also want to add some files with different characteristics to try with different sorts.

Figure 13-4. *Using the Apache web server to share files displays a sortable index*

Right click a couple files and select **Save link as** from the pop-up menu to download them. The default directory for downloads is ~/Downloads. Look for the downloaded files there.

We also have a couple command-line tools, **wget** and **curl**, to use for downloading files from web sites. Let's look first at **wget** which should already be installed. We touched on the wget command briefly in Volume 1, Chapter 12, and we installed and used it to download companion files for this course from the Apress Git repository.

As the student user on StudentVM1, make ~/Downloads the PWD. Delete all of the files in this directory. Use **wget** to download a single file. Use a file that you have in your html/downloads directory; I will use file-27.txt.

```
[student@studentvm1 Downloads]$ wget http://www2.example.com/downloads/file-
27.txt
--2019-08-12 11:04:24--  http://www2.example.com/downloads/file-27.txt
Resolving www2.example.com (www2.example.com)... 192.168.56.1
Connecting to www2.example.com (www2.example.com)|192.168.56.1|:80...
connected.
HTTP request sent, awaiting response... 200 OK
Length: 33 [text/plain]
Saving to: 'file-27.txt'

file-27.txt            100%[==============================>]      33  --.-
KB/s    in 0s

2019-08-12 11:04:24 (5.03 MB/s) - 'file-27.txt' saved [33/33]

[student@studentvm1 Downloads]$ ll
total 4
-rw-rw-r-- 1 student student 33 Aug 12 08:50 file-27.txt
[student@studentvm1 Downloads]$
```

Now download several files that match a file glob pattern.

```
[student@studentvm1 Downloads]$ wget http://www2.example.com/downloads/file-*
Warning: wildcards not supported in HTTP.
--2019-08-12 11:14:41--  http://www2.example.com/downloads/file-*
Resolving www2.example.com (www2.example.com)... 192.168.56.1
Connecting to www2.example.com (www2.example.com)|192.168.56.1|:80...
connected.
HTTP request sent, awaiting response... 404 Not Found
2019-08-12 11:14:41 ERROR 404: Not Found.
```

You will see the warning message that wildcards (globbing) are not supported using the HTTPD protocol. The wget utility can be used to download using FTP as well as HTTPD, and sets are supported when using FTP. Ensure that the VSFTP server is running on StudentVM2 and download some files using wild cards from the anonymous FTP site.

```
[student@studentvm1 Downloads]$ wget ftp://studentvm2.example.com/FTP-
file-1*.txt
```

The **curl** utility can use regular expressions such as sets to download multiple files for many protocols. The **curl** tool supports all of the following protocols: DICT, FILE, FTP, FTPS, GOPHER, HTTP, HTTPS, IMAP, IMAPS, LDAP, LDAPS, POP3, POP3S, RTMP, RTSP, SCP, SFTP, SMB, SMBS, SMTP, SMTPS, TELNET, and TFTP. It can also handle user IDs and passwords, as well as certificates. As a result, it can be used in a great many situations where a single downloading solution is desirable, such as in scripts. It is an excellent tool for use in scripted automation.

The **curl** utility is already installed so we do not need to do that. Download one file using the syntax below. The -O (uppercase alpha character O, not zero) specifies that the file name used in the download, file-12.txt, is the file name to be used to save the file locally.

```
[student@studentvm1 Downloads]$ curl -O http://www2.example.com/downloads/
file-12.txt ; ll
  % Total    % Received % Xferd  Average Speed   Time    Time
Time  Current
                                 Dload  Upload   Total   Spent    Left  Speed
100    33  100    33    0     0  11000      0 --:--:-- --:--:-- --:--:-- 11000
total 4
-rw-rw-r-- 1 student student 33 Aug 12 11:47 file-12.txt
```

What happens if you do not use the -O option when doing the preceding download? The alternate form of doing a download is to use the -o (lowercase alpha) option to specify the output file name.

```
[student@studentvm1 Downloads]$ curl http://www2.example.com/downloads/file-
13.txt -o file-13.txt ; ll
  % Total    % Received % Xferd  Average Speed   Time    Time
Time  Current
                                 Dload  Upload   Total   Spent    Left  Speed
100    33  100    33    0     0  6600       0 --:--:-- --:--:-- --:--:--  6600
total 8
-rw-rw-r-- 1 student student 33 Aug 12 11:47 file-12.txt
-rw-rw-r-- 1 student student 33 Aug 12 11:53 file-13.txt
[student@studentvm1 Downloads]$
```

This requires more typing than using -O and more code in a script so, unless there is a specific reason not to, I suggest using the -O option. Note the use of the set [0-9] instead of file globs, ? or *.

```
[student@studentvm1 Downloads]$ curl -O http://www2.example.com/downloads/
file-1[0-9].txt
<snip>
[student@studentvm1 Downloads]$ ll
total 40
-rw-rw-r-- 1 student student 33 Aug 12 12:46 file-10.txt
-rw-rw-r-- 1 student student 33 Aug 12 12:46 file-11.txt
-rw-rw-r-- 1 student student 33 Aug 12 12:46 file-12.txt
-rw-rw-r-- 1 student student 33 Aug 12 12:46 file-13.txt
-rw-rw-r-- 1 student student 33 Aug 12 12:46 file-14.txt
-rw-rw-r-- 1 student student 33 Aug 12 12:46 file-15.txt
-rw-rw-r-- 1 student student 33 Aug 12 12:46 file-16.txt
-rw-rw-r-- 1 student student 33 Aug 12 12:46 file-17.txt
-rw-rw-r-- 1 student student 33 Aug 12 12:46 file-18.txt
-rw-rw-r-- 1 student student 33 Aug 12 12:46 file-19.txt
[student@studentvm1 Downloads]$
```

Download a file using FTP.

```
[student@studentvm1 Downloads]$ curl -O ftp://studentvm2.example.com/FTP-
file-02.txt
  % Total    % Received % Xferd  Average Speed   Time    Time
Time  Current
                                 Dload  Upload   Total   Spent    Left  Speed
100    16  100    16    0     0    410      0 --:--:-- --:--:-- --:--:--   421
[student@studentvm1 Downloads]$ ll
total 48
-rw-rw-r-- 1 student student  33 Aug 12 12:46  file-10.txt
-rw-rw-r-- 1 student student  33 Aug 12 12:46  file-11.txt
-rw-rw-r-- 1 student student  33 Aug 12 12:46  file-12.txt
-rw-rw-r-- 1 student student  33 Aug 12 12:46  file-13.txt
-rw-rw-r-- 1 student student  33 Aug 12 12:46  file-14.txt
-rw-rw-r-- 1 student student  33 Aug 12 12:46  file-15.txt
-rw-rw-r-- 1 student student  33 Aug 12 12:46  file-16.txt
-rw-rw-r-- 1 student student  33 Aug 12 12:46  file-17.txt
-rw-rw-r-- 1 student student  33 Aug 12 12:46  file-18.txt
-rw-rw-r-- 1 student student  33 Aug 12 12:46  file-19.txt
-rw-rw-r-- 1 student student  16 Aug 12 13:57  FTP-file-02.txt
[student@studentvm1 Downloads]$
```

And now do multiple files over FTP with a set.

```
[student@studentvm1 Downloads]$ curl -O ftp://studentvm2.example.com/FTP-
file-2[1-3].txt

[1/3]: ftp://studentvm2.example.com/FTP-file-21.txt --> FTP-file-21.txt
--_curl_--ftp://studentvm2.example.com/FTP-file-21.txt
  % Total    % Received % Xferd  Average Speed   Time    Time
Time  Current
                                 Dload  Upload   Total   Spent    Left  Speed
100    16  100    16    0     0    410       0 --:--:-- --:--:-- --:--:--   410

[2/3]: ftp://studentvm2.example.com/FTP-file-22.txt --> FTP-file-22.txt
--_curl_--ftp://studentvm2.example.com/FTP-file-22.txt
100    16  100    16    0     0   8000       0 --:--:-- --:--:-- --:--:--  8000

[3/3]: ftp://studentvm2.example.com/FTP-file-23.txt --> FTP-file-23.txt
--_curl_--ftp://studentvm2.example.com/FTP-file-23.txt
100    16  100    16    0     0   8000       0 --:--:-- --:--:-- --:--:--  8000
[student@studentvm1 Downloads]$ ll
total 12
-rw-rw-r-- 1 student student 16 Aug 12 14:00 FTP-file-21.txt
-rw-rw-r-- 1 student student 16 Aug 12 14:00 FTP-file-22.txt
-rw-rw-r-- 1 student student 16 Aug 12 14:00 FTP-file-23.txt
[student@studentvm1 Downloads]$
```

So we have discovered that **wget** can use file globs but not REGEXes like sets when downloading FTP. It cannot use any form of glob or REGEX with HTTPD. The **curl** utility can use REGEXes but not file globs – at least on the protocols we have tested.

The **wget** and **curl** man pages have good descriptions and examples of their many features.

Chapter summary

This chapter has shown us some tools for sharing files on a file server. We used FTP, SAMBA, and NFS on StudentVM2 to share directories with users on StudentVM1. FTP in any form, SAMBA, and NFS all require some nontrivial setup to work in a nonsecure mode. Even more work is required to provide a secure environment on those that support it.

We have also seen that tools we already have available, SSH and Midnight Commander can work together to provide a very powerful, secure, and flexible yet easy-to-use file sharing solution that just works. Midnight Commander can be used without SSH to access FTP sites and with SSL to access VSFTP sites. MC can also be used with SSH to connect to a shell session on a remote host, one which one has a user account. We have also explored **wget** and **curl** as command line tools for downloading files with HTTPD and FTP protocols. The curl utility can download using many different types of protocols and it can use regular expressions to do so.

There are a lot of options available to us to share files as well as to use for downloading those files. We have not covered all of them, but the ones we did cover should give you a good start.

Exercises

Perform these exercises to complete this chapter.

1. Monitor the packet data stream on StudentVM1 as you use FTP to connect to the VSFTP server. Examine the resulting TCP conversation and identify the components of the FTP initiation sequence.

2. As root on your student host, mount the NFS export on /mnt. Change the PWD to the stuff subdirectory and verify that the files you copied to it are there.

3. Attempt to add a new file. What message do you get?

4. Create mount new point and an entry in the fstab for the ACS share created on StudentVM1 and mount the filesystem as a test. Reboot StudentVM1 and verify that /acs is mounted during startup.

5. Monitor the packet data stream on StudentVM1 as you use Midnight Commander as the student user on StudentVM1 to connect to StudentVM2 using various methods. Use FTP, SFTP, a shell link, and an SMB link. Observe which of these connections are encrypted and which are not.

6. Configure the VSFTP server to allow anonymous uploads.

7. Use Midnight Commander to copy files from the student account on StudentVM1 to the VSFTP server.

8. Why did you not need a user ID and password in Experiment 13-14 when using Midnight Commander to connect to the server using a shell link?

9. What directory is the PWD when you open a shell link to the server?

10. Use wget to download some files from our FTP server.

Be sure to shut down all file sharing client and server tools and services after completing these exercises.

## CHAPTER 14

Remote Desktop Access

Objectives

In this chapter, you will learn

- To define remote desktop access

- To install and configure TigerVNC, a remote desktop system

- To connect to the remote VNC server and perform typical desktop tasks

- To configure an encrypted VNC connection to a remote server

Introduction

Sometimes there is a need for remote desktop access (RDA) that cannot be fulfilled in any other way. This type of access connects to a remote computer using tools that enable you as the user to work on a graphical desktop as easily as if you were sitting in front of the remote host with physical access to it. VNC[1] stands for Virtual Network Computing and it is the tool that enables use of remote graphical desktops. TigerVNC[2] is the VNC of choice for Fedora and RHCE as well as other distributions.

In Chapter 5 of this volume, we explored X-forwarding in which we used SSH to login to a remote host using the -X option and then started a single GUI application whose window appeared on our local host. The vast majority of the time, if I need remote GUI access, it is usually for a single application so that is a perfect solution.

---

[1]Wikipedia, *VNC*, `https://en.wikipedia.org/wiki/Virtual_Network_Computing`
[2]TigerVNC Web site, `https://tigervnc.org`

© David Both 2020
D. Both, *Using and Administering Linux: Volume 3*, https://doi.org/10.1007/978-1-4842-5485-1_14

However, using VNC can be useful if I need to perform multiple GUI-based tasks on a remote host. In a case such as this, I must set up a VMC server, such as TigerVNC,[3] on the remote host and then use a client to connect with that server. The result is that a GUI desktop hosted by that remote host is displayed on my local desktop.

VNC works by transmitting keyboard and mouse events that originate on the VNC client to the remote VNC server. The VNC server performs the necessary tasks and returns any screen updates back to the client so that the VNC client window may be updated.

TigerVNC

TigerVNC is a fairly standard implementation of VNC. The VNC protocols were originally developed by the Olivetti & Oracle Research Lab in Cambridge, England.[4] VNC allows multiple clients to connect to the server, and is platform-independent in that it allows compatible VNC clients for different operating systems to connect to the server. TigerVNC clients can also connect to compatible VNC servers on other operating systems.

The TigerVNC installation instructions are available in the Fedora[5] specifically the *Infrastructure Services* section of the *System Administrator's Guide*. This information can be found in the same location for RHEL 7 in the Red Hat documentation.[6] I have not found VNC in the RHEL 8 documentation, possibly because the documentation structure has been changed significantly.

EXPERIMENT 14-1

Start this experiment as root on StudentVM2. We will install the TigerVNC server, the client, and configure the server and the firewall. Install the server with the following command.

```
[root@studentvm2 ~]# dnf -y install tigervnc-server tigervnc
```

---

[3]Wikipedia, *TigerVNC*, https://en.wikipedia.org/wiki/TigerVNC

[4]Wikipedia, *Olivetti Research Laboratory*, https://en.wikipedia.org/wiki/Olivetti_Research_Laboratory

[5]Fedora Documentation, https://docs.fedoraproject.org/en-US/docs/

[6]RHEL Documentation, https://access.redhat.com/documentation/

It is necessary to add a rule to the /etc/sysconfig/iptables file. Add the following lines to the Filter table INPUT chain. Note that this one rule allows a range of six ports.

```
# This line is for TigerVNC
-A INPUT -p tcp -m state --state NEW -m tcp --dport 5900:5905 -j ACCEPT
```

Be sure to save the revised IPTables rule set.

There is very little configuration required for Tiger VNC, but one thing you must do is to create a VNC password that the remote clients will use.

As the user student on StudentVM2, issue the **vncpasswd** command and set the password. Answer **n** for No to the question about a view-only password. That would allow you to see what was happening on the remote desktop but not to interact with it. This would be useful for viewing the user's actions on the host but would prevent the remote TigerVNC viewer from interacting with the desktop in any way.

```
[student@studentvm2 ~]$ vncpasswd
Password:<Enter Password>
Verify:<Enter Password>
Would you like to enter a view-only password (y/n)? n
[student@studentvm2 ~]$
```

Warning   This password is not encrypted. Anyone with access to your home directory on the server will be able to read this file and your password.

There are a couple ways in which you can test the VNC server. You can go to another host and connect to the VNC server from there or you can connect to your own server using the client. Let's start by testing on StudentVM2, which is why we also installed the client on it.

As user student on StudentVM2, start the VNC server in the background with its simplest form. The ampersand (&) causes the server to run in the background. This allows us to log in using SSH to a remote host and start the server and then to log out.

```
[student@studentvm2 ~]$ vncserver &
[1] 24984
[student@studentvm2 ~]$
New 'studentvm2.example.com:1 (student)' desktop is studentvm2.example.com:1
```

Creating default startup script /home/student/.vnc/xstartup

Creating default config /home/student/.vnc/config

Starting applications specified in /home/student/.vnc/xstartup

Log file is /home/student/.vnc/studentvm2.example.com:1.log

<Press the Enter key>

```
[1]+  Done                    vncserver
[student@studentvm2 ~]$ ps -ef | grep vnc
student  24997    1  0 11:06 pts/0    00:00:00 /usr/bin/Xvnc :1 -auth /var/
run/lightdm/student/xauthority -desktop studentvm2.example.com:1 (student)
-fp catalogue:/etc/X11/fontpath.d -geometry 1024x768 -pn -rfbauth /home/
student/.vnc/passwd -rfbport 5901 -rfbwait 30000
student  25484 22352  0 11:07 pts/0    00:00:00 grep --color=auto vnc
[student@studentvm2 ~]$
```

We can see that the server is running and the default geometry of the screen as well as the port number and the display number. Be sure to make note of the display number assigned to the session. It should be :1. Multiple displays are possible, and if you run the above command again, the next display would be :2.

This invocation of the VNC Server defaults to a remote screen size of 1024x768.

Using the application launcher, open **Applications ➤ Internet** and click the **TigerVNC Viewer** icon. In the small **VNCViewer Connection Details** window shown in Figure 14-1, type the name of your VNC server and the display number, that is, studentvm2:1, and press the **Connect** button.

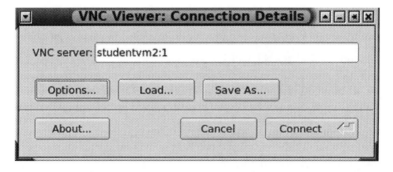

Figure 14-1. *Enter the DNS name of the VNC server and the display number, and then press the Connect button*

The VNC authentication window is displayed. Notice that it has a red band at the top with a message to indicate that the connection is not secure. In the VNC authentication window, type the password you previously set. The remote desktop window will open on your desktop as shown in Figure 14-2.

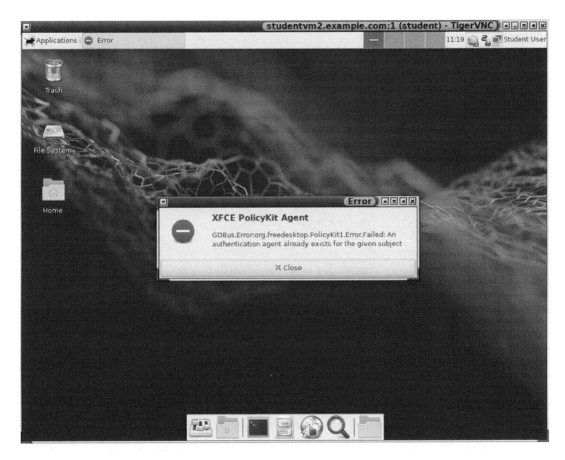

Figure 14-2. *The VNC desktop*

I received an error in the TigerVNC desktop window. You may see this also, but it is fine to ignore it and click **Close**.

Now that the window is open, you can resize it to the dimensions of your liking. You can use the remote desktop just as you would if you were sitting in front of the physical screen with a keyboard and mouse for the remote host.

Launch a couple programs like a terminal emulator and the file manager. You should explore the home directory a bit and you will see that the files and directories are those of the student user. When you have finished your explorations, close all of the programs running in the TigerVNC viewer window.

Now close the remote desktop simply by clicking the "X" button to close the TigerVNC viewer window. Terminate the VNC Server. You must use the display number to ensure that you kill the correct display.

```
[student@studentvm2 ~]$ vncserver -kill :1
Killing Xvnc process ID 24997
[student@studentvm2 ~]$
```

As the root user on StudentVM1, install the TigerVNC viewer. We don't need to install the server on this host.

```
[root@studentvm1 ~]# dnf -y install tigervnc
```

As the student user on StudentVM2, start the VNC server and set the initial screen geometry for the VNC Server to 1100x1200 with the following command. As we have seen, the screen can be resized after it is started.

```
[student@studentvm2 ~]$ vncserver -geometry 1100x900 &
```

Back as the student user on StudentVM1, launch the TigerVNC viewer and log in to the VNC server on StudentVM2 as we did above.

You will see the TigerVNC viewer window similar to that in Figure 14-3. This shows the StudentVM1 desktop and the TigerVNC remote desktop viewer connected to the StudentVM2 host. I have resized the windows to be small enough that they fit the page in a readable size.

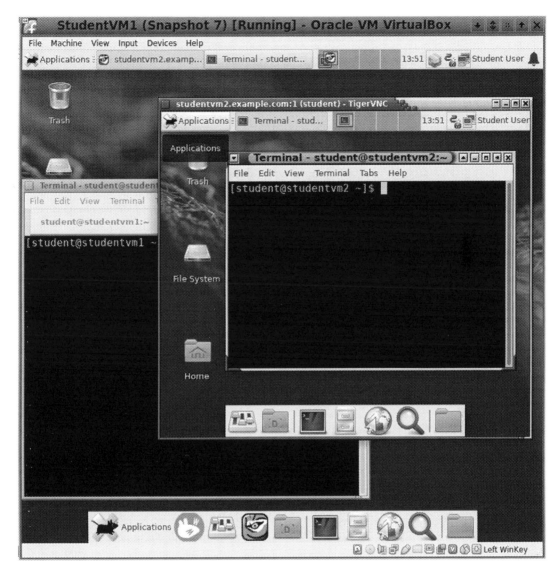

Figure 14-3. *The StudentVM1 desktop with the TigerVNC viewer containing the remote desktop for StudentVM2*

Security

VNC uses unencrypted connections by default. In fact, remote desktop access in general adds a security risk to your environment, but the unencrypted connection is horrible. This could result in your data being intercepted and easily accessed. We can use the **via** option of the **vncviewer** utility to create an SSH tunnel to encrypt the connection from the client to the server.

EXPERIMENT 14-2

In this experiment, we will use SSH to encrypt our connection to the server. To begin, as the student user on StudentVM2, ensure that the **vncserver** is running for display :1.

As the student user on StudentVM1, create an encrypted SSH tunnel to the server using the following command. We have specifically created this tunnel to port 5901 on the VNC server.

```
[student@studentvm1 ~]$ ssh -L 5901:localhost:5901 studentvm2
Last login: Sat Aug 24 09:47:26 2019 from 192.168.56.21
[student@studentvm2 ~]$
```

This terminal session is now a tunnel to for the student user to the StudentVM2 host.

In another terminal session as the student user, connect to the VNC server.

```
[student@studentvm1 ~]$ vncviewer -via localhost

TigerVNC Viewer 64-bit v1.9.0
Built on: 2018-09-25 10:36
Copyright (C) 1999-2018 TigerVNC Team and many others (see README.rst)
See http://www.tigervnc.org for information on TigerVNC.
```

The **Connection Details** dialog window is displayed. Click the **Connect** button. In the terminal session, you will be asked for the student user's password. Enter the password for the student user to continue.

```
student@localhost's password: <Enter Paswword>

Sat Aug 24 10:05:37 2019
 DecodeManager: Detected 2 CPU core(s)
 DecodeManager: Creating 2 decoder thread(s)
 CConn:        connected to host localhost port 40013

Sat Aug 24 10:05:38 2019
 CConnection: Server supports RFB protocol version 3.8
 CConnection: Using RFB protocol version 3.8
 CConnection: Choosing security type VeNCrypt(19)
 CVeNCrypt:   Choosing security type TLSVnc (258)
```

Now the VNC Authentication dialog is displayed. Note that, for me at least, it still has the red banner proclaiming the connection as insecure. Type the VNC authentication password for the student user – this is a different password than the student user's Linux login password – and click the OK button.

At this point, the VNC session window to StudentVM2 is displayed. Experiment with this for a bit, but the remote desktop should work no differently than it did when it was not encrypted.

When finished, terminate all VNC viewer and server sessions.

Problems

I have run into one perplexing problem when using TigerVNC.

Blank TigerVNC view screen

I had installed TigerVNC on one of my smaller hosts to do some experimentation and research before starting work on this course. I had a problem accessing the VNC session after getting everything set up, including the firewall. All the VNC viewer would display was a black screen and sometimes an "X" cursor. A lot of research on Google did not provide an exact solution, primarily due to the age of some of the information and the various configuration files that appear in different distributions and at different times. That research did lead me to synthesize my own related solution to the problem.

When using TigerVNC to log in as a user on a remote host, the VNC configuration is maintained in some files in the ~/.vnc directory. The ~/.vnc/xstartup script file on the server, SudentVM2 in this case, needs to be modified to start a specific desktop rather than the default xinitrc script. Add or modify the lines highlighted in bold as required to resolve this problem if you encounter it.

```
#!/bin/sh

unset SESSION_MANAGER
unset DBUS_SESSION_BUS_ADDRESS
# comment out the following line
# exec /etc/X11/xinit/xinitrc
# Add the following line to resolve the blank screen problem
startxfce4
```

You can see in the ~/.vnc/xstartup file that I have commented out the xinitrc line and added the startxfce4 statement at the bottom of the file. This will start the Xfce desktop. Use the start command for your favorite desktop in your own file. The VNC desktop can be different from the default login desktop.

I did not see this problem when using Xfce, or LXDE as the desktops on my hosts, but I did see it with KDE on the TigerVNC server. I did not experience this during my research for this course, but you may run into it "in the wild."

Note   This solution only works for the specific user account for which this change has been made.

Chapter summary

This chapter has guided us through our exploration of configuring VNC remote desktop sessions. We used TigerVNC for this, but other VNC tools are available. Some of those tools are commercial.

TigerVNC is the default VNC software for many Linux distributions including Fedora. It provides us with the capability to create encrypted or unencrypted desktop connections to one or more remote servers. The server also allows multiple incoming connections so that multiple users can simultaneously use a VNC desktop on the server.

VNC is not always the correct solution for remote GUI access, but it can be the best option for some uses.

Exercises

Perform the following exercises to complete this chapter.

1. Is the client server terminology used in VNC consistent with its use in the standard X-Window system and X-forwarding? Why do you think that might be?

2. On StudentVM2, start two VNC servers using screen :1 and screen :2. Use the TigerVNC viewer to connect to one screen from the localhost, StudentVM2. Also connect to StudentVM2 from StudentVM1 so that you have two VNC sessions running simultaneously.

3. View the TCP packet stream as you open a VNC session from StudentVM1 to StudentVM2 and perform some simple tasks.

## CHAPTER 15

Network Time Protocol

Objectives

In this chapter, you will learn

- Why accurate timekeeping is essential

- The structure of the Internet's NTP infrastructure

- The two implementations of the NTP protocol

- How to configure an NTP client using Chrony

- How to configure and test an NTP server using Chrony

- The importance of time zones

- How to change the system's time zone

Linux and time

> *Does anybody really know what time it is? Does anybody really care?*
>
> —Chicago, 1969

Perhaps that rock group didn't care what time it was, but our computers really need to know the exact time. Timekeeping is very important to computer networks. In banking, stock markets, and other financial businesses, transactions must be maintained in the proper order, and exact time sequences are critical for that. For SysAdmins and DevOps following the trail of email through a series of servers or determining the exact sequence of events, using log files on geographically dispersed hosts can be much easier when exact times are kept on the computers in question.

© David Both 2020
D. Both, *Using and Administering Linux: Volume 3*, https://doi.org/10.1007/978-1-4842-5485-1_15

I used to work at one organization that received over 20 million emails per day and which had four servers just to accept and do a basic filter on the incoming flood of email. From there, emails were sent to one of four more servers to perform more complex anti-spam assessments and then deliver the email to one of several additional servers where the messages were placed in the correct inboxes. At each layer, the emails would be sent to one of the servers at the next level selected only by the randomness of round-robin DNS. Sometimes we needed to trace the arrival of a new message through the system until we could determine where it "got lost," according to the pointy haired bosses. We had to do this with frightening regularity.

Most of that email turned out to be spam. Some people actually complained that their [Joke, cat pic, recipe, inspirational saying, and a few even more strange emails]-of-the-day was missing and asked us to find it. We did reject those opportunities.

Our email searches, as well as other transactional searches, were all aided by logs entries with timestamps that – today – can resolve down to the nanosecond in even the slowest of modern Linux computers. In very high-volume transaction environments, the difference of a few microseconds of difference in the system clocks can mean thousands of transactions to be sorted through in order to find the correct ones.

The NTP server hierarchy

NTP is the Network Time Protocol, and it is used by computers worldwide to synchronize their times with Internet standard reference clocks via a hierarchy of NTP servers. The primary servers are at stratum 1 and they are connected directly to various national time services at stratum 0 via satellite, radio, or even modems over phone lines in some cases. Those time services at stratum 0 may be an atomic clock, a radio receiver that is tuned to the signals broadcast by an atomic clock, or a GPS receiver using the highly accurate clock signals broadcast by GPS satellites.

To prevent time requests from time servers lower in the hierarchy, that is, with a higher stratum number, from overwhelming the primary reference servers, there are several thousand public NTP stratum 2 servers that are open and available for all to use. Many users and organizations, myself included, with large numbers of their own hosts that need an NTP server, set up their own time servers so that only one local host actually accesses the stratum 2 time servers. The remaining hosts in our networks are all configured to use the local time server which, in the case of my home network, is a stratum 3 server.

NTP choices

The original NTP daemon, ntpd, has been joined by a newer one, chronyd. Both perform the task of keeping the time of the local host synchronized with the time server. Both services are available and I have seen nothing to indicate that this will change any time soon.

Chrony has some features which make it the better choice for most environments. Some of the primary advantages of using chrony are shown in this list.

- Chrony can synchronize to the time server much faster than ntp. This is good for laptops or desktops that do not run constantly.

- It can compensate for fluctuating clock frequencies such as when a host hibernates, enters a sleep mode, or when the clock speed varies due to frequency stepping that slows clock speeds when loads are low.

- It handles intermittent network connections and bandwidth saturation.

- It adjusts for network delays and latency.

- After the initial time sync is accomplished, Chrony never steps the clock. This ensures stable and consistent time intervals for many system services and applications that require that.

- Chrony can work even without a network connection of any type. In this case, the local host or server could be updated manually.

Both the NTP and Chrony RPM packages are available from standard Fedora repositories. It is possible to install both and switch between them, but modern releases of Fedora CentOS and RHEL have moved from NTP to Chrony as the default time-keeping implementation. I have found that Chrony works well, provides a better interface for the SysAdmin, and presents much more information and increases control.

So just to make it clear, NTP is a protocol that is implemented on the local host with either NTP or Chrony. We will explore only Chrony for both client and server configuration on a Fedora host. Configuration for current releases of CentOS and RHEL is the same.

There is an interesting web site that provides a comparison between NTP and Chrony as implementations of the NTP protocol.[1] This is the Chrony web site and contains a great deal of other information about Chrony.

Chrony structure

Chrony consists of two major components. The Chrony daemon, `chronyd`, runs in the background and monitors the time and status of the time server specified in the chrony.conf file. If the local time needs to be adjusted, chronyd does so smoothly without the programmatic trauma that would occur if the clock were to be instantly reset to a new time.

Chrony also provides the `chronyc` tool that allows us to monitor the current status of Chrony and to make changes if necessary. The chronyc utility can be used as a command that accepts sub-commands, or it can be used as an interactive text mode program. We will use it both ways in this chapter.

Client configuration

The NTP client configuration is simple and requires little or no intervention. The NTP server is defined during the Linux installation or it can be provided by the DHCP server at boot time. The default /etc/chrony.conf file shown below in its entirety requires no intervention to work properly as a client. For Fedora, Chrony uses the Fedora NTP pool. CentOS and RHEL also have their own NTP server pools. Like many Red Hat based distributions, the configuration file is well commented as you can see in Figure 15-1.

---

[1]Chrony web site, *Chrony*, `https://chrony.tuxfamily.org/comparison.html`

```
# Use public servers from the pool.ntp.org project.
# Please consider joining the pool (http://www.pool.ntp.org/join.html).
pool 2.fedora.pool.ntp.org iburst

# Record the rate at which the system clock gains/losses time.
driftfile /var/lib/chrony/drift

# Allow the system clock to be stepped in the first three updates
# if its offset is larger than 1 second.
makestep 1.0 3

# Enable kernel synchronization of the real-time clock (RTC).
rtcsync

# Enable hardware timestamping on all interfaces that support it.
#hwtimestamp *

# Increase the minimum number of selectable sources required to adjust
# the system clock.
#minsources 2

# Allow NTP client access from local network.
#allow 192.168.0.0/16

# Serve time even if not synchronized to a time source.
#local stratum 10

# Specify file containing keys for NTP authentication.
keyfile /etc/chrony.keys

# Get TAI-UTC offset and leap seconds from the system tz database.
leapsectz right/UTC

# Specify directory for log files.
logdir /var/log/chrony

# Select which information is logged.
#log measurements statistics tracking
```

Figure 15-1. *The default Chrony configuration file*

Let's look at the current status of NTP on StudentVM2. The `chronyc` command is our primary administrative tool for interacting with Chrony. When used with the `tracking` sub-command, chronyc provides statistics that tell us the time discrepancy between the local system and the reference server.

EXPERIMENT 15-1

Perform this experiment as root on StudentVM2. The tracking sub-command provides information about the accuracy of our own host.

```
[root@studentvm2 ~]# chronyc tracking
Reference ID    : C11D3F96 (hydra.spiderspace.co.uk)
Stratum         : 3
Ref time (UTC)  : Sat Aug 24 15:29:51 2019
System time     : 0.000002236 seconds fast of NTP time
Last offset     : -0.001532960 seconds
RMS offset      : 0.001532960 seconds
Frequency       : 0.488 ppm slow
Residual freq   : +38.487 ppm
Skew            : 1.435 ppm
Root delay      : 0.047432110 seconds
Root dispersion : 0.002641887 seconds
Update interval : 2.2 seconds
Leap status     : Normal
[root@studentvm2 ~]#
```

The Reference ID in the first line of the result is the server to which our host is synchronized. That server is a stratum 3 reference server which was last contacted by our host at Sat Aug 24 15:29:51 2019. The rest of these lines are described in the chronyc(1) man page.

The other sub-command I find interesting and useful is `sources` which provides information about the time source configured in chrony.conf

```
[root@studentvm2 ~]# chronyc sources
210 Number of sources = 4
```

```
MS Name/IP address          Stratum Poll Reach LastRx Last sample
===============================================================================
^+ 4.53.160.75                2  10   377    476  -4269us[-4364us] +/-   62ms
^* hydra.spiderspace.co.uk    2  10   377    412  +2528us[+2433us] +/-   21ms
^- ntp.xtom.com               2  10   377    769  +1415us[+1324us] +/-   76ms
^+ time.richiemcintosh.com    2  10   377    309  -7290us[-7290us] +/-   39ms
[root@studentvm2 ~]#
```

These sources were provided by the pool. Note that the "S" column – Source State – indicates that the server with an asterisk (*) in that line is the one to which our host is currently synchronized. This is consistent with the data from the tracking sub-command.

Note that the -v option provides a nice description of the fields in this output. The data is the same but it is displayed with more explanatory information.

```
[root@studentvm2 ~]# chronyc sources -v
210 Number of sources = 4

  .-- Source mode  '^' = server, '=' = peer, '#' = local clock.
 / .- Source state '*' = current synced, '+' = combined , '-' = not combined,
| /   '?' = unreachable, 'x' = time may be in error, '~' = time too variable.
||                                                 .- xxxx [ yyyy ] +/- zzzz
||      Reachability register (octal) -.          |  xxxx = adjusted offset,
||      Log2(Polling interval) --.      |         |  yyyy = measured offset,
||                              \        |         |  zzzz = estimated error.
||                               |       |          \
MS Name/IP address          Stratum Poll Reach LastRx Last sample
===============================================================================
^+ 4.53.160.75                2  10   377    981  -4269us[-4364us] +/-   62ms
^* hydra.spiderspace.co.uk    2  10   377    916  +2528us[+2433us] +/-   21ms
^- ntp.xtom.com               2  10   377    241  +1430us[+1430us] +/-  100ms
^+ time.richiemcintosh.com    2  10   377    811  -7290us[-7290us] +/-   39ms
[root@studentvm2 ~]#
```

Configuring NTP with Chrony

The nice thing about the Chrony configuration file is that this single file is used to configure the host as both a client and a server. So all we need to do to add server function to our host – it will always be a client, obtaining its time from a reference server – is to make only a couple changes to the Chrony configuration and then configure the host's firewall to accept NTP requests.

Configuring the NTP server

The Chrony server requires little additional configuration.

EXPERIMENT 15-2

Perform this experiment as root on StudentVM2.

Use your favorite editor to modify the /etc/chrony.conf file. Uncomment the line

```
# local stratum 10
```

This enables the Chrony NTP server to continue to act as if it were connected to a remote reference server if the connection to the Internet fails. Thus, this host can continue to be an NTP server to other hosts on the local network.

Let's restart chronyd and then track how the service is working for a few minutes. We are not yet an NTP server but we want to test a bit before we go there. Run the following command line program to initiate this test.

```
[root@studentvm2 ~]# systemctl restart chronyd ; watch -n 1 chronyc tracking
```

The results should look like this. The watch command runs the chronyc tracking command once every second and allows us to watch changes occur over time.

Note   It may take a few seconds for the Chrony to locate, connect with, and sync up with the NTP server. Just keep watching.

```
Every 1.0s: chronyc tracking                studentvm2.example.com: Sat Aug
                                            24 20:59:13 2019

Reference ID    : 45A4C6C0 (linode.ibendit.com)
Stratum         : 3
Ref time (UTC)  : Sun Aug 25 00:59:02 2019
System time     : 0.000000766 seconds slow of NTP time
Last offset     : +0.001268859 seconds
RMS offset      : 0.001268859 seconds
Frequency       : 0.225 ppm slow
Residual freq   : +600.482 ppm
Skew            : 0.084 ppm
Root delay      : 0.090373300 seconds
Root dispersion : 0.042884983 seconds
Update interval : 1.7 seconds
Leap status     : Normal
```

Synchronizing directly to the Fedora pool machines would usually result in synchronization at stratum 2 or 3. This depends upon what stratum the pool server is at. Notice also that, over time, the amount of error will decrease. It should eventually stabilize with a tiny variation about a fairly small range of error. The size of the error depends upon the stratum and other network factors. After a few minutes, use Ctrl-C to break out of the watch loop.

Be sure to watch the **System time** line. This shows the difference between the system hardware time and the NTP time. This difference is reduced slowly so as to prevent problems with internal system timers, cron jobs, and systemd timers. This prevents the possibility of jobs being skipped if the correction were to be made as a single jump.

You can rerun the command line program to start this over so you can watch it more than once in case you might have missed something.

To make the StudentVM2 host into an NTP server, we need to allow it to listen on the local network. Uncomment the "allow" line to allow hosts on the local network to access our NTP server and set the network IP address to that of our internal network.

```
# Allow NTP client access from local network.
allow 192.168.56.0/24
```

Note that the server can listen for requests on any local network to which it is attached. Now restart chronyd.

In order to allow other hosts on your network to access this NTP server, it is necessary to configure the firewall to allow inbound UDP packets on port 123. Note that NTP uses UDP packets and not TCP packets. Do that now.

At this point, this host is an NTP server. We can test it with another host or a VM that has access to the network on which the NTP server is listening.

Configuring the client and testing

We will configure the client, StudentVM1, to use the new NTP server as the preferred server in the /etc/chrony.conf file. Then we will monitor that client using the chronyc tools we have already explored.

EXPERIMENT 15-3

Perform this experiment as the root user on StudentVM1. Start by viewing the tracking and sources information to determine the current time source and statistics

```
[root@studentvm1 ~]# chronyc sources
210 Number of sources = 5
MS Name/IP address         Stratum Poll Reach LastRx Last sample
===============================================================================
^+ 192.168.0.52                 3    8   377     57  +1968us[+1968us] +/-   33ms
^- zinc.frizzen.net             3   10   377    909  +1587us[+1409us] +/-  100ms
^- ns3.weiszhosting.com         2   10   377    783    -39us[  -39us] +/-  147ms
^* clock1.alb1.inoc.net         1   10   377    865  -1208us[-1392us] +/-   27ms
^- LAX.CALTICK.NET              2   10   377    31m   -815us[ -727us] +/-  101ms
[root@studentvm1 ~]# watch -n 1 chronyc tracking
Reference ID    : 40F6840E (clock1.alb1.inoc.net)
Stratum         : 2
Ref time (UTC)  : Sun Aug 25 12:48:34 2019
System time     : 0.000490161 seconds fast of NTP time
Last offset     : -0.000184654 seconds
RMS offset      : 0.000759893 seconds
```

```
Frequency        : 0.187 ppm slow
Residual freq    : -0.170 ppm
Skew             : 0.556 ppm
Root delay       : 0.044264890 seconds
Root dispersion  : 0.008576056 seconds
Update interval  : 1037.8 seconds
Leap status      : Normal
```

Add the following line to the /etc/chrony.conf file. I usually place this line just above the first pool server statement near the top of the file as shown in the following. There is no special reason for this except that I like to keep the server statements together. It would work just as well at the bottom of the file, and I have done that on several hosts. This configuration file is not sequence-sensitive.

```
server 192.168.56.1 iburst prefer
# Use public servers from the pool.ntp.org project.
# Please consider joining the pool (http://www.pool.ntp.org/join.html).
pool 2.fedora.pool.ntp.org iburst
```

The prefer option marks this as the preferred reference source. As such, this host will always be synchronized with this reference source so long as it is available. You could also use the fully qualified hostname for a remote reference server, or the hostname only without the domain name for a local reference time source so long as the search statement is set in the /etc/resolv.conf file. I prefer the IP address to ensure that the time source is accessible even if DNS is not working. In most environments, the server name is probably the better option because NTP will continue to work even if the IP address of the server is changed.

Restart Chrony and continue to observe the chronyc tracking output as it updates every second. The results should eventually sync up to StudentVM2 as the Reference ID server.

```
Reference ID     : C0A83801 (studentvm2.example.com)
Stratum          : 3
Ref time (UTC)   : Sun Aug 25 13:10:15 2019
System time      : 0.000000001 seconds slow of NTP time
Last offset      : +0.000002270 seconds
RMS offset       : 0.000002270 seconds
Frequency        : 0.237 ppm slow
Residual freq    : +0.897 ppm
Skew             : 1.328 ppm
Root delay       : 0.030728187 seconds
```

```
Root dispersion : 0.052947082 seconds
Update interval : 2.0 seconds
Leap status     : Normal
[root@studentvm1 ~]#
```

At this point, our StudentVM1 client is using StudentVM2 as its NTP time source. Adding more hosts in our network to use StudentVM2 as the time source is as simple as adding the same line to their chrony.conf files and restarting the Chrony daemon.

chronyc as an interactive tool

I mentioned near the beginning of this chapter that chronyc can be used as an interactive command tool. Simply run the command without a sub-command to display a chronyc command prompt. From there, just type in the sub-commands which can save typing if we need to issue multiple chronyc commands.

EXPERIMENT 15-4

Perform this experiment as the root user on StudentVM1.

```
[root@studentvm1 ~]# chronyc
chrony version 3.4
Copyright (C) 1997-2003, 2007, 2009-2018 Richard P. Curnow and others
chrony comes with ABSOLUTELY NO WARRANTY.  This is free software, and
you are welcome to redistribute it under certain conditions.  See the
GNU General Public License version 2 for details.

chronyc>
```

Enter the Help sub-command to view a list of all the possible sub-commands. Now you can enter just the sub-commands. Try using the tracking, ntpdata, and sources sub-commands. The chronyc command line allows command recall and editing for chronyc sub-commands.

Setting the hardware clock

One thing I like to do after my client computers have synchronized with the NTP server is to set the system hardware clock from the system (OS) time. This is useful because it will take longer to synchronize the host to the NTP time if the hardware clock is very far off. The operating system gets its initial time set from the hardware clock located on the motherboard. If that clock is off, the initial system time will be incorrect.

Of course, our systems are virtual machines, but they also have virtual hardware clocks, so this experiment works as it should.

EXPERIMENT 15-5

Perform this experiment as root on StudentVM2. First read the current value of and then set the hardware clock from the system (Operating System) clock. And then read the hardware clock again.

```
[root@studentvm2 ~]# hwclock -r ; hwclock --systohc --localtime ; hwclock -r
2019-08-25 16:04:56.539023-04:00
2019-08-25 16:04:57.823655-04:00
[root@studentvm2 ~]#
```

The --localtime option ensures that the hardware clock is set to local time rather than UTC. Now do this on the StudentVM1 host.

```
[root@studentvm1 ~]# hwclock -r ; hwclock --systohc --localtime ; hwclock -r
2019-08-25 12:07:24.793523-04:00
2019-08-25 16:07:26.152275-04:00
```

Notice that there was a significant difference in the hardware clock on my instance of StudentVM2. Because the difference was almost exactly 4 hours, I suspect it was a time-zone difference in the hardware clock.

The hwclock command can be added as a cron job or a script in cron.daily to keep the hardware clock synced with the system time.

About time zones

Early timekeeping was based on astronomical observation; specifically, when the sun was at the zenith, it was considered to be high noon. This is called local solar time. This was fine until the railroads came into existence. Because their speed enabled them to travel quickly between locations, it became very complex to calculate and define their schedules in terms of local solar times. This is especially true because local and solar times can differ by as much as 15 minutes throughout the year.

The railroads needed more consistency so they, the communications industries, and others, worked to create a standardized set of time zones. The function of a time zone[2] is to provide large geographical regions with standard times. Every location within a given time zone uses the same time.

Computers sometimes need to have their time zone changed. The computer might be relocated or the organization might decide to convert to UTC as they grow. We can do that easily from the command line. The time zone is set in Fedora by a symlink, /etc/localtime, which points to a file in the /usr/share/zoneinfo directory.

EXPERIMENT 15-6

Perform this experiment as root on StudentVM1. We will look at the current setting, change the system time zone to UTC, and then change it back to the correct time zone for your locale.

First, do a long listing of the /etc/localtime file.

```
[root@studentvm1 ~]# ll /etc/localtime
lrwxrwxrwx. 1 root root 38 Dec 22  2018 /etc/localtime -> ../usr/share/
zoneinfo/America/New_York
[root@studentvm1 ~]#
```

This tells us a lot about time zone configuration. Primarily we find that /etc/localtime is where the system looks for its time zone configuration file. It also tells us that those files are all located in /usr/share/zoneinfo/ and its subdirectories. By using a symbolic link, we can link to any time zone configuration file in the zoneinfo directory tree.

Spend some time exploring this directory tree to see the many files that are there.

---

[2]timeanddate.com, *Time Zones*, `www.timeanddate.com/time/time-zones.html`

We could look for time zones or change the time zone manually, but we do not need to. Modern Fedora systems that use systemd have a tool that makes this a bit easier. The timedatectl utility allows us to list all available time zones and to change the system time zone. Let's start by listing all time zones. This utility dumps its output to the less utility so we can scroll through the many lines of data.

```
[root@studentvm1 ~]# timedatectl list-timezones
Africa/Abidjan
Africa/Accra
Africa/Addis_Ababa
Africa/Algiers
Africa/Asmara
Africa/Bamako
Africa/Bangui
Africa/Banjul
Africa/Bissau
Africa/Blantyre
Africa/Brazzaville
Africa/Bujumbura
Africa/Cairo
Africa/Casablanca
<snip>
Pacific/Noumea
Pacific/Pago_Pago
Pacific/Palau
Pacific/Pitcairn
Pacific/Pohnpei
Pacific/Port_Moresby
Pacific/Rarotonga
Pacific/Saipan
Pacific/Tahiti
Pacific/Tarawa
Pacific/Tongatapu
Pacific/Wake
Pacific/Wallis
UTC
lines 385-426/426 (END)
```

We can also look at the current time zone settings. This command provides the data in a form readable to the machine if we want to use it in a later command.

```
[root@studentvm1 ~]# timedatectl show
Timezone=America/New_York
LocalRTC=yes
CanNTP=yes
NTP=yes
NTPSynchronized=yes
TimeUSec=Sun 2019-08-25 21:40:40 EDT
RTCTimeUSec=Sun 2019-08-25 17:40:40 EDT
[root@studentvm1 ~]#
```

Or this way in more human readable format. It is fine to ignore this warning in most environments. It might be an issue if you are using a real-time clock (RTC) for process control.

```
[root@studentvm1 ~]# timedatectl status
               Local time: Sun 2019-08-25 21:44:12 EDT
           Universal time: Mon 2019-08-26 01:44:12 UTC
                 RTC time: Sun 2019-08-25 21:44:12
                Time zone: America/New_York (EDT, -0400)
System clock synchronized: yes
              NTP service: active
          RTC in local TZ: yes

Warning: The system is configured to read the RTC time in the local time
zone.
         This mode cannot be fully supported. It will create various problems
         with time zone changes and daylight saving time adjustments. The RTC
         time is never updated, it relies on external facilities to maintain it.
         If at all possible, use RTC in UTC by calling
         'timedatectl set-local-rtc 0'.
```

Set the time zone to UTC and verify the change.

```
[root@studentvm1 ~]# timedatectl set-timezone UTC ; date
Mon Aug 26 01:50:26 UTC 2019
[root@studentvm1 ~]#
```

Note that the system time has changed. The GUI desktop clock in the top panel also shows the new time. Look at the localtime file.

```
[root@studentvm1 ~]# ll /etc/localtime
lrwxrwxrwx 1 root root 25 Aug 26 01:50 /etc/localtime -> ../usr/share/
zoneinfo/UTC
[root@studentvm1 ~]#
```

Change the time zone back to your correct local time zone. In my case, that is

```
[root@studentvm1 ~]# timedatectl set-timezone America/New_York ; date
Sun Aug 25 21:55:27 EDT 2019
[root@studentvm1 ~]#
```

Wikipedia has an interesting history of timekeeping in its Time Zone article.[3]

Chapter summary

Chrony is a powerful tool for synchronizing the times of client hosts whether they are all on the local network or scattered around the globe. It is easy to configure because, despite the large number of configuration options available, only a few are required in most circumstances.

Chrony and NTP (the service) both use the same configuration and the files' contents are interchangeable. The man pages for chronyd, chronyc, and chrony.conf contain an amazing amount of information that can help you get started or learn about some esoteric configuration option.

We looked at time zones, their importance, how they are configured, and how to change them

---

[3]Wikipedia, *Time Zones*, https://wikipedia.org/wiki/Time_zone

Exercises

Perform the following exercises to complete this chapter.

1. Why is it important to synchronize the times on all of the computers in a network?

2. When using the `chronyc` tracking command – along with the watch command to observe changes as they occur – what happens to the update interval and why?

3. You may not see this on your host, but in the list of NTP time sources for *my* instance of StudentVM1, there is an entry for 192.168.0.52. What is this entry and why does it appear in the list of sources?

4. Why might it make sense for global organizations to set all of their computers to UTC rather than to local times?

CHAPTER 16

Security

Objectives

In this chapter, you will learn

- Advanced security tools and techniques
- How to enhance security for DNS using chroot
- To modify kernel parameters to enhance network security
- Some advanced IPTables security tips
- Advanced backup techniques
- The use of ClamAV to check for viruses
- To configure basic intrusion detection using TripWire
- To detect root kits using Root Kit Hunter and chkrootkit
- To use SELinux to prevent crackers from modifying critical system files

Introduction

Security is often overlooked or only considered as an afterthought. Despite the fact that this chapter comes near the end of this course, security has been a primary consideration throughout. We have looked at many aspects of security as we explored the administration of Fedora.

There are still some things we need to consider and this chapter looks at aspects of security that have not yet been discussed. It is important to realize that security is obtrusive. It will get in your way and frustrate you when you least need that. Security that does not cause you at least some inconvenience is not going to deter any decent cracker.

345

© David Both 2020
D. Both, *Using and Administering Linux: Volume 3*, https://doi.org/10.1007/978-1-4842-5485-1_16

Advanced DNS security

The BIND DNS service is not especially secure and, with certain vulnerabilities, allow a malicious user to gain access to the root filesystem and possible privilege escalation. This issue is easily resolvable with the use of the BIND chroot package.

We have already had a brief brush with the chroot command in Volume 1, Chapter 19, but did not cover it in any detail. Tightening security on BIND DNS requires that we use chroot, so let's take a closer look.

About chroot

The chroot tool is used to create a secure copy of parts of the Linux filesystem. In this way, if a cracker does force a vulnerability in BIND to access the filesystem, this chroot'ed copy of the filesystem is the only thing at risk. A simple restart of BIND is sufficient to revert to a clean and unhacked version of the filesystem. The chroot utility can be used for more than adding security to BIND, but this is one of the best illustrations for its use.

Enabling bind-chroot

It takes only a little work to enable the chroot'ed BIND environment. We installed the bind-chroot package in Chapter 4 of this volume and we will now put it to use.

EXPERIMENT 16-1

Perform this task as the root user on StudentVM2. Because the bind-chroot package was previously installed, we need only to stop and disable the named service and then enable and start the named-chroot service.

First, explore the /var/named directory. It already contains the chroot subdirectory because we installed the bind-chroot package. Explore the contents of the /var/named/chroot directory for a few moments. Note that there are directories for /dev, /etc, /run, /usr, and /var. Each of those directories contains copies of only the files required to run a chroot'ed version of BIND. This if a cracker gains access to the host via BIND, these copies are all that they will have access to.

Notice also that there are no zone or other configuration files in the /var/named/chroot/var/ named/ directory structure.

Make /var/named the PWD. Stop and disable NAMED.

```
[root@studentvm2 ~]# systemctl disable named ; systemctl stop named
Removed /etc/systemd/system/multi-user.target.wants/named.service.
[root@studentvm2 ~]#
```

Now start and enable the named-chroot service.

```
[root@studentvm2 ~]# systemctl enable named-chroot ; systemctl start named-chroot
Created symlink /etc/systemd/system/multi-user.target.wants/named-chroot.
service → /usr/lib/systemd/system/named-chroot.service.
[root@studentvm2 ~]#
```

Now examine the /var/named/chroot/var/named/ directory and see that the required configuration files are present. Verify the status of the named-chroot service.

```
[root@studentvm2 ~]#  systemctl status named-chroot
• named-chroot.service - Berkeley Internet Name Domain (DNS)
   Loaded: loaded (/usr/lib/systemd/system/named-chroot.service; enabled;
   vendor preset: disabled)
   Active: active (running) since Mon 2019-08-26 13:46:51 EDT; 2min 43s ago
  Process: 20092 ExecStart=/usr/sbin/named -u named -c ${NAMEDCONF} -t /var/
  named/chroot $OPTIONS (code=>
  Process: 20089 ExecStartPre=/bin/bash -c if [ ! "$DISABLE_ZONE_CHECKING" ==
  "yes" ]; then /usr/sbin/na>
 Main PID: 20093 (named)
    Tasks: 5 (limit: 4696)
   Memory: 54.7M
   CGroup: /system.slice/named-chroot.service
           └─20093 /usr/sbin/named -u named -c /etc/named.conf -t /var/
              named/chroot

Aug 26 13:46:51 studentvm2.example.com named[20093]: network unreachable
resolving './DNSKEY/IN': 2001:5>
Aug 26 13:46:51 studentvm2.example.com named[20093]: network unreachable
resolving './NS/IN': 2001:503:b>
Aug 26 13:46:51 studentvm2.example.com named[20093]: network unreachable
resolving './DNSKEY/IN': 2001:5>
```

Aug 26 13:46:51 studentvm2.example.com named[20093]: network unreachable resolving './NS/IN': 2001:500:2>

Aug 26 13:46:51 studentvm2.example.com named[20093]: network unreachable resolving './DNSKEY/IN': 2001:5>

Aug 26 13:46:51 studentvm2.example.com named[20093]: network unreachable resolving './NS/IN': 2001:500:2>

Aug 26 13:46:51 studentvm2.example.com named[20093]: network unreachable resolving './DNSKEY/IN': 2001:d>

Aug 26 13:46:51 studentvm2.example.com named[20093]: network unreachable resolving './NS/IN': 2001:dc3::>

Aug 26 13:46:51 studentvm2.example.com named[20093]: managed-keys-zone: Key 20326 for zone . acceptance >

Aug 26 13:46:51 studentvm2.example.com named[20093]: resolver priming query complete

lines 1-21/21 (END)

Now do a lookup to further verify that it is working as it should. Check that the server that responds to this query has the correct IP address for StudentVM2.

[root@studentvm2 ~]# **dig studentvm1.example.com**

```
; <<>> DiG 9.11.6-P1-RedHat-9.11.6-2.P1.fc29 <<>> studentvm1.example.com
;; global options: +cmd
;; Got answer:
;; ->>HEADER<<- opcode: QUERY, status: NOERROR, id: 50661
;; flags: qr aa rd ra; QUERY: 1, ANSWER: 1, AUTHORITY: 1, ADDITIONAL: 2

;; OPT PSEUDOSECTION:
; EDNS: version: 0, flags:; udp: 4096
; COOKIE: dff58dbd1c4a55385fc785a65d641d0c5ea6f3a3d5550099 (good)
;; QUESTION SECTION:
;studentvm1.example.com.                IN      A

;; ANSWER SECTION:
studentvm1.example.com. 86400   IN      A       192.168.56.21

;; AUTHORITY SECTION:
example.com.            86400   IN      NS      studentvm2.example.com.

;; ADDITIONAL SECTION:
studentvm2.example.com. 86400   IN      A       192.168.56.1
```

```
;; Query time: 0 msec
;; SERVER: 192.168.56.1#53(192.168.56.1)
;; WHEN: Mon Aug 26 13:55:24 EDT 2019
;; MSG SIZE  rcvd: 136

[root@studentvm2 ~]#
```

You should also check to see if the correct results are returned for external domains such as www.example.org, opensource.com, and apress.com.

Note   When using the chroot'ed version of named, changes to the zone files must be made in /var/named/chroot/var/named.

It is also possible to add ACL (Access Control List) to specify which hosts are allowed to access the name server. These ACL definitions and host lists are added to the /etc/named.conf file. Hosts can be explicitly allowed or denied. Figure 16-1 shows how this can be configured. These statements would be added to the options section of /etc/named.conf.

```
acl block-these {
 10.0.2.0/24;
};
acl allow-these {
 192.168.56.0/24;
};
options {
 blackhole { block-these; };
 allow-query { allow-these; };
};
```

Figure 16-1. *Sample ACL entries for named.conf*

In the simple example shown in Figure 16-1, we allow queries from the local network and block queries from the network that leads to the outside world.

Hardening the network

There are some additional steps we can take to harden our network interfaces. Several lines can be added to the /etc/sysctl.d/98-network.conf file which will make our network interfaces more secure. This is highly advisable on the firewall/router.

EXPERIMENT 16-2

Begin this experiment as the root user on StudentVM2.

Add the entries shown to the /etc/ sysctl.d/98-network.conf file so that the file looks like that shown in Figure 16-2. We created this file in Chapter 6 of this volume when we made our StudentVM2 host into a router. we added two lines to this file, one of which is a comment.

These changes will take effect at the next boot. Of course, you can also enable them immediately without a reboot by making the appropriate changes to the associated files in the /proc filesystem.

```
# Controls IP packet forwarding so this host acts as a router

# This setting makes our host a router.
# If we want to turn off routing, change this to a 0
net.ipv4.ip_forward = 1

# Since we *DO* want to act as a router, we need to comment these out
# If the host is not a router, then uncomment these.
# net.ipv4.conf.all.send_redirects = 0
# net.ipv4.conf.default.send_redirects = 0

# Don't reply to broadcasts. Prevents joining a smurf attack
net.ipv4.icmp_echo_ignore_broadcasts = 1

# Enable protection bad icmp error messages
net.ipv4.icmp_ignore_bogus_error_responses = 1

# Enable syncookies SYN flood attack protection
net.ipv4.tcp_syncookies = 1

# Log spoofed, source routed, and redirects packets.
net.ipv4.conf.all.log_martians = 1
net.ipv4.conf.default.log_martians = 1

# Don't allow source routed packets
net.ipv4.conf.all.accept_source_route = 0
net.ipv4.conf.default.accept_source_route = 0

# Turn on reverse path filtering
net.ipv4.conf.all.rp_filter = 1
net.ipv4.conf.default.rp_filter = 1

# Disallow outsiders alter the routing tables
net.ipv4.conf.all.accept_redirects = 0
net.ipv4.conf.default.accept_redirects = 0
net.ipv4.conf.all.secure_redirects = 0
net.ipv4.conf.default.secure_redirects = 0
```

Figure 16-2. *These entries to the /etc/sysctl.conf file provide additional network security*

After making the above additions to the /etc/ sysctl.d/98-network.conf file, reboot the computer. We don't really need to reboot, but it is faster for the purposes of this experiment – unless you want to make these changes directly to the specified files in the /proc filesystem. In my opinion, testing these changes with a reboot is the correct way to test this because the file is intended to set these variable values during the Linux startup.

After the reboot, verify in the /proc filesystem that the variables have their values set as defined in the sysctl.conf file.

It is difficult to test how the changes themselves work without a way in which to generate offending packets. What we can test is that things still work as they should. Ping each host from the other and login to each from the other using SSH. From StudentVM1, ping a host outside the local network, use SSH to log in to an external host, send email, and use a browser to view an external web site. If these tests work, then everything should be in good shape.

I found an error during this testing, so you might also. In my case, I had not set ip_forward to 1 in order to configure StudentVM2 as a router. As a result, I could not ping hosts outside the local network.

These changes can be added to all Linux hosts on a network but should always be added to a system acting as a router with an outside connection to the Internet. Be sure to change the statements related to routing as required for a non-routing host.

Advanced iptables

We have been working throughout this course but especially in this volume, with IPTables to provide firewall rules for our hosts. There are some additional things we can do to improve the efficacy of our firewall.

The primary method for enhancing our IPTables rule set is to specify the network from which the firewall will accept packets requesting a connection either to the firewall or to an external network. We do this with the -s (source) option which allows us to specify a network or specific hosts by IP address. We could also specify the source by interface name such as enp0s3.

EXPERIMENT 16-3

Start this experiment as the root user on StudentVM2. Let's start by performing a test to verify that an SSH connection can be made from the external network, 10.0.2.0/24.

Testing from the outside network is a bit complicated, but we can do it. Remember our StudentVM3 virtual machine? We can use that VM for this purpose. It should already be configured to use the outside network, "StudentNetwork," and it should still be configured to boot from the Live USB image. Because the external network is not configured for DHCP, we must configure the network after the VM has completed its startup.

To make this a little easier, before starting StudentVM3, open the general settings page for StudentVM3 and configure the shared clipboard to be bidirectional. You should also power off StudentVM2 and do the same thing.

Boot StudentVM2 and then Boot StudentVM3 to the Fedora Live image. When the startup has completed, open a terminal session and su to root. Add a new file, /etc/sysconfig/network-scripts/ifcfg-enp0s3, and add the following content. I did this easily; I copied the content of the ifcfg-enp0s3 from StidentVM2. I then opened a new enp0s3 file in an editor on StudentVM3 and pasted the data into it. I made the changes necessary to create the file below and saved it.

I removed the UUID line and set the IPADDR to 10.0.2.31. Everything else can stay the same.

```
TYPE=Ethernet
PROXY_METHOD=none
BROWSER_ONLY=no
BOOTPROTO=none
IPADDR=10.0.2.31
PREFIX=24
GATEWAY=10.0.2.1
DNS1=192.168.56.1
DNS2=10.0.2.1
DEFROUTE=yes
IPV4_FAILURE_FATAL=no   ·
IPV6INIT=yes
IPV6_AUTOCONF=yes
IPV6_DEFROUTE=yes
IPV6_FAILURE_FATAL=no
IPV6_ADDR_GEN_MODE=stable-privacy
```

```
NAME=enpOs3
DEVICE=enpOs3
ONBOOT=yes
```

It should not be necessary to enable the connection as that should happen almost immediately after the file is saved. If it does not start, you can use the **ip** command.

```
[liveuser@localhost-live ~]$ ip link set enpOs3 up
```

Now we can do our initial testing. As the root user on StudentVM3, open an SSH connection to StudentVM2. Because we do not have a valid name server that will resolve studentvm2, we must use its IP address.

```
[root@localhost-live ~]# ssh 10.0.2.11
The authenticity of host '10.0.2.11 (10.0.2.11)' can't be established.
ECDSA key fingerprint is SHA256:NDM/B5L3eRJaalex6IOUdnJsE1smOSiQNWgaI8BwcVs.
Are you sure you want to continue connecting (yes/no)? yes
Warning: Permanently added '10.0.2.11' (ECDSA) to the list of known hosts.
Password: <Enter Password>
Last login: Tue Aug 27 10:41:45 2019 from 10.0.2.31
[root@studentvm2 ~]#
```

So before changing the IPTables rules, we can open an SSH connection to StudentVM2 from StudentVM3.

Now edit the /etc/sysconfig/iptables file on StudentVM2 and change the filter table rule for SSH from this:

```
-A INPUT -p tcp -m state --state NEW -m tcp --dport 22 -j ACCEPT
```

to this:

```
-A INPUT -s 192.168.56.0/24 -p tcp -m state --state NEW -m tcp --dport 22 -j
ACCEPT
```

The CIDR notation for our internal network IP address range allows SSH connections from our internal network and no other. SSH connection attempts from the outside network, 10.0.2.0/24 are rejected by the last rule in the filter table because the packets do not match any other rules.

Save the file and activate the revised rule set.

```
[root@studentvm2 ~]# cd /etc/sysconfig/ ; iptables-restore iptables
```

Begin testing this by ensuring that an SSH connection can still be initiated from StudentVM1.

```
[root@studentvm1 ~]# ssh studentvm2
Last login: Mon Aug 26 16:41:27 2019
[root@studentvm2 ~]# exit
logout
Connection to studentvm2 closed.
[root@studentvm1 ~]#
```

As root on StudentVM3, ping StudentVM2 just to verify the connection.

```
[root@localhost-live ~]# ping -c2 10.0.2.11
PING 10.0.2.11 (10.0.2.11) 56(84) bytes of data.
64 bytes from 10.0.2.11: icmp_seq=1 ttl=64 time=0.450 ms
64 bytes from 10.0.2.11: icmp_seq=2 ttl=64 time=0.497 ms
```

Now try to initiate an SSH connection from StudentVM3.

```
--- 10.0.2.11 ping statistics ---
2 packets transmitted, 2 received, 0% packet loss, time 56ms
rtt min/avg/max/mdev = 0.450/0.473/0.497/0.032 ms
[root@localhost-live ~]# ssh 10.0.2.11
ssh: connect to host 10.0.2.11 port 22: No route to host
[root@localhost-live ~]#
```

This attempt now generates a "No route to host" error message.

Allow StudentVM3 to continue to run because you will need it for the exercises at the end of the chapter. If you turn it off, you will need to reconfigure the network by adding the ifcfg-enp0s3 file again.

Advanced backups

We have already discussed backups as a necessary part of a good security policy, but we did not go into any detail. Let's do that now and look at the **rsync** utility as a tool for backups.

rsync

None of the commercial or more complex open source backup solutions fully met my needs, and restoring from a tarball can be time-consuming and sometimes a bit frustrating. I also really wanted to use another tool I had heard about, **rsync**.[1]

I had been experimenting with the **rsync** command which has some very interesting features that I have been able to use to good advantage. My primary objectives were to create backups from which users could locate and restore files quickly without having to extract data from a backup tarball and to reduce the amount of time taken to create and the backups.

This section is intended only to describe my own use of **rsync** in a backup scenario. It is not a look at all of the capabilities of **rsync** or the many other interesting ways in which it can be used.

The **rsync** command was written by Andrew Tridgell and Paul Mackerras and first released in 1996. The primary intention for **rsync** is to remotely synchronize the files on one computer with those on another. Did you notice what they did to create the name there? **rsync** is open source software and is provided with all of the distros with which I am familiar.

The **rsync** command can be used to synchronize two directories or directory trees whether they are on the same computer or on different computers, but it can do so much more than that. **rsync** creates or updates the target directory to be identical to the source directory. The target directory is freely accessible by all the usual Linux tools because it is not stored in a tarball or zip file or any other archival file type; it is just a regular directory with regular Linux files that can be navigated by regular users using basic Linux tools. This meets one of my primary objectives.

One of the most important features of **rsync** is the method it uses to synchronize preexisting files that have changed in the source directory. Rather than copying the entire file from the source, it uses checksums to compare blocks of the source and target files. If all of the blocks in the two files are the same, no data is transferred. If the data differs, only the blocks that have changed on the source are transferred to the target. This saves an immense amount of time and network bandwidth for remote sync. For example, when I first used my **rsync** Bash script to back up all of my hosts to a large external USB hard drive, it took about 3 hours. That is because all of the data had to be transferred because none of it had been previously backed up. Subsequent backups

---

[1]Wikipedia, *rsync*, https://en.wikipedia.org/wiki/Rsync

took between 3 and 8 minutes of real time, depending upon how many files had been changed or created since the previous backup. I used the **time** command to determine this, so it is empirical data. Last night, for example, it took 3 minutes and 12 seconds to complete a backup of approximately 750GB of data from 6 remote systems and the local workstation. Of course, only a few hundred megabytes of data were actually altered during the day and needed to be backed up.

The simple **rsync** command shown in Figure 16-3 can be used to synchronize the contents of two directories and any of their subdirectories. That is, the contents of the target directory are synchronized with the contents of the source directory so that at the end of the sync, the target directory is identical to the source directory.

```
rsync -aH sourcedir targetdir
```
The -a option is for archive mode which preserves permissions, ownerships and symbolic (soft) links. The -H is used to preserve hard links rather than creating a new file for each hard link. Note that either the source or target directories can be on a remote host.

Figure 16-3. *The minimum command necessary to synchronize two directories using rsync*

Let's see how this works.

EXPERIMENT 16-4

Start this experiment as the student user on StudentVM2. Note the current contents of the student user's home directory. On StudentVM1, also note the contents of the student user's home directory. They should be quite different.

Now we want to sync the student user's home directory on StudentVM1 to that on StudentVM2. As the student user on StudentVM1, use the following command to do that.

```
[student@studentvm1 ~]$ time rsync -aH . studentvm2:/home/student
Password: <Enter password>

real    0m7.517s
user    0m0.101s
sys     0m0.172s
[student@studentvm1 ~]$
```

That was easy! Now check the home directory for the student user on StudentVM2. All of the student user's file that were present on StudentVM1 are now on StudentVM2.

Now let's change a file and see what happens when we run the same command. Pick and existing file and append some more data to it. I did this.

```
[student@studentvm1 ~]$ dmesg >> file7.txt
```

Verify the file sizes on both VMs. they should be different. Now run the previous command again.

```
[student@studentvm1 ~]$ time rsync -aH . studentvm2:/home/student
Password: <Enter password>

real    0m3.136s
user    0m0.021s
sys     0m0.052s
[student@studentvm1 ~]$
```

Verify that file7.txt (or whichever file you chose to work with) is not the same, larger size on both hosts. Compare the times for both instances of the command. The real time is not important because that includes the time we took to type in the password. The important times are the amount of user and system time used by the commands which is significantly less during the second invocation. Although some of that savings may be due to caching, on a system where the command is run once a day to synchronize huge amounts of data, the time savings is very noticeable.

Now let's assume that yesterday we used **rsync** to synchronize two directories. Today we want to re-synchronize them, but we have deleted some files from the source directory. The normal way in which **rsync** would work using the syntax we used in Experiment 16-4 is to simply copy all the new or changed files to the target location and leave the deleted files in place on the target. This may be the behavior you want, but if you would prefer that files deleted from the source also be deleted from the target, that is, the backup, you can add the --delete option to make that happen.

Another interesting option, and my personal favorite because it increases the power and flexibility of rsync immensely, is the --link-dest option. The --link-dest option uses hard links[2,3] to create a series of daily backups that take up very little additional space for each day and also take very little time to create.

Specify the previous day's target directory with this option and a new directory for today. The **rsync** command then creates today's new directory and a hard link for each file in yesterday's directory is created in today's directory. So we now have a bunch of hard links to yesterday's files in today's directory. No new files have been created or duplicated. After creating the target directory for today with this set of hard links to yesterday's target directory, **rsync** performs its sync as usual, but when a change is detected in a file, the target hard link is replaced by a copy of the file from yesterday and the changes to the file are then copied from the source to the target.

So now our command looks like that in Figure 16-4. This version of our rsync command first creates hard links in today's backup directory for each file in yesterday's backup directory. The files in the source directory – the one being backed up – are then compared to the hard links that were just created. If there are no changes to the files in the source directory, no further action is taken.

```
rsync -aH --delete --link-dest=yesterdaystargetdir sourcedir todaystargetdir
```

Figure 16-4. *This command uses hard links to link unchanged files from yesterday's directory to today's. This saves a lot of time*

If there are changes to files in the source directory, rsync deletes the hard link to the file in yesterday's backup directory and makes an exact copy of the file from yesterday's backup. It then copies the changes made to the file from the source directory to today's target backup directory. It also deletes files on the target drive or directory that have been deleted from the source directory.

There are also times when it is desirable to exclude certain directories or files from being synchronized. We usually do not care about backing up cache directories and, because of the large amount of data they can contain, the amount of time required to back them up can be huge compared to other data directories. For this there is the

---

[2]Wikipedia, *Hard Links*, https://en.wikipedia.org/wiki/Hard_link

[3]Both, David, DataBook for Linux, *Using hard and soft links in the Linux filesystem*, www.linux-databook.info/?page_id=5087

--exclude option. Use this option and the pattern for the files or directories you want to exclude. You might want to exclude browser cache files so your new command will look like Figure 16-5.

```
rsync -aH --delete --exclude Cache --link-dest=yesterdaystargetdir sourcedir todaystargetdir
```

Figure 16-5. *This syntax can be used to exclude specified directories or files based on a pattern*

Note that each file pattern you want to exclude must have a separate exclude option.

The **rsync** command has a very large number of options that you can use to customize the synchronization process. For the most part, the relatively simple commands that I have described here are perfect for making backups for my personal needs. Be sure to read the extensive man page for rsync to learn about more of its capabilities as well as details of the options discussed here.

Performing backups

I automated my backups because – "automate everything." I wrote a Bash script, rsbu, that handles the details of creating a series of daily backups using **rsync**. This includes ensuring that the backup medium is mounted, generating the names for yesterday and today's backup directories, creating appropriate directory structures on the backup medium if they are not already there, performing the actual backups, and unmounting the medium.

The end result of the method in which I employ the rsync command in my script is that I end up with a date-sequence of backups for each host in my network. The backup drives end up with a structure similar to the one shown in Figure 16-6. This makes it easy to locate specific files that might need to be restored.

So, starting with an empty disk on January 1, the rsbu script makes a complete backup for each host of all the files and directories that I have specified in the configuration file. This first backup can take several hours if you have a lot of data like I do.

On January 2, the rsync command uses the –link-dest= option to create a complete new directory structure identical to that of January 1; then it looks for files that have changed in the source directories. If any have changed, a copy of the original file from January 1 is made in the January 2 directory and then the parts of the file that have been altered are updated from the original.

After the first backup onto an empty drive, the backups take very little time because the hard links are created first, and then only the files that have been changed since the previous backup need any further work.

```
/-
  |
  /-path to backup media
           |
          /Backups
             |
             |--/host1
             |    |--/2018-01-01
             |    |      |--/etc
             |    |      |--/home
             |    |      |--/var
             |    |      |--/usr/local
             |    |--2018-01-02
             |    |      |--/etc
             |    |      |--/home
             |    |      |--/var
             |    |      |--/usr/local
             |    |--2018-01-03
             |    |      |--/etc
             |    |      |--/home
             |    |      |--/var
             |    |      |--/usr/local
             |   etc
             |--host2
             |    |--2018-01-01
             |    |      |--/etc
             |    |      |--/home
             |    |      |    |
             |    |      |    |--/student
             |    |      |    |    |
             |    |      |    |    |--/file1.txt (Unchanged)
             |    |      |   etc   etc
             |    |      |--/var
             |    |      |--/usr/local
             |    |--2018-01-02
             |    |      |--/etc
             |    |      |--/home
             |    |      |    |
             |    |      |    |--/student
             |    |      |    |    |
             |    |      |    |    |--/file1.txt (Unchanged)
             |    |      |   etc   etc
             |    |      |--/var
             |    |      |--/usr/local
             |    |--2018-01-03
             |    |      |--/etc
             |    |      |--/home
             |    |      |    |
             |    |      |    |--/student
             |    |      |    |    |
             |    |      |    |    |--/file1.txt  (Changed)
             |    |      |   etc   etc
             |    |      |--/var
             |    |      |--/usr/local
            etc etc     etc
```

Figure 16-6. *The directory structure for my backup data disks*

Figure 16-6 also shows a bit more detail for the host2 series of backups for one file, /home/student/file1.txt, on the dates January 1, 2, and 3. On January 2, the file has not changed since January 1. In this case, the rsync backup does not copy the original data from January 1. It simply creates a directory entry with a hard link in the January 2 directory to the January 1 directory which is a very fast procedure. We now have two directory entries pointing to the same data on the hard drive. On January 3, the file has been changed. In this case, the data for ../2018-01-02/home/student/file1.txt is copied to the new directory, ../2018-01-03/home/student/file1.txt and any data blocks that have changed are then copied to the backup file for January 3. These strategies, which are implemented using features of the `rsync` program, allow backing up huge amounts of data while saving disk space and much of the time that would otherwise be required to copy data files that are identical.

One of my procedures is to run the backup script twice each day from a single cron job. The first iteration performs a backup to an internal 4TB hard drive. This is the backup that is always available and always at the most recent version of all my data. If something happens and I need to recover one file or all of them, the most I could possibly lose is a few hours' worth of work.

The second backup is made to one of a rotating series of 4TB external USB hard drive. I take the most recent drive to my safe deposit box at the bank at least once per week. If my home office is destroyed and the backups I maintain there are destroyed along with it, I just have to get the external hard drive from the bank and I have lost at most a single week of data. That type of loss is easily recovered.

The drives I am using for backups, not just the internal hard drive but also the external USB hard drives that I rotate weekly, never fill up. This is because the `rsbu` script I wrote checks the ages in days of the backups on each drive before a new backup is made. If there are any backups on the drive that are older than the specified number of days, they are deleted. The script uses the `find` command to locate these backups. The number of days is specified in the rsbu.conf configuration file.

Of course, after a complete disaster, I would first have to find a new place to live with office space for my wife and I, purchase parts and build new computers, restore from the remaining backup, and then recreate any lost data.

My script, rsbu, is available along with its configuration file, rsbu.conf, and a READ.ME file as a tarball, rsbu.tar, from `https://github.com/Apress/using-and-administering-linux-volume-3/raw/master/rsbu.tar.gz`.

You can use that script as the basis for your own backup procedures. Be sure to make any modifications you need and test thoroughly.

Recovery testing

No backup regimen would be complete without testing. You should regularly test recovery of random files or entire directory structures to ensure not only that the backups are working, but that the data in the backups can be recovered for use after a disaster. I have seen too many instances where a backup could not be restored for one reason or another and valuable data was lost because the lack of testing prevented discovery of the problem.

Just select a file or directory to test and restore it to a test location such as /tmp so that you won't overwrite a file that may have been updated since the backup was performed. Verify that the files' contents are as you expect them to be. Restoring files from a backup made using the preceding rsync commands is simply a matter of finding the file you want to restore from the backup and then copying it to the location to which you want to restore it.

I have had a few circumstances where I have had to restore individual files and, occasionally, a complete directory structure. I have had to restore the entire contents of a hard drive on a couple occasions. Most of the time this has been self-inflicted when I accidentally deleted a file or directory. At least a few times it has been due to a crashed hard drive. So those backups do come in handy.

Restrict SSH remote root login

Sometimes it is necessary to allow SSH connections from external sources and it may not be possible to specify which IP addresses might be the source. In this situation we can prevent root logins via SSH entirely. It would be necessary to login to the firewall host as a non-root user and then su to root or SSH to an internal host as that non-root user and then su to root.

```
                    EXPERIMENT 16-5
```

As the root user on StudentVM1, login to StudentVM2 via SSH. You should be able to do this. After confirming that you have logged into your neighbor's computer, log out again.

On StudentVM2, edit the etc/ssh/sshd_config file and change the following line:

`#PermitRootLogin yes`

To:

`PermitRootLogin no`

And restart SSHD to enable the change. As the root user on StudentVM1, try to log in to StudentVM2 as root.

You should receive a "Permission denied" error. Also be sure to verify that you can login to StudentVM2 as the student user.

Change this back and revert to allowing remote root login on SSH and test to ensure that you can login to StudentVM2 as root.

Malware

Protecting our systems against malware like viruses, root kits, and Trojan horses is a big part of security. We have several tools we can use to do this, four of which we will cover here. Viruses and Trojan horses are usually delivery agents and can be used to deliver malware such as root kits.

Root kits

A root kit is malware that replaces or modifies legitimate GNU Utilities to both perform its own activities and to hide the existence of its own files. For example, a root kit can replace tools like **ls** so that it won't display any of the files installed by the root kit. Other tools can scan log files and remove any entries that might betray the existence of files belonging to the root kit.

Most root kits are intended to allow a remote attacker to take over a computer and use it for their own purposes. With this type of malware, the objective of the attacker is to remain undetected. They are not usually after ransom or to damage your files.

There are two good programs that can be used to scan your system for rootkits. The chkrootkit[4] and Root Kit Hunter[5] tools are both used to locate files that may have been infected, replaced, or compromised by root kits.

Root Kit Hunter also checks for network breaches such as backdoor ports that have been opened. normal services that are listening on various ports such as HTTP and IMAPS. If those services are listening, a warning is printed.

EXPERIMENT 16-6

Perform this experiment as root on StudentVM2. Install the chkrootkit and rkhunter RPMs.

```
[root@studentvm2 ~]# dnf -y install chkrootkit rkhunter
```

Run the **chkrootkit** command. You should get a long list of tests as they are run.

```
[root@studentvm2 ~]# chkrootkit
ROOTDIR is `/'
Checking `amd'... not found
Checking `basename'... not infected
Checking `biff'... not found
Checking `chfn'... not infected
Checking `chsh'... not infected
Checking `cron'... not infected
Checking `crontab'... not infected
Checking `date'... not infected
Checking `du'... not infected
Checking `dirname'... not infected
Checking `echo'... not infected
Checking `egrep'... not infected
<snip>
Searching for Hidden Cobra ... nothing found
Searching for Rocke Miner ... nothing found
```

---

[4]Web site, *chkrootkit*, www.chkrootkit.org

[5]Web site, *Root Kit Hunter*, http://rkhunter.sourceforge.net/

Searching for suspect PHP files... nothing found

Searching for anomalies in shell history files... nothing found

Checking `asp'... not infected

Checking `bindshell'... not infected

Checking `lkm'... chkproc: nothing detected

chkdirs: nothing detected

Checking `rexedcs'... not found

Checking `sniffer'... enp0s3: PF_PACKET(/usr/sbin/NetworkManager)

enp0s8: PF_PACKET(/usr/sbin/dhcpd, /usr/sbin/NetworkManager)

Checking `w55808'... not infected

Checking `wted'... 2 deletion(s) between Sat Dec 22 12:59:04 2018 and Sat Dec 22 13:16:15 2018

2 deletion(s) between Sat Dec 22 13:22:00 2018 and Sat Dec 22 14:28:58 2018

2 deletion(s) between Sat Dec 22 14:29:23 2018 and Sat Dec 22 20:45:25 2018

Checking `scalper'... not infected

Checking `slapper'... not infected

Checking `z2'... chklastlog: nothing deleted

Checking `chkutmp'... The tty of the following user process(es) were not found
 in /var/run/utmp !

```
! RUID          PID TTY     CMD
! student      2310 pts/0  bash
! student      2339 pts/0  su -
! root         2344 pts/0  -bash
! root         2367 pts/0  screen
```

! -oPubkeyAcceptedKeyTypes=rsa-sha256,rsa-sha2-256-cert-v01@openssh.
com,ecdsa-sha2-nistp256,ecdsa-sha2-nistp256-cert-v01@openssh.com,ecdsa-sha2-nistp384,ecdsa-sha2-nistp384-cert-v01@openssh.com,rsa-sha2-512,rsa-sha2-512-cert-v01@openssh.com,ecdsa-sha2-nistp521,ecdsa-sha2-nistp521-cert-v01@op 28783 sh-ed25519-cert-v01@openssh.com,-oPubkeyAcceptedKeyTypes=rsa-sha256,rsa-sha2-256-cert-v01@openssh.com,ecdsa-sha2-nistp256,ecdsa-sha2-nistp256-cert-v01@openssh.com,ecdsa-sha2-nistp384,ecdsa-sha2-nistp384-cert-v01@openssh.com,rsa-sha2-512,rsa-sha2-512-cert-v01@openssh.com,ecdsa-sha2-nistp521,ecdsa-sha2-nistp521-cert-v01@op 256,rsa-sha2-256-cert-v01@openssh.com,ecdsa-sha2-nistp256,ecdsa-sha2-nistp256-cert-v01@openssh.com,ecdsa-sha2-nistp384,ecdsa-sha2-nistp384-cert-v01@openssh.com,rsa-sha2-512,rsa-sha2-512-cert-v01@openssh.com,ecdsa-sha2-nistp521,ecdsa-sha2-nistp521-cert-v01@opchkutmp: nothing deleted

Checking `OSX_RSPLUG'... not tested

You can see all of the checks performed by this tool. Any anomalies would be noted. There is no man page for **chkrootkit** but there is some documentation in /usr/share/doc/chkrootkit. Be sure to read that for additional information.

I think that the Root Kit Hunter program is a better and more complete program. It is more flexible because it can update the signature files without upgrading the entire program. Like chkrootkit, it also checks for changes to certain system executable files that are frequently targeted by crackers.

Before running RootKit Hunter the first time, update the signature files.

```
[root@testvm3 sbin]# rkhunter --update
Checking rkhunter data files...
  Checking file mirrors.dat                          [ Updated ]
  Checking file programs_bad.dat                     [ Updated ]
  Checking file backdoorports.dat                    [ No update ]
  Checking file suspscan.dat                         [ Updated ]
  Checking file i18n/cn                              [ No update ]
  Checking file i18n/de                              [ Updated ]
  Checking file i18n/en                              [ No update ]
  Checking file i18n/tr                              [ Updated ]
  Checking file i18n/tr.utf8                         [ Updated ]
  Checking file i18n/zh                              [ Updated ]
  Checking file i18n/zh.utf8                         [ Updated ]
  Checking file i18n/ja                              [ Updated ]
[root@studentvm2 ~]#
```

Now create the initial database of critical files.

```
[root@studentvm2 ~]# rkhunter --propupd
[ Rootkit Hunter version 1.4.6 ]
File created: searched for 177 files, found 138
[root@studentvm2 ~]#
```

Note   The rkhunter --propupd command should be run after updates are installed and after upgrades to new releases such as from Fedora 29 to Fedora 30.

Now run the command to check for rootkits. The --sk option skips the normal pause between the different tests. The -c option tells rkhunter to check for rootkits.

```
[ Rootkit Hunter version 1.4.6 ]

Checking system commands...

  Performing 'strings' command checks
    Checking 'strings' command                          [ OK ]

  Performing 'shared libraries' checks
    Checking for preloading variables                   [ None found ]
    Checking for preloaded libraries                    [ None found ]
    Checking LD_LIBRARY_PATH variable                   [ Not found ]

  Performing file properties checks
    Checking for prerequisites                          [ OK ]
    /usr/sbin/adduser                                   [ OK ]
    /usr/sbin/chkconfig                                 [ OK ]
<snip>
    Knark Rootkit                                       [ Not found ]
    ld-linuxv.so Rootkit                                [ Not found ]
    LiOn Worm                                           [ Not found ]
    Lockit / LJK2 Rootkit                               [ Not found ]
    Mokes backdoor                                      [ Not found ]
    Mood-NT Rootkit                                     [ Not found ]
    MRK Rootkit                                         [ Not found ]
    NiO Rootkit                                         [ Not found ]
    Ohhara Rootkit                                      [ Not found ]
    Optic Kit (Tux) Worm                                [ Not found ]
    Oz Rootkit                                          [ Not found ]
    Phalanx Rootkit                                     [ Not found ]
    Phalanx2 Rootkit                                    [ Not found ]
    Phalanx2 Rootkit (extended tests)                   [ Not found ]
    Portacelo Rootkit                                   [ Not found ]
    R3dstorm Toolkit                                    [ Not found ]
<snip>
```

This program also displays a long list of tests and their results as it runs, along with a nice summary at the end. You can find a complete log with even more detailed information at /var/log/rkhunter/rkhunter.log.

Note that the installation RPM for Root Kit Hunter sets up a daily cron job with a script in /etc/cron.daily. The script performs this check every morning at about 3 a.m. If a problem is detected, an email message is sent to root. If no problems are detected, no email or any other indication that the rkhunter program was even run is provided.

Clam-AV

ClamAV is one open source anti-virus program. There are others and there are some that are not Open Source. ClamAV can be used to scan a computer for viruses.

ClamAV is not installed on your host by default. It will be installed with an empty database file and will fail when run if a valid database is not installed. We will install the ClamAV update utility which will also install all dependencies. Installing the clamav-update package allows easy update of the ClamAV database using the freshclam command.

EXPERIMENT 16-7

Perform this experiment as the root user on StudentVM2. First, install clamAV and clamav-update.

```
[root@studentvm2 ~]# dnf -y install clamav clamav-update
```

Now edit the /etc/freshclam.conf file and delete or comment out the "Example" line. Update the ClamAV database.

```
[root@studentvm2 ~]# freshclam
ClamAV update process started at Thu Aug 29 12:17:31 2019
WARNING: Your ClamAV installation is OUTDATED!
WARNING: Local version: 0.101.3 Recommended version: 0.101.4
DON'T PANIC! Read https://www.clamav.net/documents/upgrading-clamav
Downloading main.cvd [100%]
main.cvd updated (version: 58, sigs: 4566249, f-level: 60, builder: sigmgr)
Downloading daily.cvd [100%]
daily.cvd updated (version: 25556, sigs: 1740591, f-level: 63, builder: raynman)
Downloading bytecode.cvd [100%]
bytecode.cvd updated (version: 330, sigs: 94, f-level: 63, builder: neo)
Database updated (6306934 signatures) from database.clamav.net (IP:
104.16.219.84)
[root@studentvm2 ~]#
```

You will notice that there are a couple warnings in that output data. ClamAV needs to be updated, but the latest version has not yet been uploaded to the Fedora repository.

Now you can run the clamscan command on arbitrary specified directories. Using the -r option scans directories recursively. The output data stream is a list of files. Those that are not infected have OK at the end of the line.

```
[root@studentvm2 ~]# clamscan -r /root /var/spool /home
/root/.viminfo: OK
/root/.local/share/mc/history: OK
/root/.razor/server.c303.cloudmark.com.conf: OK
/root/.razor/server.c302.cloudmark.com.conf: OK
/root/.razor/server.c301.cloudmark.com.conf: OK
/root/.razor/servers.nomination.lst: OK
/root/.razor/servers.discovery.lst: OK
/root/.razor/servers.catalogue.lst: OK
/root/.config/htop/htoprc: OK
/root/.config/mc/panels.ini: Empty file
<snip>
/home/student/.thunderbird/w453leb8.default/AlternateServices.txt: Empty file
/home/student/.thunderbird/w453leb8.default/SecurityPreloadState.txt: Empty
file
/home/student2/.bash_logout: OK
/home/student2/.bashrc: OK
/home/student2/.bash_profile: OK
/home/student2/.bash_history: OK
/home/email1/.bash_logout: OK
/home/email1/.bashrc: OK
/home/email1/.esd_auth: OK
/home/email1/.bash_profile: OK
/home/email1/.config/pulse/b62e5e58cdf74e0e967b39bc94328d81-default-source:
OK
/home/email1/.config/pulse/b62e5e58cdf74e0e967b39bc94328d81-device-volumes.
tdb: OK
/home/email1/.config/pulse/b62e5e58cdf74e0e967b39bc94328d81-card-database.
tdb: OK
/home/email1/.config/pulse/b62e5e58cdf74e0e967b39bc94328d81-stream-volumes.
tdb: OK
```

```
/home/email1/.config/pulse/cookie: OK
/home/email1/.config/pulse/b62e5e58cdf74e0e967b39bc94328d81-default-sink: OK
/home/smauth/.bash_logout: OK
/home/smauth/.bashrc: OK
/home/smauth/.bash_profile: OK

----------- SCAN SUMMARY -----------
Known viruses: 6296694
Engine version: 0.101.3
Scanned directories: 431
Scanned files: 3463
Infected files: 0
Data scanned: 574.65 MB
Data read: 489.07 MB (ratio 1.17:1)
Time: 479.099 sec (7 m 59 s)
[root@studentvm2 ~]#
```

This command emits a very long data stream, so I reproduced only a bit of it here. Using the **tee** command records the data stream in the specified file while also sending it on to STDOUT. This makes it easy to use different tools and searches on the file.

View the content of the clamscan.txt file. See if you can find files that do not have "OK" appended to the end of the line.

The **clamscan** utility should be run on a regular basis to ensure that no viruses have penetrated your defenses.

Tripwire

Tripwire is intrusion detection software. It can report on system files that have been altered in some way, possibly by malware installed as part of a root kit or Trojan horse. Like many tools of this type, Tripwire cannot prevent an intrusion; it can only report on one after it has occurred and left behind some evidence that can be detected and identified.

Tripwire[6] is also a commercial company that sells a version of Tripwire and other cybersecurity products. We will install an open source version of Tripwire and configure it for use on our server.

---

[6]Tripwire, https://www.tripwire.com

EXPERIEMNT 16-8

Perform this experiment as the root user on StudentVM2. First, install Tripwire.

[root@studentvm2 ~]# **dnf -y install tripwire**

The Tripwire RPM for Fedora does not create a complete and working configuration. The documentation in the /usr/share/doc/tripwire/README.Fedora file contains instructions for performing that configuration. I strongly suggest you read that file, but we will proceed here with the bare minimum required to get Tripwire working.

Next we need to create the tripwire keyfiles that will be used to encrypt and sign the database files.

[root@studentvm2 tripwire]# **tripwire-setup-keyfiles**

```
----------------------------------------------

The Tripwire site and local passphrases are used to sign a  variety  of
files, such as the configuration, policy, and database files.

Passphrases should be at least 8 characters in length and contain  both
letters and numbers.

See the Tripwire manual for more information.

----------------------------------------------
Creating key files...

(When selecting a passphrase, keep in mind that good passphrases typically
have upper and lower case letters, digits and punctuation marks, and are
at least 8 characters in length.)

Enter the site keyfile passphrase:<Enter passphrase>
Verify the site keyfile passphrase:<Enter passphrase>
Generating key (this may take several minutes)...Key generation complete.

(When selecting a passphrase, keep in mind that good passphrases typically
have upper and lower case letters, digits and punctuation marks, and are
at least 8 characters in length.)
```

Enter the local keyfile passphrase:**<Enter passphrase>**
Verify the local keyfile passphrase:**<Enter passphrase>**
Generating key (this may take several minutes)...Key generation complete.

Signing configuration file...
Please enter your site passphrase: **<Enter passphrase>**
Wrote configuration file: /etc/tripwire/tw.cfg

A clear-text version of the Tripwire configuration file:
/etc/tripwire/twcfg.txt
has been preserved for your inspection. It is recommended that you
move this file to a secure location and/or encrypt it in place (using a
tool such as GPG, for example) after you have examined it.

Signing policy file...
Please enter your site passphrase: **<Enter passphrase>**
Wrote policy file: /etc/tripwire/tw.pol

A clear-text version of the Tripwire policy file:
/etc/tripwire/twpol.txt
has been preserved for your inspection. This implements a minimal
policy, intended only to test essential Tripwire functionality. You
should edit the policy file to describe your system, and then use
twadmin to generate a new signed copy of the Tripwire policy.

Once you have a satisfactory Tripwire policy file, you should move the
clear-text version to a secure location and/or encrypt it in place
(using a tool such as GPG, for example).

Now run "tripwire --init" to enter Database Initialization Mode. This
reads the policy file, generates a database based on its contents, and
then cryptographically signs the resulting database. Options can be
entered on the command line to specify which policy, configuration, and
key files are used to create the database. The filename for the
database can be specified as well. If no options are specified, the
default values from the current configuration file are used.

[root@studentvm2 tripwire]#

Now we need to initialize the Tripwire database. This command scans the files and creates a signature for each file. It encrypts and signs the database to ensure that it cannot be altered without alerting us to that fact. This command can take several minutes to complete. We can use the --init option or its synonym, -m i.

```
[root@studentvm2 ~]# tripwire --init
```

You will see some warnings about files that the default policy expects to see. You can ignore those for this experiment, but for a production environment, you would want to create a policy file that reflects the files you actually have and the actions to be taken if one changes.

```
We can now run an integrity check of our system.
```

```
[root@studentvm2 tripwire]# tripwire --check | tee /root/tripwire.txt
```

Once again, Tripwire generates the same warnings. Explore the Tripwire report file we created which contains a nice summary near the beginning.

Note that the file created by Tripwire, /var/lib/tripwire/report/studentvm2.example.com-20190829-144939.twr is an encrypted file. It can only be viewed using the twprint utility to view those files.

```
[root@studentvm2 ~]# twprint --print-report --twrfile /var/lib/tripwire/
report/studentvm2.example.com-20190829-144939.twr | less
```

SELinux

We disabled SELinux early in this course so we would not need to deal with side effects in other experiments caused by this important security tool. SELinux was developed by the NSA to provide a highly secure computing environment. True to the GPL, they have made this code available to the rest of the Linux community, and it is included as part of nearly every mainstream distribution.

I have no idea how much we should trust the NSA itself, but because the code is open source and can be and has been examined by many programmers around the world, the likelihood of it containing malicious code is quite low. With that said, SELinux is an excellent security tool.

SELinux provides Mandatory Access Control (MAC) which ensures that users must be provided explicit access rights to each object in the host system. The objective of SELinux[7] is to prevent a security breach – an intrusion – and to limit the damage that they may wreak if they do manage to access a protected host. It accomplishes this by labeling every filesystem object and processes. It uses policy rules to define the possible interactions between labeled objects and the kernel enforces these rules.

Red Hat has a well-done document that covers SELinux.[8] Although written for RHEL 7, it will also apply to all current versions of RHEL, CentOS, Fedora, and other Red Hat-derived distributions.

Under Fedora, SELinux has provided three sets of policy files, although you can create your own and other distros may have other pre-configured policies. By default, only the Targeted policy files are installed by Fedora. Figure 16-7 shows the pre-configured policies along with a short description of each.

SELinux Policy Name	Description
Minimum	A very limited policy that protects very little. A good starting place for testing and learning in a real-world environment.
Targeted	A policy that targets only specific processes and files. Daemons for dhcpd, httpd, named, nscd, ntpd, portmap, snmpd, squid, and syslogd may be protected – the specific ones depend upon the distribution and release. Anything unprotected runs in the unconfined_t domain which allows subjects and objects with that security context to operate using standard Linux security.
Multi-level Security (MLS)	This policy gives full SELInux protection to all objects.

Figure 16-7. *These are the three default SELinux policies provided by Fedora*

SELinux also has three modes of operation, enforcing and permissive, as described in Figure 16-8.

---

[7]Opensource.com, A sysadmin's guide to SELinux: 42 answers to the big questions, `https://opensource.com/article/18/7/sysadmin-guide-selinux`

[8]Red Hat, *Selinux User's And Administrator's Guide,* `https://access.redhat.com/documentation/en-us/red_hat_enterprise_linux/7/html/selinux_users_and_administrators_guide/index`

SELinux Mode	Description
Disabled	SELinux is disabled.
Permissive	Behaves as if it were enforcing the active policy, including labeling objects and adding entries to log files. It does not however enforce the policy. This mode could be used to test SELinux policies while not interfering with any aspect of the system.
Enforcing	Enforces the current policy.

Figure 16-8. *SELinux operational modes*

In this section, we will explore some basic SELinux tasks.

EXPERIMENT 16-9

Perform this experiment as the root user on StudentVM2.

Go to the /etc/selinux directory and view the directories there. You should see that, by default, only the Targeted policy files are installed by Fedora. Install the MLS and Minimal SELinux policy files and look at the contents of this directory again.

[root@studentvm2 selinux]# **dnf install -y selinux-policy-minimum selinux-policy-mls**

Each policy is installed in a subdirectory of /etc/selinux. Look at the contents of the /etc/selinux directory again and notice the new minimum and mls subdirectories for their respective policy files.

First, let's see if there are any man pages to which we can refer if we have questions.

[root@david ~]# **apropos selinux**

No pages are listed so we should also install the SELinux man pages and documentation.

[root@david ~]# **dnf install selinux-policy-doc**

Now look for SELinux man pages. Still nothing. We forgot to rebuild the man page database.

[root@david ~]# **mandb**

You should now find over 900 relevant man pages.

The default mode for SELinux is "Targeted – Permissive." An early experiment had you disable SELinux. Edit the /etc/selinux/config file and set the following options.

```
SELINUX=permissive
SELINUXTYPE=targeted
```

Reboot the system. It will take several minutes during the first reboot while SELinux relabels the targeted files and directories. This can be seen in Figure 16-9. Labeling is the process of assigning a security context to a process or a file. The system will reboot again at end of the relabel process.

Figure 16-9. *SELinux relabels system objects during a reboot*

Login to the desktop as student. Open a terminal session as student and another as root. Run the command id -Z in both terminals. The results should be the same, with both IDs being completely unconfined.

```
[root@studentvm2 ~]# id -Z
unconfined_u:unconfined_r:unconfined_t:s0-s0:c0.c1023
```

As root, use the getenforce command to verify the current state of enforcement.

```
[root@studentvm2 ~]# getenforce
Permissive
```

Run the **sestatus** command to view an overall status for SELinux. The following sample output shows typical results.

```
[root@studentvm2 etc]# sestatus -v
SELinux status:                 enabled
SELinuxfs mount:                /sys/fs/selinux
SELinux root directory:         /etc/selinux
Loaded policy name:             targeted
Current mode:                   permissive
Mode from config file:          permissive
Policy MLS status:              enabled
Policy deny_unknown status:     allowed
Memory protection checking:     actual (secure)
Max kernel policy version:      31

Process contexts:
Current context:                unconfined_u:unconfined_r:unconfined_t:s0-
                                s0:c0.c1023
Init context:                   system_u:system_r:init_t:s0
/usr/sbin/sshd                  system_u:system_r:sshd_t:s0-s0:c0.c1023

File contexts:
Controlling terminal:           unconfined_u:object_r:user_devpts_t:s0
/etc/passwd                     system_u:object_r:passwd_file_t:s0
/etc/shadow                     system_u:object_r:shadow_t:s0
/bin/bash                       system_u:object_r:shell_exec_t:s0
/bin/login                      system_u:object_r:login_exec_t:s0
/bin/sh                         system_u:object_r:bin_t:s0 ->
                                system_u:object_r:shell_exec_t:s0
```

```
/sbin/agetty                    system_u:object_r:getty_exec_t:s0
/sbin/init                      system_u:object_r:bin_t:s0 ->
                                system_u:object_r:init_exec_t:s0
/usr/sbin/sshd                  system_u:object_r:sshd_exec_t:s0
[root@studentvm2 ~]#
```

Run the following command to set the mode to enforcing. Run the sestatus -v command to verify that the SELinux mode is set to "enforcing". Run the id command to determine the user's context. The user should still be unconfined.

```
[root@studentvm2 ~]# setenforce enforcing
```

Start the HTTPD service if it is not already running, and run the command

```
[root@studentvm2 ~]# ps -efZ
```

to display the context of the running processes. Note that many processes are unconfined but that some processes, such as various kernel and HTTPD ones, are running in the system_u:system_r context. Some services run in the kernel_t domain while the HTTPD service tasks run in a special httpd_t domain.

Users who do not have authority for those contexts are unable to manipulate those processes, even when they su to root. However, the "targeted enforcing" mode allows all users to have all privileges so it would be necessary to restrict some or all users in the seusers file.
To see this, as root, stop the HTTPD service and verify that it has stopped.

Logout of the user student session. As root, add the following line to the /etc/selinux/targeted/seusers file. Note that each policy has its own seusers file.

```
student:user_u:s0-s0:c0.c1023
```

It is not necessary to reboot or restart SELinux. Now log in as the user student and su to root. What happens? What is the user's current context?

This is a rather blunt approach, but SELinux does allow you to get much more granular. Creating and compiling those more granular policies is beyond the scope of this course.

Now set the policy mode to "permissive" using the setenforce command and try again to su to root. What happens?

Do a bit of cleanup and edit the /etc/selinux/config file again and set SELINUX=disabled. Reboot your studentvm2 host.

Additional SELinux considerations

Making changes to the filesystem while SELinux is disabled may result in improperly labeled objects and possible vulnerabilities. The best way to ensure that everything is properly labeled is to add an empty file named /.autorelabel in the root directory and reboot the system.

SELinux is intolerant of extra whitespace. Be sure to eliminate extra whitespace in SELinux configuration files in order to ensure that there are no errors.

Social engineering

There is not room or time to delve into all the ways that crackers can use social engineering to convince users to click a URL that will take them to a web site that will infect their computer with some form of malware. The human factor is well beyond the scope of this book, but there are some excellent web sites that can be used as references to help users understand the online threats and how to protect themselves. Figure 16-10 lists some of these web sites.

Name	URL	Notes
Organization for Social Media Safety	https://ofsms.org	Aimed at youth and parents especially and provides information about how to be safe when using social media.
Safe Connects	https://www.netliteracy.org/safe-connects/	More on-line safety aimed at teens.
Kaspersky	https://usa.kaspersky.com/resource-center/preemptive-safety/top-10-internet-safety-rules-and-what-not-to-do-online	General tips for protecting your financial and identity information as well as general safety information.
Web MD	https://www.webmd.com/parenting/guide/internet-safety#1	Again, generally aimed at parents but really applies to all.
Center for Cyber Safety and Education	https://www.iamcybersafe.org/	A good site for anyone with sections for children, parents and senior citizens.

Figure 16-10. *A few of the many web sites that provide Internet-safety materials*

A search on "Internet safety" will result in a huge number (well over a billion) of hits, but the best results will be in the first few pages. Many are aimed at youth, teens, and parents, but they have good information for everyone.

Chapter summary

This chapter has explored some additional security precautions that we can take to further harden our Fedora systems against various types of cracking attacks. It also explored some advanced backup techniques because, failing all else, good, usable backups can allow us to recover from most any disaster including crackers.

None of the tools discussed in this chapter provide a single solution for Linux system security – there is no such thing. Taken together in combinations that make sense for your environment, as well as along with all of the other security we have previously implemented in this course, these tools can significantly improve the security of any Linux host. Although our virtual network and the virtual machines contained in it are now safer, there is always more that can be done. The question we need to ask is whether the cost of the effort required to lock down our systems and networks even more is worth the benefits accrued by doing so.

Remember, like most of the subjects we have covered in this course, we have just touched the surface. You should now be aware of a few of the dangers and some of the tools we have to counter those threats. This is only the beginning and you should explore these tools and others not covered here, in more depth in order to ensure that the security of Linux hosts for which you have responsibility are secured to the greatest extent possible.

Exercises

Perform the following exercises to complete this chapter.

1. In Experiment 16-3, there is no valid DNS server that can be used for our SSH command to StudentVM2. Why does the name server on StudentVM2 not work for this?

2. On StudentVM2, identify the network ports that we have open with IPTables rules and which should be open only on the internal network and not the external network. Modify those rules to accept connections only from the internal network. Test the results.

3. If you have not already, download the rsbu.tar.gz file from the Apress web site `https://github.com/Apress/using-and-administering-linux-volume-3/raw/master/rsbu.tar.gz` and install it. Using the enclosed script and configuration file, set up a simple backup configuration that runs once per day and backs up the entire home directories of both StudentVM1 and StudentVM2.

4. With SELinux enabled, determine the student user's context.

5. Why should clamscan be run on the /home directory of a mail server?

6. Configure Tripwire to the files that do not exist on StudentVM2. Initialize the database and run the integrity check.

7. Why are the Tripwire report files encrypted?

8. What other services, besides HTTPD, have their own SELinux domains?

CHAPTER 17

Advanced Package Management

Objectives

In this chapter, you will learn

- To prepare an rpmbuild directory structure to contain RPMs for different architectures

- To generate an RPM specification (spec) file that defines the structure of the generated RPM package and the files and embedded scripts to be included in it

- To build an RPM package that contains user generated scripts and configuration files

Introduction

I have used RPM-based package managers to install software on Red Hat, CentOS, and Fedora since I started using Linux over 20 years ago. From the RPM program itself, to YUM, and then DNF, which is a close descendant of YUM, I have used these tools to install and update packages on my Linux hosts. But that was all about installing packages. The YUM and DNF tools are wrappers around the RPM utility and provide additional functionality such as the ability to find and install package dependencies.

Over the years I have created a number of Bash scripts, some of which have separate configuration files, that I like to install on most of my new computers and virtual machines. It finally reached the point that it took a great deal of time to install all of these packages. I decided to automate that process by creating an RPM package that I could

© David Both 2020
D. Both, *Using and Administering Linux: Volume 3*, https://doi.org/10.1007/978-1-4842-5485-1_17

copy to the target hosts and install all of these files in their proper locations. Although the RPM tool was formerly used to build RPM packages, that function of RPM was removed and moved a new tool; RPMBUILD was created to build new RPMs.

When I started this project, I found very little information about creating RPM packages but managed to find a book, Maximum RPM, that enabled me to figure it out. That hard-copy book is now somewhat out of date as is the vast majority of information I have found. It is also out of print, and used copies go for hundreds of dollars. The online version of Maximum RPM[1] is available at no charge and is apparently being kept up to date. The RPM web site also has links to other web sites that have a lot of documentation about RPM. What other information there is tends to be very brief and apparently assumes that you already have a good deal of knowledge about the process.

Another good resource for the RPM tools that I have found is at RPM.org. This web page lists most of the available online documentation for RPM. It is mostly link to other web sites and information about RPM itself. I especially like the Fedora RPM Guide.

All of the documents I found assumes that the code needs to be compiled from sources as in a development environment. I am not a developer, I am a SysAdmin, and we SysAdmins have different needs because we don't – well shouldn't – be compiling code to use for administrative tasks; we should be using shell scripts. So we have no source code in the sense that it is something that needs to be compiled into binary executables. What we have is source code that is also the executable.

For the most part, the experiments in this chapter should be performed as the non-root user, student. RPMs should never be built by root but only by non-privileged users.

Preparation

There are some things we need to do in order to prepare for building RPMs. This includes installing the rpmbuild software, downloading the tarball that contains the files we will be including in the RPM as well as the spec file used to build the RPM, and creating the build directory structure.

---

[1]Bailey, Edward C., et al, *Maximum RPM*, `http://ftp.rpm.org/max-rpm/`, Red Hat, 2000

EXPERIMENT 17-1

Start this experiment as the root user – one of few exceptions – on StudentVM1. We will install the rpm-build and rpmdevtools packages as they are most likely not already installed. Install it now as root.

```
[root@studentvm1 ~]# dnf install -y rpm-build rpmdevtools
```

Now, as the student user, make your home directory (~) the PWD and download[2] a tarball that I have prepared of a development directory structure, utils.tar, using the following command.

```
[student@studentvm1 ~]# wget https://github.com/Apress/using-and-
administering-linux-volume-3/raw/master/utils.tar
```

This tarball includes all of the files and BASH scripts that will be installed by the final RPM. There is also a complete spec file which you can use to build the RPM. We will go into detail about each section of the spec file. We installed the RPM created from this tarball in Chapter 12 of Volume 1.

As user student, using your home directory as your present working directory (PWD), untar the tarball.

```
[student@studentvm1 ~]$ tar -xvf utils.tar
./
./development/
./development/scripts/
./development/scripts/create_motd
./development/scripts/die
./development/scripts/mymotd
./development/scripts/sysdata
./development/spec/
./development/spec/utils.spec
./development/license/
./development/license/Copyright.and.GPL.Notice.txt
./development/license/GPL_LICENSE.txt
[student@studentvm1 ~]$
```

---

[2]This utils.tar tarball is also available at my own download page. www.linux-databook.info/
downloads/

Verify that the directory structure of ~/development and the contained files looks like the following output.

```
[student@studentvm1 ~]$ tree development/
development/
├── license
│   ├── Copyright.and.GPL.Notice.txt
│   └── GPL_LICENSE.txt
├── scripts
│   ├── create_motd
│   ├── die
│   ├── mymotd
│   └── sysdata
└── spec
    └── utils.spec

3 directories, 7 files
[student@studentvm1 ~]$
```

Change ownership of these files and directories to student.student.

The mymotd script creates a "Message Of The Day" data stream that is sent to STDOUT. The create_motd script runs the mymotd scripts and redirects the output to the /etc/motd file. This file is used to display a daily message to users who login remotely using SSH.

The die script is my own script that wraps the kill command in a bit of code that can find running programs that match a specified string and kill them. It uses kill -9 to ensure that they cannot ignore the kill message. The sysdata script can spew tens of thousands of lines of data about your computer hardware, the installed version of Linux, all installed packages, and the metadata of your hard drives. I use it to document the state of a host at a point in time. I can later use that information for reference. I used to do this to maintain a record of hosts that I installed for customers.

Most of the files and directories in this tree will be installed on Fedora systems by the RPM you create during this project. Some are used to build the RPM.

Now let's create the build directory structure. The rpmbuild command requires a very specific directory structure. You must create this directory structure yourself because no automated way is provided to do it.

EXPERIMENT 17-2

As the student user on StudentVM1, create the following directory structure in your home directory.

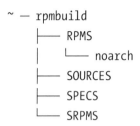

```
~ — rpmbuild
    ├── RPMS
    │   └── noarch
    ├── SOURCES
    ├── SPECS
    └── SRPMS
```

The ~/rpmbuild/RPMS directory contains subdirectories for the finished RPMs based on their architecture. Here is one way to create these directories

```
[student@studentvm1 ~]$ mkdir rpmbuild
[student@studentvm1 ~]$ cd rpmbuild/
[student@studentvm1 rpmbuild]$ mkdir -p RPMS/noarch SOURCES SPECS SRPMS
[student@studentvm1 rpmbuild]$ tree
.
├── RPMS
│   └── noarch
├── SOURCES
├── SPECS
└── SRPMS

5 directories, 0 files
```

Here is another way to create these directories. So we can see how this works, first delete the directory tree ~/rpmbuild. Then use the following command, which is part of the rpmdevtools package, to create the ~rpmbuild tree.

```
[student@studentvm1 ~]$ rpmdev-setuptree
[student@studentvm1 ~]$ tree rpmbuild/
rpmbuild/
├── BUILD
├── RPMS
├── SOURCES
├── SPECS
└── SRPMS
```

```
5 directories, 0 files
[student@studentvm1 ~]$
```

Note that the RPM build process will create the rest of the required directories.

We did not create architecture-specific directories such as the ~/rpmbuild/RPMS/X86_64 directory because our RPM is not architecture specific. We have shell scripts that are not specific to any CPU architecture. In reality we won't be using the SRPMS directory, either, which would contain source files for the compiler.

Examining the spec file

Each spec file has a number of sections, some of which may be ignored or omitted, depending upon the specific circumstances of the RPM build. This particular spec file is not an example of a minimal file required to work, but it is a good example of a moderately complex spec file that packages files that do not need to be compiled. If a compile were required, it would be performed in the %build section which is omitted from this spec file because it is not required.

As you proceed through this section, change the provided spec file as suggested to be specific for you.

Preamble

This is the only section of the spec file that does not have a label. It consists of much of the information you see when the command **rpm -qi [Package Name]** is run. Each datum is a single line which consists of a tag which identifies it and text data for the value of the tag.

```
###############################################################################
# Spec file for utils
###############################################################################
# Configured to be built by user student or other non-root user
###############################################################################
#
Summary: Utility scripts for testing RPM creation
```

```
Name: utils
Version: 1.0.0
Release: 1
License: GPL
URL: http://www.both.org
Group: System
Packager: David Both
Requires: bash
Requires: screen
Requires: mc
Requires: dmidecode
BuildRoot: ~/rpmbuild/

# Build with the following syntax:
# rpmbuild --target noarch -bb utils.spec
```

Comment lines are ignored by the rpmbuild program. I always like to add a comment to this section that contains the exact syntax of the rpmbuild command required to create the package. The Summary tag is a short description of the package. The Name, Version, and Release tags are used to create the name of the RPM file, as in utils-1.00-1.rpm. Incrementing the release and version numbers enables creating RPMs that can be used to update older ones.

The License tag defines the license under which the package is released. I always use a variation of the GPL. Specifying the license is important in order to prevent confusion about the fact that the software contained in the package is open source. This is also why I included the license and GPL statement in the files that will be installed.

The URL is usually the web page of the project or project owner. In this case, it is my personal web page. If you have a web page, you can change this to that URL.

The Group tag is interesting and is usually used for GUI applications. The value of the Group tag determines which group of icons in the Applications menu will contain the icon for the executable in this package. Used in conjunction with the Icon tag, which we are not using here, the Group tag allows adding the icon and the required information to launch a program into the Applications menu structure.

The Packager tag is used to specify the person or organization responsible for maintaining and creating the package.

The Requires statements define the dependencies for this RPM. Each is a package name. If one of the specified packages is not present, the dnf installation utility will try to locate it in one of the defined repositories defined in /etc/yum.repos.d and install it if it exists. If dnf cannot find one or more of the required packages, it will trow an error indicating which packages are missing and terminate.

The BuildRoot line specifies the top-level directory in which the rpmbuild tool will find the spec file and in which it will create temporary directories while it builds the package. The finished package will be stored in the noarch subdirectory that we specified earlier. The comment showing the command syntax used to build this package includes the option --target noarch which defines the target architecture. Because these are Bash scripts, they are not associated with a specific CPU architecture. If this option were omitted, the build would be targeted to the architecture of the CPU on which the build is being performed.

The rpmbuild program can target many different architectures and using the --target option allows us to build architecture specific packages on a host with a different architecture from the one on which the build is performed. So I could build a package intended for use on an i686 architecture on an x86_64 host, and vice versa.

Change the packager name to yours and the URL to your own web site, if you have one.

%description

The %description section of the spec file contains a description of the RPM package. It can be very short or can contain many lines of information. Our %description section is rather terse.

```
%description
A collection of utility scripts for testing RPM creation.
```

%prep

The %prep section is a script that is the first one executed during the build process. This script is not executed during the installation of the package.

This script is just a Bash shell script. It prepares the build directory, creating directories used for the build as required and copying the appropriate files into their respective directories. This would include the sources required for a complete compile as part of the build.

The $RPM_BUILD_ROOT directory represents the root directory of an installed system. The directories created in the $RPM_BUILD_ROOT directory are fully qualified paths such as /user/local/share/utils, /usr/local/bin and so on, in a live filesystem.

In the case of our package, we have no pre-compile sources because all of our programs are BASH scripts. So we simply copy those scripts and other files into the directories where they belong in the installed system.

```
%prep
###############################################################################
# Create the build tree and copy the files from the development directories   #
# into the build tree.                                                        #
###############################################################################
echo "BUILDROOT = $RPM_BUILD_ROOT"
mkdir -p $RPM_BUILD_ROOT/usr/local/bin/
mkdir -p $RPM_BUILD_ROOT/usr/local/share/utils

cp /home/student/development/utils/scripts/* $RPM_BUILD_ROOT/usr/local/bin
cp /home/student/development/utils/license/* $RPM_BUILD_ROOT/usr/local/share/utils
cp /home/student/development/utils/spec/* $RPM_BUILD_ROOT/usr/local/share/utils

exit
```

Note that the exit statement at the end of this section is required.

%files

This section of the spec file defines the files to be installed and their locations in the directory tree. It also specifies the file attributes and the owner and group owner for each file to be installed. The file permissions and ownerships are optional, but I recommend that they be explicitly set to eliminate any chance for those attributes to be incorrect or ambiguous when installed. Directories are created as required during the installation if they do not already exist.

```
%files
%attr(0744, root, root) /usr/local/bin/*
%attr(0644, root, root) /usr/local/share/utils/*
```

%pre

This section is empty in our lab project's spec file. This would be the place to put any scripts that are required to run during installation of the RPM but prior to the installation of the files.

%post

This section of the spec file is another Bash script. This one runs after the installation of files. This section can be pretty much anything you need or want it to be, including creating files, running system commands, and restarting services to reinitialize them after making configuration changes. The %post script for our RPM package performs some of those tasks.

```
%post
###########################################################################
# Set up MOTD scripts                                                     #
###########################################################################
cd /etc
# Save the old MOTD if it exists
if [ -e motd ]
then
    cp motd motd.orig
fi
# If not there already, Add link to create_motd to cron.daily
cd /etc/cron.daily
if [ ! -e create_motd ]
then
    ln -s /usr/local/bin/create_motd
fi
# create the MOTD for the first time
/usr/local/bin/mymotd > /etc/motd
```

The comments included in this script should make its purpose clear.

%postun

This section contains a script that would be run after the RPM package is uninstalled. Using rpm or dnf to remove a package removes all of the files listed in the %files section, but it does not remove files or links created by the %post section, so we need to handle that in this section.

This script usually consists of cleanup tasks that simply erasing the files previously installed by the RPM cannot accomplish. In the case of our package, it includes removing the link created by the %post script and restoring the saved original of the motd file.

```
%postun
# remove installed files and links
rm /etc/cron.daily/create_motd

# Restore the original MOTD if it was backed up
if [ -e /etc/motd.orig ]
then
   mv -f /etc/motd.orig /etc/motd
fi
```

%clean

This BASH script performs cleanup after the RPM build process. The two lines in the %clean section below remove the build directories created by the rpm-build command. In many cases, additional cleanup may also be required.

```
%clean
rm -rf $RPM_BUILD_ROOT/usr/local/bin
rm -rf $RPM_BUILD_ROOT/usr/local/share/utils
```

%changelog

This optional text section contains a list of changes to the RPM and files it contains. The newest changes are recorded at the top of this section.

```
%changelog
* Wed Aug 29 2018 Your Name <Youremail@yourdomain.com>
  - The original package includes several useful scripts. it is
    primarily intended to be used to illustrate the process of
    building an RPM.
```

Replace the data in the header line with your own name and email address.

Building the RPM

The spec file must be in the SPECS directory of the rpmbuild tree. I find it easiest to create a link to the actual spec file in that directory so that it can be edited in the development directory and there is no need to copy it to the SPEC directory.

EXPERIMENT 17-3

As the student user, make the SPECS directory the PWD and then create a link to the spec file.

```
[student@studentvm1 ~]# cd ~/rpmbuild/SPECS/
[student@studentvm1 ~]# ln -s ~/development/spec/utils.spec ; ll
total 0
lrwxrwxrwx 1 student student 41 Aug 31 11:43 utils.spec -> /home/student/
development/spec/utils.spec
[student@studentvm1 SPECS]$
```

Run the following command to build the RPM. It should only take a moment to create the RPM if no errors occur.

```
[student@studentvm1 ~]# rpmbuild --target noarch -bb utils.spec
Building target platforms: noarch
Building for target noarch
Executing(%prep): /bin/sh -e /var/tmp/rpm-tmp.QaPvYe
+ umask 022
+ cd /home/student/rpmbuild/BUILD
+ echo 'BUILDROOT = /home/student/rpmbuild/BUILDROOT/utils-1.0.0-1.noarch'
BUILDROOT = /home/student/rpmbuild/BUILDROOT/utils-1.0.0-1.noarch
+ mkdir -p /home/student/rpmbuild/BUILDROOT/utils-1.0.0-1.noarch/usr/local/
bin/
+ mkdir -p /home/student/rpmbuild/BUILDROOT/utils-1.0.0-1.noarch/usr/local/
share/utils
+ cp /home/student/development/scripts/create_motd /home/student/development/
scripts/die /home/student/development/scripts/mymotd /home/student/
development/scripts/sysdata /home/student/rpmbuild/BUILDROOT/utils-1.0.0-1.
noarch/usr/local/bin
```

```
+ cp /home/student/development/license/Copyright.and.GPL.Notice.txt /home/
student/development/license/GPL_LICENSE.txt /home/student/rpmbuild/BUILDROOT/
utils-1.0.0-1.noarch/usr/local/share/utils
+ cp /home/student/development/spec/utils.spec /home/student/rpmbuild/
BUILDROOT/utils-1.0.0-1.noarch/usr/local/share/utils
+ exit
Processing files: utils-1.0.0-1.noarch
Provides: utils = 1.0.0-1
Requires(interp): /bin/sh /bin/sh /bin/sh
Requires(rpmlib): rpmlib(CompressedFileNames) <= 3.0.4-1 rpmlib(FileDigests)
<= 4.6.0-1 rpmlib(PayloadFilesHavePrefix) <= 4.0-1
Requires(pre): /bin/sh
Requires(post): /bin/sh
Requires(postun): /bin/sh
Requires: /bin/bash /bin/sh
Checking for unpackaged file(s): /usr/lib/rpm/check-files /home/student/
rpmbuild/BUILDROOT/utils-1.0.0-1.noarch
Wrote: /home/student/rpmbuild/RPMS/noarch/utils-1.0.0-1.noarch.rpm
Executing(%clean): /bin/sh -e /var/tmp/rpm-tmp.9fGPUM
+ umask 022
+ cd /home/student/rpmbuild/BUILD
+ rm -rf /home/student/rpmbuild/BUILDROOT/utils-1.0.0-1.noarch/usr/local/bin
+ rm -rf /home/student/rpmbuild/BUILDROOT/utils-1.0.0-1.noarch/usr/local/
share/utils
+ exit 0
[student@studentvm1 SPECS]$
```

Check in the ~/rpmbuild/RPMS/noarch directory to verify that the new RPM exists there.

```
[student@studentvm1 SPECS]$ cd ~/rpmbuild/RPMS/noarch/ ; ll
total 24
-rw-rw-r-- 1 student student 24372 Aug 31 11:45 utils-1.0.0-1.noarch.rpm
[student@studentvm1 noarch]$
```

Now let's look at the contents of our ~/rpmbuild directory.

```
[student@studentvm1 ~]$ tree ~/rpmbuild/
/home/student/rpmbuild/
├── BUILD
├── BUILDROOT
│   └── utils-1.0.0-1.noarch
│       └── usr
│           └── local
│               └── share
├── RPMS
│   └── noarch
│       └── utils-1.0.0-1.noarch.rpm
├── SOURCES
├── SPECS
│   └── utils.spec -> /home/student/development/spec/utils.spec
└── SRPMS
```

Testing the RPM

As root, install the RPM to verify that it installs correctly and that the files are installed in the correct directories. The exact name of the RPM will depend upon the values you used for the tags in the Preamble section, but if you used the ones in the sample, the RPM name will be as shown in the sample command below.

EXPERIMENT 17-4

Perform this experiment as the root user. We will use RPM to install the package and not DNF.

```
[root@studentvm1 ~]# cd /home/student/rpmbuild/RPMS/noarch/ ; ll
total 24
-rw-rw-r-- 1 student student 24372 Aug 31 11:45 utils-1.0.0-1.noarch.rpm
[root@studentvm1 noarch]# rpm -ivh utils-1.0.0-1.noarch.rpm
Verifying...                          ############################### [100%]
Preparing...                          ############################### [100%]
Updating / installing...
   1:utils-1.0.0-1                     ############################### [100%]
[root@studentvm1 noarch]#
```

The -i option specifies an install. A -u would indicate performing an upgrade of a newer package over an older one. The -v means verbose and -h means we want to display the progress hash marks.

Check /usr/local/bin to ensure that the new files are there. You should also verify that the create_motd link in /etc/cron.daily has been created.

Use the following command to view the changelog. View the files installed by the package using the rpm -ql utils command. (That is a lowercase L in ql.)

```
[root@studentvm1 noarch]# rpm -q --changelog utils
* Wed Aug 29 2018 Your Name <Youremail@yourdomain.com>
- The original package includes several useful scripts. it is
    primarily intended to be used to illustrate the process of
    building an RPM.

[root@studentvm1 noarch]# rpm -ql utils
/usr/local/bin/create_motd
/usr/local/bin/die
/usr/local/bin/mymotd
/usr/local/bin/sysdata
/usr/local/share/utils/Copyright.and.GPL.Notice.txt
/usr/local/share/utils/GPL_LICENSE.txt
/usr/local/share/utils/utils.spec
[root@studentvm1 noarch]#
```

Experimenting

Let's do some experimenting.

EXPERIMENT 17-5

As the root user, remove the installed package. The -e option stands for erase.

```
[root@studentvm1 noarch]# rpm -e utils
```

Now you will change the spec file to require a package that does not exist. This will simulate a dependency that cannot be met. Add the following line immediately under the existing Requires line.

```
Requires: badrequire
```

Build the package and attempt to install it. What message is displayed?

We used the rpm command to install and delete the utils package. Try installing the package with DNF. You must be in the same directory as the package or specify the full path to the package for this to work.

Rebuilding a corrupted RPM database

I have occasionally encountered errors that indicate the RPM database is corrupted when upgrading, updating, or installing RPMs. This can occur for various reasons, but I have found that I can cause it by breaking out of a running task such as an update or installation.

The RPM database can be easily rebuilt.

EXPERIMENT 17-6

Perform this experiment as the root user. We will rebuild the RPM database even though there is nothing wrong with it. We use the -vv option to display a lot of verbose output that enables you to see what is happening.

```
[root@studentvm1 noarch]# rpm --rebuilddb -vv
```

Rerun the command without the -vv option.

Chapter summary

There are many tags and a couple sections that we did not cover in this look at the basics of creating an RPM package. Building RPM packages is not difficult, one just needs the right information. I hope this chapter helps you because it took me months to figure things out on my own.

We did not cover building from source code but, if you are a developer, that should be a simple step from this point.

Creating RPM packages is another good way to be a lazy SysAdmin and save time and effort. It provides an easy method for distributing and installing the scripts and other files that we as SysAdmins need to install on many hosts.

Exercises

Perform the following exercises to complete this chapter.

1. Try building the utils package using X86_64 as the target architecture. Remove the existing version of the package, install the X86_64 version, and test the programs. Does this cause a problem? Why? Remove this version.

2. Create a short script of your own and include it in the RPM. Increment the release number and build the revised RPM.

3. Install the original noarch RPM again. Then use DNF to upgrade the RPM to the new version.

4. What happens if you make a change to the RPM spec file and rebuild the RPM without updating the release number? Is this also true for the version number?

## CHAPTER 18

Where Do I Go from Here?

Introduction

Wow! You made it all the way through this massive Linux course. That is impressive all by itself, but are you ready to take the next steps?

In truth, we have only just begun. I find that no matter how much I learn there is always more. Despite the amount of material in this course, I have only introduced you to many of these subjects. How you proceed from here is up to you, but it can make all the difference in your future.

Curiosity

There is an old – and I think incredibly stupid – saying that "curiosity killed the cat." I had this used on me as a kid, fortunately not by my parents. I think this dumb saying is used mostly to stifle kids when their questions and inquisitiveness takes them to places that some parents, teachers, and caregivers would rather not take the time to deal with. This is one of the ways in which the boxes were built around us.

My personal saying is that "curiosity solves problems." Following our curiosity leads us to places that are outside the box, places that allow us to solve our problems in ways that we could not otherwise. Sometimes curiosity can lead me directly to the cause of a problem and other times the connection is indirect.

Learning never stops. Every time I teach a class or write an article – or book – I learn new things. This is all about my innate curiosity.

© David Both 2020
D. Both, *Using and Administering Linux: Volume 3*, https://doi.org/10.1007/978-1-4842-5485-1_18

I have a whole chapter dedicated to curiosity in my book *The Linux Philosophy for SysAdmins.*[1] I look at how my curiosity led me to Linux and how it helps me to solve problems. I also discuss how a bit of curiosity about log entries on my firewall system led me down the path to some of the tools we explored in Chapter 16 of this volume.

> *I have not failed. I've just found 10,000 ways that won't work.*
>
> —Thomas A. Edison

Although the failure of thousands of specific combinations of individual materials and fabrication technologies during testing did not lead to a viable light bulb, Edison continued to experiment. Just so, the failure to resolve a problem or create code that performs its defined task does not mean that the project or overall goal will fail. It means only that the specific tool or approach did not result in a successful outcome.

I have learned much more through my failures than I have in almost any other manner. I am especially glad for those failures that have been self-inflicted. Not only did I have to correct the problems I caused myself, but I also still had to find and fix the original problem. This always led to a great deal of research which caused me to learn much more than if I had solved the original problem quickly.

This is just my nature, and I think it is the nature of all good SysAdmins to look upon these situations as learning opportunities. As mentioned previously, I have spent many years as a trainer and some of the most fun experiences were when demonstrations, experiments, and lab projects would fail while I was teaching. Those were fantastic learning experiences for me as well as for the students in my class. Sometimes I even incorporated those accidental failures into later classes because they enabled me to teach something important.

Convert

Although I started using Linux in about 1996, I really did not start to learn it in any depth until I converted all of the computers in my home lab from OS/2 to Linux. I liked OS/2 and was comfortable with it but I could see that I would always return to it to do those tasks that I had not yet figured out how to do in Linux. I was never going to be a Linux expert that way.

---

[1]Both, David, *The Linux Philosophy for SysAdmins,* Apress, 2018, 417

Everyone learns best in their own way. As a trainer, I saw this every time I taught a class, regardless of the subject. Following our curiosity is the same – we all have that spark that leads us to discover more. Our methods may not be the same, but they will lead us all to greater knowledge and skill.

I started by installing Linux on all of my computers at home. This forced me to learn Linux and not look back. So long as I had a means to go back to my old and well-known way of doing things, it was never necessary for me to truly learn Linux. This is what I did when I decided I wanted to learn Linux, and it has taught me a large part of what I know. I had several computers and created a complete internal network in my home office. Over the years, my network has grown and changed and I have learned more with every alteration. Much of this was driven by my curiosity rather than any specific need.

I have static IP addresses from my ISP and two firewalls to provide outside access and protect my internal network. I have had Intel boxes with Fedora and CentOS on them over the years. I learned a lot about using both in roles as a firewall and router.

I have a server that runs DHCP, HTTP, SMTP, IMAP, NTP, DNS, and other services to provide them to my internal network and to make some of those services available to the outside world, such as my web site and incoming email. I have learned a great deal about using Linux in a server role in general. I have learned an incredible amount about implementing and managing each of these services.

All of this translated into usable skills in the job market. And I learned even more in those jobs.

Tools

In this course, we have looked at doing things at the command line, learning the very low-level tools for managing Linux hosts. We also created some of our own automated tools to make our administration tasks easier. I believe that it is necessary for good SysAdmins to understand the underlying tasks that need to be performed before engaging any of the more complex tools available.

There are many higher-level tools available that provide a great degree of automation and ease of use that we have not even covered. Many of these tools are also free, open source software and can be downloaded from the Fedora repositories. Most are also available for other distributions as well. You should spend some time learning about tools like Ansible and Webmin.

Ansible is an advanced tool that can automate many administrative tasks, things that we talked about automating with scripts. Webmin is a web-based administration tool that wraps and uses many of the tools we have studied in this course. It provides a flexible canter for managing Linux hosts and many of the services they provide.

There are many other tools of all kinds out there. These two will give you a starting point for advanced automation.

Resources

I have listed in the Bibliography a large number of resources, web sites, and hard-copy books that you can use to further your Linux education. Many are directly related to this course, but others not so much. They will all help you learn more.

I have two favorite web sites that I can count on for accurate and current information, technical as well as nontechnical. Opensource.com[2], a Red Hat web site, contains technical and nontechnical articles about Linux, open source software, the open organization, DevOps, being a SysAdmin, and much more. The relatively new Red Hat *Enable Sysadmin*[3] site has articles especially for SysAdmins and can be an excellent resource for all of us who do SysAdmin work. The Enable SysAdmin site has an especially good article on learning to be a SysAdmin.[4]

You may also find my personal web sites informative. The DataBook for Linux[5] is my technical web site. It has information about problems I have found and fixed, articles covering how to do things that were difficult to find information about, and more. It is loosely structured into a book-like format, but it is strictly a reference and is not at all like this self-study course.

My other web site is related to my published books. It is my "meet the author"[6] web site, so it contains information about me and my books.

There are many other excellent sources of information out there, both for Red Hat–based distributions and many of the other distributions. With a bit of searching, you can

---

[2]Red Hat, Opensource.com, `https://opensource.com`

[3]Red Hat, Enable SysAdmin, `www.redhat.com/sysadmin/`

[4]Brown, Taz, *Learn the technical ropes and become a sysadmin*, `www.redhat.com/sysadmin/ learn-technical-ropes`

[5]The DataBook for Linux, `www.linux-databook.info`,

[6]David Both, `www.both.org`

find plenty of information about Linux, almost every distribution ever created, and tens of thousands of specific problems.

Just be careful because there are many web pages with outdated or incorrect information. If you need to try out a fix or solution to a problem, be sure to do so on an expendable VM first.

And that virtual network, the one we created for this course or one like it, should also be one of your resources. Use it for testing everything you want to do on your physical network like we did in the many experiments we performed in this course.

Contribute

As I have mentioned, teaching and writing helps me to learn. So write an article – or two or three – for Opensource.com, Enable SysAdmin, or any of the other distribution-related web sites out there. Most of this type of web sites have information on how you can contribute. Writing about something I have learned or am trying to learn helps me to clarify what I already know about a subject and gives me an opportunity to expand my knowledge.

The staff at Opensource.com in particular are able to assist you through the entire writing and web publishing process. Several of us who have published articles on Opensource.com also have published books, so you never know where that might lead.

Skip this

Most lists of things to do ignore the bits you don't really need to do. Here is one I can suggest you skip as not being worth the time you might invest.

Compiling the kernel

Don't bother. This might be a nice exercise if you are a developer or trying to get the last bit of CPU efficiency in a supercomputer and really want to do massive kernel mods, but most SysAdmins will never need to do this. You might also want to do this if the certification you are working on requires it, but other than that, you are pretty much wasting your time to do this.

The fact is that the kernel is compiled with a really good set of options for the vast majority of today's desktop and server needs. If you are having performance issues, you would be better off to determine whether the culprit really is the CPU, and if it is, install a bigger and faster CPU. Sometimes faster memory will help rather than a faster CPU. You just need to research it and figure out what the real problem is.

If changes to the kernel are required, altering one or more of the kernel tuning parameters in the /proc filesystem will most likely be the best way to resolve the problem.

We have already seen one interesting example of why most SysAdmins will never need to compile the kernel. Way back in Volume 1 of this course, we installed VirtualBox on a Linux host. We also needed to install some Linux development tools. The reason those tools were required is that VirtualBox compiles its own kernel module on the system on which it is installed. It does this the first time it starts on that system, and it also checks to see whether the kernel has been updated in which case it recompiles its kernel modules again. The VirtualBox developers have automated that necessary task so that users do not need to know how to do it.

Of course, if you are just curious...

Chapter summary

To me, curiosity is the driving force behind learning. I can't just sit in a classroom because someone says I need to learn a particular thing and be successful at it. I need to have some interest in the subject and something about it needs to pique my curiosity. That propensity to work harder on the subjects I liked was very evident during my school years as I did well in the subjects that intrigued me.

By using my home network for indulging my curiosity, I had lots of safe space in which to fail catastrophically and to learn the best ways to recover from that. And there are lots of ways to fail, so I learned a lot. I learned the most when I accidentally broke things, but I also learned a great deal when I would intentionally bork things. In these instances, I knew what I wanted to learn and could target the breakage in ways that would enable me to learn about those specific things.

I was also fortunate because I had a few jobs that required or at least allowed me to take classes on various aspects of Unix and Linux. For me, classroom work is a way to validate and reinforce what I learn on my own. It gave me the opportunity to interact with – for the most part – knowledgeable instructors who could aid and clarify my understanding of the bits and pieces that I could not make sense of on my own.

Those of us who are successful at Unix and Linux System Administration are by our very nature inquisitive and thoughtful. We take every opportunity to expand our knowledge base.

We like to experiment with new knowledge, new hardware, and new software, just out of curiosity and "because it is there." We relish the opportunities that are opened to us when computer things break. Every problem is a new possibility for learning. We enjoy attending technical conferences as much for the access to other SysAdmins they afford as for the amazing amount of new information we can gather from the scheduled presentations.

Rigid logic and rules do not give us SysAdmins enough flexibility to perform our jobs efficiently. We don't especially care about how things "should" be done. SysAdmins are not easily limited by the "shoulds" that others try to constrain us with. We use logical and critical thinking that is flexible and that produces excellent results. We create our own ways of doing things with independent, critical thinking and integrated reasoning, which enables us to learn more while we are at it.

We SysAdmins are strong personalities – we need to be in order to do our jobs and especially to do things the "right" way. This is not about how we "should" perform the tasks we need to do, rather it is about using best practices and ensuring that the end result conforms to those practices.

We don't just think outside the box. We are the ones who destroy the boxes that others try to make us work inside. For us, there is no "should."

Be the curious SysAdmin. It worked for me.

Bibliography

Books

Binnie, Chris, *Practical Linux Topics*, Apress 2016, ISBN 978-1-4842-1772-6

Both, David, The Linux Philosophy for SysAdmins, Apress, 2018, ISBN 978-1-4842-3729-8

Gancarz, Mike, *Linux and the Unix Philosophy*, Digital Press – an imprint of Elsevier Science, 2003, ISBN 1-55558-273-7

Kernighan, Brian W.; Pike, Rob (1984), *The UNIX Programming Environment*, Prentice Hall, Inc., ISBN 0-13-937699-2

Libes, Don, *Exploring Expect*, O'Reilly, 2010, ISBN 978-1565920903

Nemeth, Evi [et al.], *The Unix and Linux System Administration Handbook*, Pearson Education, Inc., ISBN 978-0-13-148005-6

Matotek, Dennis, Turnbull, James, Lieverdink, Peter; *Pro Linux System Administration*, Apress, ISBN 978-1-4842-2008-5

Raymond, Eric S., *The Art of Unix Programming*, Addison-Wesley, September 17, 2003, ISBN 0-13-142901-9

Siever, Figgins, Love & Robbins, *Linux in a Nutshell 6th Edition*, (O'Reilly, 2009), ISBN 978-0-596-15448-6

Sobell, Mark G., *A Practical Guide to Linux Commands, Editors, and Shell Programming Third Edition,* Prentice Hall; ISBN 978-0-13-308504-4

van Vugt, Sander, *Beginning the Linux Command Line,* Apress, ISBN 978-1-4302-6829-1

Whitehurst, Jim, *The Open Organization*, Harvard Business Review Press (June 2, 2015), ISBN 978-1625275271

Torvalds, Linus and Diamond, David, Just for Fun, HarperCollins, 2001, ISBN 0-06-662072-4

© David Both 2020
D. Both, *Using and Administering Linux: Volume 3*, https://doi.org/10.1007/978-1-4842-5485-1

Web sites

BackBlaze, Web site, *What SMART Stats Tell Us About Hard Drives*, www.backblaze.com/blog/what-smart-stats-indicate-hard-drive-failures/

Both, David, *8 reasons to use LXDE*, https://opensource.com/article/17/3/8-reasons-use-lxde

Both, David, *9 reasons to use KDE*, https://opensource.com/life/15/4/9-reasons-to-use-kde

Both, David, *10 reasons to use Cinnamon as your Linux desktop environment*, https://opensource.com/article/17/1/cinnamon-desktop-environment

Both, David, *11 reasons to use the GNOME 3 desktop environment for Linux*, https://opensource.com/article/17/5/reasons-gnome

Both, David, *An introduction to Linux network routing*, https://opensource.com/business/16/8/introduction-linux-network-routing

Both, David, *Complete Kickstart*, www.linux-databook.info/?page_id=9

Both, David, *Making your Linux Box Into a Router*, www.linux-databook.info/?page_id=697

Both, David, *Network Interface Card (NIC) name assignments*, www.linux-databook.info/?page_id=4243

Both, David, *Using hard and soft links in the Linux filesystem*, www.linux-databook.info/?page_id=5087

Both, David, *Using rsync to back up your Linux system*, https://opensource.com/article/17/1/rsync-backup-linux

Bowen, Rich, *RTFM? How to write a manual worth reading*, https://opensource.com/business/15/5/write-better-docs

Charity, *Ops: It's everyone's job now*, https://opensource.com/article/17/7/state-systems-administration

Dartmouth University, *Biography of Douglas McIlroy*, www.cs.dartmouth.edu/~doug/biography

DataBook for Linux, www.linux-databook.info/

Digital Ocean, *How To Use journalctl to View and Manipulate Systemd Logs*, www.digitalocean.com/community/tutorials/how-to-use-journalctl-to-view-and-manipulate-systemd-logs

Edwards, Darvin, Electronic Design, *PCB Design And Its Impact On Device Reliability*, www.electronicdesign.com/boards/pcb-design-and-its-impact-device-reliability

Engineering and Technology Wiki, *IBM 1800*, `http://ethw.org/IBM_1800`

Fedora Magazine, *Tilix*, `https://fedoramagazine.org/try-tilix-new-terminal-emulator-fedora/`

Fogel, Kark, *Producing Open Source Software*, `https://producingoss.com/en/index.html`

Free On-Line Dictionary of Computing, *Instruction Set*, `http://foldoc.org/instruction+set`

Free Software Foundation, *Free Software Licensing Resources*, `www.fsf.org/licensing/education`

gnu.org, *Bash Reference Manual – Command Line Editing*, `www.gnu.org/software/bash/manual/html_node/Command-Line-Editing.html`

Harris, William, *How the Scientific Method Works*, `https://science.howstuffworks.com/innovation/scientific-experiments/scientific-method6.htm`

Heartbleed web site, `http://heartbleed.com/`

How-two Forge, *Linux Basics: How To Create and Install SSH Keys on the Shell*, `www.howtoforge.com/linux-basics-how-to-install-ssh-keys-on-the-shell`

Kroah-Hartman, Greg, Linux Journal, *Kernel Korner – udev – Persistent Naming in User Space*, `www.linuxjournal.com/article/7316`

Krumins, Peter, *Bash emacs editing*, `www.catonmat.net/blog/bash-emacs-editing-mode-cheat-sheet/`

Krumins, Peter, *Bash history*, `www.catonmat.net/blog/the-definitive-guide-to-bash-command-line-history/`

Krumins, Peter, *Bash vi editing*, `www.catonmat.net/blog/bash-vi-editing-mode-cheat-sheet/`

Kernel.org, *Linux allocated devices (4.x+ version)*, `www.kernel.org/doc/html/v4.11/admin-guide/devices.html`

Linux Foundation, *Filesystem Hierarchical Standard (3.0)*, `http://refspecs.linuxfoundation.org/fhs.shtml`

Linux Foundation, *MIT License*, `https://spdx.org/licenses/MIT`

The Linux Information Project, *GCC Definition*, `www.linfo.org/gcc.html`

Linuxtopia, *Basics of the Unix Philosophy*, `www.linuxtopia.org/online_books/programming_books/art_of_unix_programming/ch01s06.html`

LSB Work group - The Linux Foundation, *Filesystem Hierarchical Standard V3.0, 3*, `https://refspecs.linuxfoundation.org/FHS_3.0/fhs-3.0.pdf`

Opensource.com, `https://opensource.com/`

Opensource.com, *Appreciating the full power of open*, `https://opensource.com/open-organization/16/5/appreciating-full-power-open`

Opensource.com, David Both, *SpamAssassin, MIMEDefang, and Procmail: Best Trio of 2017*, Opensource.com, `https://opensource.com/article/17/11/spamassassin-mimedefang-and-procmail`

Opensource.org, *Licenses*, `https://opensource.org/licenses`

opensource.org, *The Open Source Definition (Annotated)*, `https://opensource.org/osd-annotated`

OSnews, *Editorial: Thoughts on Systemd and the Freedom to Choose*, `www.osnews.com/story/28026/Editorial_Thoughts_on_Systemd_and_the_Freedom_to_Choose`

Peterson, Christine, Opensource.com, *How I coined the term 'open source'*, `https://opensource.com/article/18/2/coining-term-open-source-software`

Petyerson, Scott K, *The source code is the license*, Opensource.com, `https://opensource.com/article/17/12/source-code-license`

Princeton University, *Interview with Douglas McIlroy*, `www.princeton.edu/~hos/frs122/precis/mcilroy.htm`

Raspberry Pi Foundation, `www.raspberrypi.org/`

Raymond, Eric S., *The Art of Unix Programming*, `www.catb.org/esr/writings/taoup/html/index.html/`

Wikipedia, *The Unix Philosophy, Section: Eric Raymond's 17 Unix Rules*, `https://en.wikipedia.org/wiki/Unix_philosophy#Eric_Raymond%E2%80%99s_17_Unix_Rules`

Raymond, Eric S., *The Art of Unix Programming, Section The Rule of Separation*, `www.catb.org/~esr/writings/taoup/html/ch01s06.html#id2877777`

Understanding SMART Reports, `https://lime-technology.com/wiki/Understanding_SMART_Reports`

Unnikrishnan A, Linux.com, *Udev: Introduction to Device Management In Modern Linux System*, `www.linux.com/news/udev-introduction-device-management-modern-linux-system`

Venezia, Paul, *Nine traits of the veteran Unix admin*, InfoWorld, Feb 14, 2011, `www.infoworld.com/t/unix/nine-traits-the-veteran-unix-admin-276?page=0,0&source=fssr`

Wikipedia, *Alan Perlis*, `https://en.wikipedia.org/wiki/Alan_Perlis`

Wikipedia, *Christine Peterson*, `https://en.wikipedia.org/wiki/Christine_Peterson`

Wikipedia, *Command Line Completion*, https://en.wikipedia.org/wiki/Command-line_completion

Wikipedia, *Comparison of command shells*, https://en.wikipedia.org/wiki/Comparison_of_command_shells

Wikipedia, *Dennis Ritchie*, https://en.wikipedia.org/wiki/Dennis_Ritchie

Wikipedia, *Device File*, https://en.wikipedia.org/wiki/Device_file

Wikipedia, *Gnome-terminal*, https://en.wikipedia.org/wiki/Gnome-terminal

Wikipedia, *Hard Links*, https://en.wikipedia.org/wiki/Hard_link

Wikipedia, *Heartbleed*, https://en.wikipedia.org/wiki/Heartbleed

Wikipedia, *Initial ramdisk*, https://en.wikipedia.org/wiki/Initial_ramdisk

Wikipedia, *Ken Thompson*, https://en.wikipedia.org/wiki/Ken_Thompson

Wikipedia, *Konsole*, https://en.wikipedia.org/wiki/Konsole

Wikipedia, *Linux console*, https://en.wikipedia.org/wiki/Linux_console

Wikipedia, *List of Linux-supported computer architectures*, https://en.wikipedia.org/wiki/List_of_Linux-supported_computer_architectures

Wikipedia, *Maslow's hierarchy of needs*, https://en.wikipedia.org/wiki/Maslow%27s_hierarchy_of_needs

Wikipedia, *Open Data*, https://en.wikipedia.org/wiki/Open_data

Wikipedia, *PHP*, https://en.wikipedia.org/wiki/PHP

Wikipedia, *PL/I*, https://en.wikipedia.org/wiki/PL/I

Wikipedia, *Programma 101*, https://en.wikipedia.org/wiki/Programma_101

Wikipedia, *Richard M. Stallman*, https://en.wikipedia.org/wiki/Richard_Stallman

Wikipedia, *Rob Pike*, https://en.wikipedia.org/wiki/Rob_Pike

Wikipedia, *rsync*, https://en.wikipedia.org/wiki/Rsync

Wikipedia, *Rxvt*, https://en.wikipedia.org/wiki/Rxvt

Wikipedia, *SMART*, https://en.wikipedia.org/wiki/SMART

Wikipedia, *Software testing*, https://en.wikipedia.org/wiki/Software_testing

Wikipedia, *Terminator*, https://en.wikipedia.org/wiki/Terminator_(terminal_emulator)

Wikipedia, *Tony Hoare*, https://en.wikipedia.org/wiki/Tony_Hoare

Wikipedia, *Unit Record Equipment*, https://en.wikipedia.org/wiki/Unit_record_equipment

Wikipedia, *Unix*, https://en.wikipedia.org/wiki/Unix

BIBLIOGRAPHY

Wikipedia, *Windows Registry*, https://en.wikipedia.org/wiki/Windows_Registry
Wikipedia, *Xterm*, https://en.wikipedia.org/wiki/Xterm
WikiQuote, *C._A._R._Hoare*, https://en.wikiquote.org/wiki/C._A._R._Hoare
WordPress, *Home page*, https://wordpress.org/

Index

© David Both 2020
D. Both, *Using and Administering Linux: Volume 3*, https://doi.org/10.1007/978-1-4842-5485-1

G

H

List of operators